Visual Studio Extensibility Development

Extending Visual Studio IDE for Productivity, Quality, Tooling, Analysis, and Artificial Intelligence

Second Edition

Rishabh Verma

Apress®

Visual Studio Extensibility Development: Extending Visual Studio IDE for Productivity, Quality, Tooling, Analysis, and Artificial Intelligence

Rishabh Verma
Hyderabad, India

ISBN-13 (pbk): 978-1-4842-9874-9   ISBN-13 (electronic): 978-1-4842-9875-6
https://doi.org/10.1007/978-1-4842-9875-6

Managing Director, Apress Media LLC: Welmoed Spahr
Acquisitions Editor: Smriti Srivastava
Development Editor: Laura Berendson
Editorial Project Manager: Jessica Vakili

Cover designed by eStudioCalamar

Cover image by Omid Moradi on Unsplash (www.unsplash.com)

Distributed to the book trade worldwide by Springer Science+Business Media New York, 1 New York Plaza, Suite 4600, New York, NY 10004-1562, USA. Phone 1-800-SPRINGER, fax (201) 348-4505, e-mail orders-ny@springer-sbm.com, or visit www.springeronline.com. Apress Media, LLC is a California LLC and the sole member (owner) is Springer Science + Business Media Finance Inc (SSBM Finance Inc). SSBM Finance Inc is a **Delaware** corporation.

For information on translations, please e-mail booktranslations@springernature.com; for reprint, paperback, or audio rights, please e-mail bookpermissions@springernature.com.

Apress titles may be purchased in bulk for academic, corporate, or promotional use. eBook versions and licenses are also available for most titles. For more information, reference our Print and eBook Bulk Sales web page at http://www.apress.com/bulk-sales.

Any source code or other supplementary material referenced by the author in this book is available to readers on GitHub (https://github.com/Rishabh-V/Visual-Studio-Extensibility-Development-2). For more detailed information, please visit https://www.apress.com/gp/services/source-code.

Paper in this product is recyclable

To my wonderful, loving, and caring wife Neha.

To our precious son, Ram, whose joyful giggles, adorable cuteness, and boundless curiosity fill our hearts with love and wonder.

And to the dedicated scientists at ISRO whose remarkable achievements inspire us to reach for the stars and beyond.

Table of Contents

About the Author

Rishabh Verma is a Microsoft Certified Professional and currently serves as a Senior Developer Relations Engineer at Google India, where he contributes to the development of Google Cloud's C# SDK. With a background in electronic engineering, he boasts over 15 years of hands-on experience in hard-core development within the .NET technology stack. Rishabh is driven by his passion for creating tools, Visual Studio extensions, and utilities aimed at boosting developer productivity.

His areas of interest include the .NET Compiler Platform (Roslyn), Visual Studio extensibility, code generation, and .NET Core. Rishabh is an active member of the .NET Foundation and has previously authored books on .NET Core 2.0, .NET Core 3.1, and Visual Studio Extensibility Development before undertaking this revision. He occasionally blogs at https://rishabhverma.net/. His Twitter ID is @VermaRishabh and his LinkedIn page is www.linkedin.com/in/rishabhverma/.

Acknowledgments

I would like to express my heartfelt gratitude to Microsoft and the Visual Studio team for creating the wonderful Visual Studio IDE, a tool cherished and utilized by millions of developers every day. Without them, we wouldn't have been here discussing this.

I extend my sincere thanks to Google for providing me with generous paternity leave, allowing me the time to write this book and share my knowledge.

Special appreciation goes to Mads Kristensen, my Visual Studio extensibility guru! This work would not have been possible without him. It is by means of his blogs, talks, videos, and extensions that I have learned about Visual Studio extensibility.

I am deeply grateful to my reviewer, Damien Foggon, for his meticulous review and proofreading. He painstakingly combed through the entire content, offering corrections, enhancements, and edits that have greatly improved this book.

A solid support system at home is the foundation of every achievement. I want to express my heartfelt thanks to my parents Smt. Pratibha Verma and Shri R. C. Verma and my brother Rishi Verma for their unwavering support and boundless energy.

I owe a special debt of gratitude to my son, Ram, and my wife, Neha. They sacrificed countless weekends and provided unwavering support, helping me meet my deadlines. This book is as much their accomplishment as it is mine.

Last, but certainly not least, I want to thank my acquisitions editor, Smriti Shrivastava, for granting me with this incredible opportunity to share my knowledge and contribute to the community. Heartfelt appreciation to my project coordinator, Shobana Srinivasan, who worked patiently and persistently alongside me.

Introduction

Welcome to the latest and most comprehensive edition of *Visual Studio Extensibility Development*, thoughtfully updated for Visual Studio 2022. We are glad to have you join us in our journey of learning Visual Studio Extensibility.

Our journey begins with a solid foundation in the essential concepts to extend Visual Studio, encompassing crucial data structures and design patterns. This introduction ensures that you feel at ease as we navigate through the depths of extensibility. This introductory section is designed to provide you with the confidence and clarity needed to fully embrace the content that follows.

Next, we'll dive into the setup process, preparing the perfect launchpad for your exploration of the extensibility realm. You'll be introduced to the boilerplate extension, gaining insights into the structure and anatomy of a Visual Studio extension. Discover how Visual Studio seamlessly discovers and loads these extensions, setting the stage for your own development endeavors.

Our journey continues as we unravel the intricate extensibility model of Visual Studio. You'll become well acquainted with the Visual Studio SDK, a vital tool in your extensibility toolkit. Armed with this knowledge, you'll embark on the creation of a basic extension, crafting custom commands that can be seamlessly integrated into the code window, tool menu, and solution explorer.

We'll then explore how to develop an extension that empowers users to search code within the search engine of their choice. You'll learn how to leverage the Options dialog to customize the extension according to user preferences. Dive into the world of notifications in Visual Studio and discover how to effectively communicate with users. You'll also master the development of an extension that generates C# POCO classes from JSON and how to leverage extensions to develop a Connected Service.

Our journey takes us to the heart of Visual Studio – the code editor. Here, we'll create code analyzers, implement light bulb-style code fix suggestions, and develop code refactoring extensions. You'll unlock the potential to extend IntelliSense, providing custom code suggestions and completions. You also learn to harness the might of AI as we integrate it into our extension, enabling developers to review, explain, and optimize code seamlessly and making their development experience better.

We'll delve into the development of extensions that distribute code snippets, enhancing developer productivity and ensuring the correct usage of APIs. You'll also gain expertise in creating Project Item and Project templates.

Explore the process of publishing an extension to the Visual Studio Marketplace, making your creation accessible to the wider developer community. Our journey continues with an in-depth look at deploying extensions using continuous integration.

As we conclude, we'll unveil a treasure trove of invaluable tips and tricks for navigating Visual Studio like a pro. Discover a curated selection of indispensable extensions that can supercharge your development workflow. You also learn about the future of Visual Studio Extensibility and the new out-of-process extensibility model that is out now in preview version.

By the time you close the final chapter of *Visual Studio Extensibility Development*, you will possess the expertise to develop, debug, customize, and publish an extension.

Who This Book Is For

This book is meticulously crafted for individuals who are truly passionate about software development and aspire to unlock the full potential of Visual Studio. Whether you're a seasoned developer with years of experience under your belt or embarking on the exciting journey of coding for the first time, our comprehensive approach caters to every skill level. Developers, programmers, engineers, architects, instructors, innovators, students, and technology enthusiasts, all leveraging the power of the Visual Studio IDE, will find immense value in these pages.

My dedicated editorial team and I have invested considerable effort to provide you with the most comprehensive and accurate information. However, should you have any constructive suggestions or feedback regarding the content of this book, I would greatly appreciate it if you could reach out to me at rishabhv@live.com. Your insights will help us continue to enhance and improve this valuable resource.

CHAPTER 1

Basics Primer

This chapter marks the beginning of our journey toward learning and developing Visual Studio (VS) extensions. To pave this path, we will provide a quick refresher of the fundamentals that will be required through the book and are prerequisites for developing Visual Studio extensions. This chapter will act as a primer for the fundamentals and can be skipped by the reader if they are well versed with the topics covered here.

Before we delve into the fundamentals, the first and foremost question that comes to mind is this: "Why should I extend Visual Studio?" So let us first answer it.

Why Should I Extend Visual Studio?

Why should I bother extending Visual Studio IDE?

I have heard this question many times and have seen numerous software developers asking this very pertinent question. So, why are we here? Visual Studio is a great integrated development environment (IDE) and makes the developer very productive in coding, developing, debugging, and troubleshooting. Then, why should I even bother extending it? Well – there are numerous reasons to do so. A few of the top ones are the following:

- Customize Visual Studio to suit your needs and environment.

- To avoid repetitive or tedious work. With extensions, it can be done just by a click of a button.

- Do things faster, as it is something that can increase your productivity. It can be in the form of a snippet, or a tool to generate a GUID (globally unique identifier), or code analysis, or code refactoring, or a project/item template, or anything else that can get the developer's job done faster. There are numerous extensions that can make even extension development faster!

© Rishabh Verma 2024
R. Verma, *Visual Studio Extensibility Development*, https://doi.org/10.1007/978-1-4842-9875-6_1

- Higher-quality development: There are a few great examples of extensions like Roslyn analyzers, StyleCop, FxCop, CodeMaid, and ReSharper, to name a few, which help the developer to identify the issues while coding. This avoids unnecessary bugs in the future, and the code can be compliant to coding standards, resulting in better quality.

- Enforce policies or settings across teams. There are extensions that can help you get code consistency and uniformity even across a large team. For example, a check-in policy extension can ensure that each code check-in has a work item associated with it and has 0 StyleCop and FxCop violations. Without this, the code would not check in.

- Extending Visual Studio is a great learning opportunity. Developers can gain deep insights into the inner working of a complex IDE like Visual Studio and understand coding and architecture patterns and improve their C# and .NET knowledge.

- Visual Studio extensibility allows developers to contribute to open source extensions and/or collaborate on projects that can improve the overall experience for the community.

- To foster innovation and experimentation, developers can explore new ideas and leverage cutting-edge technologies to extend Visual Studio. With the recent fast-paced development in the field of artificial intelligence (AI), there are lots of opportunities to experiment and innovate with AI-driven extensions. The AI-based extensions can automate repetitive tasks, enhance code analysis, review, provide intelligent code completions, and much more. We will explore this bit in the upcoming chapters.

- Of course, fame and fortune: You can either contribute to the community by sharing your great extension in the marketplace for free or monetize it and charge a fee from consumers to use it. You get a name, fame, and can also make some money, if you create great extensions.

- It would be cool if... Mads Kristensen is one of the most popular extension writers in the Visual Studio Marketplace with 125+ extensions to his credit. In one of his talks on Visual Studio extensibility, he explained how he thinks about a new Visual Studio extension and framed it beautifully: "It would be cool if..."

There are numerous great extensions for Visual Studio for improving developer productivity, quality, refactoring, editors, and controls available in the Visual Studio Marketplace: `https://marketplace.visualstudio.com/`. As of today, there are more than 12.8K extensions in the marketplace with more than 45 million downloads and counting.

Let us now start our quest of brushing up on the fundamentals.

Compiler

Let's start with the fundamental definition of a compiler. A compiler is a software that translates a computer program written in a high-level programming language, which are easier for humans to understand (like C#, Java, etc.) language into a low-level language or binary code that computers can execute. High-level languages resemble human-readable languages like English, which low-level languages consists of 0s and 1s, understood by the computer processors.

Now, there is another important thing that is called CPU architecture. The CPU processing the instructions may be a 32-bit processor (x86) or a 64-bit processor (x64). The memory space and the instruction set vary for both of these architectures. An x64 processor has a 64-bit address and memory space and hence can work on larger memory addresses. They also have a few new instructions as optimizations for faster execution. Therefore, for proper utilization of the processor, the right-processor specific machine codes should be generated. This presents a challenge that if a developer builds the code, on one hand, in the x86 architecture of CPU and ships the software, it would work well in both x86- and x64-based systems, but it would not be making optimal use of the x64 processor. On the other hand, if a developer builds the code on an x64 processor, it will not work on x86 processor-based systems.

Note   Visual Studio 2022 is a x64-based application. Until Visual Studio 2019, it was x86-based application.

For a C# .NET-based application, this is not generally an issue, as .NET compiler compiles the code into Microsoft Intermediate Language, or MSIL, which is independent of processor architecture. At the first time of execution, this MSIL is converted into the platform architecture-specific machine code. To leverage this, we can choose the .NET project platform (in project properties) as "Any CPU."

The high-level flow of how the C# code executes in a machine is depicted in Figure 1-1.

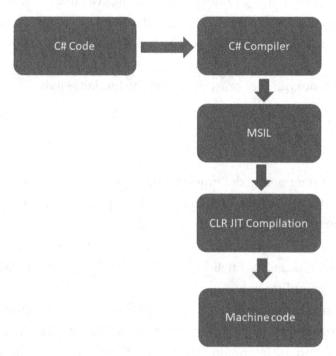

Figure 1-1. *C# code execution flow*

As an example, here is a computer program that does an operation of displaying a message on a console. It is written in the C# language using a code editor. It is a sample program of printing "Hello World!" text on a console:

```
using System;

namespace BasicsPrimer
{
    class Program
    {
        static void Main(string[] args)
```

```
        {
            Console.WriteLine("Hello World!");
        }
    }
}
```

This code will print the desired text on the console if run on a computer. The only problem we'll face is that a computer doesn't understand this code. It understands only binary language of 0s and 1s. So, we must convert this program into binary language so that the computer can understand and run it. The compiler converts the code into MSIL. When executing the program, .NET Common Language Runtime (CLR) does a just-in-time (JIT) compilation of this MSIL into machine-specific code, which the microprocessor understands and then executes the converted machine code to display "Hello World!" on the console window as shown in Figure 1-2.

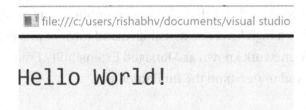

Figure 1-2. *Hello World!*

While writing extensions, we will come across the term Visual Studio SDK, so let us discuss what SDK means.

What Is Software Development Kit (SDK)?

A software development kit (SDK), as the name implies, is a collection of tools designed to facilitate software development. To better understand it, let us first understand the concept of a development kit.

A kit refers to a set of essential tools for creating something (e.g., a carpenter's kit contains tools like a hammer, chisel, etc., to make furniture). Similarly, in software development, we require a comprehensive toolset or development kit, known as software development kit, or SDK. An SDK typically includes DLLs and libraries that support, assist, and streamline the development process with a specific development environment.

For instance, when developing an application on the .NET platform, we would need the .NET SDK. The SDK encompasses various components, including but not limited to:

- Common Language Runtime (CLR) required for running/debugging applications during development

- Base Class Library (BCL) DLLs to use built-in functions of .NET Framework, etc.

Different SDKs will offer different content depending upon what the developer will require while developing software using that particular SDK.

Let's explore another relevant example related to the subject matter covered in this book. To develop Visual Studio extensions, you need to use the Visual Studio SDK (VSSDK). When you add the relevant workloads (covered in the next chapter) during Visual Studio installation, you're essentially installing the SDK required to develop Visual Studio extensions. We will discuss Visual Studio SDK through this book, while developing the extensions, and also delve into its components, as needed.

Visual Studio offers a high level of extensibility, and most of this extensibility is based on the extensibility framework known as Managed Extensibility Framework (MEF). Let's now delve into MEF and understand the fundamentals.

Managed Extensibility Framework (MEF)

To understand Managed Extensibility Framework (MEF), we need to understand the first two parts of its name, that is, "Managed" and "Extensibility." Let us understand these terms one by one:

- Managed: Any code that runs under the context of Common Language Runtime (CLR) is called managed code.

- Extensibility: A way of extending the features/behavior of a class, component, framework, tool, IDE, browser, etc. is called extensibility.

Now let's see the formal definition of MEF taken from the official Microsoft documentation page:

The Managed Extensibility Framework or MEF is a library for creating lightweight, and extensible applications. It allows application developers to discover and use extensions with no configuration required. It also lets

extension developers easily encapsulate code and avoid fragile hard depen-
dencies. MEF not only allows extensions to be reused within applications,
but across applications as well.

MEF was shipped by the .NET Framework team with version 4.0 to make an add-in- or plug-in-based extensible application easily on .NET Framework. MEF is an integral part of .NET Framework 4.0 and above, and it is available wherever the .NET Framework is used. You can use MEF in your client applications, whether they use Windows Forms, WPF, or any other technology, or in server applications that use ASP.NET.

The fundamental and simplified theory of MEF is that an application is composed of parts. So, an application can be extended by exporting parts, importing parts, and composing parts, without a need for configuration. MEF provides

- A standard for extensibility

- A declarative, attribute-based programming model

- Tools for discovery of parts implicitly, via composition at runtime

- A rich metadata system

The assembly System.ComponentModel.Composition provides the MEF. Just importing this namespace would enable us to use MEF. Let us see the high-level basic architecture of MEF (Figure 1-3).

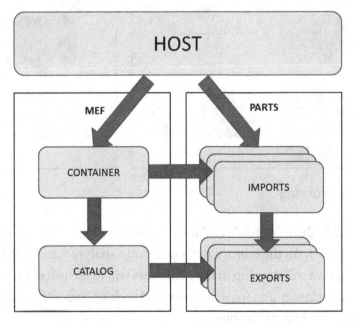

Figure 1-3. *MEF basic architecture*

An MEF component called a part declaratively specifies its dependencies, called imports, as well as its capabilities, called exports. When a part is created, the MEF composition engine satisfies its imports from the other parts that are available. Because of the declarative model (attributes), the imports and exports can be discovered at runtime, without depending on hardly coupled and referenced assemblies or error-prone configuration files. MEF allows the application to discover parts via metadata.

An application leveraging MEF declares imports for its dependencies, for example, in a constructor or in a property, and may also declare exports that can be used to expose service to other parts. This way, component parts are also extensible. A diagram depicting the high-level working of MEF is shown in Figure 1-4. The host application can have several catalogs and parts. A catalog contains the parts (exports as well as imports). There are several types of catalogs, like Directory catalog, Assembly catalog, Type catalog, etc. Each part has some dependencies that are decorated with Import or ImportMany attributes. This way they advertise their dependencies and requirements. There are some parts that expose services. They are decorated with Export or ExportMany attributes and provide or fulfill the service. Then there is an MEF container that takes the MEF catalog and composes the parts if there are matching exports and imports.

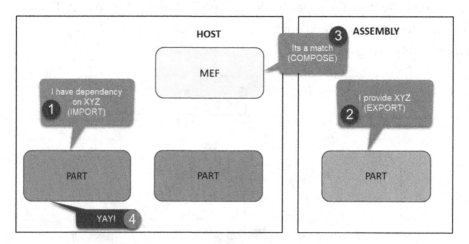

Figure 1-4. *MEF working*

Visual Studio is highly extensible and makes extensive use of MEF to extend its various components. All the editor extensions, code analyzers, code refactoring extensions, etc. that we will develop in later chapters will make use of MEF and we will need to decorate the classes that we write to extend with an Export attribute or other attributes derived from Export attributes.

For a quick recap on MEF, I would highly recommend the readers to read this good documentation by Microsoft at `https://docs.microsoft.com/en-us/dotnet/framework/mef/`.

Please note that Visual Studio extensions can be built using .NET Framework. However, please be aware that .NET Core is not supported for extension development in Visual Studio as of writing this edition.

While writing extensions, we will come across a vsixmanifest file, which is an XML file; and while publishing the extension to the marketplace, we will be creating a publishManifest file, which is a JSON file, so for the benefit of new and beginner developers, let us have a quick tour of XML and JSON.

XML and JSON

XML and JSON are the two most common data formats for exchanging information over the Internet. Let us recap them one by one.

XML stands for E**x**tensible **M**arkup **L**anguage. It is a markup language like **H**ypertext **M**arkup **L**anguage (HTML). It is self-descriptive in nature. The very famous SOAP protocol used in service-oriented architecture (SOA) also uses XML format to define its Web Services Description Language (WSDL). We will see while developing Visual Studio extensions that the vsixmanifest file that defines the extension metadata is an XML. Let us see a sample XML file:

```xml
<?xml version="1.0" encoding="utf-8"?>
<PackageManifest Version="2.0.0" xmlns="http://schemas.microsoft.com/
developer/vsx-schema/2011" xmlns:d="http://schemas.microsoft.com/developer/
vsx-schema-design/2011">
  <Metadata>

    <Identity Id="VarToStrongType..b0eb46a5-106e-44f0-ad4a-bb66f19335a8"
    Version="1.0" Language="en-US" Publisher="rishabhv"/>
    <DisplayName>VarToStrongType</DisplayName>

    <Description xml:space="preserve">This is a sample code refactoring
    extension for the .NET Compiler Platform ("Roslyn").</Description>
  </Metadata>

</PackageManifest>
```

This is a sample XML showing Visual Studio extension's package manifest.

You can read about XML in greater detail on the World Wide Web Consortium's official page: `www.w3.org/XML/`.

JSON stands for JavaScript Object Notation. This data format was first introduced in the front-end/web world. Douglas Crockford of *JavaScript: The Good Parts* fame is considered to be the man behind the fame of JSON format. It is an efficient data transfer format and better than XML. As of today, it is being used in all back-end technologies equally. While developing modern web applications, we will see that most application configurations are now JSON based, including in ASP.NET Core. While developing Visual Studio extension pack, we will see that it makes use of JSON.

Key points to know about JSON syntax are the following:

- Data is in name/value pairs.

- Data is separated by commas.

- Curly braces hold objects.

- Square brackets hold arrays or collections.

- Values must be one of the following data types:

  a. A string

  b. A number

  c. An object (JSON object)

  d. An array

  e. A Boolean

  f. Null

Here is how a typical JSON format data looks:

```
{
    "name":"Sachin",
    "age":46,
    "city":"Mumbai"
}
```

Let us do a quick dissection of this example to understand it better:

```
"name" is a key
"Sachin" is a value
"name":"Sachin" is a tuple
```

Visual Studio makes extensive use of serialization and deserialization while persisting the files and in various other places; let us have a quick recap.

Serialization and Deserialization

Before discussing serialization and deserialization, let's understand why it is required in the first place.

We live in the world of the Internet where computers talk to each other and share data. When you call a method of a web service using a SOAP or REST protocol, some data gets shared between the client PC and the server. This data sharing among computers happens via network cables. The data sharing over wire between two processes running on different PCs requires the data to be converted into a format that can be transferred over wire, and then at the receiver's end, this formatted information should be reconstructed back to the data. This, in essence, is the concept of serialization and deserialization.

So, in the context of data storage or data sharing, serialization is the process of translating data structures or object states into a format that can be stored or transmitted over wire so that it can be reconstructed to its original form at a later point in time. Deserialization is just the opposite of serialization. Serialization happens on a source machine. Deserialization happens on a remote/target machine. Figure 1-5 summarizes the process of serialization and deserialization.

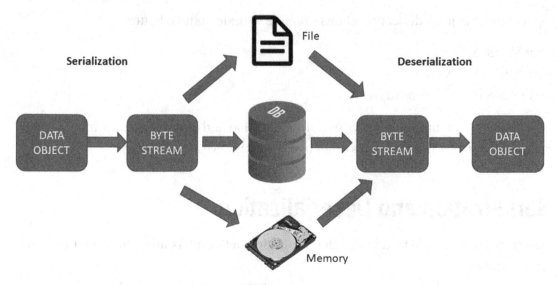

Figure 1-5. *Serialization and deserialization*

If you use a Windows operating system and have ever hibernated your system, it serves as an example of serialization. When you hibernate, the operating system serializes the state of your machine and persists it in disk. When you boot the system again, the operating system checks the disk and deserializes the data to restore the state of your machine, so you resume from where you left off.

For any .NET project that involves JSON-based data exchange, Newtonsoft.Json NuGet package is one of the popularly used packages. This library contains various classes in which you can serialize or deserialize JSON data to and from your domain model objects.

I would encourage you to learn more about it on its website here: `www.newtonsoft.com/json/help/html/SerializingJSON.htm`.

Visual Studio and its extensions make extensive use of known and popular design patterns. A few of the commonly used design patterns are visitor design patterns while working with Roslyn syntax trees, singleton design patterns in initializing the custom command, abstract factory in menus, and so on. Let us revisit few of the important design patterns.

Revisiting Visitor, Abstract Factory, and Factory Design Patterns

Design Pattern

Design patterns are standardized and reusable solutions to common problems in software design. They are also referred to as Gang of Four (GoF) design patterns, as they were initially defined by a group of four authors way back in 1994. All the design patterns are divided into three broad categories as shown in Table 1-1.

Table 1-1. *Design Patterns*

Creational design patterns	Behavioral design patterns	Structural design patterns
Abstract factory	Chain of responsibility	Adapter
Builder	Command	Bridge
Factory method	Interpreter	Composite
Singleton	Iterator	Decorator
Prototype	Mediator	Façade
	Memento	Flyweight
	Observer	Proxy
	State	
	Strategy	
	Template method	
	Visitor	

Out of this huge list, we'll be discussing only three design patterns that are going to be used in this book.

Factory Method Pattern

Factory method pattern (a.k.a. factory design pattern) is a creational design pattern, that is, it is related to object creation. It defines an interface for creating an object but lets the classes that implement the interface decide which class to instantiate. The factory method lets a class defer instantiation to subclasses.

An increasingly popular definition of factory method is a static method of a class that returns an object of that class type. But unlike a constructor, the actual object it returns might be an instance of a subclass. Unlike a constructor, an existing object might be reused in place of creating a new object. Unlike a constructor, factory methods can have different and more descriptive names.

Abstract Factory

Abstract factory is also a creational design pattern, that is, it is related to how objects are created in your application. It provides an interface for creating families of related or dependent objects without specifying their concrete classes. This pattern is generally used in the creation of menus.

Abstract factory pattern implementation provides a framework that allows us to create objects that follow a general pattern. So, at runtime, an abstract factory is coupled with any desired concrete factory, which can create objects of a desired type.

Let us see the definition given by the Gang of Four (GoF) for an abstract factory pattern:

- AbstractFactory: Declares an interface for operations that create abstract product objects

- ConcreteFactory: Implements the operations declared in the AbstractFactory to create concrete product objects

- Product: Defines a product object to be created by the corresponding concrete factory and implements the AbstractProduct interface

- Client: Uses only interfaces declared by AbstractFactory and AbstractProduct classes

Thus, the abstract factory provides interfaces for creating families of related or dependent objects without specifying their concrete classes (Figure 1-6).

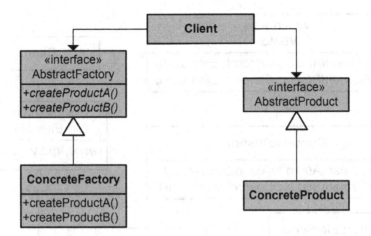

Figure 1-6. *Abstract factory design pattern*

Note   The Gang of Four published a seminal design patterns book in 1994. It's a good place to start to learn more: *Design Patterns: Elements of Reusable Object-Oriented Software* (Addison-Wesley, 1994).

Client application creates a concrete implementation of the abstract factory and then uses the generic interfaces to create the concrete objects that are part of the family of objects. The client does not know or care which concrete objects it gets from each of these concrete factories since it uses only the generic interfaces of their products.

Visitor Pattern

Visitor pattern is one of the behavioral design patterns. It is used when we have to perform an operation on a group of similar kinds of objects. With the help of a visitor pattern, we can move the operational logic from the objects to another class.

There are important parts of a visitor pattern that we need to know:

1. A method called "Visit," which is implemented by the visitor and is called for every element in the data structure

2. Visitable classes providing "Accept" methods that accept a visitor

Now let us understand the various design components involved in this pattern with the help of the UML diagram shown in Figure 1-7.

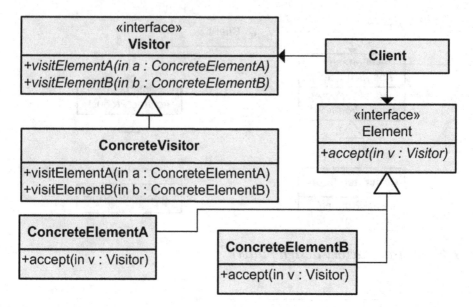

Figure 1-7. *Visitor design pattern*

- Client: The Client class is a consumer of the classes of the visitor design pattern. It has access to the data structure objects and can instruct them to accept a Visitor to perform the appropriate processing.

- Visitor: This is an interface or an abstract class used to declare the visit operations for all the types of visitable classes.

- ConcreteVisitor: For each type of visitor, all the visit methods declared in abstract visitor must be implemented. Each visitor will be responsible for different operations.

- Element: This is an interface that declares the accept operation. This is the entry point that enables an object to be "visited" by the visitor object.

- ConcreteElementA and ConcreteElementB: These classes implement the Element interface and define the "accept" operation. The visitor object is passed to this object using the "accept" operation.

A great benefit of Visual Studio being extensible is that we can plug in our code to the various solution and build events to take action when an event occurs. A few of the events of interest for developers are related to build. Visual Studio makes use of the MSBuild engine behind the scenes to build the code, so let us refresh the fundamentals of MSBuild.

MSBuild Basics

Before we talk about MSBuild, we should first understand the difference between a compilation process and a build process.

What Is Code Compilation?

Compilation is the process through which your language compiler validates the syntax of your code whether it is right or wrong. If it is right, then compilation says it is okay or else it throws compilation errors.

What Happens When We Say That We're Building the Code?

Build is the process through which a tool packages the compiled code and creates output files on disk, for example, EXE, DLL, etc.

So, MSBuild is a build tool that performs the packaging task in Visual Studio after your .NET or C++ code has been compiled successfully by respective language compilers.

How Do We Use MSBuild in Visual Studio?

It is very simple. Once you've opened any project supported by Visual Studio, go to the Build menu and click the "Build Solution" option as shown in the screenshot in Figure 1-8. The same happens when you build, rebuild, or debug your code via Visual Studio. That's all you need to do. Thereafter, Visual Studio does everything required to compile and build the project.

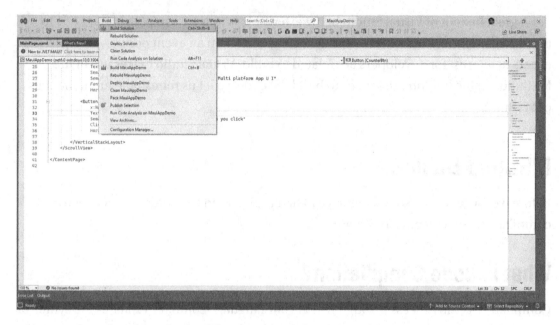

Figure 1-8. *Visual Studio build menu*

Whenever you build a project in Visual Studio, it happens in the following mentioned steps:

1. Compilation of source code

2. Packaging of compiled code

Visual Studio (VS) acts as the orchestrator in this process. It controls both the compiler and MSBuild. VS first asks the compiler whether the current code is compilable or not. If the compiler says yes, then VS asks MSBuild to trigger the build process to generate the build output binaries.

MSBuild tool comes preinstalled when you install Visual Studio, and it works in background without your knowledge. You can also use it from the command line once you've installed Visual Studio on your computer machine.

If you don't have Visual Studio installed (e.g., in your build server where your CI pipeline will be building the code for your extension), then you'll have to install either .NET software development kit (SDK) or Microsoft Build tools separately to get the MSBuild EXE, which is the starting point to run MSBuild. As of today, MSBuild is available as an extension in Visual Studio Code as well if you want to build any code and package using MSBuild.

To know about the internals of MSBuild, I would encourage you to follow its open source repository hosted on GitHub – https://github.com/microsoft/msbuild.

In modern programming, asynchrony is the part of mainstream coding and should not be an afterthought. Writing extensions is no different. While writing extensions, we will make use of asynchronous loading of packages and use async APIs for better and efficient usage of threads. To that end, let us revisit async await.

async await

async await makes up the language features in C# language that help developers to do asynchronous programming easily. How? Well, C# 5 (.NET Framework 4.5) introduced keywords async and await, so that developers can write async methods directly. Since, it's a language feature exposed via keywords, the burden of complicated code is offloaded from the developer to the compiler. With async await keywords, a developer can just write an async method and the compiler takes the responsibility of writing the complex code behind the scenes and optimizes it as well. Therefore, async await is also called "syntactic sugar." Let's create our first async method using async await keywords and understand it's working. To do so, first let us write a synchronous code and then convert it to the async method:

```
private static void DownloadData(string url, string path)
{
    // Create a new web client object.
    using (WebClient client = new WebClient())    //1
    {
        // Add user-agent header to avoid forbidden errors.
        client.Headers.Add("user-agent", "Mozilla/5.0 (Windows NT
        10.0; WOW64)"); //2

        // Download data from url.
        byte[] data = client.DownloadData(url);    //3

        // Write data in file.
        using (var fileStream = File.OpenWrite(path))  //4
        {
            fileStream.Write(data, 0, data.Length); //5
```

```
            }
        }
    }
```

We have a simple `DownloadData` method that takes two arguments of type string, namely, url and path. The code is straightforward and self-explanatory, by means of comments, but let's go through it to set the foundation for `async await`. Each line of the program is marked with a comment for clarity.

1. We create a new `WebClient` object. `WebClient` provides APIs for sending and receiving the data from a web resource using HTTP requests and responses.

2. The user-agent header information of `HttpRequest` is set.

3. The `DownloadData` method of the client is called with the URL as a parameter. This method is synchronous and may take some time to complete. The executing thread will block and wait until the statement completes successfully or encounters an error. Eventually, a result would be obtained and it would be stored in a local variable named data of type `byte[]`.

4. We have the data downloaded from the URL, so we want to save this data in a file path. So, we create a new `FileStream` object, passing the path as a parameter.

5. We invoke the Write method on the `FileStream` object and write the downloaded data to the file.

Since both `WebClient` and `FileStream` implement `IDisposable`, we have wrapped their object creation code inside the `using` block, which would ensure that once the object is no longer used, the memory of these objects is reclaimed by the CLR via garbage collection (GC).

C# is a high-level language. The code that we write in C# is for the application layer. For the same reason, it is more or less independent of the type of computer hardware, and anything that we write in C# undergoes multiple transformations before they get converted into assembly language that the CPU understands and processes. C# doesn't communicate to hardware directly. In the async sample program with method `DownloadDataAsync`, we have two instances where we need to communicate with the computer hardware to do the job. Generally, a programmer need not understand these low-level details, and only knowing to use the APIs correctly is sufficient. However, understanding these fundamentals can help us appreciate the benefits that `async await` brings to the table.

In line #3, we call the `DownloadData` method on the web client object, which is synchronous. The `DownloadData` method downloads the data from the specified URL and returns it as a byte array. Depending on factors like size of data, network speed, and other computer configuration parameters, it may take a while for this method to complete.

Now, consider this scenario in an ASP.NET Core or ASP.NET application. When this method is executed, the framework allocates one of the `ThreadPool` threads to handle the request. The thread executes the code until it reaches the `DownloadData` method call. Behind the scenes, the call goes from managed code (C# .NET) to the native code. The native code would talk to the hardware and instruct it to download the data from the specified URL. During this time, the thread allocated by ThreadPool in the managed code has nothing to do but just wait and wait. Sometime in the future, the hardware would finish its job and return the data to native code, which would in turn return the data in byte [] to the managed code. An operation in which a thread's primary task is just to wait for the operation is the I/O-bound operation. This indeed is an I/O-bound operation. Under the hood, a CLR thread pool makes use of an I/O port to schedule the threads for I/O operations. These threads are referred to as I/O completion port (IOCP) threads. A similar thing happens in line #5 as well. Here the data is written to the hard-disk drive of the computer, which is an I/O operation, and during this time, as well, the managed thread is just sitting idle and waiting!

Since the code is running in a web application, it is common to expect a scenario in which a burst of requests arrives at the server. ThreadPool would allocate a thread per request, so depending upon the number of requests, we may have a large number of threads trying to execute this code; and like we saw earlier, there would be a period of time in which all of these threads would just sit and wait for the data to be downloaded and returned back to it. Later, the data would be fetched and returned to the thread. Even in this case, depending upon the number of cores in the server, only that many threads would at the best be able to run concurrently and others would just wait for the context switch to happen. Recall that context switches are expensive, and so we have been following highly expensive observations in the preceding code:

- We are unnecessarily allocating a thread per request. (Threads are expensive.)

- The thread spends a considerable amount of time doing nothing and just waiting for an I/O operation to complete. (Wasting resources.)

- When the data returns, since we have many threads (more than CPU cores), the threads would compete for the context switch to happen to continue further processing. (Context switches are expensive.)

- This wasting of resources is happening twice in the method. See line #3 and line #5.

Due to the preceding reasons, the synchronous I/O operations are not scalable, and we may soon reach the memory and CPU limits as we are wasting or not utilizing the resources optimally. This is assuming we have enough threads in the ThreadPool, or else there may be other serious issues like thread exhaustion due to ThreadPool throttling or an HttpRequest getting queued. We will see how leveraging asynchronous methods via `async await` would solve this issue and enable the path for making highly scalable solutions. Before we dive into the async version of the preceding code, let us quickly see how we can invoke the code earlier from a console app.

To call this method from the console app, we need the following lines of code:

```
static void Main(string[] args)
{

        // Set the url to a website from which content needs to be
        downloaded.
        string url = " https://www.apress.com/in/apress-open/
        apressopen-titles";

        // Path where downloaded data needs to be saved.
        string path = "C:\\Rishabh\\download.txt";
        // Call the method.
        DownloadData (url, path);
}
```

Upon executing this code, the data would be downloaded from the specified URL and dumped into the file name `download.txt` in the specified location. This code is simple and executes synchronously.

Let's convert our `DownloadData` method into an asynchronous method, leveraging `async await` keywords. The rewritten method would look like this:

```csharp
private static async Task DownloadDataAsync(string url,
string path)
{
    // Create a new web client object.
    using (WebClient client = new WebClient()) //1
    {
        // Add user-agent header to avoid forbidden errors.
        client.Headers.Add("user-agent", "Mozilla/5.0 (Windows NT
        10.0; WOW64)"); //2

        // Download data from url.
        byte[] data = await client.DownloadDataTaskAsync(url); //3

        // Write data in file.
        using (var fileStream = File.OpenWrite(path)) //4
        {
            await fileStream.WriteAsync(data, 0, data.Length); //5
        }
    }
}
```

Pretty simple, right! The following changes are worth noting in this rewritten asynchronous method:

1. Though it may not always be the case, there is no change in the number of lines of code from the synchronous version of the method.

2. There is a new access modifier async added to the method definition.

3. The return type of method has changed from void to Task, though keeping the return type as void would have compiled as well. But it is highly NOT recommended to code that way. We will talk about this later in our discussion of exception handling.

4. We have changed the method name from DownloadData to DownloadDataAsync to indicate that this method is asynchronous. Although there is no hard-and-fast rule like this, it is recommended to have an async suffix in the method names that arc asynchronous, just to make it easier for API consumers as well as for maintenance and readability.

5. The two important operations where data was getting downloaded, and downloaded data was being written to files, now have an await keyword before their invocation, and they make use of an async version of methods instead of their synchronous method counterparts.

With just these few changes, our synchronous method has been changed to an asynchronous method. This is the USP of the `async await` keywords that it makes writing asynchronous methods easier than ever. Though there is a lot that happens behind the scenes, abstracted away from the developer, the compiler does all the hard part and makes the life of the developer easy. The calling method will also undergo a change that we will see a little later.

Based on this description, we can devise a simple step-by-step technique to convert any synchronous method to an asynchronous method and they are the following:

*   Introduce the async keyword in the method definition.

*   Replace the return type of the method according to Table 1-2.

Table 1-2. *Return Types for async Method*

Synchronous method Return Type	Async method Return Type
T	Task<T>
void	Task
void	void (only for top-level event handlers, like button click)

Add an async suffix in the method name to declare to the world that the method is asynchronous.

Inside the method, look for method invocations that have asynchronous versions available (end with async and have task-based return types). If yes, use the async version with the await keyword.

Okay! We have the async version of method. But, how is it better than the synchronous version of the method we saw earlier? Let's see the line-by-line execution of code to understand this. Like earlier, we have the line number appended as a suffix in each line of code.

1. We create a new WebClient object. WebClient provides APIs for sending and receiving the data from a web resource using HTTP requests and responses. (It is the same as the synchronous version.)

2. The user-agent header information of HttpRequest is set. (It is the same as the synchronous version.)

3. The `DownloadDataTaskAsync` method of the client is called with the URL as a parameter. This method is asynchronous and is prefixed with an await keyword. This is where the compiler will play a part. To simplify and make it comprehensive, the thread executing this code would return to the caller method upon encountering the await keyword. If it's a GUI application, and the method is invoked from a top-level event handler, then the main thread will return to process the message pump and hence the UI will remain responsive. If it's a server-side code and ThreadPool thread is executing it, then this thread will return to the caller function and hence remain available for further processing (instead of sitting there and waiting!). In the future, when the `DownloadDataTaskAsync` method completes its work and returns the data in byte[], ThreadPool may allocate the same or different thread to resume the method from the same place and continue with the rest of the code. In this sense, `async await` enables the ThreadPool threads to return to the caller method (top-level awaits may return the thread to the pool) and enter the method multiple times (as many times as await appears).

4. We have the data downloaded from the URL, so we want to save this data in a file path. So, we create a new `FileStream` object, passing the path as a parameter. (This is the same as the synchronous version.)

5. We invoke the `WriteAsync` method on the `FileStream` object and await it to write the downloaded data to the file. This will have the same behavior as we discussed in step #3. Basically, the compiler transforms the method using `async await` into a state machine, where thread can enter multiple times. This way threads remain free because they are used optimally. They are freed up and return

to the caller upon encountering the await statement and can be used elsewhere, increasing scalability and minimizing resource wastage. Therefore, methods using `async await` make the code more scalable and are highly recommended to be used in the server-side applications as well as in GUI-based applications to keep the UI responsive.

Tip   To grasp the fundamental of `async await`, I suggest thinking of the await keyword as the `ContinueWith` construct. The compiler transforms the code after the await statement inside a `ContinueWith` construct. As soon as an await keyword is encountered, the executing thread returns to the caller. Upon completion of that statement, a thread executes the code wrapped inside the `ContinueWith` construct. This can be on a different thread or the same thread depending upon if `ConfigureAwait(false)` is used or not used, respectively. This happens for all await statements.

Let's have a look at the next code using `async await`. Please pay special attention to the numbered steps.

```csharp
static async Task Main(string[] args)
{
    //                          1
    // Call the asynchronous method.
    await DownloadDataAsync(url, path);     // 2
    // Prevent the program from exiting unless you press enter.
    Console.ReadLine();                     // 5
}

1 reference | Rishabh Verma, 28 minutes ago | 1 author, 1 change
private static async Task DownloadDataAsync(string url, string path)
{
    // Create a new web client object
    using (WebClient client = new WebClient())
    {
        // Add user-agent header to avoid forbidden errors.
        client.Headers.Add("user-agent", "Mozilla/5.0 (Windows NT 10.0; WOW64)"); //2
        // download data from Url
        byte[] data = await client.DownloadDataTaskAsync(url); //3
        // Write data in file.
        using (var fileStream = File.OpenWrite(path))
        {
            await fileStream.WriteAsync(data, 0, data.Length);    // 4
        }
    }
}
```

Figure 1-9. async await control flow

In Figure 1-9, the high-level steps of the execution flow are marked. Let's discuss these steps to understand the control flow.

We know that our Main method is async as we added an async modifier in the Main method definition. As we will see in the next section, when a method is marked with an async modifier, the compiler transforms the method's code into a type that implements a state machine. The executing thread continues until it encounters an await keyword and then returns to the caller.

In our case, the main thread enters the Main method (the entry point) and starts executing the code. It continues to execute the code until it encounters the await statement, marked as step 2.

The main thread passes the url and path parameters and invokes the DownloadDataAsync, which is also asynchronous and is awaited. Inside the DownloadDataAsync method, a Task object is created and returned to the Main method. At this point, the await keyword wires up the callback method ContinueWith on this returned Task object and passes the method that resumes the state machine and then the main thread returns from the Main method.

The DownloadDataAsync method would run on the main thread until it encounters its first await statement. This can be seen by printing the Thread.CurrentThread. ManagedThreadId before and after await statements in the Main as well as in DownloadDataAsync methods.

Upon encountering an await statement like await client.DownloadDataTaskAsync, a Task object is created and returned to the DownloadDataAsync method. The await keyword wires up the callback method ContinueWith on the Task object, and the thread returns back to DownloadDataAsync.

Sometime later, the HttpClient will complete downloading the data from the URL, and a ThreadPool thread will notify the Task object, which would result in the activation of the callback method ContinueWith and the thread would resume the method from the await statement.

Now, the DownloadDataTaskAsync method of HttpClient could have completed the task successfully or may have encountered a network error. All these status checks are done by the compiler-generated code behind the scenes, and the method execution continues on the ThreadPool thread, which will then create a FileStream and call its WriteAsync method. Again, the await operator calls a ContinueWith on the task object returned from WriteAsync method passing in the callback method name to resume the method, and the thread returns from DownloadDataAsync method again.

After some time, the write operation would complete. A ThreadPool thread will notify the completion and the thread will resume the `DownloadDataAsync` method until its completion and return to the Main method. The compiler will generate the code to ensure that Main method knows that the `DownloadDataAsync` method is now complete and it has no further await statements. This is done by marking the status of Task returned from `DownloadDataAsync` method as Completed. The thread then waits at `Console.ReadLine()` waiting for a user enter to exit the console.

This concludes our quick refresher on `async await`. In the next section, we will see .NET Compiler platform and conclude this chapter.

.NET Compiler Platform (Roslyn)

Until not so long ago, C# and VB compilers used to be black boxes for developers. With the advent of .NET compiler platform (Roslyn), this changed and now developers have compiler as a service, which they can use to extend the compiler and display custom warnings and errors and build amazing developer tools. .NET compiler platform is built upon several APIs and services. Visual Studio extensibility for code fixes, refactoring, and light bulb-style code actions is provided by the.NET compiler platform.

Figure 1-10 displays the high-level architecture of the .NET compiler platform.

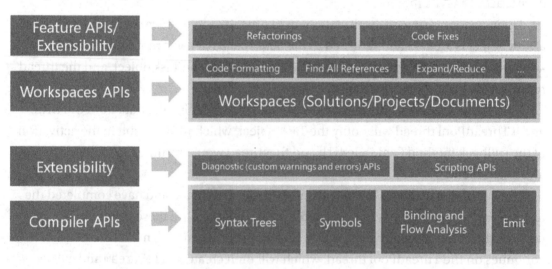

Figure 1-10. *.NET Compiler platform architecture*

There are three main layers in the .NET compiler platform:

- Compiler APIs: This layer provides an object model that holds the syntax and semantic information exposed at each phase of the compiler pipeline. This layer exposes the immutable syntax trees, symbols, code files, options, and assembly references. There is a layer of extensibility above this layer which can be used to tap on to the diagnostics and scripting APIs.

- Workspaces APIs: This layer exposes the object model that holds the information of solutions. Workspaces APIs can be used to perform code analysis, formatting across the solution.

- Feature APIs: This layer exposes the APIs to perform code analysis fixes and refactoring.

The .NET compiler platform has opened the door for the plethora of opportunities like the following:

- Enforcing best practices and standards, for example, StyleCop, FxCop, and code analyzers

- Code-aware libraries

- Code generation

- Scripting (interactive window of Visual Studio is an example)

It is also the right time to state that Visual Studio 2022 makes use of the .NET Compiler platform, and the code editor is built on top of the .NET Compiler platform.

To leverage the .NET compiler platform in your project, you need to add a NuGet package `Microsoft.CodeAnalysis`, which is a superset of all the assemblies.

This is a huge topic and deserves a book in itself to do full justice. Here, we will just present a quick overview so that the reader can understand and get started with the .NET compiler platform.

There are primarily two types of analysis that you can perform on code:

- Syntax analysis: In this case, we make use of the compiler APIs. We parse the source code and get a Syntax tree represented by `Microsoft.CodeAnalysis.SyntaxTree`. This represents the lexical and syntactic structure of the code. Once we have a syntax tree, we can get the compilation unit root and all the other nodes that are its descendants.

- Semantic model: The semantic model represents the semantic information for a source code and is represented by `Microsoft.CodeAnalysis.SemanticModel`. This is helpful to work with symbols – to evaluate the type of result of an expression, find references of a symbol, and perform flow analysis – and is also helpful in code fixes and refactoring.

Visual Studio comes with an extension named Syntax Visualizer (Go to View ➤ Other Windows ➤ Syntax Visualizer) that can be used to see the Syntax tree from the source code. This is shown in Figure 1-11.

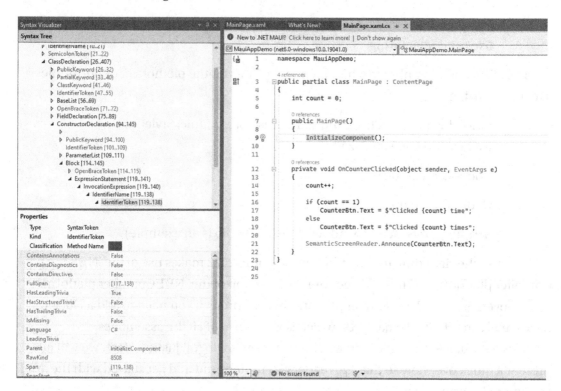

Figure 1-11. *Syntax Visualizer showing Syntax tree on the left for the source code*

The syntax trees are immutable. In fact, most of the types exposed by the .NET Compiler platform are immutable. This is deliberately done via design for thread safety, so that these types can be edited/updated without the need to acquire a lock. Therefore, every time you modify/update a type, you will get a new type object, which the existing type object remains unmodified.

Syntax Visualizer is a must-use tool for any developer working on the .NET Compiler platform to learn and understand what node of SyntaxTree maps with the code. The SyntaxTree window keeps in sync with the code on the editor. Clicking the code would focus the node in the Syntax Visualizer and vice versa. This is where we can find out that class declaration maps to ClassDeclarationSyntax in tree, method maps to MethodDeclarationSyntax, and so on.

We can also visualize the directed syntax graph of any node, in the syntax tree from the Syntax Visualizer as shown in Figure 1-12. Just right-click the node in the Syntax Visualizer and choose View Directed Syntax Graph on the context menu.

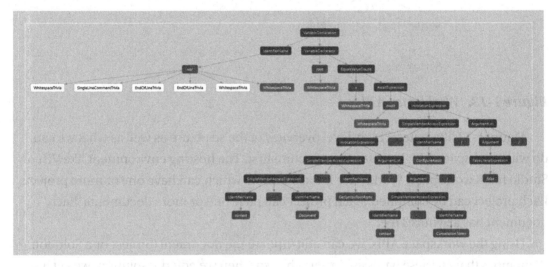

Figure 1-12. *Directed syntax graph*

Let us quickly see the usage for APIs by means of images.

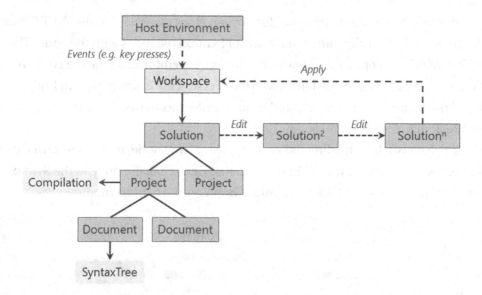

Figure 1-13. *Workspace API*

Figure 1-13 illustrates a high-level overview of the structure as well as what we can do with workspace API. Let's see the structure first. The hosting environment like Visual Studio has a workspace. Workspace has a Solution, which can have one or more projects. Each project can be compiled. Each project can have one or more documents. Each document has a Syntax Tree.

Using the workspace APIs, we can edit/update the document/project or a Solution. Remember that all these types are immutable, so when we edit the solution, we get a new solution and this can go on. Once the changes are done and you apply the changes, then the solution gets updated in the workspace.

Next, let's look at the Syntax Tree API.

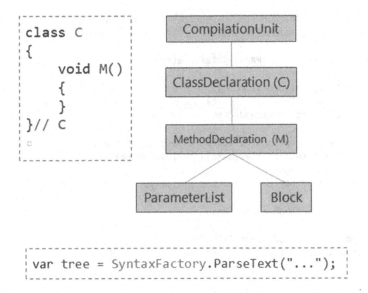

Figure 1-14. *Syntax tree API*

Figure 1-14 displays three things of interest:

- On the left is the sample C# code, having a bare minimum class definition of class named C and a single method named M returning void.

- On the bottom part is the code to parse the code into the Syntax tree. We read the code as string and invoke the SyntaxFactory.ParseText to get the syntax tree.

- The tree is depicted via blocks on the right side of the image.

This way SyntaxTree API can be used to parse the code and then conduct tests, validations, or diagnostics. We will use SyntaxTree API later in the book to write our code analyzer. A good getting-started code to parse the code into SyntaxTree and print class, methods, properties, and fields is shown in Figure 1-15. The code is well documented and self-explanatory.

```
// get the code directly or read code as string from C# file path
string text = @"class C { void M() {} }"; // System.IO.File.ReadAllText(path);
// Get the syntax tree
SyntaxTree tree = SyntaxFactory.ParseSyntaxTree(text);
// Get the compilation unit root
var root = tree.GetCompilationUnitRoot();
// Get anything you want, like, class, its name and other details, properties, fields, methoc
var classDeclarations = root.DescendantNodes().OfType<ClassDeclarationSyntax>();
// get the first class
var className = classDeclarations.FirstOrDefault().Identifier.Text;
Console.WriteLine($"The {nameof(className)} is {className}");
// get all method declarations
var methodDeclarations = root.DescendantNodes().OfType<MethodDeclarationSyntax>();

foreach (var method in methodDeclarations)
{
    string methodName = method.Identifier.Text;
    Console.WriteLine($"The {nameof(methodName)} is {methodName}");
}

// Same way Get all property declarations, field declarations ( We don't have any)
var propertyDeclarations = root.DescendantNodes().OfType<PropertyDeclarationSyntax>();
var fieldDeclarations = root.DescendantNodes().OfType<FieldDeclarationSyntax>();
```

Figure 1-15. *Working with SyntaxTree*

The whitespaces are represented as SyntaxTrivia and braces are represented
as SyntaxToken in the SyntaxTree. SyntaxTrivia and SyntaxTokens are displayed in
Figures 1-16 and 1-17.

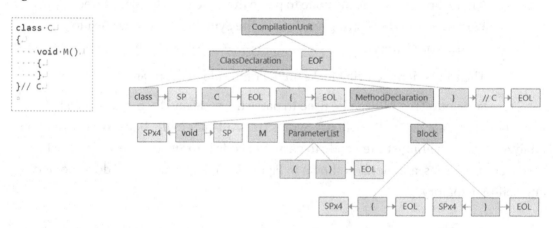

Figure 1-16. *SyntaxTrivia*

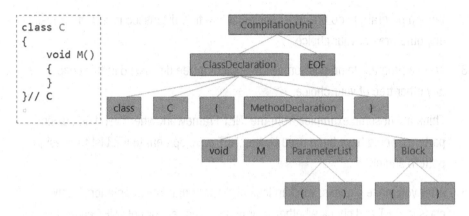

Figure 1-17. SyntaxTokens

A good resource to get acquainted with Roslyn is the documentation at `https://github.com/dotnet/roslyn/wiki/Roslyn%20Overview`.

I would highly recommend readers to get their hands on SyntaxTree and SemanticModel APIs, so that they can comfortably develop code analyzers, code fixes, and refactorings.

Summary

In this chapter, we started our journey toward understanding and developing Visual Studio extensibility by understanding why we should care about extending Visual Studio. Next, we started our revisiting quest and quickly discussed compiler, SDK, MEF, Visual Studio, XML, JSON, serialization, deserialization, design patterns, MSBuild, `async` `await`, and the .NET Compiler platform (Roslyn). In the next chapter, we will learn the anatomy of Visual Studio extensions and see how extensions are discovered and loaded.

EXERCISES

The following activities should give you a deep understanding of the fundamentals we discussed in this chapter:

1. Write a program to do in-order traversal of a tree discussed in this chapter or any other tree of your choice.

2. Write a program to do pre-order traversal of a tree discussed in this chapter or any other tree of your choice.

3. Write a program to do post-order traversal of a tree discussed in this chapter or any other tree of your choice.

4. Think about some examples from the .NET Framework where you think design patterns would have been used by the .NET development team. List the design pattern and class.

5. After you make a guess, you can look at the internal implementation of any class in .NET and check whether your guess is correct or not. .NET code is available as shared source code at the following location: `https://referencesource.microsoft.com`.

6. Read and familiarize yourself with the official Roslyn documentation at `https://github.com/dotnet/roslyn/wiki/Roslyn%20Overview`.

7. Write a console app to get SyntaxTree and SemanticModel of the source code given as input to the console.

CHAPTER 2

Getting Started

In this chapter, we will get started with the fundamentals of Visual Studio extensibility. We start by creating our very first Visual Studio 2022 extension, which does nothing. We will then dissect this created extension and understand its structure, format, and what files comprise a Visual Studio extension. Next, we will see the code walkthrough of a sample Visual Studio extension and understand the purpose of each file that comes up with the default Visual Studio boilerplate template code. We will conclude this chapter by seeing how Visual Studio discovers and loads an extension. We have a lot to cover, so let's get the ball rolling!

The Setup

At the time of writing this revision, Visual Studio 2022 stands as the latest version of the Visual Studio IDE. Visual Studio is offered in multiple editions, namely, Community, Professional, and Enterprise (`https://visualstudio.microsoft.com/vs/compare/`). The discussion in this book will center around the Visual Studio Community 2022 edition but are applicable to other editions unless explicitly specified otherwise. Visual Studio Community 2022 edition can be downloaded and installed from `https://visualstudio.microsoft.com/`. The installation is pretty straightforward but requires appropriate workloads to be selected. For extensibility, Visual Studio extensions development workload must be selected.

Creating Your First Visual Studio 2022 Extension

We have Visual Studio 2022 installed, with the required workloads chosen for developing and building Visual Studio extensions. You can refer to Figure 2-1 to ensure the appropriate workload is selected during your Visual Studio installation. You'll find it under "Other Toolsets" section in the "Workloads" tab.

© Rishabh Verma 2024
R. Verma, *Visual Studio Extensibility Development*, https://doi.org/10.1007/978-1-4842-9875-6_2

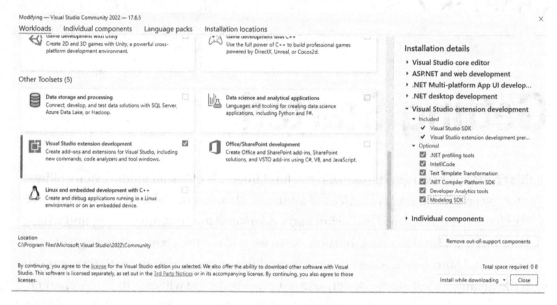

Figure 2-1. *Required workload in Visual Studio installation*

It is recommended that the "IntelliCode" component shown in the right pane is checked. Let's create our very first extension. This is a "getting started" extension, so the intent is to learn the fundamentals and not on what we achieve with this extension. We will see the step-by-step process to create your first Visual Studio 2022 extension:

1. Open Visual Studio 2022.

2. Create a new project.

3. This will display all the project templates that we can leverage to create a new project. Since we would be working with C#, choose the Language as C#. But you can also choose Visual Basic (VB) if you are comfortable with VB. The scope of this book is limited to C# only though.

4. Select the Project type drop-down value as "Extensions." This would filter the project templates as shown in Figure 2-2.

Figure 2-2. *"Create a new project" dialog filtered with Language as C# and Project type as Extensions*

Tip   If Visual Studio 2022 is installed with the correct workloads, only then would the extension project templates show up. Please refer to Figure 2-1 to select the required workloads during installation. If you do not see a VSIX Project template, you should modify your Visual Studio 2022. The official recommendation is to search for "Installer"/"Visual Studio Installer" after pressing the Windows key. Then launch the Visual Studio Installer and modify the installation of Visual Studio.

---

5. Select VSIX Project and click the Next button.

6. Next, you will see the "Configure your new project" screen. Enter the name you wish to give to your extension in Project name, the location where you wish to create this project in your file system in Location, and the name of solution in the Solution name. The values I provided in the sample are shown in Figure 2-3.

Configure your new project

VSIX Project   C#   Windows   Extensions

Project name

VSIXAnatomy

Location

C:\Users\rishabhv\source\repos\

Solution name ⓘ

VSIXAnatomy

☑ Place solution and project in the same directory

Project will be created in "C:\Users\rishabhv\source\repos\VSIXAnatomy\"

Figure 2-3. *Configure your new project*

7.   Click the "Create" button.

That's it! The code for your very first Visual Studio extension is generated by Visual Studio. Figure 2-4 is how the Solution Explorer view (View ➤ Solution Explorer or alternatively pressing the combination of Ctrl+Alt+L) in Visual Studio would look.

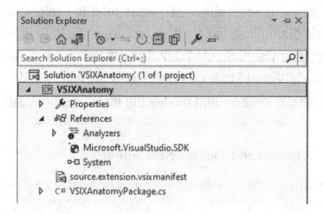

Figure 2-4. *Solution Explorer view*

8.   Build the project. It should build successfully. This is the boilerplate code that comes packaged with the VSIX Project template, so if installation was done correctly, it should build just fine. We will learn about creating a project and item templates later in the book.

Note   The flow of screens discussed earlier is specific to Visual Studio 2022. Microsoft takes user feedback seriously and may experiment and modify the user interface to suit the needs of end users. So, the screen flow and screen we discussed earlier may change in the future, but the fundamental steps would remain the same.

9. Now let's check the project properties in the Solution Explorer view to find out the output directory where our extension output would be created. To see it, click Properties ➤ Build and check the value in the Output path. You can also see the output directory by looking at the Output window of the Visual Studio after building the project. The Output Window of Visual Studio can be launched by clicking View ➤ Output or alternatively by the keyboard using the key combination of Ctrl+Alt+O.

10. Now that we know the output directory, let's check the build output of our extension. Figure 2-5 is how it looks in my machine.

This PC › SSD (C:) › Users › rishabhv › source › repos › VSIXAnatomy › bin › Debug

Name	Date modified	Type	Size
extension.vsixmanifest	08-08-2023 22:58	Extension Manifest	1 KB
VSIXAnatomy.dll	08-08-2023 22:58	Application extension	6 KB
VSIXAnatomy.pdb	08-08-2023 22:58	Program Debug Database	16 KB
VSIXAnatomy.pkgdef	08-08-2023 22:58	Package Definition Registration File	1 KB
VSIXAnatomy.vsix	08-08-2023 22:58	Microsoft Visual Studio Extension	10 KB

Figure 2-5. Output

We see a number of files in the output. However, the most important one is VSIXAnatomy.vsix file. This is the Visual Studio extension.

11. We can double-click this file and it would get installed. Let's do this installation by double-clicking the .vsix file shown in Figure 2-5. This would launch the VSIX Installer and would show a summary in its landing screen as seen in Figure 2-6.

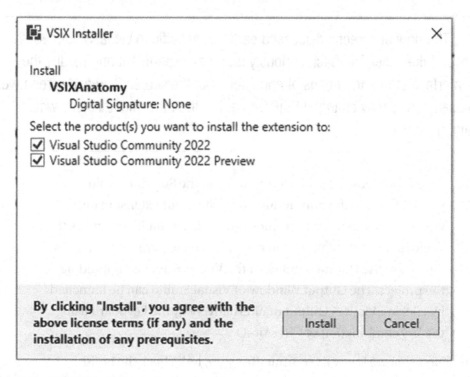

Figure 2-6. *VSIX Installer*

Please note that the screenshot showcases both Visual Studio Community 2022 and Visual Studio Community 2022 Preview. This is due to the fact that, during the time of writing this chapter, numerous highly upvoted Visual Studio feature requests from the developer community are being made accessible in a preview release (17.7, 17.8, etc.). It is important to understand that a preview release is not intended for production use. Its purpose is to provide customers with a glimpse of forthcoming functionalities and gather their feedback. I have installed both versions, which is why we see two distinct 2022 versions displayed.

VSIX Installer, as the name suggests, installs (as well as uninstalls) the VSIX in the machine so that Visual Studio can discover an extension next time it is started. It is developed in WPF and has improved over the years and become sophisticated. When Visual Studio starts, it starts and hosts numerous services to run and do its work. If any of these services locks the file or folder, then installation (or uninstallation) of extensions may fail or not work correctly. To circumvent this situation, the installer displays the processes that must be ended for the install to be successful.

12. Click the Install button. In my case, Visual Studio 2022 in which I created this extension and built is still running, so I see the screen in Figure 2-7, which asks me to shut down certain processes that may interfere in the installation of the extension.

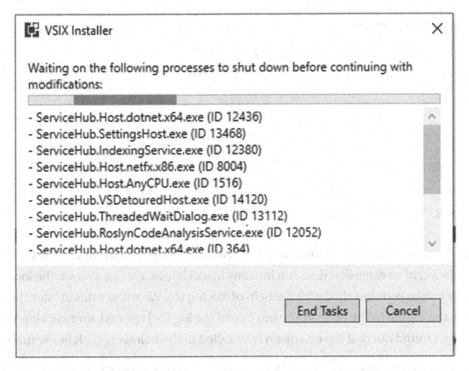

Figure 2-7. *End processes*

Clicking the "End Tasks" button would end these processes and install the extension. The progress bar would show up to keep the user updated with the progress of installation. It generally finishes very quickly, so progress may show for a small duration. Once the installation is done, the user sees the "Install Complete" screen as shown in Figure 2-8.

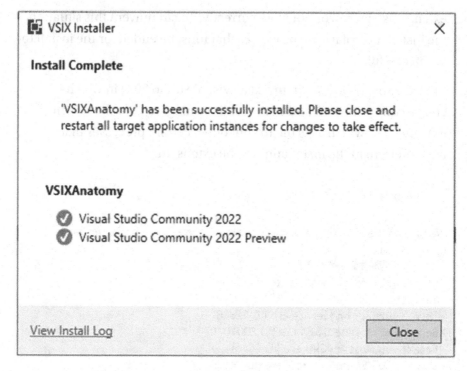

Figure 2-8. *Install Complete*

Notice in the bottom left, there is a link "View Install Log," which we can use to debug the installation of an extension if we run into any install issues. We can also see the location where our extension is installed with the help of this log file. We will see this in later chapters.

From the log file (to be precise, the last line of the log file) opened after clicking View Install Log, I found out that the extension is installed in the following path in my machine:

C:\Users\rishabhv\AppData\Local\Microsoft\VisualStudio\17.0_b10098a9\ Extensions\stqij2tk.yoh

This path is one of the paths that Visual Studio would look for while starting. We can say this because the extension is installed by the VSIX Installer at this path, and hence Visual Studio is already aware of it. This path can be split into three parts as shown as follows:

- C:\Users\rishabhv\AppData\Local\

- Microsoft\VisualStudio*17.0_b10098a9**Extensions*\

- stqij2tk.yoh

The first part is specific to the logged-in user and varies from machine to machine and user to user. This path is the local `Appdata` folder of the user and can be accessed directly by the environment variable `%LOCALAPPDATA%`.

The second part is the relative part where the extensions are installed. The path comprises the folder structure, starting with Microsoft, which contains a folder named `VisualStudio`, followed by the version of Visual Studio, which would vary for Visual Studio versions.

The third and final part is a folder name that the VSIX Installer generates for the extension to keep it unique. We will discuss this folder name in the later chapters.

What's inside this folder? Inside this folder are the files that extend Visual Studio. Figure 2-9 illustrates the basic minimum files that would show up in a typical extension that you would develop and deploy.

Name	Date modified	Type	Size
catalog.json	08-08-2023 23:11	JSON File	1 KB
extension.vsixmanifest	08-08-2023 23:11	Extension Manifest	1 KB
manifest.json	08-08-2023 23:11	JSON File	1 KB
VSIXAnatomy.dll	08-08-2023 23:11	Application extension	6 KB
VSIXAnatomy.pkgdef	08-08-2023 23:11	Package Definition Registration File	1 KB

Figure 2-9. *Installed extension*

We see five files in the folder. We will discuss these files later in the chapter, when we discuss anatomy of an extension.

The Install Complete screen (Figure 2-8) also tells us that we need to restart Visual Studio, so that it can load this extension. Since our extension does nothing, we will skip this exercise until we develop something meaningful. But right now, we have created our first extension and deployed it with the intent of grasping the fundamentals. Toward the end of this chapter, we will modify this code and display a message via our extension code.

VSIX follows Open Packaging Convention a.k.a. OPC. It's important to know about it to better understand a VSIX file and its anatomy. Let's have a look.

Open Packaging Convention

Open Packaging Convention (OPC) refers to the file technology that represents the implementation of an ECMA 376 standard. It doesn't have a specific file format but is a file technology that is used to a design file format with a shared base architecture. So, OPC is an ISO and ECMA industry standard for creating new file formats. OPC file format was created by Microsoft for storing XML and non-XML files in a compressed container. So many new formats supported by Microsoft products use OPC as the base technology for packaging.

The OPC file itself is referred to as a **package**. These OPC-based packages are zip archives, zip-based containers, meaning they can be renamed to a zip file extension and extracted to the file system to see the package contents. The files contained inside the package are called **parts**. These individual parts can be related to other parts in the package or external files via **relationships**. Relationships can be of the following types:

- **Package-level relationships**, which define the relation between the package itself with one of its parts (a file within the package) or an external resource or file

- **Part-level relationships**, which define the relation between a part in the package with another part in the package or an external resource or file

A few of the common examples of OPC that we can see in our daily usage are Word (.docx), Excel (xlsx), and PowerPoint (pptx) files, which leverage the OPC file technology. It's good to point out that although these formats share OPC file technology as a foundation, the data contained in a package file depends on the specific format and may vary from package to package, depending upon format. OPC amalgamates the best of zip, xml, and web technologies into an open-industry standard that makes it really simple to structure, store, and transport application data. Figure 2-10 depicts various OPC packages that we commonly see.

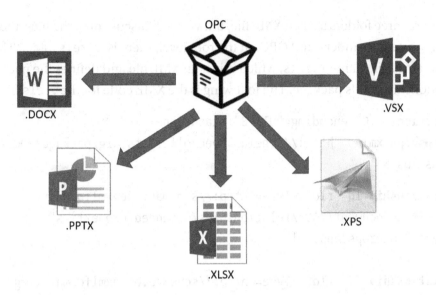

Figure 2-10. *OPC*

Let us try and understand file structure in the OPC package by a simple example. In your laptop, create any Microsoft Office file. I will create a Word file in my desktop for the purpose of this demonstration. Please ensure that you create a brand-new file or make a backup of the Office file you choose, as we will be playing around with it, so there is a risk of losing data. Follow the following steps in order:

1. Open the file, enter some text, and save it.

2. Rename the file extension of the office file to `.zip`. In my case, I created a new Word file with the name, `Demo.docx`. After renaming, it became `Demo.docx.zip`.

3. Right-click the file and extract the contents of this zip file. This extracted folder looks, for me, as shown in Figure 2-11.

Figure 2-11. *Extracted docx package*

There are three folders and an XML file, but we shall discuss only the files and folders that are important to understand OPC. At the root level, there is a _rels folder. This folder contains a file named .rels, which is just an XML file and defines the package-level relationship of this package. The following is the XML code for the .rels file:

```
<?xml version="1.0" encoding="UTF-8" standalone="yes"?>
<Relationships xmlns="http://schemas.openxmlformats.org/package/2006/
relationships">

    <Relationship Id="rId3" Type="http://schemas.openxmlformats.
    org/officeDocument/2006/relationships/extended-properties"
    Target="docProps/app.xml"/>

    <Relationship Id="rId2" Type="http://schemas.openxmlformats.org/
    package/2006/relationships/metadata/core-properties" Target=
    "docProps/core.xml"/>

    <Relationship Id="rId1" Type="http://schemas.openxmlformats.org/
    officeDocument/2006/relationships/officeDocument" Target="word/
    document.xml"/>

    <Relationship Id="rId4" Type="http://schemas.openxmlformats.org/
    officeDocument/2006/relationships/custom-properties" Target=
    "docProps/custom.xml"/>
</Relationships>
```

The word folder has another _rels folder that contains a file named document.xml. rels. This file is also an XML file and defines the part-level relationships. This explains the organization of relationships inside the package. The following are the important points to grasp:

- Relationships are defined in the XML file.

- Package-level relationships are defined in the root level _rels folder.

- Part-level relationships are defined in another _rels folder present inside some other folder in the package.

Another important file is [Content_Types].xml located in the root folder. This file defines the different file formats contained in the package. The types for specific parts may be overridden using the Override tag, which overrides any Default tag for the file type. These are the two tags defined in this XML file. The contents of this XML file are shown as follows:

```
<?xml version="1.0" encoding="UTF-8" standalone="yes"?>
<Types xmlns="http://schemas.openxmlformats.org/package/2006/
content-types">

    <Default Extension="rels" ContentType="application/vnd.openxmlformats-
    package.relationships+xml"/>
    <Default Extension="xml" ContentType="application/xml"/>

    <Override PartName="/word/document.xml" ContentType="application/
    vnd.openxmlformats-officedocument.wordprocessingml.document.main+xml"/>

    <Override PartName="/word/styles.xml" ContentType="application/vnd.
    openxmlformats-officedocument.wordprocessingml.styles+xml"/>

    <Override PartName="/word/settings.xml" ContentType="application/
    vnd.openxmlformats-officedocument.wordprocessingml.settings+xml"/>

    <Override PartName="/word/webSettings.xml" ContentType="application/
    vnd.openxmlformats-officedocument.wordprocessingml.webSettings+xml"/>

    <Override PartName="/word/footnotes.xml" ContentType="application/
    vnd.openxmlformats-officedocument.wordprocessingml.footnotes+xml"/>

    <Override PartName="/word/endnotes.xml" ContentType="application/
    vnd.openxmlformats-officedocument.wordprocessingml.endnotes+xml"/>

    <Override PartName="/word/fontTable.xml" ContentType="application/
    vnd.openxmlformats-officedocument.wordprocessingml.fontTable+xml"/>

    <Override PartName="/word/theme/theme1.xml" ContentType="application/
    vnd.openxmlformats-officedocument.theme+xml"/>
```

```
<Override PartName="/docProps/core.xml" ContentType="application/
vnd.openxmlformats-package.core-properties+xml"/>

<Override PartName="/docProps/app.xml" ContentType="application/
vnd.openxmlformats-officedocument.extended-properties+xml"/>

<Override PartName="/docProps/custom.xml" ContentType="application/
vnd.openxmlformats-officedocument.custom-properties+xml"/>
</Types>
```

The OPC package file provides a flexibility to contain relational structure and package web-accessible content. They provide more security and robustness by providing the ability to digitally sign the package, which ensures authenticity and validates that the content has not been altered after signing.

To summarize, the following are a few of the advantages of using OPC for packaging:

- Zip-based container system

- Web-accessible content

- Relational data structure

- Robustness

- Compact size

- Web accessibility

- ISO and ECMA industry standard acceptance

For a detailed and better understanding of OPC, I would highly recommend the readers to visit the following link:

https://learn.microsoft.com/en-us/previous-versions/windows/desktop/opc/open-packaging-conventions-overview

VSIX

VSIX stands for **V**isual **S**tudio **I**ntegration **E**xtension.

Info   The Visual Studio Extensibility team didn't intend an acronym for the Visual Studio extension. They didn't want VSI as it stood for **V**isual **S**tudio **I**nstaller. This was the time when all the file extensions created by Microsoft were being suffixed or marked with **x** like doc**x**, ppt**x**, xls**x**, etc., so the extension name vsi**x** came up. There were thoughts to use vsx (as it could mean Visual Studio extension); however, Visio had already used this file extension.

A **VSIX** package is a `.vsix` file that contains one or more Visual Studio extensions. The package is *self-describing* as it also contains the metadata that Visual Studio uses to classify and install the extensions. `Manifest` and `[Content_Types].xml` files contain this metadata information. A VSIX package may also contain one or more of the following:

- `.vsixlangpack` files to localize the extension
- VSIX packages to install dependencies
- Binary file that contains the core functionality of the extensions

A VSIX file is the basic unit of deployment for Visual Studio. Visual Studio Installer recognizes this extension and installs it to the location where it can be discovered and loaded by the Visual Studio when it starts and loads.

Note   The names of the files included in the VSIX packages must not include whitespaces. Characters reserved in Uniform Resource Identifiers (URI) are also not allowed in the file names included in VSIX packages. This is defined under [RFC2396].

Grokking the Structure of a Boilerplate Extension

Now that we know the basics of VSIX, let us explain the boilerplate code and its structure that comes with the default VSIX template. The solution structure of the default VSIX Project template contains the following files.

VSIXAnatomyPackage.cs File

The name of this file is of the format {ProjectName}Package.cs. This class implements the package that would be exposed by the assembly created by building this project. Now, the question comes to mind of what constitutes a valid Visual Studio package? Any class that implements an IVsPackage interface and registers itself with the Visual Studio Shell satisfies the minimum criteria to be considered a valid Visual Studio package. In the older SDK, Microsoft.VisualStudio.Shell.Package used to be the abstract class that one used to derive from to create a valid package. Loading and initializing a package can result in disk I/O, and if this happens on the UI thread, it can lead to responsiveness issues as the Main/UI thread is doing I/O instead of keeping the UI responsive. This is the drawback of this class and costs startup performance of Visual Studio for auto-load extensions.

To improve this, with Visual Studio 2015, Microsoft introduced the Microsoft.VisualStudio.Shell.AsyncPackage abstract class that derives from Package class. Leveraging this class, we can opt in asynchronous loading of the extension and reduce performance costs and maintain responsiveness of the UI. Starting Visual Studio 2019, synchronous loading of extensions is turned off by default so that Visual Studio starts up faster and performs better while launching, as the UI thread is less rigorously used. However, to maintain the previous extensions in a working state, you can always enable synchronous loading of extensions as shown in Figure 2-12.

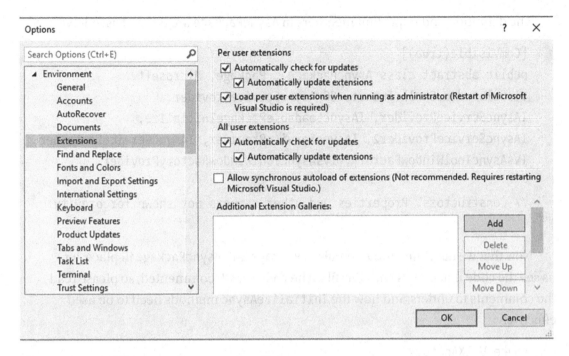

Figure 2-12. *Allow synchronous loading*

However, I would strongly discourage using this option for the extensions developed or maintained by you as you should update your extensions to use asynchronous loading. Also observe the two small sections for "Per user extensions" and "All user extensions," as extensions can be installed on a per-user basis or for all users. The following is how the Package class is defined:

```
[ComVisible(true)]
[PackageRegistration]

public abstract class Package : IVsPackage, OLE.Interop.
IServiceProvider, IOleCommandTarget, IVsPersistSolutionOpts,
IServiceContainer, System.IServiceProvider, IVsUserSettings,
IVsUserSettingsMigration, IVsUserSettingsQuery, IVsToolWindowFactory,
IVsToolboxItemProvider,IVsToolboxItemProvider2
{

    //// Constructors, Properties and other members not shown for brevity.

}
```

The definition and important members in AsyncPackage are defined as follows:

```
[ComVisible(true)]
public abstract class AsyncPackage : Package, Microsoft.
VisualStudio.Shell.Interop.COMAsyncServiceProvider.
IAsyncServiceProvider, IAsyncLoadablePackageInitialize,
IAsyncServiceProvider2, IAsyncServiceProvider, IAsyncServiceContainer,
IVsAsyncToolWindowFactory, IVsAsyncToolWindowFactoryProvider
{
    // Constructors, Properties and other members not shown for brevity.
}
```

Now that we have the fundamentals of Package and AsyncPackage in place, let us see the code that comes with this file. The code is well commented, so please read the comments to understand how the InitializeAsync methods need to be used effectively:

```
namespace VSIXAnatomy
{

    [PackageRegistration(UseManagedResourcesOnly = true,
    AllowsBackgroundLoading = true)]
    [Guid(VSIXAnatomyPackage.PackageGuidString)]
    public sealed class VSIXAnatomyPackage : AsyncPackage
    {

        public const string PackageGuidString = "94eea500-2b7b-4701-
        bf8e-0f6cd169f9ff";
        /// <summary>

        /// Initialization of the package; this method is called right
        after the package is sited, so this is the place where you can
        put all the initialization code that rely on services provided by
        VisualStudio.

        /// </summary>
```

```
/// <param name="cancellationToken">A cancellation token to monitor
for initialization cancellation, which can occur when VS is
shutting down.</param>
/// <param name="progress">A provider for progress updates.</param>

/// <returns>A task representing the async work of package
initialization, or an already completed task if there is none. Do
not return null from this method.</returns>

protected override async Task InitializeAsync(CancellationToken
cancellationToken, IProgress<ServiceProgressData> progress)
{
    // When initialized asynchronously, the current thread may
    be a background thread at this point. Do as much work in
    background as you can before switching to UI thread to keep
    responsiveness.

    // Do any initialization that requires the UI thread after
    switching to the UI thread.

    await this.JoinableTaskFactory.SwitchToMainThreadAsync
    (cancellationToken);
    //// We will discuss JoinableTaskFactory and other threading
    constructs specific to Visual Studio in the later chapters.
    }
}   }
```

The [PackageRegistration] attribute on top of the class is responsible for registering the package with the Visual Studio Shell. This attribute also tells the pkgdef creation utility what data to put in the resulting .pkgdef created during build. AllowBackgroundLoading flag allows package services to be loaded in the background, and the resulting .pkgdef file will have this information as well. The GUID (globally unique identifier) attribute associates a unique identifier to the package. There are a few other attributes that can be present on the class, which we will discuss as we use them while creating extensions and packages. The files generated from the boilerplate extension template along with analyzers are shown in Figure 2-13.

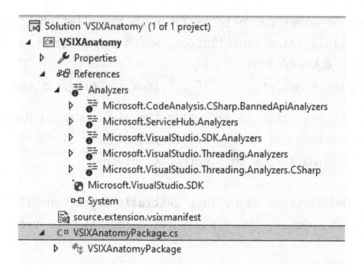

Figure 2-13. *Boilerplate code in Solution Explorer Source.extension.*
`vsixmanifest` *File*

This is another important file that can be seen in Figure 2-14. It contains all the
metadata information that the extension needs like product identifier, product name,
author of the product, version, description of the product, and what it does and where
it can be used, supported language, license information for the end user, icon of the
product, associated tags to search it quickly in the marketplace, release notes, getting
started guide, website URL of the product, etc. It also defines the installation type and
target of the extension, that is, whether the product would be deployed as a Visual Studio
extension or as an extension SDK. This is also the file where we define the supported
Visual Studio version for this product; based on the version range specified here, your
product may work for only Visual Studio 2022 or other versions of Visual Studio as well.
Apart from these, any other dependencies, prerequisites, and assets that the product
needs can be specified here. Figure 2-14 shows the metadata view of the manifest editor
in Visual Studio.

| Product Name: | VSIXAnatomy | | | | | | Author: | Rishabh Verma |
| Product ID: | VSIXAnatomy.e5b888da-d141-4371-9f30-f9cc5d181511 | | | | | | Version: | 1.0 |

Metadata	Description:	Empty VSIX Project.	
Install Targets			
Assets			
Dependencies			
Prerequisites	Language:	English (United States)	▾
	License:	LICENSE.txt	▾	Browse...
	Icon:	icon.ico	▾	Browse...
	Preview Image:	PreviewImage.png	▾	Browse...
	Tags:	VSIX,Anatomy,Sample, Extension	
	Release Notes:		▾	Browse...
	Getting Started Guide:		▾	Browse...

Figure 2-14. *Manifest editor*

References

These are regular references that we see in other project types as well. One of the things to note here is that the default boilerplate template comes up with the NuGet reference to the following package:

- `Microsoft.VisualStudio.SDK`

There is a reference to the `System` assembly as well. Apart from the references, we can also see several analyzers for SDK, banned APIs and threading, which ensure that using the SDK, threading code is done right and banned APIs are not used. We shall discuss these analyzers in later chapters while we write actual meaningful extensions.

Properties

Like any other .NET project, clicking Properties displays the project properties. There is an `AssemblyInfo.cs` file where assembly information like assembly name, version, company name, etc. are specified.

With the code walkthrough done, let us understand the VSIX that is generated by building this project.

Anatomy of Extension

As discussed earlier, VSIX follows OPC and its content can be seen by changing the file extension from .vsix to .zip, so let's make this change in the VSIX file generated earlier in this chapter.

So, I would rename the file VSIXAnatomy.vsix to VSIXAnatomy.vsix.zip and then extract the contents of this zip file. Post extraction, Figure 2-15 shows what my extracted folder looks like.

Name ^	Type	Size
[Content_Types].xml	XML Document	1 KB
catalog.json	JSON File	1 KB
extension.vsixmanifest	Extension Manifest	2 KB
manifest.json	JSON File	1 KB
VSIXAnatomy.dll	Application extension	6 KB
VSIXAnatomy.pkgdef	Package Definition Registration File	1 KB

Figure 2-15. *Anatomy of extension*

We see a total of six files here. Compare it with Figure 2-9, where we saw the files in the installed extension and there were five files in that case. All of those five files are in this folder and there is an additional [Content_Type].xml file, which as we discussed defines the files contained in this extension.

Please note that if you have specified the license, icon, release notes, preview image, etc. in the vsixmanifest file, those will show up in both the places. I haven't shown them here for brevity.

Examining the Files

Let us discuss each of these six files and understand their purpose.

[Content_Types].xml

As discussed earlier in the OPC section, [Content_Types].xml file identifies the file types contained in the .vsix file or package. Visual Studio Installer uses [Content_Types].xml during installation of the package but does not install it. That is why we did not see this file in the preceding install directory.

```xml
<?xml version="1.0" encoding="utf-8"?>
<Types xmlns="http://schemas.openxmlformats.org/package/2006/
content-types">
  <Default Extension="vsixmanifest" ContentType="text/xml" />
  <Default Extension="dll" ContentType="application/octet-stream" />
  <Default Extension="pkgdef" ContentType="text/plain" />
  <Default Extension="json" ContentType="application/json" />
</Types>
```

Catalog.json

This is a JSON file generated and packaged inside the VSIX at the time of build. This JSON file contains the manifest and packages information for the extension. The manifest section defines the type, ID, and version of manifest, while the packages section defines the component and vsix details like version, identifier, dependencies, localization information, extension directory, etc. A typical catalog.json is shown as follows:

```json
{
  "manifestVersion": "1.1",
  "info": {
    "id": "VSIXAnatomy.e5b888da-d141-4371-9f30-f9cc5d181511,version=1.0",
    "manifestType": "Extension"
},
  "packages": [
    {
      "id": "Component.VSIXAnatomy.e5b888da-d141-4371-9f30-f9cc5d181511 ",
      "version": "1.0",
      "type": "Component",
      "extension": true,
      "dependencies": {
        "VSIXAnatomy.e5b888da-d141-4371-9f30-f9cc5d181511 ": "1.0",
        "Microsoft.VisualStudio.Component.CoreEditor": "[17.0,18.0)"
      },
      "localizedResources": [
        {
```

```
      "language": "en-US",
      "title": "VSIXAnatomy",

      "description": "Empty VSIX Project." // Put your description here.
    }
  ]
},
{
  "id": "VSIXAnatomy.e5b888da-d141-4371-9f30-f9cc5d181511 ",
  "version": "1.0",
  "type": "Vsix",
  "payloads": [
    {
      "fileName": "VSIXAnatomy.vsix",
      "size": 26194
    }
  ],
  "vsixId": "VSIXAnatomy.e5b888da-d141-4371-9f30-f9cc5d181511",

  "extensionDir": "[installdir]\\Common7\\IDE\\Extensions\\jkrfgyhb.f2n",
  "installSizes": { "targetDrive": 20641 }
}
  ]
}
```

We will discuss `Catalog.json` structure in detail in a later chapter when we learn to migrate an extension from Visual Studio 2019 to Visual Studio 2022.

Extension.`vsixmanifest`

This file contains information about the extension to be installed and follows the VSX Schema. The VSIX manifest must be named extension.vsixmanifest when it is included in a VSIX file. This is the only mandatory file in the extension.

```
<PackageManifest Version="2.0.0" xmlns="http://schemas.microsoft.com/
developer/vsx-schema/2011">
  <Metadata>
```

```
    <Identity Id="VSIXAnatomy.e5b888da-d141-4371-9f30-f9cc5d181511"
    Version="1.0" Language="en-US" Publisher="Rishabh Verma" />
    <DisplayName>VSIXAnatomy</DisplayName>
    <Description>Empty VSIX Project.</Description>
  </Metadata>
  <Installation>

    <InstallationTarget Id="Microsoft.VisualStudio.Community"
    Version="[17.0, 18.0)" />
  </Installation>
  <Dependencies>

    <Dependency Id="Microsoft.Framework.NDP" DisplayName="Microsoft .NET
    Framework" Version="[4.5,)" />
  </Dependencies>
  <Prerequisites>

    <Prerequisite Id="Microsoft.VisualStudio.Component.CoreEditor"
    Version="[17.0,18.0)" DisplayName="Visual Studio core editor" />
  </Prerequisites>
  <Assets>

    <Asset Type="Microsoft.VisualStudio.VsPackage" Path="VSIXAnatomy.
    pkgdef" />
  </Assets>
</PackageManifest>
```

Manifest.json

This is another JSON file generated and packaged inside the VSIX at the time of build. This JSON file contains the manifest information in the JSON format. This came into existence in the new extension schema. The sample JSON from the boilerplate extension is shown in the following code, which contains the file list as well as dependencies:

```
{
  "id": "VSIXAnatomy.e5b888da-d141-4371-9f30-f9cc5d181511",
  "version": "1.0",
  "type": "Vsix",
  "vsixId": "VSIXAnatomy.e5b888da-d141-4371-9f30-f9cc5d181511",
```

```
  "extensionDir": "[installdir]\\Common7\\IDE\\Extensions\\jkrfgyhb.f2n",
  "files": [
  {
    "fileName": "/extension.vsixmanifest",
    "sha256": null
  },
  {
    "fileName": "/VSIXAnatomy.dll",
    "sha256": null
  },
  {
    "fileName": "/VSIXAnatomy.pkgdef",
    "sha256": null
  }
  ],
  "installSizes": { "targetDrive": 20641 },
  "dependencies": { "Microsoft.VisualStudio.Component.CoreEditor":
  "[17.0,18.0)" }
}
```

VSIXAnatomy.dll

This is the binary that contains the Visual Studio package exposed by the VSIX. This will contain all the functionality and features that we code. We can develop a template or toolbox item or any other extension for Visual Studio. The main binary would invariably contain the code for it.

VSIXAnatomy.pkgdefs

A .pkgdef file encapsulates configuration information in an easily editable, distributable, and deployable form. It has been in existence from the Visual Studio 2008 days. The following code is a snippet of a .pkgdef file generated during build, which registers the VSIXAnatomy class written as a Visual Studio package with the IDE:

```
[$RootKey$\Packages\{fcd9b5c2-3cb8-455e-b702-9d090bd06870}]
@="VSIXAnatomyPackage"
"InprocServer32"="$WinDir$\SYSTEM32\MSCOREE.DLL"
```

```
"Class"="VSIXAnatomy.VSIXAnatomyPackage"
"CodeBase"="$PackageFolder$\VSIXAnatomy.dll"
"AllowsBackgroundLoad"=dword:00000001
```

Folks who work with the Registry often may see a similarity between this content and the .reg file exported from the Registry editor tool of Windows. However, there is a visible key difference. Instead of seeing HKEY_LOCAL_MACHINE or HKEY_CURRENT_USER or other such root values from the Registry, we see an abstraction token as $RootKey$, which represents HKEY_LOCAL_MACHINE\SOFTWARE\Microsoft\VisualStudio\<Version>\. The <Version> would vary based on the version of Visual Studio. For Visual Studio 2022, this value is 17.0. For other versions, Table 2-1 shows the version values.

Table 2-1. *Visual Studio Version and Name Mappings*

Version	Name
8.0	Visual Studio 2005
9.0	Visual Studio 2008
10.0	Visual Studio 2010
11.0	Visual Studio 2012
12.0	Visual Studio 2013
14.0	Visual Studio 2015
15.0	Visual Studio 2017
16.0	Visual Studio 2019
17.0	Visual Studio 2022

Using tokens makes the .pkgdef files reusable for multiple applications and easily distributable. This is why you would find the .pkgdef files in the Visual Studio installed location in your machine also. Since a .pkgdef file is used to register the package, it was named "pkgdef". We will discuss more about .pkgdef files a little later in the chapter when we see how Visual Studio discovers and loads an extension.

Examining the Other Parts of the Extension

Apart from the files we saw earlier in our sample extension, VSIX package may also contain the following: language packs, dependencies, and other references.

Language Packs

A VSIX package may contain one or more `extension.vsixlangpack` files to provide localized text during installation.

Dependencies and Other References

VSIX package may also contain other VSIX packages as references or dependencies. Each of these other packages must include its own VSIX manifest.

If a user tries to install an extension that has dependencies, the installer verifies that the required assemblies are installed on the machine. If the required assemblies are not found, a list of the missing assemblies is displayed. If a project in a multi-project solution includes a reference to another project in the same solution, the VSIX package includes the dependencies of that project. NuGet packages referred to in the project are also included as dependencies.

VSIX can be installed either for all the users in the machine or only for a specific user. We saw earlier in the chapter from the VSIX installer log file that VSIX Installer installed the extension in a directory structure under `%LocalAppData%`. So, by default, the installation is done only for the current user. However, if we set the check box, "The VSIX is installed for all users" in the manifest (see Figure 2-16), the extension will be installed under the directory `..\<VisualStudioInstallationFolder>\Common7\IDE\Extensions` and will be available to all users of the computer.

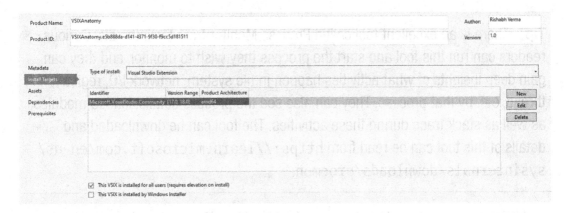

Figure 2-16. *Install for all users*

An important point to note in the last figure is the "Product Architecture" column, which has a value of "amd64". Up until and including Visual Studio 2019, Visual Studio had an x86 (32-bit) architecture. However, Visual Studio 2022 has transitioned to an x64 (64-bit) architecture. Consequently, extensions designed to work with Visual Studio 2022 (64-bit) may not be compatible with earlier versions of Visual Studio, and the reverse is also true.

Let us see how Visual Studio discovers and loads an extension.

How Does Visual Studio Discover and Load an Extension?

Visual Studio uses the following two technologies to deploy Visual Studio extensions:

- Pkgdef files

- VSIX file

Registry plays a pivotal role in the product deployments on Windows operating systems. Visual Studio extension/package deployment is no different. However, by virtue of pkgdef files, Visual Studio packages need not write to Registry directly. Registration information in pkgdef takes care of putting this information in appropriate places in the Registry, via the installation subsystem.

Tip   There is an excellent tool called Process Monitor from Sysinternals. Curious readers can run this tool and start the process they wish to monitor, and they can gain deep insights of what activities happen in file system, network I/O, registry, thread, etc. by that process. They can also see the process details, loaded modules, as well as stack trace during these activities. The tool can be downloaded and details of this tool can be read from `https://learn.microsoft.com/en-us/sysinternals/downloads/procmon`.

When you launch Visual Studio, by clicking the Visual Studio icon in the installed programs menu, it executes a process named `devenv.exe`, which is in `<VsInstallRootFolder>\Common7\IDE`. `devenv.exe` first executes the important steps like command-line parsing and Watson integration initialization (the technology for managing crash/hang dumps). Then it initializes the `PkgDef` management logic. This can be seen using the Sysinternals Process Monitor tool as shown in Figure 2-17.

Process Name	PID	Operation	Path	Result
devenv.exe	15684	CreateFile	C:\Program Files\Microsoft Visual Studio\2022\Community\Common7\IDE\devenv.exe	SUCCESS
devenv.exe	15684	QueryBasicInformationFile	C:\Program Files\Microsoft Visual Studio\2022\Community\Common7\IDE\devenv.exe	SUCCESS
devenv.exe	15684	CloseFile	C:\Program Files\Microsoft Visual Studio\2022\Community\Common7\IDE\devenv.exe	SUCCESS
devenv.exe	15684	CreateFile	C:\Program Files\Microsoft Visual Studio\2022\Community\Common7\IDE\devenv.exe	SUCCESS
devenv.exe	15684	QueryBasicInformationFile	C:\Program Files\Microsoft Visual Studio\2022\Community\Common7\IDE\devenv.exe	SUCCESS
devenv.exe	15684	CloseFile	C:\Program Files\Microsoft Visual Studio\2022\Community\Common7\IDE\devenv.exe	SUCCESS
devenv.exe	15684	CreateFile	C:\Program Files\Microsoft Visual Studio\2022\Community\Common7\IDE\devenv.exe	SUCCESS
devenv.exe	15684	QueryBasicInformationFile	C:\Program Files\Microsoft Visual Studio\2022\Community\Common7\IDE\devenv.exe	SUCCESS
devenv.exe	15684	CloseFile	C:\Program Files\Microsoft Visual Studio\2022\Community\Common7\IDE\devenv.exe	SUCCESS
devenv.exe	15684	CreateFile	C:\Program Files\Microsoft Visual Studio\2022\Community\Common7\IDE\devenv.PkgDef	NAME NOT FOUND
devenv.exe	15684	CreateFile	C:\Program Files\Microsoft Visual Studio\2022\Community\Common7\IDE\master.pkgdef	SUCCESS
devenv.exe	15684	QueryBasicInformationFile	C:\Program Files\Microsoft Visual Studio\2022\Community\Common7\IDE\master.pkgdef	SUCCESS
devenv.exe	15684	CloseFile	C:\Program Files\Microsoft Visual Studio\2022\Community\Common7\IDE\master.pkgdef	SUCCESS
devenv.exe	15684	QueryBasicInformationFile	C:\Windows	SUCCESS
devenv.exe	15684	CreateFile	C:\Windows	SUCCESS
devenv.exe	15684	CreateFile	C:\Windows	SUCCESS
devenv.exe	15684	CreateFile	C:\Windows\System32	SUCCESS
devenv.exe	15684	QueryBasicInformationFile	C:\Windows\System32	SUCCESS
devenv.exe	15684	CloseFile	C:\Windows\System32	SUCCESS
devenv.exe	15684	CreateFile	C:\Users\HP\Documents	SUCCESS
devenv.exe	15684	QueryBasicInformationFile	C:\Users\HP\Documents	SUCCESS
devenv.exe	15684	CloseFile	C:\Users\HP\Documents	SUCCESS
devenv.exe	15684	CreateFile	C:\Program Files	SUCCESS
devenv.exe	15684	QueryBasicInformationFile	C:\Program Files	SUCCESS
devenv.exe	15684	CloseFile	C:\Program Files	SUCCESS
devenv.exe	15684	CreateFile	C:\Program Files\Common Files	SUCCESS
devenv.exe	15684	QueryBasicInformationFile	C:\Program Files\Common Files	SUCCESS
devenv.exe	15684	CloseFile	C:\Program Files\Common Files	SUCCESS

Figure 2-17. *pkgdef initialization*

`PkgDef` management logic is initialized by reading the file `devenv.pkgdef`, which used to be located in the same directory as `devenv.exe`. However, this seems to have changed since Visual Studio 2019 as we see its status as "NAME NOT FOUND", and this file doesn't exist in the same directory. `master.pkgdef` is instead read immediately after looking for `devenv.pkgdef`. `master.pkgdef` file defines the locations where Visual Studio should be looking for other `pkgdef` files as well as installed VSIX extensions.

If we see the contents of the directory containing devenv.exe, we do see master.pkgdef (but not devenv.pkgdef) as shown in Figure 2-18.

PC › SSD (C:) › Program Files › Microsoft Visual Studio › 2022 › Community › Common7 › IDE

Name	Type
BlendDesc-Ln.dll	Application extension
BlendMnu.dll	Application extension
CodeMarkersEtw.man	MAN File
CodeMarkersEtwRc.dll	Application extension
compluslm.dll	Application extension
concrt140.dll	Application extension
DbgComposition.dll	Application extension
DDConfigCA.exe	Application
DeployAppRecipe.exe	Application
DeployAppRecipe.exe.config	XML Configuration File
devenv.com	MS-DOS Application
devenv.exe	Application
devenv.exe.config	XML Configuration File
devenv.isolation.ini	Configuration settings
devenv.prf	PICS Rules File
devenv.visualelementsmanifest.xml	XML Document
devenv.winprf	WINPRF File
devenvdesc.dll	Application extension
ELFBinComposition.dll	Application extension
EntityFramework.dll	Application extension
EntityFramework.SqlServer.dll	Application extension
EntityFramework.SqlServerCompact.dll	Application extension
iisresolver.dll	Application extension
master.pkgdef	Package Definition Registration File
masterX64.PkgUnDef	Unregister Package Definition File
Microsoft.Data.ConnectionUI.Dialog.dll	Application extension

Figure 2-18. *Location of devenv.exe and master.pkgdef*

Let's open the master.pkgdef file and see its content (Figure 2-19).

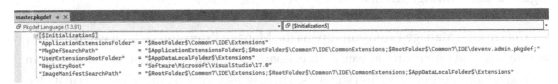

Figure 2-19. *master.pkgdef content*

Table 2-2 describes the variables that we see in the master PkgDef file.

Table 2-2. *Variables and Their Purpose*

Variable	Description
ApplicationExtensionsFolder	The root folder under which machine-wide VSIXs are deployed. The extensions that have "The VSIX is deployed for all users" check box are checked in the manifest.
PkgDefSearchPath	The list of folders to look for pkgdef files. This list may also contain pkgdef files.
UserExtensionsRootFolder	The root folder under which per-user VSIXs are deployed.
RegistryRoot	The root registry location under which user settings and configurations are stored.
ImageManifestSearchPath	The list of folders to look for in image manifest.

The primary job of PkgDef management is to locate, load pkgdef files, and merge them with the rest of the configuration data stored in the Registry. The folders and pkgdef files listed in the PkgDefSearchPath are scanned recursively and PkgDef files found under these paths are loaded. PkgDef management then scans recursively starting from extension folders under UserExtensionsRootFolder and loads only those PkgDef files that belong to enabled extensions. The extensions can be enabled/disabled from the Extension manager. In Visual Studio 2022, there is a direct top-level menu item for extensions which has an item named Manage Extensions as shown in Figure 2-20.

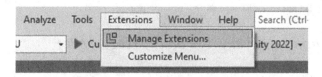

Figure 2-20. *Manage Extensions*

Clicking the Manage Extensions opens the Manage Extensions screen where we can see the installed extensions, as well as download and install new extensions online from a marketplace or other extension galleries. There is a section to update existing installed extensions as well as a roaming extension manager. We will see these in detail, in a later chapter, when we discuss about publishing our extension to the marketplace and hosting our private extension gallery. Figure 2-21 is what the UI of Manage Extensions looks like.

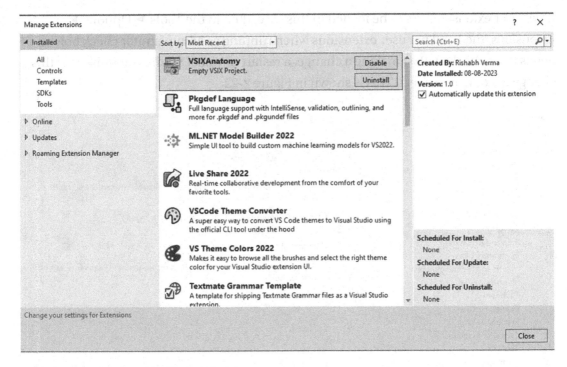

Figure 2-21. *Manage Extensions*

Notice that by selecting an extension, an Enable/Disable button is shown. The extension can be enabled or disabled from this button. Also observe that on the right panel, the extension metadata from VSIX is shown in the form of Created By and Version. There is a check box, "Automatically update this extension," which is checked.

When Visual Studio loads, it loads pkgdef files of only those extensions that are enabled. After all the Visual Studio configuration data is loaded and merged, it is cached in the Registry. Visual Studio can now use this cached configuration data to initialize its core services and build the UI. This is a very high and simplified overview of how things work and tie up. Visual Studio makes extensive use of Managed Extensibility Framework (MEF), which is basically an extensibility framework for discovering and using extensions. As Visual Studio starts, a bunch of its core services are started. One of these services is called SVsExtensionManager service. This service recursively looks at the ApplicationExtensionsFolder (defined in master.pkgdef). All the discovered extensions under this folder become available to the Visual Studio via MEF. Next, the UserExtensionsRootFolder path under which per-user extensions are installed is scanned recursively. This is a conditional step and happens only if the user is not the administrator in the machine and not running the Visual Studio as administrator.

If per-user extensions are to be loaded in this case, then in the Tools ➤ Options ➤ Extensions, the Load per user extensions when running as administrator check box needs to be checked. Post making a change, a restart of Visual Studio is required for this change to come into effect. This is shown in Figure 2-22.

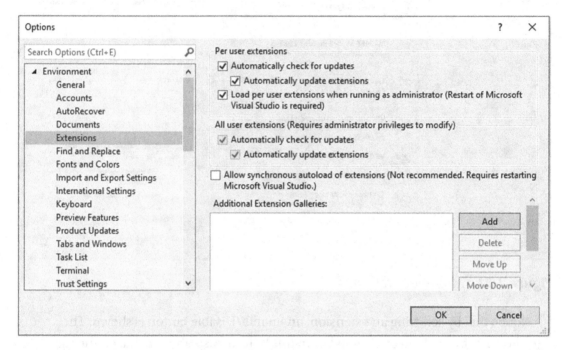

Figure 2-22. *Per-user extension loading*

This is required because all these changes are processed only one time at the startup. This is how, at a high level, Visual Studio discovers and loads the extensions.

Summary

In this chapter, we learned the basics of Visual Studio extension, the default code that comes from the template. We discussed OPC and how it is leveraged by VSIX and how using it makes it easier to distribute and deploy Visual Studio extensions. We learned about what comprises a basic Visual Studio package and how AsyncPackage should be leveraged to keep the Visual Studio responsive while loading the extension. We saw a few of the important intricacies of working with Visual Studio and how it discovers and loads an extension. In the next chapter, we shall discuss the Visual Studio extensibility model and start extending Visual Studio.

EXERCISES

Nothing will work, unless you do. —Anonymous

The following activities should give you a deep understanding of the fundamentals we discussed in this chapter:

- Read the OPC specification in detail online at `https://learn.microsoft.com/en-us/previous-versions/windows/desktop/opc/open-packaging-conventions-overview`.

- Take a Word, Excel, and PowerPoint file each and see their anatomies and details by renaming them to `.zip` and extracting them. Can you edit or add the text in the resulting file and then convert it back to the original format?

- Download and install Process Monitor (procmon) from the link shared in the chapter or by searching it online in your favorite search engine.

- Observe and infer the activities you see in procmon while installing a VSIX.

- Observe and infer the activities you see in procmon while launching Visual Studio.

- Discover the UI, Tools, and Options of Visual Studio 2022 and list the top ten things you notice that are new in Visual Studio 2022.

CHAPTER 3

Extending Visual Studio

In this chapter, we will learn about the extensibility model of Visual Studio. To do so, we will look at the Visual Studio user interface and its software development kit (SDK) and check out the extensibility points available to us. We will then develop a basic extension for a custom command and see how it can be integrated in a code window, tool menu, and solution explorer. We conclude this chapter by discussing some potent questions around the command extensibility. By the end of this chapter, we will understand the fundamentals of Visual Studio extensibility and have developed a basic extension giving us a solid foundation to create the real-world extensions for our beloved IDE.

Know Your IDE – Visual Studio 2022 User Interface

Before we can start extending, we should know the user interface (UI) of Visual Studio. The UI of Visual Studio is shown in Figure 3-1.

© Rishabh Verma 2024
R. Verma, *Visual Studio Extensibility Development*, https://doi.org/10.1007/978-1-4842-9875-6_3

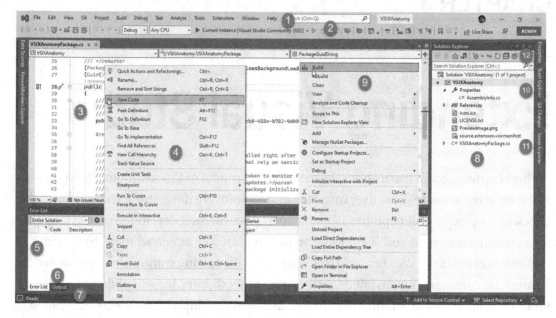

Figure 3-1. *Visual Studio 2022 user interface*

This will not only make us aware of the nomenclature and layout of Visual Studio but also help us know the extensibility points and components that we would like to extend. Figure 3-1 displays the UI of Visual Studio 2022 at the time of writing this chapter. The different sections of the UI are numbered so that we can easily identify and discuss them briefly. Let's have a look at these different components in the order in which they are numbered in the figure:

1. Menus/Menu bar: This is the topmost section of the Visual Studio and comprises the menu items that are used frequently to execute various commands and operations. A few of the notable ones with a brief description are listed as follows:

    a. File: This menu contains commands to create, open, and save files, projects, and solutions.

    b. Edit: It contains commands to modify, refactor, cut, paste, and delete the code.

    c. View: The View menu contains commands to display and view the windows in the Visual Studio IDE.

    d. Git: The commands in this menu make it easier to work with Git from the IDE itself.

    e. Project: This menu contains commands to add or remove files and dependencies in the project.

    f. Debug: This menu contains the commands to run, debug, and utilize debugging tools and windows.

    g. Architecture: It's available only in the Enterprise version of the tool and not in Community and other versions of Visual Studio. This menu contains commands to generate code map for the solution and display other windows related to architecture like UML explorer, layer explorer, class view, object browser, etc.

    h. Test: The Test menu command categorizes all the commands to discover, debug, and run the tests as well as to view windows to create test playlists and coverage results.

    i. Analyze: This menu groups the commands to analyze the code and calculate code metrics.

    j. Tools: It contains the commands to customize and change the settings of the Visual Studio IDE.

    k. Extensions: It provides a direct navigation to the Extensions and Updates window.

    l. Window: This menu contains the commands to add a new window; hide, view, dock, or tab the window; and change the layout.

    m. Help: This menu groups the commands to view the information about the Visual Studio IDE, product registration, feedback, and online documentation.

2. Toolbar: The toolbar exists just below the top menus of Visual Studio and exposes access to the contextual and most common commands. A few of the common commands that can be seen in toolbar in the last image are Save, Save All, Undo, etc.

3. Code Window: This is where the code files are edited and code is written. It can be an XML, C#, F#, txt, JavaScript, TypeScript, C++, or any other file type that the installed Visual Studio supports. We can extend the editor via IntelliSense, refactoring, and light bulb-style code suggestions via extensions in the code window. Other possible extensibility points exposed by the editor are margins, scrollbars, tags, adornments, options, etc.

4. Code Window Context menu: This may not be a universal nomenclature. When we right-click the code window, a context menu is displayed, which lists the commands that can be executed on the code file. The image displays the context menu for a C# file opened in a code window. We can extend this menu and add a new item in it.

5. Error List: As the name suggests, all the errors, warnings, and messages are listed in this window, which by default (in the default web development layout) are docked toward the bottom of Visual Studio. It can be opened from the top meu bar by clicking **View ➤ Error List** or by pressing **Ctrl+\+E**. The errors, warnings, and messages displayed in this window are produced as we write code or by IntelliSense, or by build or code analysis. Doubling-clicking an error navigates to the file and location of that error. It provides filters to display only errors, warnings, and messages or a combination of them. This window provides a drop-down at the top, by which the scope of items displayed in the window can be reduced to document(s), project(s), or solution(s). This window supports search and hence makes it easier to find a specific item. We can write extensions to display items in the Error List as well as handle what happens when an item in the Error List is clicked.

6. Output Window: This is where the status messages are displayed from various components of Visual Studio IDE like IntelliSense, Solution, Source Control, Package Manager, etc. While debugging, the output window is helpful so that we can see the debugging and error messages, warnings, as well as status messages. We can write extensions that utilize Output window, and we will see it in subsequent chapters.

7. Status bar: This is the bottommost part of Visual Studio IDE, which displays the status of the latest operation. In the last image, we see the status as Ready. We can easily write status messages in the status bar while writing our extensions.

8. Solution Explorer: This window doesn't need much description as every developer who has ever used Visual Studio is definitely familiar with Solution Explorer and has used it to add and edit files, projects, and solutions. It displays the solution, projects, and files that we are working with.

9. Solution Explorer Context Menu: When we right-click an item selected in Solution Explorer, we get a context menu that displays a list of commands that are relevant for the selected item. For example, when the project is selected, right-clicking the context menu displays items applicable to a Project like Build, Rebuild, Clean, Debug, etc. And this is the same, likewise, for the file and solution. We can extend this menu as we will see later in this chapter.

10. Git Changes: To connect and work with the Team Foundation Server (TFS), which later got renamed to Visual Studio Online (VSO), which later again got renamed to Visual Studio Team Services (VSTS), now known as Azure DevOps. We can also connect to Git repositories from here.

11. Server Explorer: As the name suggests, it provides a single and unified window to access servers either installed or connected on the system. The most common ones are database and SharePoint servers. If you connect to your Azure subscription, you can see a variety of cloud components and services like App Service, Classic Cloud Services, SQL Database, Notification Hubs, Virtual Machines, and Storages that are linked with your subscription.

12. Properties Window: This window provides an interface to display and edit (if it's not read-only) the design time properties and events of the selected item in designers like WPF designer or Windows Forms designer and editors. It can also be used to view

the file, project, and solution property selected in the Solution Explorer. To display the Properties Window, select an item in the designer or solution explorer and press F4. This window makes use of a Property Grid control to display the properties.

Now that we have revisited the user interface of Visual Studio and briefly discussed their extensibility, it's time to jump into the extensibility model of Visual Studio.

Visual Studio Extensibility Model

In this section, we discuss the Visual Studio Extensibility model. The obvious question that may cross your mind is this: "*Why do I need to know the extensibility model?*"

The answer is simple, just like without knowing WPF/Windows form/MAUI/UWP, a desktop-based GUI application for Windows cannot be created by a C# developer. Or just like without knowing ASP.NET/ASP.NET Core, a web application/API based on these frameworks cannot be created; similarly, without knowing the Visual Studio Extensibility model, it would be very difficult to create a good Visual Studio extension. Once we know the Visual Studio Extensibility model, we will be able to extend Visual Studio by creating extensions with confidence.

Recall that in the last chapter, in the section "Grokking the Structure of a Boilerplate Extension," we discussed this boilerplate extension, which has a reference to `Microsoft.VisualStudio.SDK` package. This package is a meta package and contains the Visual Studio Software Development Kit (SDK).

Info   Meta package is a special NuGet package that describes a group of packages that makes sense together. For example, Microsoft defined a meta package named `Microsoft.NETCore.App`, which contains all the NuGet packages that are needed to develop a .NET Core app. Likewise, `Microsoft.VisualStudio.SDK` is a meta package that groups a number of NuGet packages that are needed to develop extensions to extend Visual Studio.

There are 110+ NuGet packages that cumulatively constitute the Visual Studio SDK. For the current version of SDK, the dependent NuGet packages can be seen at `www.nuget.org/packages/Microsoft.VisualStudio.SDK#dependencies-body-tab`.

Discussing each of these packages is neither feasible nor required and productive, so we will discuss only the distinct and most important assemblies in this section. We also discuss the namespaces, interfaces, and classes in detail as we develop extensions through the course of this book. A few of the important namespaces that we need to know are listed in Table 3-1.

Table 3-1. *Important Namepsaces in Visual Studio SDK*

Namespace	Description
Microsoft.VisualStudio.ComponentModelHost	This namespace defines the interfaces and GuidList that are used for the Managed Extensibility Framework (MEF) in Visual Studio.
Microsoft.VisualStudio.Shell	It contains the abstract class AsyncPackage and Package from which any Visual Studio package is defined. Packages are the preferred way of extending the Visual Studio IDE. The containing assembly of this namespace is also used in creating a custom tool window and defining custom commands.
Microsoft.VisualStudio.Editor	It contains the classes used in editor like options, margins, scrollbars, etc.
Microsoft.VisualStudio.Editor	It contains the interfaces and classes used by the editor for colors, fonts, etc., and editor constants.
Microsoft.VisualStudio.Language.Intellisense	This namespace contains the interfaces and classes that are responsible for actions suggestions, light bulb, signature helpers, and IntelliSense.
Microsoft.VisualStudio.Text.*	This is where the types and interfaces that provide and expose the functionality for text selection, adornment, formatting, outlining, and tagging brace completion in the code editor.
Microsoft.VisualStudio.CommandBars	This contains the definitions of CommandBars, CommandBar button, and its events and handlers.

(continued)

Table 3-1. (*continued*)

Namespace	Description
Microsoft.VisualStudio. Threading	This namespace contains the classes and types that help us effectively leverage threading in Visual Studio. It contains Threading tools, JoinableTasks, and SingleThreaded SynchronizationContext, to name a few important types.
Microsoft.VisualStudio. ProjectAggregator	It contains two interfaces and one class, which are used for Visual Studio projects.
Microsoft.VisualStudio. Language	This namespace houses the types for code cleanup, CodeLens, and IntelliSense. It also contains other types used by the code editor of Visual Studio.
Microsoft.VisualStudio. Utilities	The attributes that would be used in our extension development are mostly defined under this namespace. NameAttribute, PriorityAttribute, DisplayAttribute, AppliesToProjectAttribute, OrderAttribute, ExportImplementationAttribute, and ImportImplementationsAttribute are a few of the common attributes defined in this namespace. It also contains classes that are used by the editor.
EnvDTE EnvDTE80 EnvDTE90 EnvDTE90a EnvDTE100	This namespace (EnvDTE) has been in the Visual Studio for quite some time now and has evolved over the years and so we see the suffixes 80, 90, 90a, and 100, which were added for different versions of Visual Studio. This namespace contains the interfaces and types that are used for automation of tasks in Visual Studio. The earlier versions (until VS 2012) of Visual Studio supported add-ins and provided a nice wizard to create an add-in, which made extensive use of this namespace. The modern VSPackage also supports leveraging the automation model.
VSLangProj*	The types and interfaces defined in these namespaces are used by the language (C#/VB) project system and their automation.
Microsoft.Build*	These namespaces (namespaces starting with Microsoft. Build) are used by the MSBuild infrastructure.

In this last table, we saw only a handful of namespaces, which is like a drop in the ocean, but these are the most frequently used ones for commonly developed Visual Studio extensions. We shall discuss a few more namespaces as we progress in this journey of extending our beloved IDE.

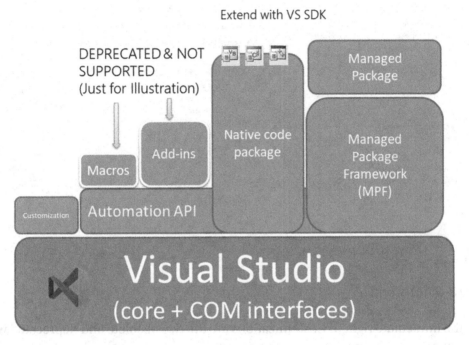

Figure 3-2. *Visual Studio Extensibility model*

Figure 3-2 illustrates a high-level extensibility model of Visual Studio. At the base of this model is the Visual Studio comprising its core components, APIs, and COM interfaces. Above it there are different ways by which Visual Studio can be extended. On the very left, the block is named customization. Visual Studio IDE is extensible even without coding, by making use of Tools ➤ Customize. This provides us the flexibility to add/remove the commands and menus and also adjust their placements. The next figure showcases this customization feature of Visual Studio. We can customize the menu bar, toolbar, or context menu commands by adding or removing the command or even changing the placement of the command. There is an option to assign the keyboard shortcuts as well, by means of the Keyboard button. I encourage readers to explore and play around with this feature on their own as it is very intuitive.

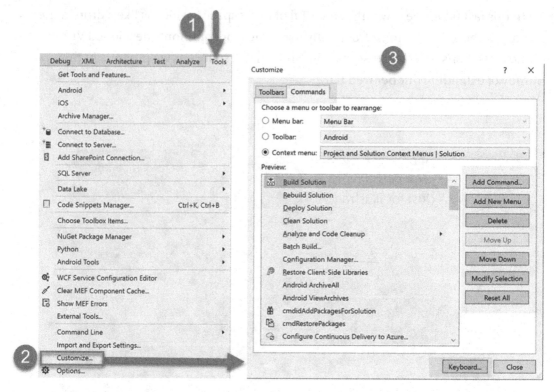

Figure 3-3. *Customize*

To the immediate right of Customizations are the two obsolete and deprecated ways of extensibility, namely, Macros and Add-ins. They were around for a long time in the Visual Studio journey and were relevant until Visual Studio 2012. They are shown in Figure 3-3 only for illustration purposes and are not supported by Visual Studio now. They were based on top of Visual Studio automation API viz EnvDTE. Then comes the Visual Studio SDK, which provides the highest degree of the extensibility, based on the VSPackage. Also, notice the height difference among the different techniques. Customization is smallest in height and Package is tallest, depicting that Package provides the highest extensibility and customization provides the lowest flexibility of extensibility. We will develop all our extensions based on VSPackage.

Knowing the important namespaces and SDK helps, but we still need to know what types and interfaces to use so that we can extend Visual Studio. For each of these namespaces, we can see and list the interfaces and types defined. However, all theory and no code would make it a little boring. So, for the remainder of this chapter, we develop an extension and discuss the important types and interfaces. Visual Studio has a bunch of extensibility templates that automatically add the required namespaces in the classes, while we develop an extension.

Extending Menus and Commands

In this section, we will develop a Visual Studio extension to extend the commands in the Tools menu. Figure 3-4 shows the menubar, menu, and commands for the Tools menu. The "Invoke MyCommand" command shown in the figure can be added simply by just using the default extensibility command template to add a command as the command template adds the command directly in the Tools menu by default.

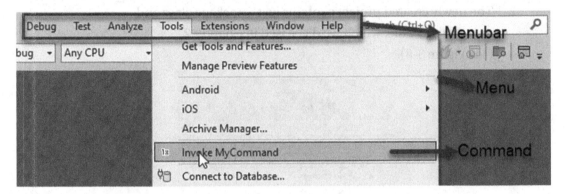

Figure 3-4. *Menu and command*

In the process, we will learn about the Visual Studio Command Table and tools that can help us edit the `.vsct` file correctly. We will also learn how to bind keyboard shortcuts to the newly added command as well as change the icons associated with them. Finally, toward the end of this section, we see how the visibility of these commands can be changed and how we can dynamically add or remove commands based on context. Let's write some code.

Tools Menu Extension

Let us follow the following steps to create an extension for the Visual Studio Tools menu:

1. Create a new Visual Studio Extensibility project by choosing the VSIX project template as shown in Figure 3-5. Please provide a meaningful name, such as "ToolsMenuCommand" or a name of your choice.

Figure 3-5. *VSIX Project template*

2. The newly created project contains just a package class and
    `vsixmanifest` file, which we discussed in Chapter 2
    (see Figure 3-6).

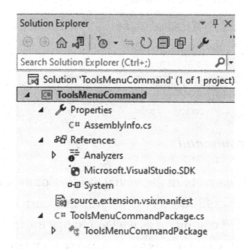

Figure 3-6. *Files in boilerplate project*

> Notice that right now, the project doesn't have any command class.

3. To add a new command, right-click the project. It will display the
    Project context menu. Then click Add ➤ New Item (or directly
    press Ctrl+Shift+A) to add a new item. This will open the Add New
    Item dialog as shown in Figure 3-7. In case you see a compact
    view, you may want to click the "Show All Templates" button.

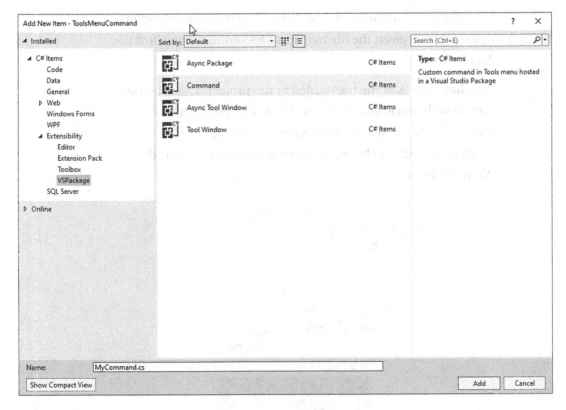

Figure 3-7. *Add New Item*

4. On the left panel, under the Extensibility category of C# Items, click VSPackage. It displays the following four item templates:

   a. Async Package: To create an async package that can be loaded in Visual Studio.

   b. Command: To create a custom command in the Tools menu.

   c. Async Tool Window: To create a custom tool window that can be hosted in Visual Studio with a command to load the tool window asynchronously.

   d. Tool Window: To create a tool window that can be hosted in Visual Studio with a command to load it synchronously. I think this is provided to support backward compatibility as the new recommendation is always to use the Async Tool Window.

We will select Command template to add a new Command in our
project. I have given the file name as MyCommand.cs. Click the
Add button.

5. Let's have a look at the files added in the project. The modified
project with newly added files is shown in Figure 3-8, and
the newly added files and references are highlighted for
easy identification. The references are added to support the
Windows form.

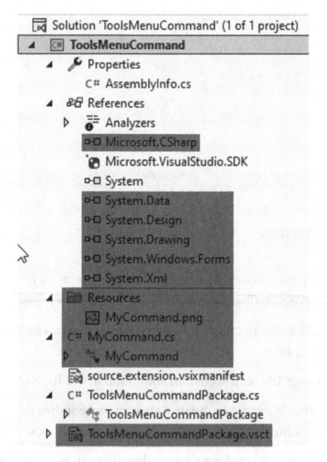

Figure 3-8. *Files added by choosing Command template*

Apart from the references, three more files are added:

a.   MyCommand.png: This is an image strip or sprite (a set of images) with the same name as the name of created command that is created inside a Resources folder. The default image sprite contains six images as shown in Figure 3-9. I have explicitly numbered the images to identify them easily.

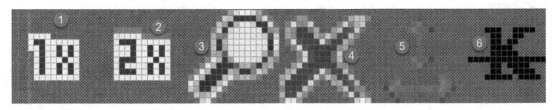

Figure 3-9. *Image sprite containing six images*

b.   MyCommand.cs: This is the C# code file that is used for adding a new command and contains the event handler to execute the code when the command is invoked. If we notice the command file, it has just three methods, in addition to a public static property named Instance that returns the instance of `MyCommand`:

   i.   A private constructor for the command, which takes `AsyncPackage` and `OleMenuCommandService` as the parameter. This is where the command is constructed and added to the command service.

   ii.   A public static `InitializeAsync` method, which takes `AsyncPackage` as a parameter and initializes the singleton instance of the command, by invoking the private constructor of command, after resolving the `OleMenuCommandService` from the `AsyncPackage`.

   iii.   A private callback method named Execute, which is the event handler to execute the command when the menu item is clicked.

Figure 3-10 summarizes this newly added command class.

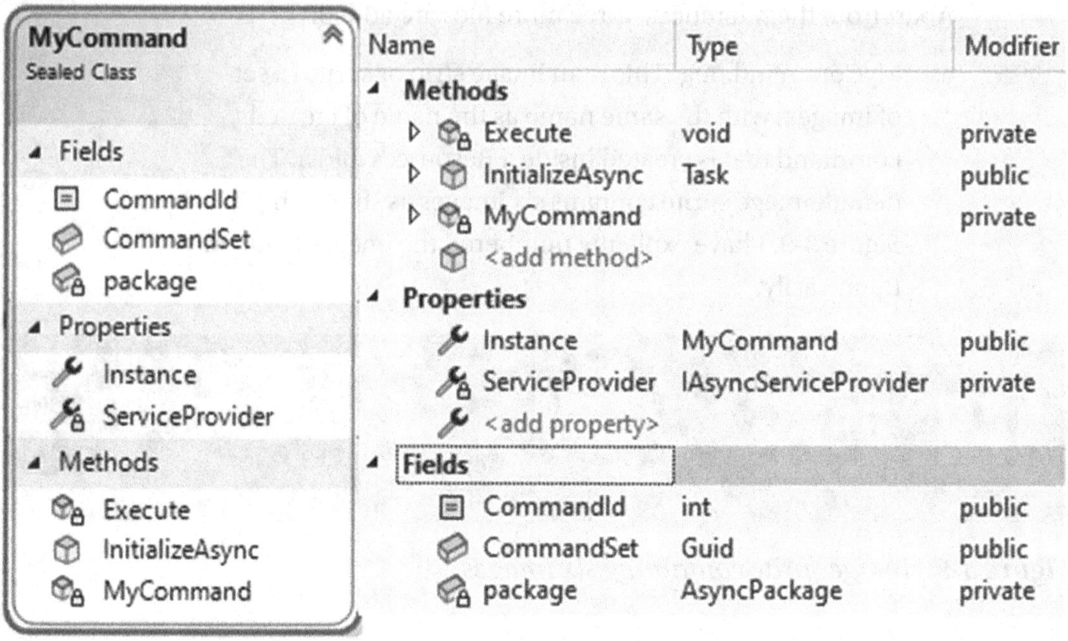

Figure 3-10. *Class diagram of MyCommand.cs*

   c.   `ToolsMenuCommandPackage.vsct`: The extension of this file
vsct stands for **V**isual **S**tudio **C**ommand **T**able (vsct). This
file is an XML configuration file that configures the Visual
Studio Command Table and describes the commands that are
contained in the VSPackage. It also controls the layout and
appearance of commands. The commands can be included
in a button, menu, toolbar, etc. When this configuration file
is passed through the VSCT compiler, it converts it into a
binary that is understood by Visual Studio. Let's just check
the code snippet that is responsible for adding a command in
the Tools menu. Figure 3-11 shows the trimmed version (with
comments removed) of the vsct file. The snippet is numbered
so that we can discuss the key concepts of a vsct file.

```xml
<?xml version="1.0" encoding="utf-8"?>
<CommandTable  1  ="http://schemas.microsoft.com/VisualStudio/2005-10-18/CommandTable" xmlns:xs="http://www.w3.org/2001/XMLSchema">
  <!--This is the file that defines the IDs for all the commands exposed by VisualStudio. -->
  <Extern href="stdidcmd.h"/>  2

  <!--This header contains the command ids for the menus provided by the shell. -->
  <Extern href="vsshlids.h"/>
   3
  <Commands package="guidToolsMenuCommandPackage">  4
    <Groups>
   5  <Group guid="guidToolsMenuCommandPackageCmdSet" id="MyMenuGroup" priority="0x0600">
        <Parent guid="guidSHLMainMenu" id="IDM_VS_MENU_TOOLS" />  6
      </Group>
    </Groups>

    <!--This section defines the elements the user can interact with, like a menu command or a button
        or combo box in a toolbar. -->
    <Buttons>  7
      <Button guid="guidToolsMenuCommandPackageCmdSet" id="MyCommandId" priority="0x0100" type="Button">  8
        <Parent guid="guidToolsMenuCommandPackageCmdSet" id="MyMenuGroup" />
        <Icon guid="guidImages" id="bmpPic1" />  9
        <Strings>
          <ButtonText>Invoke MyCommand</ButtonText>  10
        </Strings>
      </Button>
    </Buttons>

    <!--The bitmaps section is used to define the bitmaps that are used for the commands.-->
    <Bitmaps>   9         11
      <Bitmap guid="guidImages" href="Resources\MyCommand.png" usedList="bmpPic1, bmpPic2, bmpPicSearch, bmpPicX, bmpPicArrows, bmpPicStrikethrough"/>
    </Bitmaps>
  </Commands>

  <Symbols>
    <!-- This is the package guid. -->                                                    4
    <GuidSymbol name="guidToolsMenuCommandPackage" value="{c4cf0872-23e7-4230-b219-5aaf03be855c}" />

    <!-- This is the guid used to group the menu commands together -->
    <GuidSymbol name="guidToolsMenuCommandPackageCmdSet" value="{ec82d9e6-e11d-4efc-90be-5cf7b845e00d}">
      <IDSymbol name="MyMenuGroup" value="0x1020" />
      <IDSymbol name="MyCommandId" value="0x0100" />
    </GuidSymbol>
          9
    <GuidSymbol name="guidImages" value="{14d2eab7-1627-4caa-a2f9-00711401a08f}" >
      <IDSymbol name="bmpPic1" value="1" />
      <IDSymbol name="bmpPic2" value="2" />
      <IDSymbol name="bmpPicSearch" value="3" />
      <IDSymbol name="bmpPicX" value="4" />
      <IDSymbol name="bmpPicArrows" value="5" />
      <IDSymbol name="bmpPicStrikethrough" value="6" />
    </GuidSymbol>
  </Symbols>
</CommandTable>
```

```
[PackageRegistration(UseManagedResourcesOnly = true, AllowsBackgroundLoading = true)]
[Guid(ToolsMenuCommandPackage.PackageGuidString)]
[ProvideMenuResource("Menus.ctmenu", 1)]
1 reference
public sealed class ToolsMenuCommandPackage : AsyncPackage
{
    /// <summary>
    /// ToolsMenuCommandPackage GUID string.
    /// </summary>                                        4
    public const string PackageGuidString = "c4cf0872-23e7-4230-b219-5aaf03be855c";
```

Figure 3-11. *vsct file code*

From the code snippet of the vsct file, these are the following key
takeaways:

6. CommandTable element is the root node of the vsct file. The
    namespace and schema of the vsct are specified as attributes
    of this element. This element contains the definition of all the
    elements that define the command. The command may be a
    menu item, toolbar, button, or a combo box that you see in the
    Visual Studio IDE. Whatever is defined in this command table is
    the UI or layout of the commands that the containing VSPackage
    exposes to the Visual Studio IDE. CommandTable has Extern,
    Commands, and Symbols as the children. The high-level structure
    of CommandTable is as follows:

```
<CommandTable xmlns="http://schemas.microsoft.com/
VisualStudio/2005-10-18/CommandTable" xmlns:xs="http://www.
w3.org/2001/XMLSchema" >
    <Extern>... </Extern>
    <Include>... </Include>
    <Define>... </Define>
    <Commands>... </Commands>
    <CommandPlacements>... </CommandPlacements>
    <VisibilityConstraints>... </VisibilityConstraints>
    <KeyBindings>... </KeyBindings>
    <UsedCommands... </UsedCommands>
    <Symbols>... </Symbols>
</CommandTable>
```

The following sections summarize the purpose of each of these XML elements.

Extern

It is an optional element and generally contains preprocessor directives for the vsct
compiler. This element refers to any external C++ header (.h) or .vsct files to be merged
with this .vsct file at the time of compilation. The attribute href is used to refer to the
file. From the .vsct file code, we see that the file name referred to earlier is stdidcmd.h.
For example,

```
<Extern href="stdidcmd.h" />
```

Include

This is an optional element and hence is not shown in the code listing shown previously.
This element specifies a file that can be included in the current file. The attribute href is
used to refer to the file. All the symbols and types defined in the include file will be part
of the compilation output. For example,

```
<Include href="KnownImageIds.vsct" />
```

Define

This is again an optional element. Define, as the name suggests, defines a symbol and its value. It has two required attributes, name and value, and an optional attribute Condition, which can be used to evaluate the symbol. For example,

```
<Define name="Mode" value="Standard" />
```

Commands

This is also an optional element. However, this is the main element that defines the commands for the VSPackage. It has an attribute called package, the value of which should be the same as that of the Package GUID defined in the Package class as well as in the Symbols section of the `.vsct` file. In the `.vsct` code displayed in Figure 3-11, this is illustrated by the number 4 (which is used three times in the snippet). If we go from top to bottom in the `.vsct` file, we notice that #4 is first used on the Commands element, which has its attribute package set to `guidToolsMenuCommandPackage`. The next #4 can be seen inside the Symbols element where a `GuidSymbol` element is defined with the same name `guidToolsMenuCommandPackage` and its value is a globally unique identifier (GUID). Toward the bottom right of the figure, we again see #4, which is a snippet from Package class, where in the Package GUID is defined. Notice that the GUID value in code behind the (.cs) file and `.vsct` file is the same. It is because of this GUID that the commands are linked with the Package. The Commands element can have multiple children as shown in the following in the high-level structure of Commands:

```
<Commands package="guidToolsMenuPackage" >
   <Menus>... </Menus>
   <Groups>... </Groups>
   <Buttons>... </Buttons>
   <Combos>... </Combos>
   <Bitmaps>... </Bitmaps>
</Commands>
```

We see that there can be five children of Commands.

Menus

These define all the menus and toolbars that a VSPackage implements. It has an optional attribute called Condition, which can be used to render a menu based on the condition. The Menus element is a collection of Menu elements and hence can have multiple Menu elements inside it. Each Menu element represents a single menu or toolbar.

```
<Menus>
  <Menu>... </Menu>
  <Menu>... </Menu>
</Menus>
```

In Figure 3-11, we do not see this element as the package we implemented only created a command and not a menu.

The Menu element defines a single menu item. There are six different kinds of menus, namely, Context, Menu, MenuController, MenuControllerLatched, Toolbar, and ToolWindowToolbar. The syntax of Menu element is next:

```
<Menu guid="guidMyCommandSet" id="MyCommand" priority="0x100" type="Menu">
  <Parent>... </Parent>
  <CommandFlag>... </CommandFlag>
  <Strings>... </Strings>
</Menu>
```

The GUID and id attributes are required attributes of a Menu element and represents the GUID and id of the command identifier. Priority, type, and Condition are optional attributes. Priority is a numeric value that specifies the relative position of a menu in the group of menus, while type is an enumerated value that specifies the kind of element. If a type is not specified, its value is defaulted to Menu. The possible values are

- Context
- Menu
- MenuController
- MenuControllerLatched
- Toolbar
- ToolWindowToolbar

For the detailed purposes and use of these types, the reader should read the detailed documentation for Visual Studio 2022 at `https://learn.microsoft.com/en-in/visualstudio/extensibility/menu-element?view=vs-2022`.

The syntax of the Menu element shows that it has three children:

- Parent: This is an optional element. If specified, it represents the parent of the menu item.

- CommandFlag: This is a required element. The valid CommandFlag values for a Menu are as follows:

  - AlwaysCreate

  - DefaultDocked

  - DefaultInvisible

  - DontCache

  - DynamicVisibility

  - IconAndText

  - NoCustomize

  - NotInTBList

  - NoToolbarClose

  - TextChanges

  - TextIsAnchorCommand

For a detailed documentation of CommandFlag element, please read the Microsoft documentation at `https://learn.microsoft.com/en-in/visualstudio/extensibility/command-flag-element?view=vs-2022`.

- Strings: This is a required element. It can have multiple children. The ButtonText element is the required and most important child element, and it defines the text that the menu displays. An ampersand in the text string specifies the keyboard shortcut for the command. The syntax of Strings element is as shown as follows:

```
<Strings>
  <ButtonText>... </ButtonText>
```

```
    <ToolTipText>...</ToolTipText>
    <MenuText>...</MenuText>
    <CommandName>... </CommandName>
    <CanonicalName>...</CanonicalName>
    <LocCanonicalName>...</LocCanonicalName>
</Strings>
```

The purpose of these elements is discussed in the following:

- ButtonText: This element specifies the text that appears in the menu. This cannot be blank.

- ToolTipText: This element specifies the tool-tip text that appears for the menu command. If the tool-tip text is not specified, the text of ButtonText is used as a tool tip.

- MenuText: This element specifies the text that is displayed for a command if it is on the main menu, a toolbar, in a shortcut menu, or in a submenu. If the MenuText element is blank, the IDE uses the ButtonText element value. This element can also be used for localization.

- CommandName: This is the command name of the command. This command name can be seen in the Tools ➤ Customize ➤ Commands section, where all the commands are listed. The command can also be seen in the Tools ➤ Options ➤ Keyboards dialog.

CanonicalName: This is the English Canonical Name element. It specifies the name of the command in English text that can be entered in the Command window to execute the menu item. The IDE strips out any characters that are not letters, digits, underscores, or embedded periods. This text is then concatenated to the ButtonText field to define the command. For example, New Project on the File menu becomes the command, File.NewProject. If the English CanonicalName field is not specified, the IDE uses the ButtonText field and strips out all except letters, digits, underscores, and embedded periods. For example, the Button Text "&Define Commands..." becomes DefineCommands, where the ampersand, the space, and the ellipsis are removed.

- LocCanonicalName: This behaves identically to the English CanonicalName element, except that it supports localization.

  For a detailed documentation of Strings element, please read the Microsoft documentation at https://learn.microsoft.com/en-us/ visualstudio/extensibility/strings-element?view=vs-2022.

Groups

This element defines a set of Group elements representing the group of commands exposed by the VSPackage. The syntax of Groups element is shown next:

```
<Groups>
  <Group>... </Group>
  <Group>... </Group>
</Groups>
```

The Group element represents a single group of commands that follows the following syntax:

```
<Group guid="guidMyCommandSet" id="MyGroup" priority="0x101">
  <Parent>... </Parent>
</Group>
```

GUID and id are required attributes and specify the GUID and identifier of the group. The priority is a numeric value that specifies the ordering of the command group.

For a detailed documentation of Groups element, please read the Microsoft documentation at https://learn.microsoft.com/en-us/visualstudio/ extensibility/groups-element?view=vs-2022.

Buttons

The Buttons element is the grouping of Button elements that represents a command with UI, which the user can interact with. The syntax of Buttons element is this:

```
<Buttons>
  <Button>... </Button>
  <Button>... </Button>
</Buttons>
```

The Button element, which represents the command and its UI, can be of three different types: Button, MenuButton, or SplitDropDown. The syntax of Button element is this:

```
<Button guid="guidMyCommandSet" id="MyCommand" priority="0x100"
type="button">
  <Parent>... </Parent>
  <Icon>... </Icon>
  <CommandFlag>... </CommandFlag>
  <Strings>... </Strings>
</Button>
```

To avoid repetition and redundancy, we will not discuss the attributes and child elements discussed earlier. The attributes GUID, id, priority, and type have already been discussed, and they serve the same purpose for the Button element also. The child elements Parent, CommandFlags, and Strings were also discussed. There is another element Icon, which can be used to associate an icon with the command. The valid values of CommandFlags and other details of Button element can be seen at https://learn.microsoft.com/en-in/visualstudio/extensibility/button-element?view=vs-2022.

Combos

This element groups the Combo elements. It has the following syntax:

```
<Combos>
  <Combo>... </Combo>
  <Combo>... </Combo>
</Combos>
```

The Combo element defines a combo box, which can contain multiple commands. Combo box can be one of the following types: DropDownCombo, DynamicCombo, IndexCombo, or MRUCombo. The syntax of Combo element is this:

```
<Combo guid="guidMyCommandSet" id="MyCommand" defaultWidth="20"
idCommandList="MyCommandListID" priority="0x102" type="DropDownCombo">
  <Parent>... </Parent
  <CommandFlag>... </CommandFlag>
  <Strings>... </Strings>
</Combo>
```

For a detailed documentation of Combos element, please read the Microsoft documentation at `https://learn.microsoft.com/en-us/visualstudio/extensibility/combos-element?view=vs-2022`.

Bitmaps

This element groups the Bitmap element, which loads a bitmap. The syntax of the Bitmaps element is as follows:

```
<Bitmaps>
  <Bitmap>... </Bitmap>
  <Bitmap>... </Bitmap>
</Bitmaps>
```

Bitmap element, as the name suggests, defines a bitmap, which can be loaded either from the file or a resource. The syntax of Bitmap element is next:

```
<Bitmap guid="guidImages" href="Resources\MyCommand.png" usedList="img1,
img2, img3" />
```

The Bitmap element has the following attributes:

- GUID: This is a required attribute and is a unique identifier for a bitmap. This identifier is not associated with any VSPackage.

- resID: This is the resource identifier of the bitmap. One of resID's or href's attribute is required. It is an integer resource ID that determines the bitmap strip that is to be loaded during command table merging. When the command table is being loaded, the bitmaps specified by the resource ID will be loaded from the resource of the same module.

- usedList: This attribute is required if a resID attribute is used. It specifies the list of images to be used from the image strip.

- href: This specifies the path to the image file. One of a resID or href attribute is required. The path specified in this attribute is searched for by the image and embedded in the output of vsct compiler. If the usedList attribute is not present, all images in the strip are available, or else only the images specified in usedList would be used. Images may be .bmp, .png, or .gif, but it is recommended to use a .png format.

For a detailed documentation of Bitmaps element, please read the Microsoft documentation at `https://learn.microsoft.com/en-us/ visualstudio/extensibility/bitmaps-element?view=vs-2022`.

The Condition Attribute

Most of the elements we just discussed have an optional attribute called Condition. As the name suggests, this attribute is used to conditionally include the item in the output. There are predefined functions and operators that can be used to test the token. If a condition is applied to a list or group, it applies to all the child elements of the list or group. If a condition is defined in both parent and child elements, then the condition is evaluated by an AND operation. All nonzero expressions are evaluated as true. For a detailed documentation on the Condition attribute, please read the official Microsoft documentation at `https://learn.microsoft.com/en-in/visualstudio/ extensibility/vsct-xml-schema-conditional-attributes?view=vs-2022`.

The VSCT File Continued

Returning to Figure 3-11:

1. The first two child elements of `CommandTable` in the `vsct` file are Extern nodes, which reference files stdidcmd.h and vsshlids.h, that contain all the IDs of commands exposed by Visual Studio and command IDs of menus.

2. The Commands element contains Groups, Buttons, and Bitmaps elements as children. It has an attribute named package that is important and is set to the package GUID. (Please refer to all the #4s in Figure 3-11.)

3. The GUID used in the package attribute of the Commands element is defined in the `GuidSymbol` element defined in the Symbols element, and the package GUID defined in the Package class must be the same.

4. Groups (collection) can have multiple menu groups inside it. A menu group is a container for other menus or commands. Each menu group has a GUID, id, and priority.

5. Each group has a Parent element that specifies the parent menu. The id is set to ***IDM_VS_MENU_TOOLS***, which makes it clear that the parent menu of MyMenuGroup is the top **Tools menu**. Changing this value would put up this command in a different menu. By default, there is no IntelliSense support for a vsct file. However, Mads Kristensen has written an extension pack, named Extensibility Essentials 2022, which packs a number of essential extensions to extend Visual Studio 2022. Using this extension, we can get some IntelliSense support in vsct files as well. We will see this extension pack in action while we develop extensions throughout the book.

   For a detailed list of GUID and ids of the commands and menus of Visual Studio, please refer to https://learn.microsoft.com/en-in/visualstudio/extensibility/internals/guids-and-ids-of-visual-studio-menus?view=vs-2022.

6. Buttons (collection) can have multiple Button elements inside it, which represent the UI of a command. The Button can have an optional child element as Parent, which links this button or command to a menu. Button, like other elements, has the required attributes named GUID and id.

7. There is an attribute of the Button element called type, which defines the type of command. It can have the value as Button, MenuButton, or SplitDropdown. The snippet shows the value as Button.

8. The Icon element associates an icon with the command. This icon would display in the UI for this button/command. In Figure 3-11, bmpPic1 is associated with the icon for the newly added command. Changing the id of this Icon element would change the associated icon. Look at the Bitmaps element, which also has #9 assigned to it in the figure. Bitmaps element groups the Bitmap element that points to the image or defines the usedList of

images in the sprite or strip. The usedList represents the ordinal positions of the icons in the strip. The vsct file shown here has both href as well as usedList, but when href is set, all the images in the strip are used and usedList becomes optional. Otherwise, when the VSCT compiler is executed on the vsct, only the images in the strip would be compacted to only these icons. The ordinal position mapping of icons is done in the Symbols section. Please note that #9 is also assigned to the GuidSymbol element with name guidImages, which contains a number of IDSymbol elements that define the name and position of the images in the strip.

9. There is a child element of Strings called ButtonText element, which contains the name that would be displayed in UI for this command. In the current sample, the text displayed would be "Invoke MyCommand."

10. The Bitmap element has an href attribute that has the path to the image file: Resources\MyCommand.png. One of href or usedList is a required attribute as mentioned in Table 3-1 summarizing the purpose of each element in a vsct file.

Running the Code

With the files added (references, C# code, image png, .vsct file), the code is ready to be run. However, on clicking the command, nothing meaningful would happen; only a message box would show up.

1. Let's run this project, by right-clicking the project and then clicking Debug ➤ Start New Instance (or just pressing F5). This would build the project (create a vsix) and launch the new experimental instance of Visual Studio in which this extension would be loaded. You can notice that the newly launched instance of Visual Studio is an experimental instance by observing the top-right section of the newly launched instance. Figure 3-12 illustrates the normal instance of Visual Studio on the top and Experimental instance of Visual Studio on the bottom. Notice the highlighted text EXP in the bottom section, which identifies the instance as experimental.

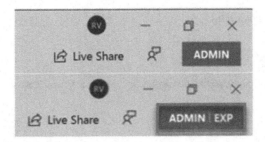

Figure 3-12. *Normal instance and Experimental instance*

2. Let's check out the Tools menu in the new instance of Visual Studio IDE. We will see a newly added command added along with its icon as shown in Figure 3-13.

Figure 3-13. *Invoke MyCommand with its icon*

3. Click this new command and it will display a message dialog as shown in Figure 3-14. This is because the default command template code adds the C# code, which just displays the message dialog. We can wire up whatever code we wish to wire up in the event handler as we will see a little later in the chapter.

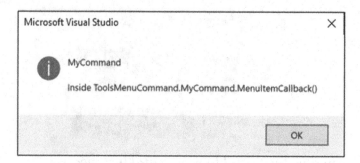

Figure 3-14. *Message dialog triggered from command*

We have just extended the Tools menu of Visual Studio with a custom command that just shows a dialog message. We didn't have to do much yet, as we just used the default Visual Studio Extensibility project item, which did all the boilerplate code for us. We checked out the newly added references and files in the project and came to know that vsct file plays a key role in extending the menu, and editing it correctly can help us extend commands and menus in the IDE. Next, let us discuss the package code that is added by the extensibility template. This way, all ground is covered and we understand what is going on.

The AsyncPackage Abstract Class

Figure 3-15 illustrates the class diagram of the AsyncPackage abstract class from which our package class derives.

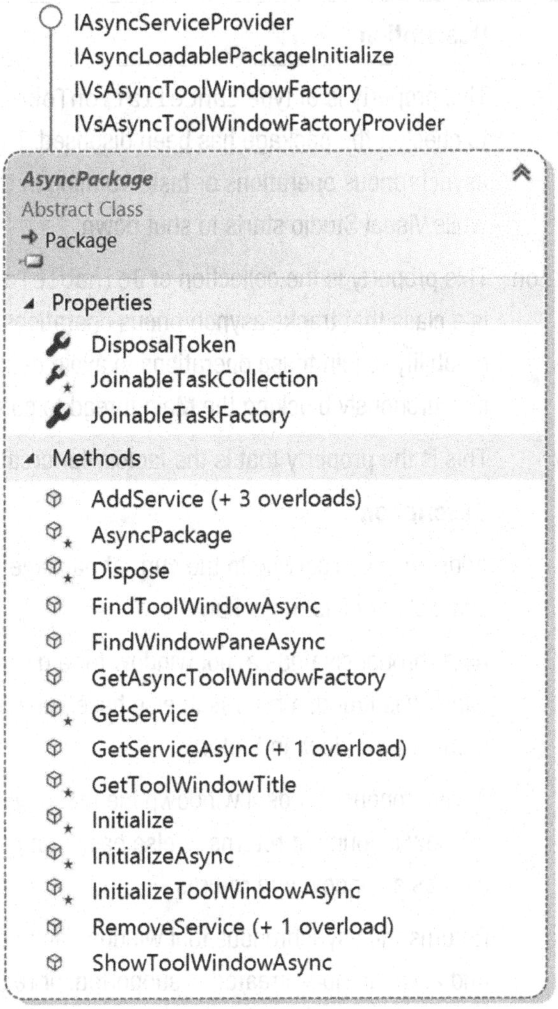

○ IAsyncServiceProvider
  IAsyncLoadablePackageInitialize
  IVsAsyncToolWindowFactory
  IVsAsyncToolWindowFactoryProvider

AsyncPackage
Abstract Class
→ Package
⊡

▲ Properties
  🔧 DisposalToken
  🔧 JoinableTaskCollection
  🔧 JoinableTaskFactory

▲ Methods
  ⬡ AddService (+ 3 overloads)
  ⬡ AsyncPackage
  ⬡ Dispose
  ⬡ FindToolWindowAsync
  ⬡ FindWindowPaneAsync
  ⬡ GetAsyncToolWindowFactory
  ⬡ GetService
  ⬡ GetServiceAsync (+ 1 overload)
  ⬡ GetToolWindowTitle
  ⬡ Initialize
  ⬡ InitializeAsync
  ⬡ InitializeToolWindowAsync
  ⬡ RemoveService (+ 1 overload)
  ⬡ ShowToolWindowAsync

Figure 3-15. AsyncPackage *class diagram*

AsyncPackage is an abstract class that derives from Package abstract class and implements the following important interfaces:

IAsyncServiceProvider, IAsyncLoadablePackageInitialize, IVsAsyncToolWindowFactory, and IVsAsyncToolWindowFactoryProvider

The important members of the class and their purpose are listed in the next table.

Property	Description
DisposalToken	This property is of type CancellationToken that can be used to check if the package has been disposed. This can happen for asynchronous operations or tasks running in the background thread while Visual Studio starts to shut down.
JoinableTaskCollection	This property is the collection of JoinableTask. JoinableTask is a class that tracks asynchronous operations and provides an ability to join those operations to avoid deadlock while synchronously blocking the Main thread to complete the operation.
JoinableTaskFactory	This is the property that is the factory for creating JoinableTask.

Method	Description
AddService	Adds an async service to the current package. The service is not available outside of package.
FindToolWindowAsync	Asynchronously finds a tool window for a given type and Id. If the window is found, it returns it; else based on parameter value, it creates a window and returns.
FindWindowPaneAsync	Asynchronously finds a windowpane for a given type and Id. If the window is found, it returns it; else based on parameter value, it creates a window and returns.
GetAsyncToolWindow Factory	Returns the asynchronous tool window factory interface if it exists and asynchronous created is supported, or returns null.
GetService	Fetches a service registered with the package, by passing the type of service as parameter.
GetServiceAsync	Fetches an async service registered with the package, by passing the type of service as parameter.
GetToolWindowTitle	Gets the title string to be used as window title.
Initialize	It is generally recommended to not use this method as it may result in deadlock. This method runs on Main/UI thread and hence any expensive operation in this method may virtually result in freezing.
InitializeAsync	This method runs on background thread and hence must be used to run the initialization code that can be run on the background thread.

Property	Description
InitializeToolWindow Async	Initializes and performs the code operations to create a tool window asynchronously.
RemoveService	Removes an async service registered with this package.
ShowToolWindowAsync	Displays the tool window of given type and id asynchronously.

Now that we know the methods, properties, and interfaces implemented by AsyncPackage and their purposes, doing a code walkthrough would be more meaningful and comprehensive. Figure 3-16 shows the code of our ToolsMenuCommandPackage file. The code is calibrated with numbers to discuss the important points.

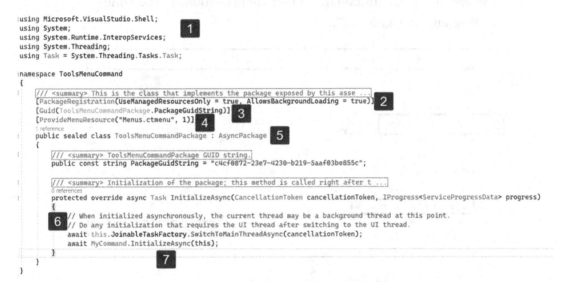

Figure 3-16. ToolsMenuCommandPackage code

1. In Figure 3-16, item #1 shows the namespace references.

2. Item #2 displays the PackageRegistration attribute. This is used on the package for registration of it. The RegPkg.exe utility uses reflection to determine the attributes that need to be registered. We see two attributes, UseManagedResourcesOnly and AllowsBackgroundLoading, which tell us that package would use only managed resources and that it's safe to load the package in the background thread.

3. Item #3 assigns the GUID to the package. We saw in the earlier section that commands are associated to the package via this GUID.

4. ProvideMenuResource attribute provides the registration information of menu resources used in the package. We see a hard-coded string "Menus.ctmenu" as the first parameter (which shouldn't be changed) and 1 as the second parameter (which is the version number) to this attribute. If we navigate to the build output of our extension and reflect on the generated dll using justDecompile or any other reverse engineering/reflection tool, we will find that under the resources of this dll, the key name of the resource is Menus.ctmenu and its value is a binary. The same is illustrated in Figure 3-17.

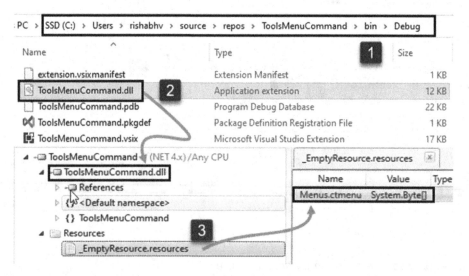

Figure 3-17. *Reflecting the extension dll*

If we see the generated.pkgdef file, which is a package definition file used for registration in the build output of the extension project, we see that all the registration information is encapsulated in the .pkgdef file. Figure 3-18 demonstrates the registration information passed in the attributes.

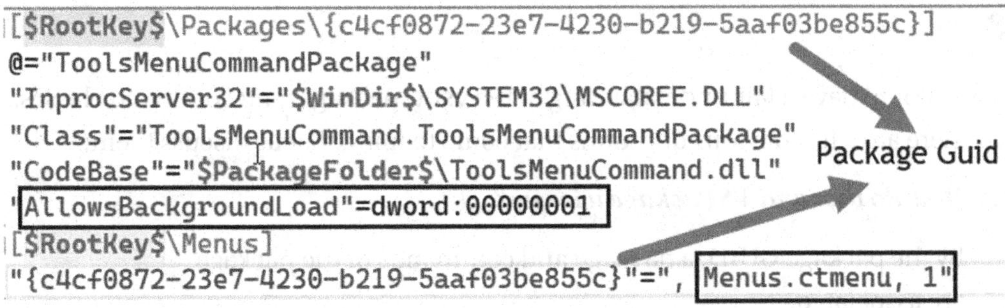

```
[$RootKey$\Packages\{c4cf0872-23e7-4230-b219-5aaf03be855c}]
@="ToolsMenuCommandPackage"
"InprocServer32"="$WinDir$\SYSTEM32\MSCOREE.DLL"
"Class"="ToolsMenuCommand.ToolsMenuCommandPackage"
"CodeBase"="$PackageFolder$\ToolsMenuCommand.dll"        Package Guid
"AllowsBackgroundLoad"=dword:00000001
[$RootKey$\Menus]
"{c4cf0872-23e7-4230-b219-5aaf03be855c}"=",  Menus.ctmenu, 1"
```

Figure 3-18. *Pkgdef file and registration information*

5. Item #5 shows that the ToolsMenuCommandPackage is a sealed class that derives from the AsyncPackage abstract class that we already discussed.

6. This is the override method for the InitializeAsync method of the base class AsyncPackage. It provides an option to cancel the initialization by means of a cancellationToken and provides the ability to report progress by passing in IProgress<ServicePro gressData> as parameters. Please read the comments carefully to understand the use of a Main/UI thread vs. a background thread. For any work or operation that needs UI thread or needs to be executed on UI thread, it's recommended to use the SwitchToMainThreadAsync method of JoinableTaskFactory. The code analyzers that come baked in as part of the project template will help you identify the APIs that need to be called on the UI thread only. So, you'll know when you need to call the SwitchToMainThreadAsync method.

7. This shows how the command is initialized from the Package. In the last line of the package, the InitializeAsync method of MyCommand is invoked, which initializes the command.

FAQs

By now, we should have a fair understanding of the vsct, package, and command classes. However, there are a few obvious questions that come to mind. Let us discuss them:

1. ***How do vsct and VSPackage wire up?***

   By the package GUID, a package and commands of the package are associated.

2. ***How can I change the icon of my newly added command?***

   This is quite simple. All we need to do is include an image of appropriate size and format in the project. Then include it in the Bitmaps section via an href or resID attribute and then specify the same GUID in the Icon element of the command. We will see a sample extension demonstrating this usage of image in the next chapter where we assign the icon to our command.

3. ***How can I bind the keyboard keys with my command?***

   Using the KeyBinding element in the vsct file. We will make use of a KeyBinding element and learn to assign keyboard shortcuts by means of an example in the subsequent chapters where we develop real-world extensions.

4. ***How can I control the visibility of my custom command?***

   Using the VisibilityConstraints and VisibilityItem elements. We will see a sample demonstrating this feature in the next chapter.

5. ***We didn't do anything in the event handler of the custom command. How can I leverage the already existing commands or services in my extension?***

   The AsyncPackage class exposes the APIs (GetService, GetServicesAsync) to find and use the existing service by just passing in the type of service. Once we use this, we can write to Statusbar, Output window, and do a bunch of other things. Also, vsct provides a feature to reuse the existing commands by means of UsedCommand element. We will create an extension that makes use of both these constructs while we develop a real-world extension in the next chapter.

6. ***How can I create a ToolsWindow extension (a window just like Solution Explorer)?***

   The AsyncPackage abstract class exposes the APIs to initialize and find a tool window. These APIs of AsyncPackage can be used to create the ToolWindow. The UI of the ToolWindow can be developed just like a WPF control. We will develop a tool window extension in the next chapter.

7. ***How can I get IntelliSense support while editing vsct file?***

   Mads Kristensen has written an awesome extension pack called Extensibility Essentials 2022, which has a bunch of cool and useful extensions for easing the development of Visual Studio extensions. One of the extensions in the pack is that of VSCT IntelliSense, which can provide IntelliSense support to the vsct files.

8. ***How does debugging the extension project start a new IDE instance?***

   Visual Studio extensions are developed for Visual Studio. Right? So, extensions can be seen and tested only in Visual Studio. Therefore, when we debug an extension, we do need an instance of VS IDE in which the extension being developed/debugged can be checked. If we check the project properties of our extensibility project, under the ***Debug*** tab, we will find that the ***Start action*** of project is set to ***Start external program***, which has the path to the devenv.exe (which is the executable that runs when you start Visual Studio IDE). Also, the command-line arguments value is set to /rootsuffix Exp, which tells the executable to launch in experimental instance. Since we created this project from a template, it was already set by default. However, if you need to debug an extension from scratch, you can use the same debug settings to debug the extension. The path of devenv.exe in my Visual Studio 2022 Community installation is "C:\Program Files\Microsoft Visual Studio\2022\ Community\Common7\IDE\devenv.exe".

Figure 3-19 illustrates the debug properties of our extensibility project.

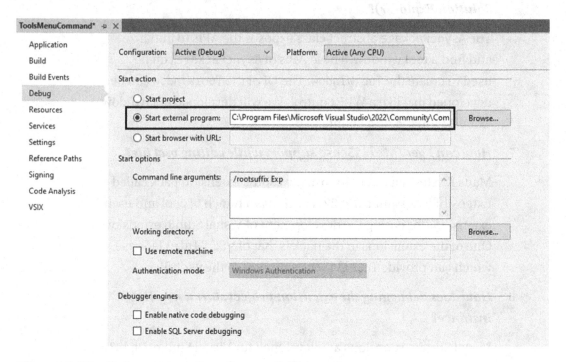

Figure 3-19. *Debug properties of extensibility project*

9. ***What is the need to use an experimental instance?***

   While developing or debugging an extension, many times the
   extension code may be half-baked or buggy. Using it with our
   normal instance may cause issues in the Visual Studio IDE
   and in certain extreme cases even cause interruption in using
   other features of Visual Studio. So, to avoid this "pollution" or
   "corruption" of a normal instance of Visual Studio IDE, Visual
   Studio SDK provides an experimental instance that can be used
   to debug extensions while developing and debugging. For code
   development, we can continue to use the same normal instance
   of Visual Studio, so no change there. In fact, it is recommended
   to use an experimental instance of Visual Studio for development
   and debugging of any VSPackage. That is why the default
   extensibility project sets the project properties to launch an
   experimental instance of Visual Studio in debug mode.

If you wish to launch the experimental instance without debugging, you can type the following command in the command prompt:

```
<VSInstallationPath>\Common7\IDE\devenv.exe /Rootsuffix Exp
```

`<VSInstallationPath>` is "C:\Program Files\Microsoft Visual Studio\2022\Community" in my machine. Depending upon the version of Visual Studio installed in your machine, the path may be slightly different.

An experimental instance is more or less the same Visual Studio; it just reads its configurations and settings from a different registry hive location than that of a normal Visual Studio instance and operates on a different AppData folder as shown in Figure 3-20. The experimental instance works on the folder that has a suffix of Exp as highlighted.

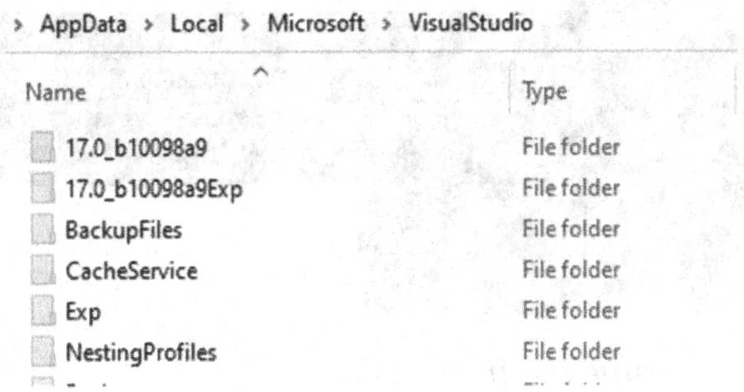

> AppData > Local > Microsoft > VisualStudio

Name	Type
17.0_b10098a9	File folder
17.0_b10098a9Exp	File folder
BackupFiles	File folder
CacheService	File folder
Exp	File folder
NestingProfiles	File folder

Figure 3-20. *Experimental instance folder of Visual Studio IDE*

When an extension is deployed, it is by default deployed to the normal instance of Visual Studio.

10. *OK. An experimental instance safeguards the normal instance of Visual Studio. What do I do if an experimental instance runs into an issue or gets corrupted?*

You can reset the experimental instance of Visual Studio by following these simple steps:

1. Press Windows key (or click the Windows icon on the bottom left of your Windows 10 operating system).

2. Type Reset. This will display Reset the Visual Studio 2022 Experimental Instance as one of the results.

3. Click it to launch the app.

4. A console application will launch, which would reset the Experimental Instance of the Visual Studio. This is shown in Figure 3-21.

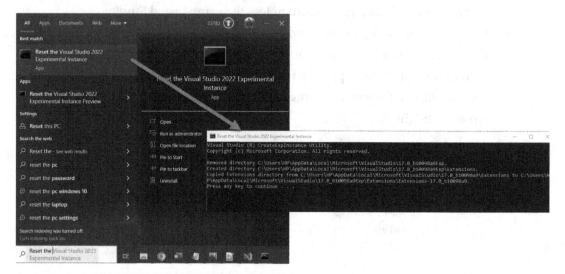

Figure 3-21. *Reset experimental instance*

It is recommended that all the instances of Visual Studio be closed before resetting the experimental instance.

Summary

In this chapter, we discussed the Visual Studio user interface and which components of the user interface that we may need to and want to extend. We learned about the extensibility model of Visual Studio and discussed the important namespaces and assemblies of Visual Studio SDK. We then created a simple extension, which adds a custom command in the Tools menu of Visual Studio. We did a walkthrough of files and code and learned how it all wires up. We discussed a few scenarios and how they can be handled. In the next chapter, we will start developing the extensions that will do something meaningful.

```
EXERCISES
```

The following activities should give you a deep understanding of the fundamentals we discussed in this chapter:

1. Read the documentation and schema of Visual Studio Command Table and all its elements from the official Microsoft Visual Studio documentation at `https://learn.microsoft.com/en-us/visualstudio/extensibility/vsct-xml-schema-reference?view=vs-2022`.

2. Read about the Visual Studio 2022 SDK from the official Microsoft Visual Studio documentation at `https://learn.microsoft.com/en-us/visualstudio/extensibility/visual-studio-sdk-reference?view=vs-2022`.

3. Try to customize your Visual Studio IDE, without writing any line of code and using the out-of-the-box features of Visual Studio. How will you do it?

4. What are `JoinableTask`, `JoinableTaskFactory`, and `JoinableTaskCollection`? Why do we need them?

5. Create an extension that adds a custom command in the following menus:

   a. Project context menu

   b. Code Window context menu

   c. File menu

Try to display different messages when the command button is clicked on each of these menus.

6. Do a code walkthrough of your extension project created earlier and list what you learned.

7. Identify the path and registry location used by the experimental instance of Visual Studio 2022 in your machine. Can you launch an experimental instance of Visual Studio? How?

CHAPTER 4

Developing Your First Extensions

In the last few chapters, we have gone through numerous theories, concepts, and fundamentals related to building Visual Studio extensions. Now it's time to translate this theory into practice. In this chapter, we will develop a pair of meaningful and useful, real-world Visual Studio extensions in a step-by-step fashion. Throughout this process, we will also learn key fundamentals, concepts, and techniques for developing a Visual Studio extension that can be shipped to the Visual Studio Marketplace or shared with a broader audience.

Extensions to Aid Development of VS Extensions

Recall that in the previous chapter, we learned that adding a custom command to Visual Studio requires modifications to the vsct file. We discovered that, by default, Visual Studio 2022 lacks IntelliSense support for editing the vsct file, which poses some challenges in editing it quickly and correctly. Visual Studio comes equipped with a multitude of images that extension writers can leverage. However, we lack knowledge on how to visualize and use them in our extensions. Thankfully, Mads Kristensen thought about these problems and developed an extension pack named "Extensibility Essentials 2022." This pack serves as a valuable resource for Visual Studio extension writers, enhancing their development experience by making it smoother, simpler, and faster. Within this extension pack, a collection of extensions is included, each designed to simplify various tasks that might otherwise seem complex. As of writing this chapter, this extension pack contains the following extensions:

© Rishabh Verma 2024

R. Verma, *Visual Studio Extensibility Development*, https://doi.org/10.1007/978-1-4842-9875-6_4

- VSIX Synchronizer: Provides the ability to generate code-behind files for `.vsixmanfiest` and `.vsct` files in managed code to make the information easy to consume from the rest of the extension

- Insert GUID: Makes it super easy to insert a new GUID into any editor and input field

- Image Manifest Tools: Makes it easier to create and maintain imagemanifest files for a Visual Studio extension

- Clean MEF Component Cache: Clears the Visual Studio Managed Extensibility Framework (MEF) component cache to fix issues with cache corruption

- `Pkgdef` Language: Full language support with `IntelliSense`, validation, outlining, and more for `.pkgdef` and `.pkgundef` files

- Extensibility Margin: Shows relevant information about the current file and language to extensibility authors

- Extensibility Template Pack 2022: A template pack for Visual Studio extension authors full of useful project and item templates

- Known Monikers Explorer 2022: A tool window for Visual Studio extension authors to explore the KnownMonikers image collection

- VSCT `IntelliSense` 2022: Gives `IntelliSense` for `.vsct` files used by Visual Studio extension authors

- Textmate Grammar Template: A template for shipping Textmate Grammar files as a Visual Studio extension

- VS Theme Colors 2022: Makes it easy to browse all the brushes and select the right theme color for your Visual Studio extension UI

- VSCode Theme Converter: A super easy way to convert VS Code themes to Visual Studio using the official CLI tool under the hood

The details for each of these extensions can be found on their respective extension pages on the Visual Studio Marketplace site (`https://marketplace.visualstudio.com/`). But there's more. Mads has also shared the GitHub URL of each of the extension in this pack. You can locate this in the project details section of each extension. This allows curious readers to delve into the inner workings of each extension and understand the magic behind them.

I strongly recommend that readers install this extension pack before embarking on the development of Visual Studio 2022 extensions. The extension can be downloaded from the Visual Studio Marketplace at `https://marketplace.visualstudio.com/items?itemName=MadsKristensen.ExtensibilityEssentials2022` and then proceed to install it. Alternatively, you can navigate to the top menu of Visual Studio by clicking Extensions ➤ Manage Extensions and then search for Extensibility Essentials 2022 as shown in Figure 4-1.

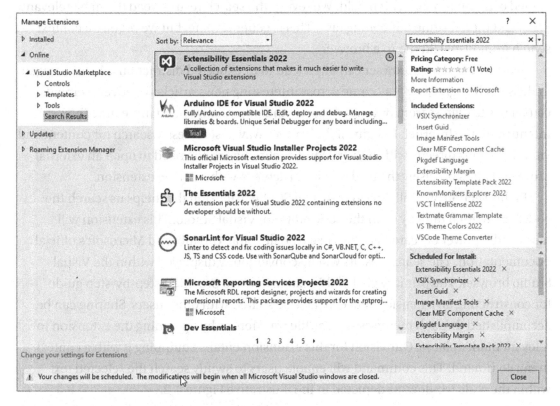

Figure 4-1. *Extensibility Essentials 2022*

Once the extension pack shows up, click the download button. The extension pack will start installation once the Visual Studio closes. Similarly, it is also recommended to install the Command Explorer extension: `https://marketplace.visualstudio.com/items?itemName=MadsKristensen.CommandExplorer`.

With this extension pack installed, we are ready to start coding our extension. The first extension that we will develop in this chapter will perform a code/text search.

Visual Studio Extension to Perform Search

Many times, while writing new code or reviewing/fixing an existing code, we come across documentation comments, keywords, types, or APIs that we aren't entirely sure about and want to explore further on the Internet. In our quest for knowledge, we typically find ourselves copying the entire text or code snippet, launching our preferred web browser, navigating to our favorite search engine like Google, and then pasting the copied content into the search field. We review the search results, read the most relevant links, and then resume our coding task. This is generally fine, but we require a context switch from Visual Studio to a browser.

Switching to a web browser can often lead to unexpected distractions. As we navigate to the search engine, we may come across interesting news articles or advertisements, causing us to digress from our initial search and potentially spend more time than intended on the Internet. Imagine if there was a way to seamlessly search for content and view the results directly within Visual Studio, eliminating the need to open an external browser. This is precisely the goal we aim to achieve with our new extension.

In this section, we will develop a Visual Studio extension that helps us search the code/text written directly from the code editor of Visual Studio. This extension will harness the power of search engines like Google, Bing, GitHub, and Microsoft's official documentation. The search results will be conveniently displayed within the Visual Studio browser. The primary goal of this extension is to provide a step-by-step guide for constructing an extension that can later be shared with other users. Sharing can be accomplished through methods such as file transfers or by uploading the extension to relevant marketplaces. Our vision for this extension entails equipping it with a context menu command. This command will enable users to swiftly search the selected text within the code window, as depicted in the illustrative Figure 4-2.

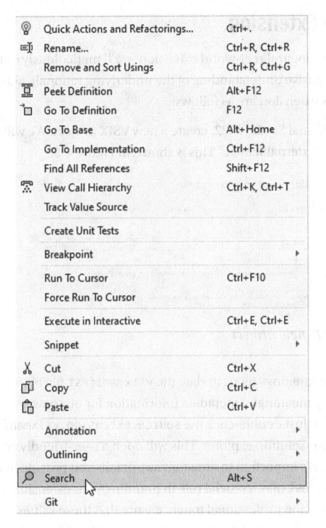

Figure 4-2. *Search command*

In addition to developing this extension, we will also learn the following:

- How to utilize the services and APIs already provided by Visual Studio within our extension?

- How to incorporate an icon into our custom command?

- How to assign a keyboard shortcut to the custom command?

- How to leverage options within extension?

Let's get going on this exciting journey.

Starting the Extension

As this marks our inaugural real-world extension, we'll meticulously outline the steps to ensure a comprehensive understanding of the underlying rationale and approach. The steps to create this extension are as follows:

1. In your Visual Studio 2022, create a new VSIX project. We will name it "ExternalSearch." This is shown in Figure 4-3.

Figure 4-3. *Create new project*

2. First and foremost, let us update the vsixmanifest file by providing meaningful metadata information for our new extension. Just double-click the source.extension.vsixmanifest file in your solution explorer. This will open a user-friendly editing window. It's important to note that any details you provide in the vsixmanifest play a crucial role in branding your extension. For a polished and professional touch, ensure that these values are correct and meaningful. The description text should describe your extension to the new users, so it should be relevant and correctly and clearly describe what your extension does. We had a quick discussion about the vsixmanifest file earlier in Chapter 2, so we will not dive into each field. However, the gist is that this file directly affects the branding of your extension and hence should always be updated. The following are a few of the pointers to update this file:

    a. Author and version are pre-populated. However, each time you release an update for your extension, ensure that this version number is incremented (like 1.1, 1.2, etc.). This has

multiple reasons. First, it lets users update the extension if
the previous version of the extension is installed, without
uninstalling, or else VSIX installer would complain that
the extension is already installed. If you have shared your
extension in Visual Studio Marketplace, then when you
upload the updated version with new features, the underlying
architecture of managed extensions would identify that the
new version of the extension is available in the marketplace
and depending upon the extension to update settings, either
a notification would be displayed or the extension would be
updated automatically. The extensions that are installed for
all users cannot be auto-updated and hence would not have
auto-update settings. The update setting of an extension in
the Manage Extensions window is shown in Figure 4-4.

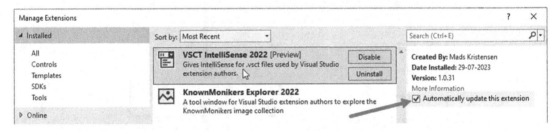

Figure 4-4. *Automatically update the extension*

b. If you plan to ship or share your extension, you can include
the license information by adding a rich text file (.rtf) or text
file in your project and then browsing it in the License section
of the manifest. We are not discussing licenses in this book,
but it's good to understand different types of licenses and
their scope. `https://opensource.org/licenses/` is a good
resource to read and learn different licenses.

c. For providing an icon and preview image of your extension,
you can either use your own image or make use of image
monikers that ship with Visual Studio. To make use of images
that ship with Visual Studio, the Known Monikers Explorer
extension can be of great help so we have already installed

it as part of the Extensibility Essentials 2022 extension pack. To use this extension, navigate to the main menu of Visual Studio, then go to View ➤ Other Windows ➤ Known Monikers Explorer. This will open a tool window that will list all the known image monikers that we can use. Select an image that we want to use for our extension. Since we are going to search in this extension, we use an image that depicts searching. This is shown in Figure 4-5. When we right-click the image, it presents a context menu, which provides a functionality to export the image. We can export the image from here and use that image for the icon and preview image in the vsix manifest file. A 32-bit PNG is the preferred format for icons, so you may want to export the 32-bit PNG format.

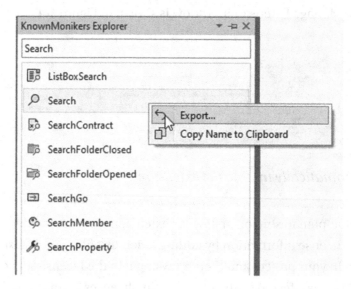

Figure 4-5. *KnownMonikers Explorer*

d. The other fields like tags, release notes, getting started guide, etc. are simple and can be updated as needed. After filling these details, the vsixmanifest looks like what is shown in Figure 4-6.

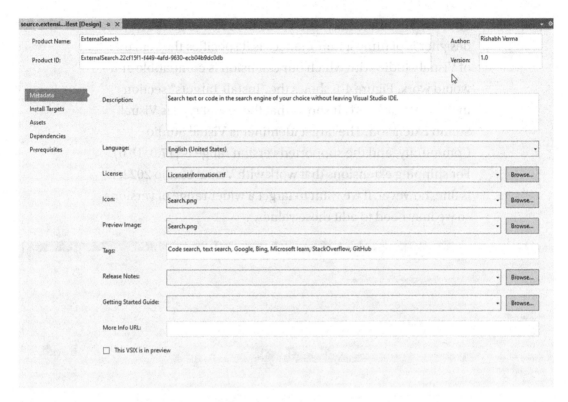

Figure 4-6. *Updated* `vsixmanifest`

e. If we tick the "This VSIX is in preview," it will mark the extension in Preview state, and [Preview] would display with the name of the extension. This can be leveraged for dogfooding your extensions. The VSCT `IntelliSense` extension is in preview state at the time of writing this chapter and can be easily identified in the marketplace as well as in the Manage Extensions dialog as shown in Figure 4-7.

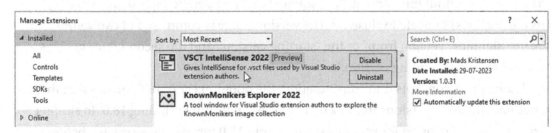

Figure 4-7. *Extension in preview*

f.   The "Install Targets" section within the vsixmanifest
designer is of utmost importance, as it specifies the versions
of Visual Studio with which our extension is compatible and
would work. Figure 4-8 shows the "Install Targets" section
in the vsixmanifest. It shows that the install type is Visual
Studio Extension. The target identifier is Visual Studio
Community, and the supported version range is [17.0, 18.0).
For shipping extensions that work with Visual Studio 2022, it
is fine, however, if we want to target a wider range of versions,
so we may need to edit these values.

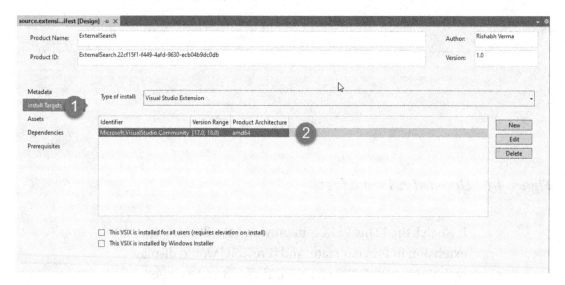

Figure 4-8. *Version range*

In Chapter 2, we explored the version and product name mapping of Visual Studio,
where 17.0 corresponds to Visual Studio 2022 and 18.0 alludes to a future version of
Visual Studio. Within this context, "[]" (square brackets) denote inclusivity, while "()"
(round brackets) indicate exclusivity. The version range is comprised of two values:
the first signifies "version from" or the "starting version" and the second one specifies
"version to" or the "ending version."

Taking these concepts into consideration, the notation [17.0, 18.0) means that the
range encompasses versions from 17.0 (inclusive) up to, but excluding 18.0. In simpler
terms, it denotes support for versions starting from 17.0 through versions just before
18.0. Furthermore, it's worth noting that identifier and version ranges can be added,

modified, or removed as needed. If an extension is compatible with the Community version of Visual Studio, it inherently supports all higher editions such as Enterprise. However, this compatibility does not extend in the reverse direction.

The "ProductArchitecture" element is crucial; Visual Studio 2022 will not install your extension without it. Valid values include "x86" and "amd64." This element specifies the platforms that the extension supports, and it is case-insensitive. Only one platform can be specified per element, and one element can be defined per "InstallationTarget" instance. For product versions earlier than 17.0, the default value is "x86" and can be omitted. However, for product versions 17.0 and later, this element is required, and there is no default value. Specifically, for Visual Studio 2022, the only valid content for this element is "amd64."

3. In the solution explorer, right-click the project. The context menu will display. On this menu, click "Add new item." Alternatively, you can click the project (to select it) and press Ctrl+Shift+A. This will open the "Add New Item" dialog. Under the Extensibility category (and VSPackage subcategory on the left panel), click the Command item template to add it to the project. I have named this new command class as SearchCommand.cs as shown in Figure 4-9.

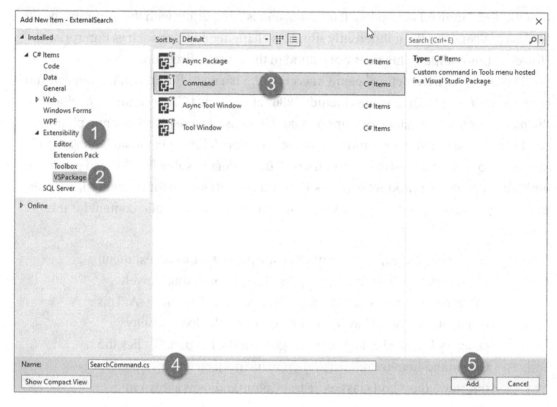

Figure 4-9. *Add new item*

This action will add several new files (`.cs`, `.vsct`, `.png`) and references. We covered the details of these files in the preceding chapter.

Adding a Command to the Menu

Building on the information provided in the previous chapter, we are aware that just upon adding the command in the project, the extension can be run, and the newly added command will appear in the Tools menu. However, placing the command in the Tools menu is not the most user-friendly and ergonomic design. It's less intuitive to select text or code within the code window and then navigate to the Tools menu to activate the command. Ideally, we would prefer the command to be readily accessible as a context menu item within the code editor window. This would allow us to select a text or code snippet and conveniently trigger the search operation by clicking this contextual command. So, this command should appear on the code editor window where we edit the code. We also want to have keyboard support for this command so that the developer using our extension can just select the code snippet/text on the code window and press the key combination to perform the search. Recall that the location of the command is specified in the Groups section of the .vsct file, specifically in the "id" attribute of the Parent element as shown in Figure 4-10.

```
<Groups>
  <Group guid="guidExternalSearchPackageCmdSet" id="MyMenuGroup" priority="0x0600">
    <Parent guid="guidSHLMainMenu" id="IDM_VS_MENU_TOOLS"/>
  </Group>
</Groups>
```

Figure 4-10. *Parent id determines the location of command*

1. We need to modify the "id" attribute of the Parent element under the Group element, such that the location of this command can be changed to the code window from the Tools menu. Now, the question comes to mind is this: What id value should I update to achieve this? Let's answer this.

   Earlier in this chapter, we installed the Extensibility Essentials 2022 extension pack. One of the extensions that is part of this pack is VSCT IntelliSense. This enables IntelliSense support in vsct file. Now, if we edit the value of id and type code (for the code window) in the vsct file, we see the valid set of id values as shown in the next figure. From the group of values, IDM_VS_CTXT_ CODEWIN sounds like context menu for code window, so it is most appropriate fit for our scenario. When I searched it online, it is indeed the correct id for the code window. However, this is a hit- and-trial approach and may not scale for other scenarios. Though IntelliSense guides us to put the correct values, it may still not be able to guide you to place your commands in the right location. Perhaps a tool tip or corresponding location glyph can help. See Figure 4-11.

```
<Groups>
  <Group guid="guidExternalSearchPackageCmdSet" id="MyMenuGroup" priority="0x0600">
    <Parent guid="guidSHLMainMenu" id="code"/>
  </Group>
</Groups>
```

IDG_VS_CODEWIN_SNIPPETS	Group/Menu
IDG_VS_CODEWIN_TEXTEDIT	Group/Menu
IDG_VS_MNUDES_VIEWCODE	Group/Menu
IDG_VS_PROJ_ADDCODE	Group/Menu
IDG_VS_VIEW_CODEBROWSENAV_WINDOWS	Group/Menu
IDG_VS_VIEW_FORMCODE	Group/Menu
IDM_VS_CTXT_CODEWIN	Group/Menu
IDM_VS_CTXT_OBJBROWSER_DESC	Group/Menu

```
<!--Buttons section. -->
<!--This section defines the elements t                                      r a button
    or combo box in a toolbar. -->
<Buttons>
  <!--To define a menu group you have t                                y priority.
      The command is visible and enable                        ty, status, etc, you can use
      the CommandFlag node.
      You can add more than one CommandFlag node e.g.:
```

Figure 4-11. *Illustrates* `IntelliSense` *support in* `.vsct` *file*

Now, our command will be placed in the code window context menu. However, we still need to provide an icon and keyboard support to make it professional and user-friendly.

Adding an Icon and Keyboard Support

When we add a command from the template, a default icon is assigned, but we want to do better. Visual Studio ships with over 4030 icons and images, which support high DPI, integrates seamlessly, and looks good in any color theme of Visual Studio IDE. Next, we will see how we can leverage these icons in our extension.

1. In the vsct file, immediately after the top two **Extern** elements, we will add a new element **Include** with the href property set to `KnownImageIds.vsct`. As soon as we type K for the href value, `IntelliSense` will display the exact file name, so you need not remember the exact name. This file contains the image symbols as shown in Figure 4-12. In my machine, this file is located at C:\ Program Files\Microsoft Visual Studio\2022\Community\VSSDK\ VisualStudioIntegration\Common\Inc.

```
KnownImageIds.vsct  ┅ ✕  Command Explorer        What's New?
    1       <?xml version='1.0' encoding='utf-8'?>
    2     ⊟<!--
    3       [auto-generated]
    4           This code was generated by the ManifestToCode tool.
    5           Tool Version: 16.0.0.1
    6       [/auto-generated]
    7       -->
    8     ⊟<CommandTable xmlns="http://schemas.microsoft.com/VisualStudio/2005-10-18/CommandTable">
    9     ⊟   <Symbols>
   10     ⊟     <GuidSymbol name="ImageCatalogGuid" value="{ae27a6b0-e345-4288-96df-5eaf394ee369}">
   11             <IDSymbol name="Abbreviation" value="0" />
   12             <IDSymbol name="AboutBox" value="1" />
   13             <IDSymbol name="AbsolutePosition" value="2" />
   14             <IDSymbol name="AbstractAssociation" value="3" />
   15             <IDSymbol name="AbstractClass" value="4" />
   16             <IDSymbol name="AbstractCube" value="5" />
   17             <IDSymbol name="Accelerator" value="6" />
   18             <IDSymbol name="AcceptEventAction" value="7" />
   19             <IDSymbol name="Accessibility" value="8" />                      I
   20             <IDSymbol name="Accordian" value="9" />
   21             <IDSymbol name="Account" value="10" />
   22             <IDSymbol name="AccountAttribute" value="11" />
   23             <IDSymbol name="AccountGroup" value="12" />
   24             <IDSymbol name="Action" value="13" />
   25             <IDSymbol name="ActionLog" value="14" />
   26             <IDSymbol name="ActionTool" value="15" />
   27             <IDSymbol name="ActivateWorkflow" value="16" />
   28             <IDSymbol name="ActiveDocumentHost" value="17" />
   29             <IDSymbol name="ActiveEnvironment" value="18" />
   30             <IDSymbol name="ActiveFluidLayout" value="19" />
   31             <IDSymbol name="ActiveServerApplication" value="20" />
   32             <IDSymbol name="ActiveXControl" value="21" />
   33             <IDSymbol name="Activity" value="22" />
   34             <IDSymbol name="ActivityDiagram" value="23" />
```

Figure 4-12. KnownImageIds.vsct

Notice that the name of the GuidSymbol element is
ImageCatalogGuid, which contains all the image symbol names
and values. This is good enough, and with IntelliSense support,
we just need to type a part of name of image that we wish to use
and IntelliSense will show the appropriate list of valid values
with a glyph. For example, since our extension will be performing
a text search in external search engines, we want an appropriate
search icon. So, under the Button element, we will edit the Icon
element properties. We first change the GUID property of the
Icon element. IntelliSense will help us edit the value of the
GUID attribute as ImageCatalogGuid, and then typing search in
the id property would help us select the right image as shown in
Figure 4-13.

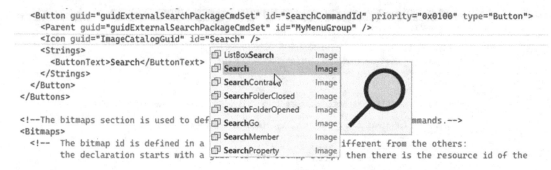

Figure 4-13. *Editing Icon – see the IntelliSense support and glyph*

2. Since we are using built-in images from the Visual Studio Image catalog, we do not require .png file in the solution. So, we do not need the Bitmaps element and the corresponding symbols defined in the vsct files. We will get rid of all these elements from the vsct file. This will, however, not work as is. We need to add a CommandFlag element (after Icon element) and specify its value as ImageIsMoniker for the icon to show up for the command. The preceding steps would enable us to make use of images that ship as part of the Visual Studio Image catalog.

3. Next, we modify the button text to Search, so our command would display in context menu as Search.

4. To add the keyboard support to our command, we will create a KeyBindings node immediately after the Commands node and then press the tab key, which will populate the snippet of KeyBindings. Now, to specify the keyboard shortcut to this command, we first need to ensure that the keyboard shortcut that we use for this command is not already being used. To do so, navigate to Tools ➤ Options ➤ Keyboard as shown in Figure 4-16. To reach here, you can search on the Options dialog as well, or directly type Keyboard on the top search text box of Visual Studio and navigate.

5. In the "Press shortcut keys" text box (marked as #2 in Figure 4-14), press the key combination that we wish to use and check if it's being used. For demonstration purposes, I pressed Ctrl+S (I know we use it to save the document). The text box gets updated with this key combination. Just below this text box is the "Shortcut currently used by" field, which gets updated and shows that this key combination is used by the File.SaveSelectedItems command. This way, we can find out if a key combination can be used or not for our custom command. Using the same exercise, I can say that Alt+S is not being used by any other command in my Visual Studio, so it seems like a good key combination for our search command.

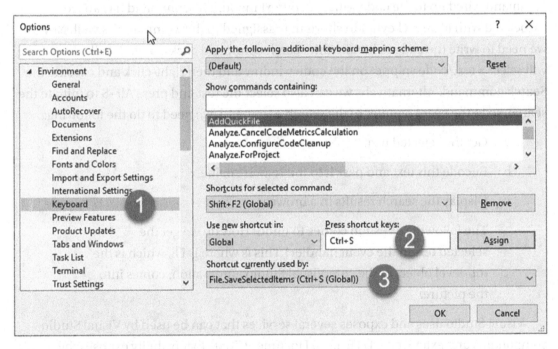

Figure 4-14. *Keyboard shortcuts*

6. To assign the key combination of Alt+S to our command, the KeyBindings element will look as shown in Figure 4-15.

```
<KeyBindings>
  <KeyBinding guid="guidExternalSearchPackageCmdSet" id="SearchCommandId" editor="guidVSStd97" key1="S" mod1="Alt">
  </KeyBinding>
</KeyBindings>
```

Figure 4-15. *KeyBindings*

IntelliSense would help us with the correct values for GUID, id (which should match the command), editor, key1, key2, mod1, and mod2. Since, we are using just Alt and S as a key combination, we got rid of key2 and mod2.

Writing the Search Functionality

With the preceding step, all the vsct file changes are completed. We have our new command wired up to the code window context menu. The command has an icon associated with it, and a keyboard shortcut is assigned to this command as well. Now, we need to write the code to handle this search command click event. Recall that we will select a text/code snippet on the code window and then right-click and execute the Search command. Alternatively, we can also select the text and press Alt+S to initiate the search, so in the event handler of the search command, we need to do the following:

    a.   Get the selected text.

    b.   Encode this text and pass it to the search engine.

    c.   Display the search results in a browser.

        The following question comes to mind: How do we get the selected text in the event handler? This is where DTE, which is the top-level object of the core Visual Studio automation, comes into the picture.

Visual Studio uses and exposes several services that can be used by Visual Studio components and extensions. DTE a.k.a. Document Tools Extensibility exposes the properties and APIs that can be used for extending and automating the documents, projects, etc. Let us quickly go through DTE, its important properties, and methods. The class diagram of DTE is shown in Figure 4-16 and the "Class References" section at the end of the chapter summarizes the properties and methods of DTE. The same can be seen online at https://learn.microsoft.com/en-us/dotnet/api/envdte. dte?view=visualstudiosdk-2022.

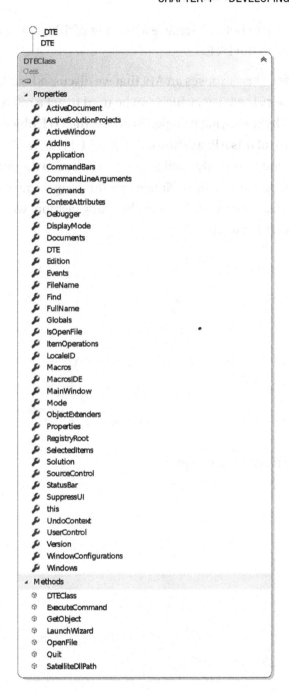

Figure 4-16. *DTE class diagram*

So, we see that DTE can help us achieve a number of things. The next thing that we need to do is get access to the DTE.

1. AsyncPackage class exposes an API that we discussed earlier
   named GetServiceAsync, which can be used to get a reference
   to a service, by specifying its type. To access the DTE object, we
   will make use of this API as shown in Figure 4-17. This API is
   very useful and frequently used to get a reference to the services
   while developing extensions. Notice that this is an async API, and
   therefore to use it correctly in a non-blocking fashion, we have
   used the await keyword.

```
1 reference
public static DTE2 DteInstance
{
    get;
    private set;
}
```

```
/// <summary> Initializes the singleton instance of the command.
1 reference
public static async Task InitializeAsync(AsyncPackage package)
{
    // Switch to the main thread - the call to AddCommand in SearchCommand's constructor requires
    // the UI thread.
    await ThreadHelper.JoinableTaskFactory.SwitchToMainThreadAsync(package.DisposalToken);
    DteInstance = await package.GetServiceAsync(typeof(DTE)) as DTE2;
```

Figure 4-17. *GetServiceAsync usage*

2. Now we have reference to the DTE2 object, but how do we get the selected text? For this, we need to use the property named ActiveDocument of DTE2, which returns the active document of Visual Studio. This property is of type Document. Before we can start using this property, let us see which properties and methods are exposed by the Document type. The class diagram of Document is as shown in Figure 4-18.

Figure 4-18. Document type

The properties and methods of the Document interface are summarized in the
"Class References" section at the end of this chapter. The documentation for the
Document type can be read online at `https://learn.microsoft.com/en-us/dotnet/
api/envdte.document?view=visualstudiosdk-2022`.

We see that Document has a property named Selection, which can help us get the
selection from the document. The EnvDTE assembly exposes a type called TextSelection
that handles the selection of text. Using them, we can get the selected text. For writing
extensions, TextSelection type can be helpful for various needs.

A high-level summary of TextSelection properties and methods from
Microsoft official documentation is listed in the "Class References" section. The
documentation can be seen and read online in the Microsoft documentation
site at `https://learn.microsoft.com/en-us/dotnet/api/envdte.
textselection?view=visualstudiosdk-2022`.

With this, we now know the APIs and properties that can be used to work with
documents and text selection. Let's put this knowledge into action.

3. We get the Selection property of the ActiveDocument property
   of DTE2 and then check if it can be cast to type TextSelection. If
   text selection is null, we have nothing to search, so we can display
   the message to the user on the StatusBar or OutputWindow of the
   Visual Studio. If we have text selection, we can construct the URL
   to search it in a search engine by opening the URL in the browser.
   This entire code flow is illustrated in Figure 4-19.

```
private void Execute(object sender, EventArgs e)
{
    ThreadHelper.ThrowIfNotOnUIThread();

    if (!(DteInstance?.ActiveDocument?.Selection is TextSelection textSelection))
    {
        DteInstance.StatusBar.Text = "The selection is null or empty";
        return;
    }

    var textToBeSearched = textSelection.Text.Trim();
    if (string.IsNullOrWhiteSpace(textToBeSearched))
    {
        DteInstance.StatusBar.Text = "The selection is null or empty";
        return;
    }

    var encodedText = HttpUtility.UrlEncode(textToBeSearched);
    DteInstance.StatusBar.Text = $"Searching {textToBeSearched}";
    OutputWindow.OutputStringThreadSafe($"Searching {textToBeSearched}");
    var url = $"https://www.google.com/search?q={encodedText}";
    DteInstance.ItemOperations.Navigate(url, vsNavigateOptions.vsNavigateOptionsDefault);
}
```

Figure 4-19. *Execute method to search selected text in Google.*

Let us discuss a few salient points and concepts demonstrated by this code:

a. We make use of the static DteInstance property to reference DTE2 instance. DTE instance should be accessed in the Main/UI thread. The snippet illustrates the API to throw an exception if the executing thread is not the Main/UI thread.

b. DTE has a StatusBar property that can be used to display text, animation, progress, etc. in the Visual Studio status bar. We can use this property to display short status messages to the user while searching or when the selected text is empty.

c. The snippet in the image also illustrates how to display text in the OutputWindow. The OutputString method can be used to write text in the Output window. However, we first need to get a reference to the OutputWindow. This is done by using the service infrastructure of Visual Studio and calling the GetServiceAsync API. This is done in the InitializeAsync method of the SearchCommand class. Visual Studio exposes the General Output window by means of the SVsGeneralOutputWindowPane that can be used directly to get reference of the General Output window as shown in Figure 4-20.

```
public static async Task InitializeAsync(AsyncPackage package)
{
    // Switch to the main thread - the call to AddCommand in SearchCommand's constructor requires
    // the UI thread.
    await ThreadHelper.JoinableTaskFactory.SwitchToMainThreadAsync(package.DisposalToken);
    DteInstance = await package.GetServiceAsync(typeof(DTE)) as DTE2;
    Assumes.Present(DteInstance);
    OutputWindow = await package.GetServiceAsync(typeof(SVsGeneralOutputWindowPane)) as IVsOutputWindowPane;
    Assumes.Present(OutputWindow);
    OleMenuCommandService commandService = await package.GetServiceAsync(typeof(IMenuCommandService)) as OleMenuCommandService;
    Instance = new SearchCommand(package, commandService);
}
```

Figure 4-20. InitializeAsync method

    d.   **Assumes** is a static helper class that exposes the APIs to check the assumption about the service instances. The **Present** method verifies if the value is not null, or else it throws an exception.

    e.   DTE2 has a property named ItemOperations that can be used to work with files and perform operations like opening a file, checking if a file is open, adding a new item to project, adding an existing item to a project, or navigating to a URL. We have used the Navigate method of ItemOperations to navigate to the search engine URL.

Testing the Extension

With the preceding steps, the first draft of our extension is ready.

    1.   Press F5 and start debugging. This will launch a new experimental instance of Visual Studio with our ExternalSearch extension installed. Then, open an existing C# project and open one of the C# files for edit in the code window.

    2.   Select a code snippet/text in the code window and right-click. This will display a context menu with our new custom command. Notice the icon, name, as well as keyboard shortcut of the Search command as shown in Figure 4-21.

Figure 4-21. *Search command*

3. Click the Search command (or alternatively press the key combination Alt+S). This will search the selected text in the Google search engine and display the results in the Visual Studio browser as shown in Figure 4-22.

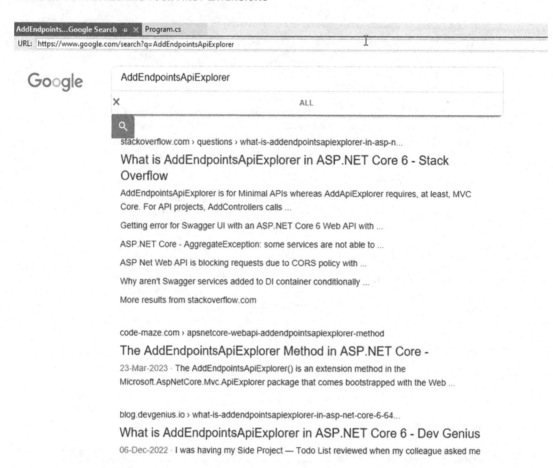

Figure 4-22. *Google search in Visual Studio browser*

With this, we have a working Visual Studio extension that can be used to search a code/text in Google search engine, directly inside Visual Studio. However, this is not ready to be shared with the community as a few users may prefer to search in Bing, or Stack Overflow, or Microsoft docs, or GitHub, or any other search engine. Our extension should be able to provide this flexibility to the user. How can we do it? Configuration is what comes to mind. If I can configure what search engine I want to use, it would solve this use case. Visual Studio extensions have a support for Options page that can be configured by the user to customize a feature/extension as per their needs. In the next steps, we will discuss how we can make our extension configurable by leveraging an Option page for our ExternalSearch extension.

4. To add an options page, we will first add a new class to our project and name it ExternalSearchOptionPage.cs.

5. The class should derive from a DialogPage class. The class diagram of DialogPage class is shown in Figure 4-23. The properties and methods of the DialogPage from the official Microsoft docs site are summarized in the "Class References" section. The documentation on DialogPage is very detailed, and it shares a great deal of insights in the working of DialogPage. I would highly encourage readers to read this documentation at `https://learn.microsoft.com/en-us/dotnet/api/microsoft.visualstudio.shell.dialogpage?view=visualstudiosdk-2022`.

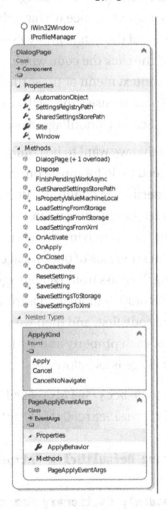

Figure 4-23. *DialogPage*

The DialogPage has APIs to save and load settings to the registry as well as on the file system, and the properties expose the location of the storage. This class can be inherited so we can override the methods to change the default implementation. In our case, the default implementation of DialogPage is sufficient as we are dealing with simple properties. The class diagram of DialogPage class is shown in Figure 4-23.

Now that we are aware of the APIs exposed by the DialogPage, let's use it.

6. To uniquely identify this newly created ExternalSearchOptionPage class as our extension's option page, we need to assign a GUID to this class by means of a GUID attribute. Since we have the Insert GUID extension installed as part of the Extensibility Essentials 2022 extension pack, we can right-click the code window and then click Insert GUID in the context menu or press the key combination of Ctrl+K, Ctrl+Space to insert the GUID in the GUID attribute on top of the ExternalSearchOptionPage class.

7. Next, we define the properties that we want to be configured. This is pretty much what we need to do for most common option page scenarios. Whatever properties we define and decorate with attributes and TypeConverters will show up in the options dialog page of the extension by the underlying infrastructure. The point is that most common scenarios of option pages can be easily handled by inheriting the class from DialogPage, defining the properties, and decorating them with attributes and TypeConverters. Let us see the code first, and then we will discuss and understand the purpose of each property and attribute. The code for ExternalSearchOptionPage is as follows:

```
[Guid("f6528658-87a9-4b49-bcc3-5647df1e68bd")]
public sealed class ExternalSearchOptionPage : DialogPage
{
    private const string DefaultUrl = "https://www.google.com/
    search?q={0}";
    private static readonly Dictionary<SearchEngines, string>
    allEngines = new Dictionary<SearchEngines, string>()
```

```csharp
{
    { SearchEngines.Google, DefaultUrl },
    { SearchEngines.Bing, "https://www.bing.com/search?q={0}" },
    { SearchEngines.MicrosoftLearn, "https://learn.microsoft.com/
    en-in/search/?terms={0}&category=All" },
    { SearchEngines.StackOverflow, "https://stackoverflow.com/
    search?q={0}" },
    { SearchEngines.GitHub, "https://github.com/search?q={0}" }
};

[DisplayName("Use Visual Studio Browser")]
[DefaultValue(true)]
[Category("General")]
[Description("A value indicating whether search should be displayed
in Visual Studio browser or external browser")]
public bool UseVSBrowser { get; set; }

[DisplayName("Search Engine")]
[DefaultValue("Google")]
[Category("General")]
[Description("The Search Engine to be used for searching")]
[TypeConverter(typeof(EnumConverter))]
public SearchEngines SearchEngine { get; set; } =
SearchEngines.Google;

[DisplayName("Url")]
[Category("General")]
[Description("The Search Engine url to be used for searching")]
[Browsable(false)]
public string Url
{
    get
    {
        var selectedEngineUrl = allEngines.FirstOrDefault(j =>
        j.Key == SearchEngine).Value;
```

```
            return string.IsNullOrWhiteSpace(selectedEngineUrl) ?
            DefaultUrl : selectedEngineUrl;
        }
    }
}
```

The file has just one static field and three properties. The static field `SearchEngines` is a dictionary of the `SearchEngines` enum as the key and string as the value. Different search engines with their URLs are added in the dictionary.

`System.ComponentModel` namespace defines a number of attributes that can be applied on the properties. These attributes are highlighted as bold in the previous code listing. The purpose of these attributes is summarized in Table 4-1.

Table 4-1. *Attributes Defined in System.ComponentModel*

Attribute Name	Description
DisplayName	Assigns a name to the property.
DefaultValue	Assigns a default value to the property.
Category	Assigns a category to the property.
Description	Assigns a description to the property.
TypeConverter	Converts the value from one type to another. For example, EnumConverter converts an enum to a string and vice versa. We can create a custom type converter for any type by inheriting a class from TypeConverter and overriding the methods for converting the types. The documentation of TypeConverters and its APIs can be seen online at https://docs.microsoft.com/en-us/dotnet/api/system.componentmodel.typeconverter?view=netframework-4.8.
Browsable	Specifies if the property should display or not in the PropertyGrid.

There may be extension users who may want to see the search results in an external browser. The property UseVSBrowser is added for that purpose. It has a default value of true, meaning by default the Visual Studio browser would be used. The other property is that of SearchEngine, which exposes the search engines to be selected by the end user. So, the user has the flexibility to choose Bing, Google, Stack Overflow, Microsoft Learn, or GitHub. The default value of the search engine is Google and the attribute

TypeConverter ensures that all the values of the enum are displayed as a drop-down in the Property grid. Once the user chooses a search engine, the corresponding URL needs to be used, so we need to do a lookup in our static dictionary to get the URL of the selected search engine. This is done in the URL property. We do not want the user to edit it, so it's only read (get only property). Also, once the search engine is selected, the URL cannot be changed, so there is no point in showing it to the user. The Browsable attribute with a false parameter hides this property.

With this, coding for our simple PropertyGrid-based DialogPage is done. We need not worry about persisting the values or loading the values as the DialogPage infrastructure takes care of it. However, there may be cases wherein we have a requirement to display a custom UI in our options page. We can achieve this custom UI scenario by inheriting the option page class from the UIElementDialogPage (instead of DialogPage) and creating a UserControl with appropriate UI.

Coming back to our current extension, we still need to wire it up with our package and then access the options in our extension code to honor the user-provided values. We will make these changes in the next steps:

1. Let's go back to our Package class and add an attribute ProvideOptionPage to wire up the options page with this package. The next code listing shows this attribute:

```
[ProvideOptionPage(typeof(ExternalSearchOptionPage),
"External Search", "General", 1, 1, true, new string[]
{ "External Search Options"})]
    public sealed class ExternalSearchPackage : AsyncPackage
```

Here's what each parameter of the ProvideOptionPage attribute does:

- typeof(ExternalSearchOptionPage): This part specifies the type of the options page associated with the attribute. It tells Visual Studio which class is responsible for providing the options settings for your extension.

- "External Search": This is a string that represents the name of the options category or group. In this case, it's named "External Search." When you access Visual Studio's options settings, you will likely see this group as a section where you can configure settings related to "External Search."

- `"General"`: This string represents the subcategory or subfolder within the "External Search" category where these options will be located. It further organizes the options settings under the "External Search" group.

- 1: This short value represents the options page's category ID. It's a unique identifier for the category, helping Visual Studio manage and organize extension-specific settings. I have used 1 but can choose any short value.

- 1: This short value represents the options page's page ID. Like the category ID, it's a unique identifier for the specific options page within the category.

- `true`: This Boolean value indicates whether the options page should be automatically loaded when Visual Studio starts. When set to true, the options page is loaded automatically.

- `new string[] { "External Search Options" }`: This is an array of string values representing the localized display names for the options page. In this case, it's an array with a single string element, "External Search Options." This is the name that users will see when they navigate to this extension's options/settings page within Visual Studio.

2. Now, we need to access the options page and then use the option properties in our extension. To do so, we first need to access the options page. We make use of `GetDialogPage` API of the package class to get the options. Once we have access to the options, we can use its properties and use either the external browser or VS browser as well as the configured search engine. The complete code listing of Execute method incorporating options is as follows:

```
private void Execute(object sender, EventArgs e)
{
    ThreadHelper.ThrowIfNotOnUIThread();
    var options = package.GetDialogPage(typeof(ExternalSearch
    OptionPage)) as ExternalSearchOptionPage;
    // Get the options.
```

```
if (!(DteInstance?.ActiveDocument?.Selection is TextSelection
textSelection))
{
    DteInstance.StatusBar.Text = "The selection is null
    or empty";
    return;
}

var textToBeSearched = textSelection.Text.Trim();
if (string.IsNullOrWhiteSpace(textToBeSearched))
{
    DteInstance.StatusBar.Text = "The selection is null
    or empty";
    return;
}
    var encodedText = HttpUtility.UrlEncode(textToBeSearched);
    DteInstance.StatusBar.Text = $"Searching
    {textToBeSearched}";
    OutputWindow.OutputStringThreadSafe($"Searching
    {textToBeSearched}");
    var url = string.Format(options.Url, encodedText);
if (options.UseVSBrowser)
{
    DteInstance.ItemOperations.Navigate(url,
    vsNavigateOptions.vsNavigateOptionsDefault);
}
else
{
    System.Diagnostics.Process.Start(url);
}
}
```

3. Now, if we debug the project, a new experimental instance of
   Visual Studio would open. Navigate to Tools ➤ Options page and
   then search for External Search. It would display the External
   Search Options dialog. The External Search Options dialog is as
   shown in Figure 4-24.

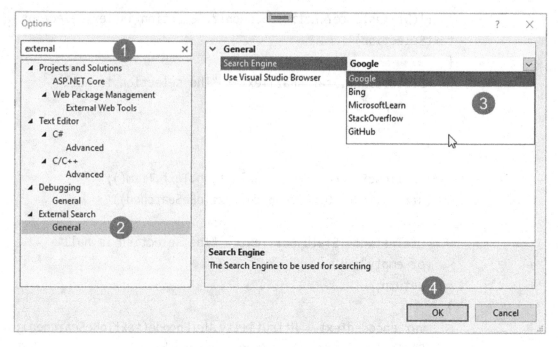

Figure 4-24. *External Search Options page*

4. Now, if we change the search engine to Bing or any other search
   engine, we will see that search engine being used for our next
   search has changed to Bing as shown in Figure 4-25.

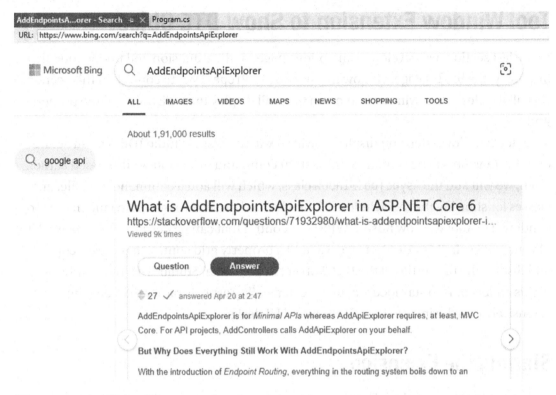

Figure 4-25. *Using Bing search*

Now our extension looks good enough to be shared with other users.

Congratulations! We have just completed a working extension that is near ready to be shared with other users (of course post testing). Microsoft extensibility has a great sample to demonstrate the options page usage, which can be seen in GitHub at `https://github.com/microsoft/VSSDK-Extensibility-Samples/tree/master/Options`. It exposes the base class and model to create an options page. Another sample demonstrating the intricacies of an options page in a thread-safe way is `https://github.com/madskristensen/OptionsSample`.

At times, we may need to develop extensions wherein we need to show a window in Visual Studio with some custom UI, like the Solution Explorer window or the Properties window. To develop them, Visual Studio has a built-in item template called `AsyncToolWindow`. In the next section, we will see how we can develop a simple tool window extension for Visual Studio.

Tool Window Extension to Show DTE Object

In the last section, we developed an options page for the extension and understood that internally, the `DialogPage` window makes use of a `PropertyGrid` control. In this section, we will develop a tool window extension that will display the DTE object in the property grid control.

A tool window extension displays a window in the Visual Studio IDE. The structure of this extension will be similar to the custom command extension we discussed earlier. Then, we will add the `AsyncToolWindow` class, which will add a command, vsct file, and classes for showing the tool window. The command provides a means to launch the tool window. The tool window hosts a WPF user control that can be designed to display a UI of your choice. In this extension, we will add a property grid control in our user control and display the properties of the DTE2 object in the Visual Studio IDE. The emphasis of this endeavor is to stay focused on the extensibility aspects rather than delving extensively into the intricacies of WPF-based UI design.

Starting the Extension

Let's develop this extension. The steps are as follows:

1. Create a new VSIX project in Visual Studio 2022. Give this project a meaningful name like PropertiesToolWindow.

2. Update the `vsixmanifest` file with the appropriate and meaningful values as discussed earlier in this chapter. The updated `vsixmanifest` file is shown in Figure 4-26.

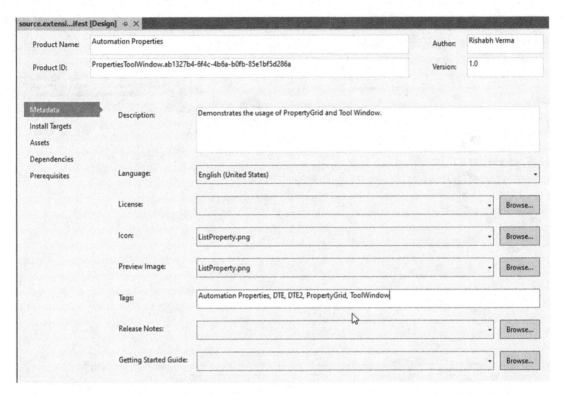

Figure 4-26. *Updated* vsixmanifest

3. Now, we will add the tool window. To do so, right-click the project in the solution explorer and then click Add ➤ New item in the context menu. This will open the Add New Item dialog. Under the Extensibility category in the left pane, click the **Async Tool Window** and name the class ToolWindow. This will add a tool window that can be hosted in the AsyncPackage and a command to load this window asynchronously. This is shown in Figure 4-27.

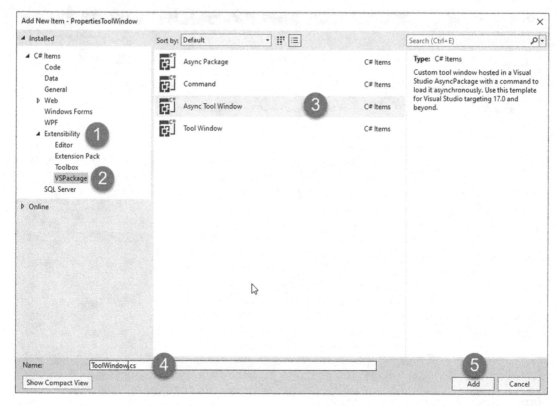

Figure 4-27. *Async Tool Window*

4. This will add a ToolWindow class that derives from the
    ToolWindowPane class, which has the default implementation for
    a tool window. Deriving from ToolWindowPane class makes our
    ToolWindow class a tool window.

Adding a ToolWindowPane

The class diagram for ToolWindowPane is shown in Figure 4-28, which lists its
properties, methods, and events. The diagram also reveals that ToolWindowPane
itself derives from the WindowPane class and implements the IVsWindowSearch
interface. The properties, methods, and events of ToolWindowPane with their purposes
are summarized in the "Class References" section. The full documentation can be
read online at https://learn.microsoft.com/en-us/dotnet/api/microsoft.
visualstudio.shell.toolwindowpane?view=visualstudiosdk-2022.

Figure 4-28. *ToolWindowPane class*

If we go through these members, we see a few members related to Search, ToolBar, and InfoBar. The search and toolbar are intuitive and previously discussed to some extent. The description makes these members comprehensive.

Writing the Extension

1. Looking at the solution explorer, we will see the following files (in addition to the ToolWindow class) added in the project:

    a. .vsct file, command class to expose a command that can be used to load the tool window

    b. A WPF user control that will be hosted by the tool window, which is itself hosted in Visual Studio

At this stage, the extension is already in a working state. If we run/debug this project, it will open a new experimental instance of Visual Studio IDE. Navigate to View ➤ Other Windows ➤ Properties Tools Window, and it will display a tool window with a button. On clicking the button, it displays a message box. We need to customize the code to meet our requirements. First, we will modify the vsct file to assign an image, proper text, and keyboard shortcut to the command. We have already seen the steps to update vsct file in the previous extension. Figure 4-29 displays the code snippet of the updated .vsct file. The changes are highlighted for easy identification.

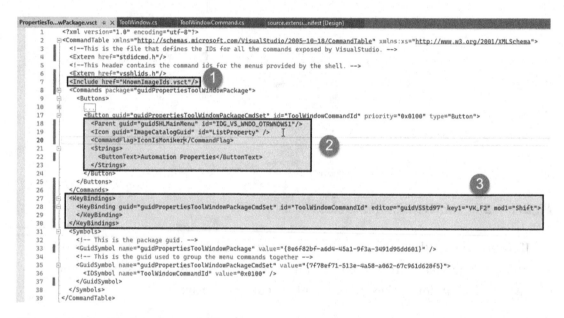

Figure 4-29. *Updated .vsct file*

Note that guidSHLMainMenu id is set to **IDG_VS_WDO_ OTRWNDWS1** that corresponds to the **View ➤ Other Windows** menu of the Visual Studio top menu. If we want to change this location, this id should be changed as discussed earlier in the chapter. The keyboard combination of Shift+F2 is assigned to the command.

2. Next, we will modify the WPF user control to have a property grid, which will show the properties of a DTE2 object. Unfortunately, the default WPF toolbox doesn't have a PropertyGrid control; Windows forms have it. But there are a few third-party packages that have the PropertyGrid control for WPF. We will make use of the Extended.WPF. Toolkit by Xceed as it has a PropertyGrid control. To do so, right-click the project references of the project and then click Manage NuGet Packages. On the browse section, search and install the Extended. WPF.Toolkit package in your project as shown in Figure 4-30.

Figure 4-30.   *Extended.WPF.Toolkit*

3. Once the package is installed, modify the user control XAML file as shown in Figure 4-31.

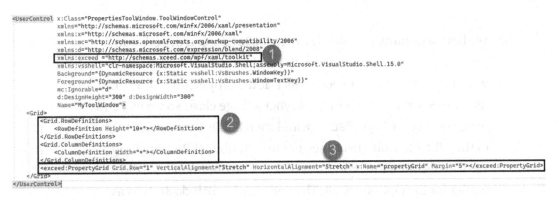

Figure 4-31.   *Updated XAML*

The following changes are made:

a.   Added xmlns for the toolkit in the UserControl element

b.   Defined Grid's row and column definitions

c.   Added PropertyGrid control

4.   Next, let's update the code-behind file of the user control. The UI
     of our user control is simple. It just has a PropertyGrid control. So,
     in the code-behind file, we should pass on the data that we want
     to be bound to this control. Let's define a new constructor for our
     User Control, which takes an entity or model (class containing
     the data to be bound) as the parameter. Let's name that class as
     ToolWindowData. Once we have the data, we just need to bind it
     to property grid. This is shown in Figure 4-32.

```
public partial class ToolWindowControl : UserControl
{
    /// <summary>
    /// Initializes a new instance of the <see cref="ToolWindowControl"/> class.
    /// </summary>
    1 reference
    public ToolWindowControl()
    {
        this.InitializeComponent();
    }

    1 reference
    public ToolWindowControl(ToolWindowData data) : this()
    {
        this.propertyGrid.SelectedObject = data;
    }
}
```

Figure 4-32. *User Control code-behind*

5.   We have a dummy class for ToolWindowData created. Let's add
     properties to it that we want to display in the tool window. We
     want to see the DTE2 object, so let's add a property for DTE2. Let
     us also see what there is in the AsyncPackage class, so we will add
     one property for AsyncPackage and then finally a property for one
     of the WPF controls, just to see the functioning of PropertyGrid.
     We will decorate the properties with the attributes like we did
     earlier for the Options page. The code for ToolWindowData is as
     follows:

```
[DisplayName("Tool Window Data")]
public class ToolWindowData
{
    [DisplayName("DTE Instance")]
```

```
[Category("General")]
[Description("The DTE Instance")]
[EditorBrowsable(EditorBrowsableState.Always)]
[TypeConverter(typeof(ExpandableObjectConverter))]
public DTE DTE { get; set; }

[DisplayName("Async Package")]
[Category("General")]
[Description("The Package")]
[EditorBrowsable(EditorBrowsableState.Always)]
[TypeConverter(typeof(ExpandableObjectConverter))]
public AsyncPackage Package { get; set; }

[DisplayName("Text Box")]
[Category("General")]
[Description("The TextBox")]
[EditorBrowsable(EditorBrowsableState.Always)]
[TypeConverter(typeof(ExpandableObjectConverter))]
public TextBox TextBox { get; set; }
}
```

I would highly encourage readers to go through the attributes used earlier in detail, specifically TypeConverters as they play a pivotal role in how data displays in the PropertyGrid control. Here, we have used an ExpandableObjectConverter, which can be used to convert the expandable or dynamic objects to other types.

6. The code added by the AsyncToolWindow template adds a WPF user control that is hosted by the tool window. The tool window invokes the parameter-less constructor of the user control that still exists. However, we have added a constructor that takes ToolWindowData as a parameter, and we want this constructor to be invoked by a tool window. To make this happen, we will modify the ToolWindow.cs file and add a constructor that takes ToolWindowData as the parameter. The code listing for ToolWindow is as follows:

```
[Guid(ToolWindow.ToolWindowId)]
public class ToolWindow : ToolWindowPane
{

    internal const string ToolWindowId = "a26b1099-
    d844-4461-9f4c-79f49c5b8257";
    public ToolWindow() : this(null)
    {
    }

    // The data should be passed from InitializeToolWindowAsync
    method in the Package class.
    public ToolWindow(ToolWindowData data) : base()
    {
        this.Caption = "Automation Properties";
        this.BitmapImageMoniker = KnownMonikers.
        ListProperty;

        // This is the user control hosted by the tool window;
        Note that, even if this class implements IDisposable,

        // we are not calling Dispose on this object. This is
        because ToolWindowPane calls Dispose on
        // the object returned by the Content property.
        this.Content = new ToolWindowControl(data);
    }
}
```

Each tool window derives from the ToolWindowPane and has a unique identifier assigned to it. Visual Studio uses this identifier to persist the size, position, state, etc. of the tool window in the settings store.

ToolWindows can exist in a number of states, like tabbed, linked, floating, MDI, etc. What state we want the tool window to be in can be set in the Package class. We will see this shortly in the steps to come. An interesting thing about tool windows is that once created, they are never destroyed, unless Visual Studio closes. Even if we close the tool window, it is actually not closed;

it's hidden. This can be confirmed by placing a breakpoint in
the ToolWindow constructor. We will find that the constructor is
called only once.

Though we have created a constructor that is accepting
ToolWindowData as a parameter, this parameter still needs
to be passed to the constructor. How do we do it? We need to
override a method named InitializeToolWindowAsync in our
Package class so that it returns the instance of the object that
needs to be passed. In the constructor, we are setting the Caption,
BitmapImageMoniker, and Content properties, which we have
already discussed. Here I have used a string directly, but it's
recommended to make use of constants.

7. Now, let's move to our Package class. This is the class that hosts
the tool window. First and foremost, we need our tool window to
be in a tabbed state just like a document, so we will update the
ProvideToolWindow attribute (which registers and tells the Visual
Studio that this package owns a tool window) on our Package class
as the following:

```
[ProvideToolWindow(typeof(ToolWindow), Style = VsDockStyle.
Tabbed, Orientation = ToolWindowOrientation.none,
Window ="DocumentWell")]
```

We have added a Style attribute, which is an enum and can have the
following values: none, MDI, Float, Linked, Tabbed, and AlwaysFloat.
The next attribute is Orientation, which is again an enum and can
have the following values: none, Top, Left, Right, and Bottom. The
window property specifies that the tool window should be tabbed in
the DocumentWell, where all the documents are opened.

ProvideToolWindowAttribute is an important attribute,
and its properties determine the fate of tool window, so
let us understand the properties exposed by this attribute
from the official Microsoft docs. The documentation can
also be read online at https://learn.microsoft.com/
en-us/dotnet/api/microsoft.visualstudio.shell.
providetoolwindowattribute?view=visualstudiosdk-2022.

Table 4-2 lists the important properties of
ProvideToolWindowAttribute.

Table 4-2. *Properties of* ProvideToolWindowAttribute

Property Name	Description
DockedHeight	Gets or sets the default height of the ToolWindow when docked.
DockedWidth	Gets or sets the default width of the ToolWindow when docked.
DocumentLikeTool	Set this property to true if you want a tool window that is like a document in its behavior and lifetime. The tool window will only be MDI or floating and will remain visible in its position across all layout changes until manually closed by the user at which point it will be destroyed. This flag implies DontForceCreate and destructive multi-instance.
Height	Gets or sets the default height of the tool window.
MultiInstances	**Determines whether multiple instances of the tool window are allowed.**
Orientation	Gets or sets the default orientation for the tool window relative to the window specified by the Window property.
PositionX	Gets or sets the default horizontal value of the top-left corner of the tool window.
PositionY	Gets or sets the vertical value of the top-left corner of the tool window.
Style	Gets or sets the default docking style for the tool window.
ToolType	Gets or sets the type of the tool window.
Transient	**Gets or sets whether the tool window should not be reopened when the IDE restarts.**
TypeID	Override the TypeID property in order to let the RegistrationAttribute-derived classes to work with System.ComponentModel.TypeDescriptor.GetAttributes (...). An attribute derived from this one will have to override this property only if it needs a better control on the instances that can be applied to a class.
Width	Gets or sets the default width of the tool window.
Window	Gets or sets the GUID of the default window on which the tool window should be docked.

The properties in bold alter the behavior of tool windows drastically. A transient property determines if the tool window should not open automatically if IDE restarts. I would encourage readers to play around with these properties and explore what properties bring about what changes in the appearance of the tool window.

8. Next, we need to override a couple of methods in the Package class `GetAsyncToolWindowFactory` and `InitializeToolWindowAsync`. We need to override them because we have customized the tool window constructor to accept a parameter. Had we used the default parameter-less constructor, we need not override these two methods. In the `GetAsyncToolWindowFactory`, we tell the underlying infrastructure to use the current Package class as the factory, and once this happens, `InitializeToolWindowAsync` method overridden in the same class gets invoked. Here, we would construct our `ToolWindowData` object and return so that it gets passed to the `ToolWindow` constructor. The code for these two overridden methods is as shown in Figure 4-33.

```
public override IVsAsyncToolWindowFactory GetAsyncToolWindowFactory(Guid toolWindowType)
{
    return toolWindowType.Equals(Guid.Parse(ToolWindow.ToolWindowId)) ? this : null;
}

0 references
protected override async Task<object> InitializeToolWindowAsync(Type toolWindowType, int id, CancellationToken cancellationToken)
{
    await JoinableTaskFactory.SwitchToMainThreadAsync(cancellationToken);
    var dte = await this.GetServiceAsync(typeof(EnvDTE.DTE)) as DTE2;
    return new ToolWindowData
    {
        DTE = dte,
        Package = this,
        TextBox = new TextBox() { Name = nameof(TextBox) }
    };
}
```

Figure 4-33. *Overridden methods to pass* `ToolWindowData` *object to* `ToolWindow` *constructor*

9. With this, all our code changes are made. However, there is one more class added in the project, which we did not see or modify. This class is the `ToolWindowCommand` class. The code for this class is the same as adding a custom command, so there is nothing new to discuss here. This class exposes a command, which when executed launches the tool window. This command is in the View | Other Windows menu. Let us see the Execute method of this class

as that is responsible for showing the tool window. The code for
Execute method is this:

```
private void Execute(object sender, EventArgs e)
{
    this.package.JoinableTaskFactory.RunAsync
    (async delegate
    {
        ToolWindowPane window = await this.package.
        ShowToolWindowAsync(typeof(ToolWindow), 0, true,
        this.package.DisposalToken);
        if ((null == window) || (null == window.Frame))
        {
            throw new NotSupportedException("Cannot create
            tool window");
        }
    });
}
```

The code in bold is responsible for showing the tool window.
There are a few important things to make note of here:

a.   Execute is a synchronous event handler method. See that the
     code to show the tool window is wrapped inside a RunAsync
     block. This shows how to execute an async operation in a
     synchronous method.

b.   Since the invocation of method is async, the tool window is
     loaded asynchronously. That is why it was referred to as an
     AsyncToolWindow.

c.   ShowToolWindowAsync method takes four parameters. First
     is the type of tool window to be created; the second is an
     identifier that specifies the instance id of the tool window.
     The third parameter is a Boolean, which determines if the tool
     window should be created if it doesn't exist. If this parameter
     is false and the tool window doesn't exist, then the window
     will be set to null. A fourth parameter is a cancellation token
     that can be used to cancel the asynchronous operation.

Running the Extension

Now to run it:

1. Press F5. In the new Visual Studio instance that opens, navigate to the View ➤ Other Windows ➤ Automation Properties as shown in Figure 4-34.

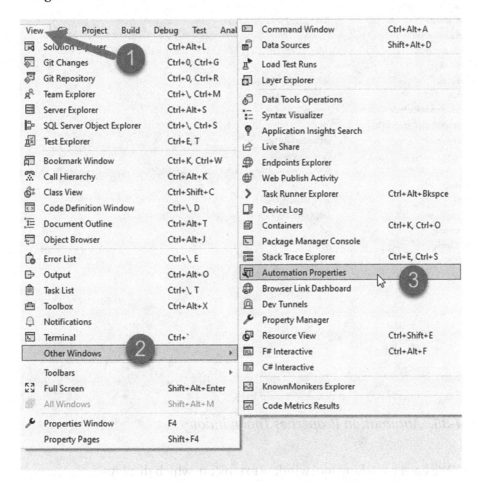

Figure 4-34. *Navigation to Automation Properties extension*

2. A tool window would show up as seen in Figure 4-35.

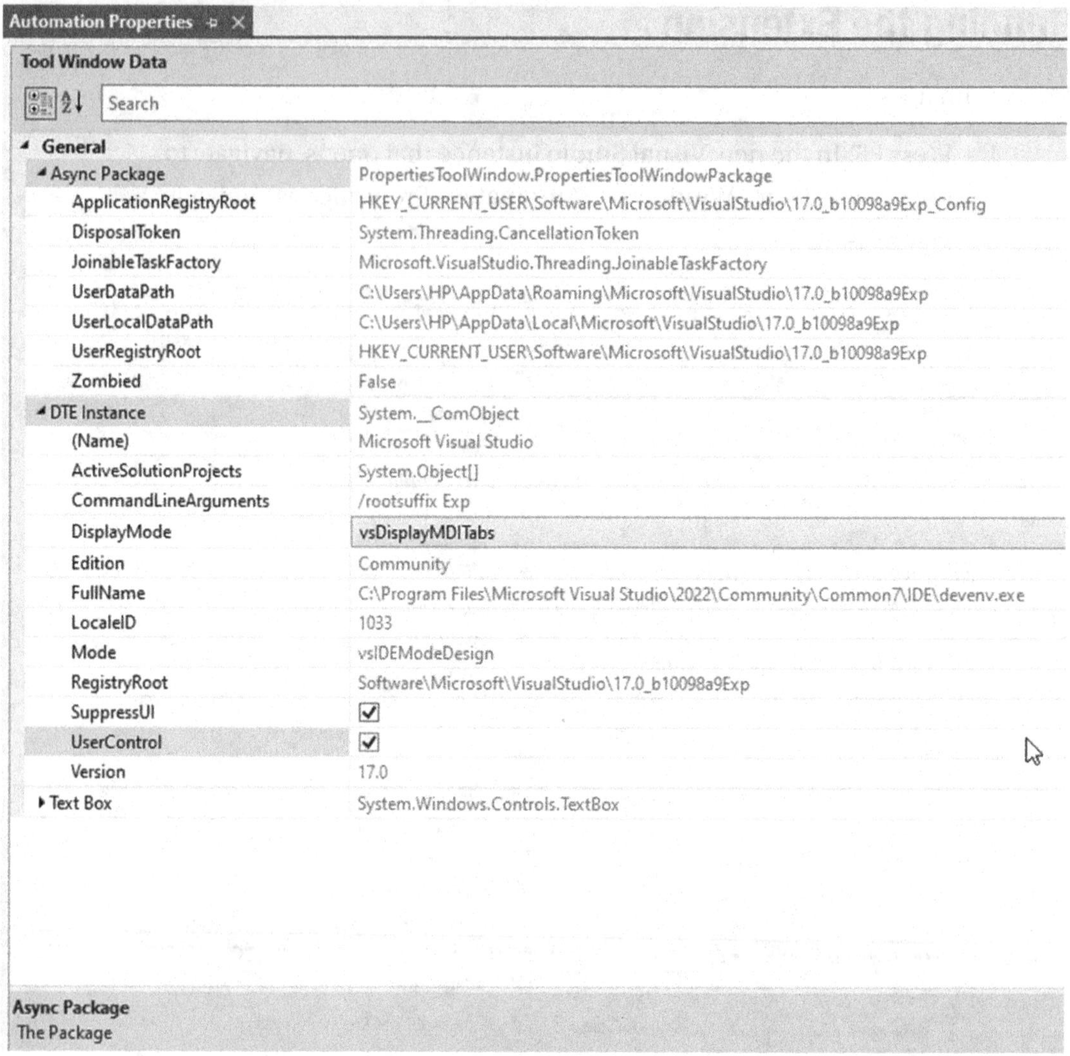

Figure 4-35. *Automation Properties Tool window*

We have a working tool window extension, which displays
the properties of AsyncPackage, DTE, and Textbox control
in the PropertyGrid control. It is a good place to see the
values of the ApplicationRegistryRoot, UserDataPath, and
UserRegistryRoot paths where the extension information gets
stored. In the DTE2 object properties, we can see the Edition,
version, command-line arguments, etc. Also notice that the
properties of the Textbox control display in the same way as we

see in the properties window while designing the XAML. So, apart
from learning to develop a tool window extension, we have also
seen the DTE2, Package object properties, and their live values
and got an exposure to `PropertyGrid` control as well. The code
map diagram of the extension code is shown in Figure 4-36.

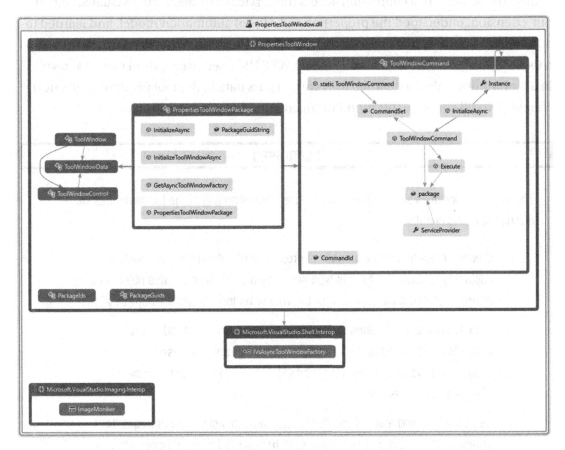

Figure 4-36. *Code map diagram of the ToolWindow extension*

This ends our chapter. The Visual Studio Extensibility team also has
a sample of the Async Tool Window in GitHub. It can be seen at the
following URL:

```
https://github.com/microsoft/VSSDK-Extensibility-Samples/
tree/master/AsyncToolWindow
```

Summary

In this chapter, we developed a couple of useful and meaningful extensions and learned a few important concepts along the way. We saw an illustration of how to add custom commands and wire up an event handler to custom commands. We learned how we can change the location of a command, access the services exposed by the Visual Studio in our extension, understood the properties and APIs of automation model, and learned to add support for the options page and use it in our extension. We also learned to develop a tool window extension and how a custom WPF UI-based user control can be shown in a tool window. We also learned how we can pass data to the tool window. In the next chapter, we will continue this momentum and develop new extensions.

EXERCISES

The following activities should give you a deeper understanding of the fundamentals we discussed in this chapter:

1. Create a class that has a number of properties of different types. Create a custom type converter for this type and display an instance of this object in a `PropertyGrid` control. Note that the WinForms toolbox has a `PropertyGrid`.

2. Explore the ways to change the visibility of a custom command. What methods do you need to use? Hint: `https://learn.microsoft.com/en-us/visualstudio/extensibility/visibilityitem-element?view=vs-2022`.

3. Read, explore, and learn about the Assets, Dependencies, and Prerequisite section of the `vsixmanifest` file. Read `https://learn.microsoft.com/en-us/visualstudio/extensibility/vsix-manifest-designer?view=vs-2022`.

4. Use the Settings Store Explorer extension and find out where the options of the extensions are stored.

5. Create a tool window extension that displays the properties of open documents and windows in Visual Studio IDE.

6. Explore the dynamic tool window. Read `https://learn.microsoft.com/en-us/visualstudio/extensibility/opening-a-dynamic-tool-window?view=vs-2022`.

7. Walk through the code of the following extensions to understand and learn more about Async Tool Windows, ImageMonikers, Commands, and displaying context menus in a tool window:

    a. Command Explorer: `https://github.com/madskristensen/CommandTableInfo`

    b. KnownMonikers Explorer: `https://github.com/madskristensen/KnownMonikersExplorer`

Class References

DTE

Property Name	Description
`ActiveDocument`	Gets the active document.
`ActiveSolutionProjects`	Gets an array of the currently selected projects.
`ActiveWindow`	Gets the currently active window or topmost window if no window is active.
`AddIns`	Gets the AddIns collection that are available. When I used it, I got NotImplementedexception as AddIns and Macros are deprecated.
`Application`	Microsoft Internal Use only.
`CommandBars`	Gets a reference to the development environment command bars.
`CommandLineArguments`	Gets a string representing the command-line arguments.
`Commands`	Gets the Commands collection.
`ContextAttributes`	Gets a collection of attributes, which allows the automation clients to add new attributes to the currently selected items in the Dynamic Help window and provide contextual help for the additional attributes.
`Debugger`	Gets the debugger objects.

(continued)

Property Name	Description
DisplayMode	Gets the display mode, either MDI or tabbed documents.
Documents	Gets the collection of open documents in the IDE.
DTE	Gets the top-level extensibility object.
Edition	Gets a description of the edition of the environment.
Events	Gets a reference to the Events object.
FileName	Microsoft Internal Use only.
Find	Gets the Find object that represents global text find operations.
FullName	Gets the full path and name of the object's file.
Globals	Gets the Globals object that contains values that may be saved in the solution (.sln) file, in the project file, or in the user's profile data. The Globals object is a cache for storing data for the duration of each session of the Visual Studio environment, as well as across sessions using the VariablePersists property.
IsOpenFile	Microsoft Internal Use only.
ItemOperations	Gets the object for performing common file actions.
LocaleID	Gets the ID of the locale in which the development environment is running.
Macros	Gets the Macros object. In Visual Studio 2019 and above, this throws NotImplementedException as Macros and AddIns are deprecated.
MacrosIDE	Gets the root of the Macros IDE's automation model.
MainWindow	Gets a window object representing the main development environment window.
Mode	Gets the mode of the development environment, either debug or design.
Name	Gets or sets the name of the topmost automation object.
ObjectExtenders	Gets the object that provides access to the automation object.
Properties [String,String]	Returns a Properties collection representing all available categories and subcategories contained in the Options dialog box on the Tools menu.

(*continued*)

Property Name	Description
RegistryRoot	Gets a string with the path to the root of the Visual Studio registry settings.
SelectedItems	Gets a collection containing the items currently selected in the environment.
Solution	Gets the Solution object that represents all open projects in the current instance of the environment and allows access to the build objects.
SourceControl	Gets a SourceControl object that allows you to manipulate the source code control state of the file behind the object.
StatusBar	Gets the StatusBar object, representing the status bar on the main development environment window.
SuppressUI	Gets or sets whether UI should be displayed during the execution of automation code.
UndoContext	Gets the global UndoContext object, which represents, as a single transaction, all operations performed on all participating open documents in Visual Studio. If its SetAborted() method is invoked, all changes made since opening the object are discarded.
UserControl	Sets or gets a value indicating whether the environment was launched by a user or by automation.
Version	Gets the host application's version number.
WindowConfigurations	Gets the collection, representing all available named window configurations, created for the environment.
Windows	Gets a Windows collection containing the windows that display in the object.
Method Name	**Description**
ExecuteCommand (String, String)	Executes the specified command. This method would easily find a place in the top drawer of an extension developer's toolkit. This method can be used in the extensions to execute any existing commands of the Visual Studio if the command is applicable while executing. This also helps achieve a lot of functionality by building on commands that are already available, rather than rediscovering the wheel.

(continued)

Property Name	Description
`GetObject(String)`	Gets an interface or object that is late-bound to the DTE object and can be accessed by name at runtime.
`LaunchWizard(String, Object[])`	Runs a wizard with the supplied parameters.
`OpenFile(String, String)`	Microsoft Internal Use only.
`Quit()`	Closes the environment.
`SatelliteDllPath (String, String)`	Returns the computed path to the satellite DLL when given the installation directory and the file name of the DLL containing localized resources.

Document Interface

Property Name	Description
`ActiveWindow`	Gets the currently active window or the topmost window if no others are active. Returns null if no windows are open.
`Collection`	Gets the collection containing the object that represents a document in the environment open for editing.
`DTE`	Gets the top-level extensibility object.
`Extender`	Returns the requested Extender if it is available for this object.
`ExtenderCATID`	Gets the Extender category ID (CATID) for the object.
`ExtenderNames`	Gets a list of available Extenders for the object.
`FullName`	Gets the full path and name of the object's file.
`IndentSize`	Microsoft Internal Use only.
`Kind`	Gets a GUID string indicating the kind or type of the object.
`Language`	Microsoft Internal Use only.
`Name`	Gets the name of the document.
`Path`	Gets the path, without file name, for the directory containing the document.

(continued)

Property Name	Description
ProjectItem	Gets the ProjectItem object associated with the Document object.
ReadOnly	Microsoft Internal Use only.
Saved	Returns true if the object has not been modified since last being saved or opened.
Selection	**Gets an object representing the current selection on the Document.**
TabSize	Microsoft Internal Use only.
Type	Microsoft Internal Use only.
Windows	Gets a Windows collection containing the windows that display in the object.

Method Name	Description
Activate	Moves the focus to the current item.
ClearBookmarks	Microsoft Internal Use only.
Close	Closes the open document and optionally saves it, or closes and destroys the window.
MarkText	Microsoft Internal Use only.
NewWindow	Creates a new window in which to view the document.
Object	Returns an interface or object that can be accessed at runtime by name.
PrintOut	Microsoft Internal Use only.
Redo	Re-executes the last action that was undone by the Undo() method or the user.
ReplaceText	Microsoft Internal Use only.
Save	Saves the document.
Undo	Reverses the action last performed by the user of the document.

TextSelection

Property Name	Description
ActivePoint	Gets the current endpoint of the selection.
AnchorColumn	Microsoft Internal Use only.
AnchorPoint	Gets the origin point of the selection.

(*continued*)

Property Name	Description
BottomLine	Microsoft Internal Use only.
BottomPoint	Gets the point at the end of the selection.
CurrentColumn	Microsoft Internal Use only.
CurrentLine	Microsoft Internal Use only.
DTE	Gets the top-level extensibility object.
IsActiveEndGreater	Gets whether the active point is equal to the bottom point.
IsEmpty	Gets whether the anchor point is equal to the active point.
Mode	Gets or sets a value determining whether dragging the mouse selects in stream or block mode.
Parent	Gets the immediate parent object of a TextSelection object.
Text	Gets or sets the text selection.
Textpane	Gets the text pane that contains the text selection.
TextRanges	Gets a TextRanges collection with one TextRange object for each line or partial line in the selection.
TopLine	Microsoft Internal Use only.
TopPoint	Gets the top end of the selection.
Method Name	**Description**
Backspace	Microsoft Internal Use only.
Cancel	Microsoft Internal Use only.
ChangeCase	Changes the case of the text selection.
CharLeft	Moves the object the specified number of characters to the left.
CharRight	Moves the object the specified number of characters to the right.
ClearBookmark	Clears any unnamed bookmarks in the current text buffer line.
Collapse	Collapses the text selection to the active point.
Copy	Copies the text selection to the clipboard.
Cut	Copies the text selection to the clipboard and deletes it from its original location.

(continued)

Property Name	Description
Delete	Deletes the text selection.
DeleteLeft	Deletes a specified number of characters to the left of the active point.
DeleteWhitespace	Deletes the empty characters (whitespace) horizontally or vertically around the current location in the text buffer.
DestructiveInsert	Inserts text, overwriting the existing text.
EndOfDocument	Moves the object to the end of the document.
EndOfLine	Moves the object to the end of the current line.
FindPattern	Searches for the given pattern from the active point to the end of the document.
FindText	Searches for the given text from the active point to the end of the document.
GotoLine	Moves to the beginning of the indicated line and selects the line if requested.
Indent	Indents the selected lines by the given number of indentation levels.
Insert	Inserts the given string at the current insertion point.
InsertFromFile	Inserts the contents of the specified file at the current location in the buffer.
LineDown	Moves the insertion point of the text selection down the specified number of lines.
LineUp	Moves the insertion point of the text selection up the specified number of lines.
MoveTo	Microsoft Internal Use only.
MoveToAbsolute Offset	Moves the active point to the given 1-based absolute character offset.
MoveToDisplay Column	Moves the active point to the indicated display column.
MoveToLineAnd Offset	Moves the active point to the given position.

(continued)

Property Name	Description
MoveToPoint	Moves the active point to the given position.
NewLine	Inserts a line break character at the active point.
NextBookmark	Moves to the location of the next bookmark in the document.
OutlineSection	Creates an outlining section based on the current selection.
PadToColumn	Fills the current line in the buffer with empty characters (whitespace) to the given column.
PageDown	Moves the active point a specified number of pages down in the document, scrolling the view.
PageUp	Moves the active point a specified number of pages up in the document, scrolling the view.
Paste	Inserts the clipboard contents at the current location.
PreviousBookmark	Moves the text selection to the location of the previous bookmark in the document.
ReplacePattern	Replaces matching text throughout an entire text document.
ReplaceText	Microsoft Internal Use only.
SelectAll	Selects the entire document.
SelectLine	Selects the line containing the active point.
SelectBookmark	Sets an unnamed bookmark on the current line in the buffer.
SmartFormat	Formats the selected lines of text based on the current language.
StartOfDocument	Moves the insertion point to the beginning of the document.
StartOfLine	Moves the object to the beginning of the current line.
SwapAnchor	Exchanges the position of the active and the anchor points.
Tabify	Converts spaces to tabs in the selection according to your tab settings.
Unindent	Removes indents from the text selection by the number of indentation levels given.
Untabify	Converts tabs to spaces in the selection according to the user's tab settings.
WordLeft	Moves the text selection left the specified number of words.
WordRight	Moves the text selection right the specified number of words.

DialogPage

Property Name	Description
AutomationObject	Gets the DTE automation model object for a given instance of a dialog page class.
SettingsRegistryPath	Gets or sets the subkey under the Visual Studio version-specific root for storing settings data for a dialog page.
SharedSettings StorePath	Gets the location where the settings are stored in the shared settings store. It's based on the SharedSettingsAttribute on your AutomationObject, or the full type name if the attribute is not specified.
Site	Gets or sets the site of the dialog page. Overrides the implementation inherited from Component.
Window	Gets the window that is used as the user interface of the dialog page.
Method Name	**Description**
Dispose	Releases the unmanaged resources that are used by a dialog page class and optionally releases the managed resources; the parent class, Component, supports unmanaged resources.
GetSharedSettings StorePath	Gets the shared settings store path for the given property.
IsPropertyValue MachineLocal	Determines whether a given value from a property on the AutomationObject is local to this machine (vs. being roamable to other machines).
LoadSettingFromStorage	Loads the setting of a given property descriptor from the storage.
LoadSettings FromStorage	Called by Visual Studio to load the settings of a dialog page from local storage, generally the registry.
LoadSettingsFromXml	Called by Visual Studio to load the settings of a dialog page from the Visual Studio settings storage on disk.
OnActivate	Handles Windows Activate messages from the Visual Studio environment.
OnApply	Handles Apply messages from the Visual Studio environment.
OnClosed	Handles Close messages from the Visual Studio environment.

(*continued*)

Property Name	Description
OnDeactivate	Handles Deactivate messages from the Visual Studio environment.
ResetSettings	Should be overridden to reset settings to their default values.
SaveSetting	Saves the setting of given property descriptor in the storage.
SaveSettingsToStorage	Called by Visual Studio to store the settings of a dialog page in local storage, typically the registry.
SaveSettingsToXml	Called by Visual Studio to store the settings of a dialog page to the Visual Studio settings storage on disk.

ToolWindowPane

Property Name	Description
BitmapImageMoniker	Gets or sets the ImageMoniker for the icon for this tool window. This property should be used instead of BitmapResource and BitmapIndex to allow for DPI-aware icons.
BitmapIndex	Gets or sets the index of the image in the bitmap strip to use for the window frame icon.
BitmapResourceID	Gets or sets the resource ID for the bitmap strip from which to take the window frame icon.
Caption	Gets or sets the caption for the tool window.
Content	Gets or sets the content of this tool window.
Frame	Gets or sets the type that provides access to behaviors and properties of environment window frames, for both tool and document windows, which host the ToolWindowPane.
Package	Gets or sets the package that owns the tool window.
SearchCategory	Gets the search category that is used for storing MRU items if the window search implementation for your tool window supports most-recently-used search strings. By default, the tool window GUID is used for the search category.

(continued)

Property Name	Description
SearchEnabled	Override this if you want to support the search in your window. You must also override other functions from the IVsWindowSearch interface, like CreateSearch, etc.
SearchFiltersEnum	Override this function if the tool window supports search filters. The class WindowSearchFilterEnumerator can be used to construct an enumerator over an array of search filters that implement the IVsWindowSearchFilter interface.
SearchHost	Gets the search host implementation associated with this tool window.
SearchOptionsEnum	Override this function if the tool window supports search options. The class T:Microsoft.VisualStudio.PlatformUI. WindowSearchOptionEnumerator can be used to construct an enumerator over an array of search options implementing the IVsWindowSearchOption interface.
ToolBar	Gets or sets a unique command identifier that consists of a numeric command ID and a GUID menu group identifier.
ToolBarCommand Target	If the tool window has a ToolBar, then you can use this property to customize its command target. If this value is null, then the window frame of this tool window is used as the command target for the ToolBar. Like other toolbar-related properties, this property must be set before the initialization of the ToolWindowPane is complete.
ToolBarDropTarget	Gets or sets the toolbar drop target.
ToolBarLocation	Gets or sets the location of the toolbar in the tool window.
ToolClsid	Gets or sets the CLSID of a tool that should be used for this tool window.
Method Name	**Description**
AddInfoBar	Adds an info bar to this ToolWindowPane. The info bar will show at the top of the pane's frame when that frame is visible onscreen.
ClearSearch	Clears the pane of the results from a previously completed or partial search.
CreateSearch	Override at least this function if you need to support a search in a tool window.

(continued)

Property Name	Description
GetIVsWindowPane	Gets the IVsWindowPane that is associated with the tool window.
OnInfoBarAction ItemClicked	Called when an action item on an info bar added via AddInfoBar is clicked. If this method is overridden, the base implementation must be called to raise the InfoBarActionItemClicked event.
OnInfoBarClosed	Called when an info bar added via AddInfoBar is closed. If this method is overridden, the base implementation must be called to raise the InfoBarClosed event.
OnNavigation KeyDown	Allows the pane to intercept certain keys after a search is started, and to navigate between the results or select one of the results displayed in the pane.
OnToolBarAdded	Called when a toolbar is added to the tool window.
OnToolWindow Created	This method can be overridden by the derived class to execute any code that must run after the creation of IVsWindowFrame.
ProvideSearch Settings	Allows override of default search settings. By default, the search is started delayed, with indefinite progress. The names of properties that can be overridden are defined in the class SearchSettingsDataSource. PropertyNames. Values that implement the IVsUIObject interface can be constructed for common types using the Microsoft.Internal. VisualStudio.PlatformUI.BuiltInPropertyValue class, or you could use helper functions like Microsoft.Internal.VisualStudio. PlatformUI.Utilities.SetValue(Microsoft.VisualStudio. Shell.Interop.IVsUIDataSource,System.String,System. Object) to set values in the data source.
RemoveInfoBar	Removes an info bar from this ToolWindowPane.
ToolWindowPane	The constructors of ToolWindowPane. One overload takes ServiceProvider as parameter. This is called by Visual Studio.
Event Name	**Description**
InfoBarActionItem Clicked	Event raised when a button or hyperlink on an info bar is associated with this ToolWindowPane.
InfoBarClosed	Event raised when an info bar associated with this ToolWindowPane is closed.

CHAPTER 5

Developing Real-World Extensions

This chapter builds on the last chapter and continues our efforts in developing Visual Studio extensions. In this chapter, we will develop a new set of extensions focused on displaying notifications and enabling custom code generation. While developing these extensions, we will simultaneously expand our knowledge and grasp new facets and concepts of Visual Studio.

Let's begin by exploring the various methods available for displaying notifications within the Visual Studio environment, along with insights into when each of these methods is most appropriate to use. The key notification mechanisms include the following:

1. InfoBar: InfoBars offer a nonintrusive means of conveying messages, warnings, or information to users. They are well suited for presenting brief updates or contextual hints directly within the interface.

2. StatusBar: The StatusBar is positioned at the bottom of the Visual Studio IDE and is ideal for indicating ongoing tasks, progress, or displaying short messages that do not require immediate user action.

3. DialogBox: Dialog boxes serve as modal windows that temporarily pause user interactions, making them suitable for obtaining user input or conveying essential information that requires immediate attention.

© Rishabh Verma 2024
R. Verma, *Visual Studio Extensibility Development*, https://doi.org/10.1007/978-1-4842-9875-6_5

4. Output Window: The Output Window is a versatile tool for displaying logs, debugging information, and detailed messages relevant to the ongoing development process. It's particularly useful for extensions and tools that require thorough communication with developers.

5. Toast notifications: Toast notifications, often linked with UWP (Universal Windows Platform) or WPF (Windows Presentation Foundation), are transient alerts that briefly appear and then fade away. Though this is not a native notification mechanism of Visual Studio, it can still be used for notification with minimal coding. They are effective for sharing noncritical updates or messages that do not require constant attention.

Each of these notification methods serves a distinct purpose based on the urgency of the message, the interaction required, and the user's workflow. By understanding these options, one can choose the appropriate notification approach that aligns with the intended user experience and the context of your Visual Studio extension or application.

In the last chapter, we saw that the ToolWindowPane class exposes infobar APIs. In the next section, we will explore the practical implementation of these APIs.

Visual Studio Extension to Display Notifications

As discussed, Infobar is one of the many ways that Visual Studio uses to display notifications and alerts that are actionable. Infobar can be placed either on a document window or tool window, so using an infobar is advantageous in scenarios where important contextual notifications need to be shown closer to the region of attention. The Visual Studio documentation offers an elaborate account of how to best utilize InfoBars, encompassing usage scenarios, best practices, and potential pitfalls to avoid. Additionally, the documentation delves into a comprehensive exploration of the array of notification and alert mechanisms that Visual Studio offers. A valuable and recommended read can be found at `https://learn.microsoft.com/en-in/visualstudio/extensibility/ux-guidelines/notifications-and-progress-for-visual-studio?view=vs-2022#BKMK_Infobars`.

Let's summarize a few of the key and salient points before we implement an extension to display an infobar.

Usage scenarios of Infobar:

- To display important contextual non-blocking and actionable messages

- To alert about detected problems, vis-à-vis crashes in an extension or an extension causing performance issues

- To present a way to easily act in scenarios like an editor-detecting file having mixed tabs and spaces

- To intimate that the UI is in a specific state that has some interaction implication, like historical debugging

Table 5-1 summarizes the dos and don'ts.

Table 5-1. *Dos and Don'ts for Visual Studio Infobar*

Do	Don't
Ensure that Infobar messages are crisp and precise.	Use an infobar to present common commands that are typically found in a toolbar.
Ensure conciseness and clarity in the text for links and buttons.	Use an infobar instead of modal dialog.
Keep the "action" options provided to the user to a minimum, displaying only required actions.	Create a floating message outside a window.
	Use multiple infobars in several locations within the same window.

Figure 5-1 shows the infobar and its four, different labeled sections.

Figure 5-1. *Infobar and its sections*

The four sections of an infobar labeled as 1–4 in Figure 5-1 comprise:

1. Icon: This is shown on the leftmost side of the infobar and is the placeholder to display the icon for the infobar. Figure 5-1 displays the information icon.

2. Text: This is the section where the message to be displayed to the user is placed.

3. Actions: The actionable links and buttons, which users can take, belong to this section.

4. Close button: The right side of the infobar is a close button to close the infobar.

Starting the Extension

Now that we have acquired ample context regarding the InfoBar, let's proceed to build an extension that serves as a practical demonstration of notifications. Our initial focus will be on showcasing the process of displaying an InfoBar at the top of the document window within Visual Studio. Subsequently, we will delve into incorporating additional notification mechanisms discussed earlier.

The procedure to add an InfoBar unfolds as follows:

1. Create a new VSIX project in Visual Studio and give it a name such as "DisplayNotifications" or any other term that holds significance.

2. Update the vsixmanifest with proper description, icons, and metadata as seen in earlier extensions. Please refer to extensions developed in the last chapter to see the detailed discussion on updating vsixmanifest.

3. Right-click the "DisplayNotifications" project in the solution explorer and then click Add ➤ New Item. The "Add New Item" dialog will display. Under the Extensibility category, choose Async Tool Window to add a tool window as shown in Figure 5-2.

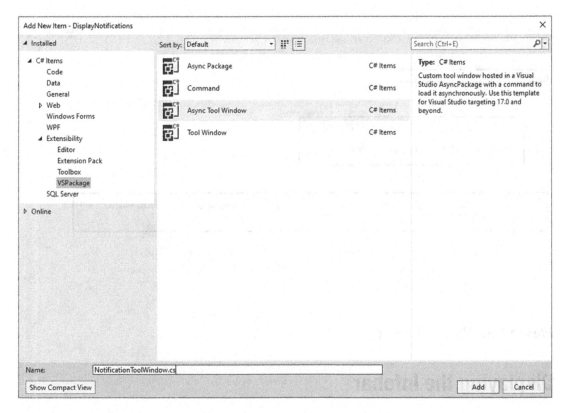

Figure 5-2. *Add Async Tool Window*

4. This will add a tool window and a command to launch it. Update
    the vsct file to associate an icon, command name, and keyboard
    shortcut to this newly added command. Please refer to the steps
    of extensions developed in Chapter 4, which discusses the details
    of updating the vsct file. The screenshot of the updated vsct file
    is shown in Figure 5-3. The changes are highlighted for easy
    reference. Please note that the KeyBinding element shown in
    Figure 5-3 is only for demonstration purposes, and readers should
    use appropriate key combinations that they can remember and
    are not already in use in Visual Studio.

```xml
<?xml version="1.0" encoding="utf-8"?>
<CommandTable xmlns="http://schemas.microsoft.com/VisualStudio/2005-10-18/CommandTable" xmlns:xs="http://www.w3.org/2001/XMLSchema">
  <!--This is the file that defines the IDs for all the commands exposed by VisualStudio. -->
  <Extern href="stdidcmd.h"/>
  <!--This header contains the command ids for the menus provided by the shell. -->
  <Extern href="vsshlids.h"/>
  <Include href="KnownImageIds.vsct"/>
  <Commands package="guidDisplayNotificationsPackage">
    <Buttons>
      <Button guid="guidDisplayNotificationsPackageCmdSet" id="NotificationToolWindowCommandId" priority="0x0100" type="Button">
        <Parent guid="guidSHLMainMenu" id="IDG_VS_WNDO_OTRWNDWS1"/>
        <Icon guid="ImageCatalogGuid" id="NotificationAlert" />
        <CommandFlag>IconIsMoniker</CommandFlag>
        <Strings>
          <ButtonText>Display Notifications</ButtonText>
        </Strings>
      </Button>
    </Buttons>
  </Commands>
  <KeyBindings>
    <KeyBinding guid="guidDisplayNotificationsPackageCmdSet" id="NotificationToolWindowCommandId" editor="guidVSStd97"
                key1="VK_F5" mod1="Control"></KeyBinding>
  </KeyBindings>
  <Symbols>
    <!-- This is the package guid. -->
    <GuidSymbol name="guidDisplayNotificationsPackage" value="{131ca5cd-ca59-45ba-b97d-db4be15fe841}" />
    <!-- This is the guid used to group the menu commands together -->
    <GuidSymbol name="guidDisplayNotificationsPackageCmdSet" value="{9ffca492-ec05-4786-8e91-b2972eb5db44}">
      <IDSymbol name="NotificationToolWindowCommandId" value="0x0100" />
    </GuidSymbol>
  </Symbols>
</CommandTable>
```

Figure 5-3. *Updated* `.vsct` *file*

Displaying the Infobar

Next, we will add a class to the project. This class will be responsible for displaying the infobar. Let us name that class as `InfobarService.cs`. Before we write the code for this class, let us discuss the different types that can create and display the infobar. These important types are illustrated in Figure 5-4.

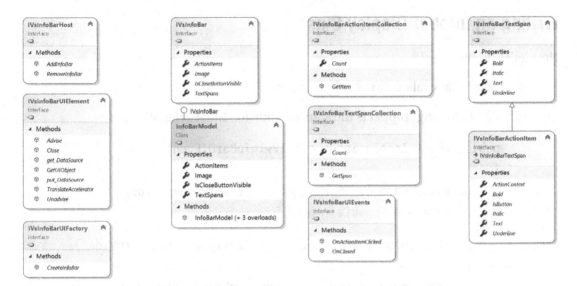

Figure 5-4. *Infobar type system*

The important types are summarized in the "Class References" section at the end of this chapter.

To display an infobar, we need to do the following:

1. Create a class that implements `IVsInfoBarUIEvents`.

2. Create an infobar model by specifying the message (making use of `InfoBarTextSpan` type that implements `IVsInfoBarTextSpan`), icon, action items (using `InfoBarActionItem` that implements `IVsInfoBarActionItem`), and optional close button.

3. Get a reference to `IVsInfoBarUIFactory` using `IServiceProvider`.

4. Invoke the method `CreateInfoBar` of the factory to get the `InfobarUIElement` of type `IVsInfoBarUIElement`.

5. Subscribe to the events that can be raised from Infobar, like button click events or hyperlink click events.

6. Get a reference to the infobar host. It can be either the main window infobar host or a tool windowpane.

7. Call the `AddInfoBar` method on the host and pass the `IVsInfoBarUIElement` object. This will display the infobar in the host.

Writing an Infobar Display Class

Now let's add the class:

1. Add a class called InfoBarService.cs.

2. The following snippet is the starting code for InfoBarService.cs:

```
public class InfoBarService : IVsInfoBarUIEvents
{
    private readonly IServiceProvider serviceProvider;
    private uint cookie;

    private InfoBarService(IServiceProvider serviceProvider)
    {
        this.serviceProvider = serviceProvider;
    }

    public static InfoBarService Instance { get; private set; }

    public static void Initialize(IServiceProvider
    serviceProvider)
    {
        Instance = new InfoBarService(serviceProvider);
    }

    public void ShowInfoBar(string message, ToolWindowPane
    toolWindow = null)
    {
        Microsoft.VisualStudio.Shell.ThreadHelper.
        ThrowIfNotOnUIThread();

        // Construct an InfoBar.
        InfoBarTextSpan text = new InfoBarTextSpan(message);
        InfoBarHyperlink yes = new InfoBarHyperlink("Yes", "yes");
        InfoBarHyperlink no = new InfoBarHyperlink("No", "no");
        InfoBarButton noButton = new InfoBarButton("No", "no");
        InfoBarTextSpan[] spans = new InfoBarTextSpan[] { text };
```

```
InfoBarActionItem[] actions = new InfoBarActionItem[]
{ yes, no, noButton };

InfoBarModel infoBarModel = new InfoBarModel(spans,
actions, KnownMonikers.StatusInformation,
isCloseButtonVisible: true);

var factory = serviceProvider.GetService(typeof
(SVsInfoBarUIFactory)) as IVsInfoBarUIFactory;
Assumes.Present(factory);

IVsInfoBarUIElement element = factory.
CreateInfoBar(infoBarModel);
element.Advise(this, out cookie);
if (toolWindow == null)
{
    var shell = serviceProvider.
    GetService(typeof(SVsShell)) as IVsShell;
    if (shell != null)
    {
        shell.GetProperty((int)__VSSPROPID7.VSSPROPID_
        MainWindowInfoBarHost, out var obj);
        var host = (IVsInfoBarHost)obj;
        if (host == null)
        {
            return;
        }
        host.AddInfoBar(element);
    }
}
else
{
    toolWindow.AddInfoBar(element);
}
}
```

```
public void OnActionItemClicked(IVsInfoBarUIElement
infoBarUIElement, IVsInfoBarActionItem actionItem)
{
    ThreadHelper.ThrowIfNotOnUIThread();
    string context = (string)actionItem.ActionContext;

    if (string.Equals(context, "yes", StringComparison.
    OrdinalIgnoreCase))
    {
        MessageBox.Show("Thanks for liking it!");
    }
    else
    {
        MessageBox.Show("Spend more time, maybe you start
        liking :)!");
    }
}

public void OnClosed(IVsInfoBarUIElement infoBarUIElement)
{
    Microsoft.VisualStudio.Shell.ThreadHelper.
    ThrowIfNotOnUIThread();
    infoBarUIElement.Unadvise(cookie);
}
} // end class
```

We can see that the class

- Implements the interface IVsInfoBarUIEvents

- Has two private fields: serviceProvider and cookie of type
  IServiceProvider and uint, respectively

- Defines a private constructor that takes IServiceProvider as a
  parameter

- Has a public static read-only property named Instance, which
  ensures that only an instance of this service is created

- Has a public static method named Initialize that takes `IServiceProvider` as a parameter and initializes the static property Instance with the new instance of the `InfoBarService`

- Defines a public instance method named `ShowInfoBar` that takes two parameters:

    - Message of type string: To display the desired message

    - An optional parameter toolWindow of type `ToolWindowPane`

This method does the following work in order:

1. Creates an infobar model. The `InfoBarTextSpan` class is used to display the text in a span. `InfoBarTextSpan` constructor takes a string parameter. This is where we pass the message to be displayed in the infobar. `InfoBarHyperlink` defines a hyperlink. `InfoBarHyperlink` constructor takes two parameters:

    - Text of type string to display the hyperlink text.

    - `ActionContext` of type dynamic, which passes the data of this hyperlink to the event handler. In this code snippet, we have used string text as the context. However, we can use any object as the context.

   We have added two hyperlinks in the action section: one for yes and another for no. Just to demonstrate that even a button can be added as an action, we have used the `InfoBarButton` as well, which takes the same parameters as `InfoBarHyperlink`.

   As discussed earlier, an infobar has four sections (icon, text, actions, close button), of which we have defined two: text and actions. We need to construct an `InfoBarModel` object. `InfoBarModel` has multiple overloads. For the purpose of demonstration, we are using the following overloaded method:

```
public InfoBarModel(IEnumerable<IVsInfoBarTextSpan> textSpans,
IEnumerable<IVsInfoBarActionItem> actionItems, ImageMoniker
image = default, bool isCloseButtonVisible = true);
```

As we can see, this overload accepts the collection or IEnumerable as the first two parameters for textSpans and actionItems, respectively. So, next we create an array of InfoBarTextSpan and InfoBarActionItem and then construct the InfoBarModel object as shown as follows:

InfoBarModel infoBarModel = new InfoBarModel(**spans, actions, KnownMonikers.StatusInformation, isCloseButtonVisible: true**);

Notice that the third parameter specifies the icon. We have used the Microsoft.VisualStudio.Imaging.KnownMonikers class to provide the icon of StatusInformation. Finally, the last parameter is specified as true, which marks the close button of an infobar as visible. With this, our InfoBar model is created.

2. Next, we get the reference to IVsInfoBarUIFactory by using the serviceProvider. Then we pass the InfoBarModel object created earlier to the CreateInfoBar method of this factory and get the infobar UI element of type IVsInfoBarUIElement.

3. We then subscribe to the events of the infobar. Notice that our InfoBarService class implements IVsInfoBarUIEvents and has event handlers OnClosed and OnActionItemClicked, which will fire when an infobar is closed or an action (hyperlink click, button click, etc.) is performed. To subscribe to the events of infobar, the Advise method of IVsInfoBarUIElement is used as

element.Advise(this, out cookie);

Advise method call on the element object is used to register an object (in this case, this, i.e., the InfoBarService) as an event listener or subscriber. It implies that the InfoBarService object has implemented or can handle the events or notifications that the element will send. The second parameter of Advise method is a cookie. The out keyword preceding cookie is used to indicate that cookie will be assigned a value by the Advise method. The cookie can be used for later unadvising or unsubscribing from events when it's no longer needed.

4. Next, it is checked if `toolWindow` is null or not. If `toolWindow` is null, we display the infobar in the main window infobar host, or else we display it in the tool windowpane. To display in main window infobar host, we first get the reference to the Visual Studio Shell and then get the host by the following code:

```
var shell = serviceProvider.
GetService(typeof(SVsShell)) as IVsShell;
if (shell != null)
{
    shell.GetProperty((int)__VSSPROPID7.VSSPROPID_
    MainWindowInfoBarHost, out var obj);
    var host = (IVsInfoBarHost)obj;
}
```

5. Once we have the host, we call the `AddInfoBar` method of the host, passing the infobar UI element parameter to show the infobar.

6. If the tool windowpane is not null, we show the infobar on the tool windowpane.

The remaining code of the class defines the `OnClosed` and `OnActionItemClicked` event handlers. The `OnClosed` method has one parameter `infoBarUIElement` that is of type `IVsInfoBarUIElement`. The `OnClosed` method is called when the infobar is closed, so at that time, we need to unsubscribe to all the infobar events. This is done by invoking the Unadvise method of the `IVsInfoBarUIElement` as shown in the following code:

```
infoBarUIElement.Unadvise(cookie);
```

The `OnActionItemClicked` method is invoked when an action item is clicked on the infobar, like a hyperlink or a button. `OnActionItemClicked` method has two parameters `infoBarUIElement` of type `IVsInfoBarUIElement` and actionItem of type `IVsInfoBarActionItem`. From the action item, we can get the action context, which can help us act based on the context. Here we have used string parameters, so we just do string comparison and display message as listed in the following code:`string context = (string)actionItem.ActionContext;`

```
string message = string.Equals(context, "yes", StringComparison.
OrdinalIgnoreCase)
    ? "Thanks for liking it!"
    : "Spend more time, maybe you'll start liking it :)!";

MessageBox.Show(message);
```

We have the `InfoBarService` code ready; however, it needs to be initialized and wired up so that it can be used. To initialize the `InfoBarService`, we have already defined a static Initialize method in `InfoBarService` class. We call this static method in the `InitializeAsync` method of the `NotificationToolWindowCommand` class as shown as follows:

```
public static async Task InitializeAsync(AsyncPackage package)
{
    // Switch to the main thread - the call to AddCommand in
       NotificationToolWindowCommand's constructor requires
    // the UI thread.
    await ThreadHelper.JoinableTaskFactory.
    SwitchToMainThreadAsync(package.DisposalToken);

    InfoBarService.Initialize(package);

    OleMenuCommandService commandService = await package.
    GetServiceAsync((typeof(IMenuCommandService))) as
    OleMenuCommandService;

    Instance = new NotificationToolWindowCommand(package,
    commandService);
}
```

We will display the infobar at two places, the main window infobar host and on tool window. When the tool window loads, we will show the InfoBar in the main window infobar host. To do so, we will write the code in the constructor of the WPF user control code behind (cs) file, which invokes the `ShowInfoBar` method of the `InfoBarService`, by passing the message to be displayed in the infobar. The code for the user control constructor looks as shown next:

```
public ToolWindowWithInfoBarControl()
{
    this.InitializeComponent();
```

```
    // Define the text to be displayed in Infobar.
    var text = "Welcome to Chapter 5. Are you liking it?";
    // Show in main window infobar host
    InfoBarService.Instance.ShowInfoBar(text);
}
```

Modifying the Event Handler

The default WPF user control that comes with the AsyncToolWindow template has a
button. We will display the next infobar on the click on this button on the tool window.
To do this, we will make the following changes:

1. Create a static read-only property named ToolWindow of type
   ToolWindowPane in the command class as illustrated:

   ```
   internal static ToolWindowPane ToolWindow { get; private set; }
   ```

2. In the command class, we will modify the event handler method
   that shows the tool window. In the Execute method of the
   command class, we will set the static ToolWindow property with
   the ToolWindowPane instance as shown in the next code listing:

```
private void Execute(object sender, EventArgs e)
{
    this.package.JoinableTaskFactory.RunAsync(async delegate
    {
        ToolWindowPane window = await this.package.ShowToolWindow
        Async(typeof(ToolWindowWithInfoBar), 0, true, this.
        package.DisposalToken);
        if ((null == window) || (null == window.Frame))
        {
            throw new NotSupportedException("Cannot create tool
            window");
        }
        ToolWindow = window;
    });
}
```

3. Coming back to the WPF user control class; in the button-click event
    handler, we will wire up the call to the ShowInfoBar method of InfoBarService,
    passing the ToolWindow instance as shown in the following code snippet:

```
private void button1_Click(object sender, RoutedEventArgs e)
{
    InfoBarService.Instance.ShowInfoBar($"This info bar is
    invoked from the tool window button. Are you liking it?",
    NotificationToolWindowCommand.ToolWindow);
}
```

With this, we are done with the code changes to display infobar in our extension.

Running the Extension

Let's run the extension. A new experimental instance of Visual Studio will launch.
Navigate to View ➤ Other Windows ➤ Display Notifications, as shown in Figure 5-5.

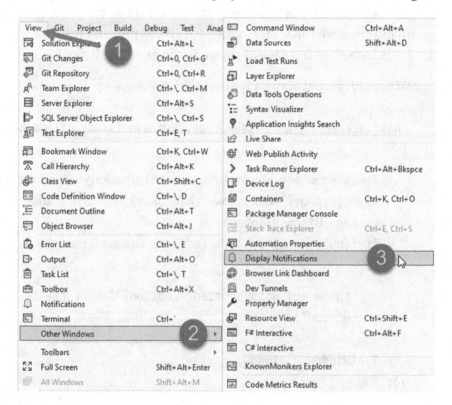

Figure 5-5. *Display Notifications*

1. A tool window would display along with an infobar above the main document window as shown in Figure 5-6.

Figure 5-6. *InfoBar above the main document window*

This also explains an important concept that a tool window is initialized only once; after that tool window is only either made visible or hidden and is not destroyed. This is precisely the reason that on repeating the navigation, View ➤ Other Windows ➤ Display Notifications doesn't display the infobar again, as the user control constructor is not called again.

2. Clicking the Yes, no hyperlink, or No button would display the message box, with appropriate messages shown based on the action context.

3. Clicking the button in the tool window displays a new infobar on top of the tool window, as shown in the Figure 5-7.

Figure 5-7. *Infobar on the tool window*

With this, we have successfully added Infobar in the extension to show a notification. Next, let's explore other notification mechanisms.

Displaying Other Notifications

The process of displaying a notification involves two fundamental steps. First, we get access to the specific Visual Studio element within which the notification is intended to appear. Subsequently, we invoke the appropriate method to display the notification. Let us see this for different notification types:

- StatusBar: We can get access to Visual Studio StatusBar in multiple ways. A couple of examples are as follows:

```
var statusbar = await package.GetServiceAsync(typeof(IVsStatus
bar)) as IVsStatusbar;
or
var dte = await package.GetServiceAsync(typeof(DTE)) as DTE2;
var statusbar = dte.StatusBar;
```

  After obtaining access, notification text can be displayed by using either the SetText method or by modifying the property as shown in next code snippet:

```
statusbar.SetText("This is a demo of notification in statusbar.");
```

  or

```
dte.StatusBar.Text = "This is a demo of notification in
statusbar.";
```

  Additionally, StatusBar supports reporting progress and animations. Chapter 9 will provide demonstrations on reporting progress and incorporating animations into the StatusBar.

- Output Window: Developers can access it via the IVsOutputWindowPane service. Messages can then be displayed by calling the appropriate methods. The next code snippet illustrates displaying notifications in the Output Window:

```
OutputWindow = await package.GetServiceAsync(typeof(IVsOutput
WindowPane)) as IVsOutputWindowPane;
OutputWindow.OutputStringThreadSafe("This is demo of writing to
Output Window");
```

- Dialog box: There are several ways to present a modal message dialog within Visual Studio. When a command is added through the default item template, it includes code for displaying a message using the MessageBox. For instance,

```
VsShellUtilities.ShowMessageBox(
package,
message,
title,
OLEMSGICON.OLEMSGICON_INFO,
OLEMSGBUTTON.OLEMSGBUTTON_OK,
OLEMSGDEFBUTTON.OLEMSGDEFBUTTON_FIRST);
```

Or alternatively, we can directly use MessageBox control from either Windows Forms or WPF. The usage of WPF control is shown in the next code listing:

```
MessageBox.Show("This is a message to display in the MessageBox.",
"MessageBox Title", MessageBoxButtons.OK, MessageBoxIcon.
Information);
```

We can replace the message text and the title as needed and also customize the buttons and icons in the MessageBox using the MessageBoxButtons and MessageBoxIcon enum, respectively.

- Toast notification: Toast notifications are particularly useful for conveying time-sensitive updates, progress updates, or alerts to users, enhancing the user experience within the IDE. As discussed earlier, they are not native to Visual Studio, but can be presented in the same way as in a UWP or WPF app. To display a toast notification, we will leverage Microsoft.Toolkit.Uwp.Notifications NuGet package:

```
public static void ShowToastNotification(string title, string
message)
{
    // Construct the toast content
    ToastContent content = new ToastContentBuilder()
        .AddText(title)
```

```
        .AddText(message)
        .GetToastContent();

    // Show the toast notification
    ToastNotificationManagerCompat.CreateToastNotifier().Show(new
    ToastNotification(content.GetXml()));
}
```

Calling this static method with appropriate title and message displays the toast notification:

```
ToastNotificationHelper.ShowToastNotification("Toast", "This is a
sample of toast notification.");
```

All the different notifications in Visual Studio are shown in Figure 5-8.

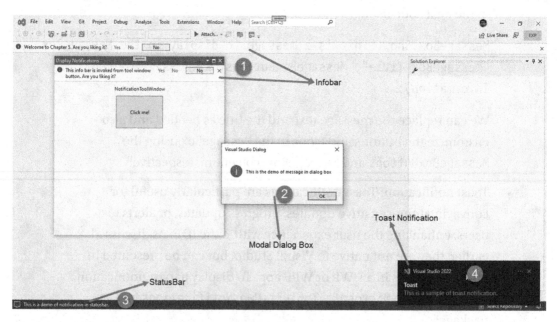

Figure 5-8. *Different notifications in Visual Studio*

This concludes our sample extension demonstrating notifications in Visual Studio. In the next section, we will develop an extension demonstrating the code generation.

Visual Studio Extension to Generate Code

In this section, we will generate a simple C# POCO class from a JavaScript Object Notation (JSON) file.

With the web applications and APIs being used more extensively than ever before, JSON has become part and parcel of every web developer's toolkit, and very often it is needed to convert JSON to C# plain old CLR object (POCO) class. Visual Studio does a great job at it. Just copy the JSON and put the cursor on the file where C# classes need to be created. Then, in the top main menu of the Visual Studio, follow the navigation, Edit ➤ Paste Special ➤ Paste JSON as Classes as shown in Figure 5-9.

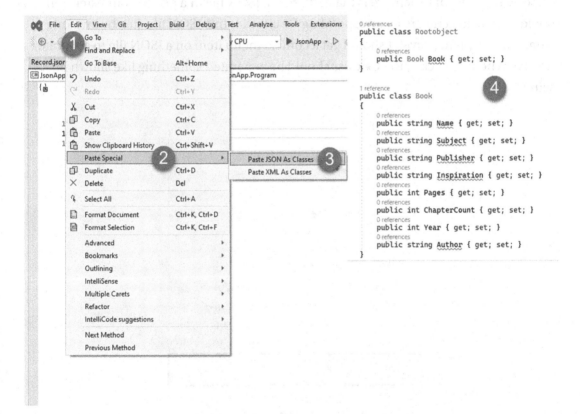

Figure 5-9. *JSON to C# POCO classes*

The C# classes corresponding to the copied JSON will be generated in the file. This is a cool trick. However, in my experience, not many web developers are aware of this cool feature of Visual Studio. In line with this functionality, we will develop an extension that generates the C# POCO class directly from the JSON file. The intention of developing this extension has many folds:

- Learn how to generate code in an extension.

- Learn the concept of dynamic visibility of command.

- Learn to apply a custom tool to a file type.

So, what we want to achieve is that if there is a JSON file in a project, our extension should be able to generate a corresponding C# class for this JSON file, just by invoking a command. At a high level, I should get a context menu item on a JSON file to generate a C# file. When we click it, the C# class should be generated something like shown in Figure 5-10.

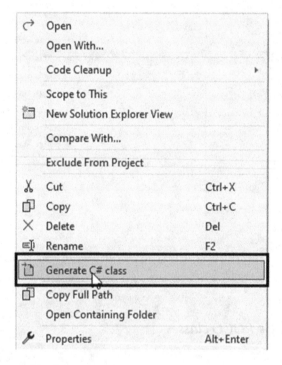

Figure 5-10. *Generate C# class*

Starting the Code Generating Extension

Let us develop this extension in a step-by-step manner. The steps are as follows:

1. Create a new VSIX project in Visual Studio and give its name as
   JsonToCSharpCodeGeneration or some other meaningful name.

2. Update the vsixmanifest with the proper description, icons, and
   metadata as seen in earlier extensions. Please refer to extensions
   developed in the last chapter to see the detailed discussion on
   updating vsixmanifest.

3. Right-click the "JsonToCSharpCodeGeneration" project in the
   solution explorer and then click Add ➤ New Item. "Add New Item"
   dialog will then display. Under the Extensibility category, choose
   Command to add ApplyCommandCodeGenerationCommand class as
   shown in Figure 5-11.

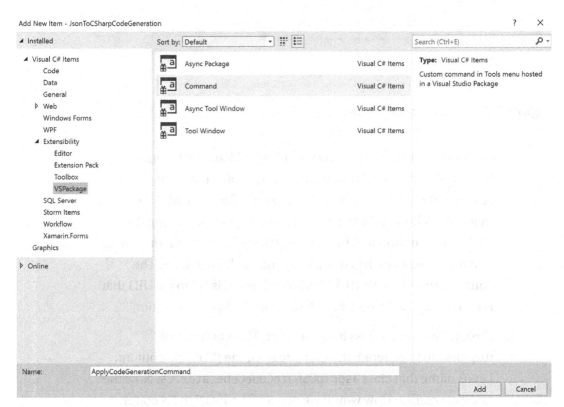

Figure 5-11. *Add Command*

4. This will add a command class. Update the vsct file to associate an icon, command name, and keyboard shortcut to this newly added command. Please refer to the steps of extensions developed in Chapter 4, which discusses the details of updating the vsct file. The screenshot of the updated vsct file is shown in Figure 5-12. The changes are highlighted for easy reference.

```
<?xml version="1.0" encoding="utf-8"?>
<CommandTable xmlns="http://schemas.microsoft.com/VisualStudio/2005-10-18/CommandTable" xmlns:xs="http://www.w3.org/2001/XMLSchema">
  <!--This is the file that defines the IDs for all the commands exposed by VisualStudio. -->
  <Extern href="stdidcmd.h"/>
  <!--This header contains the command ids for the menus provided by the shell. -->
  <Extern href="vsshlids.h"/>
  <Include href="KnownImageIds.vsct"/>
  <Commands package="guidJsonToCSharpCodeGenerationPackage">
    <Groups>
      <Group guid="guidJsonToCSharpCodeGenerationPackageCmdSet" id="MyMenuGroup" priority="0x0600">
        <Parent guid="guidSHLMainMenu" id="IDM_VS_CTXT_ITEMNODE" />
      </Group>
    </Groups>
    <Buttons>
      <Button guid="guidJsonToCSharpCodeGenerationPackageCmdSet" id="ApplyCodeGenerationCommandId" priority="0x0100" type="Button">
        <Parent guid="guidJsonToCSharpCodeGenerationPackageCmdSet" id="MyMenuGroup" />
        <Icon guid="ImageCatalogGuid" id="GenerateFile" />
        <CommandFlag>IconIsMoniker</CommandFlag>
        <CommandFlag>DynamicVisibility</CommandFlag>
        <Strings>
          <ButtonText>Generate C# class</ButtonText>
        </Strings>
      </Button>
    </Buttons>
  </Commands>
  <VisibilityConstraints>
    <VisibilityItem guid="guidJsonToCSharpCodeGenerationPackageCmdSet" id="ApplyCodeGenerationCommandId"
                    context="guidVisibilityContext"/>
  </VisibilityConstraints>
  <Symbols>
    <!-- This is the package guid. -->
    <GuidSymbol name="guidJsonToCSharpCodeGenerationPackage" value="{4fe18284-0dbd-4936-9f6e-3ff7304dc7c2}" />
    <GuidSymbol name="guidVisibilityContext" value="{878bc455-61ba-459b-b18d-6922cde6ce19}"/>
    <!-- This is the guid used to group the menu commands together -->
    <GuidSymbol name="guidJsonToCSharpCodeGenerationPackageCmdSet" value="{78327699-c6b2-4daf-a7d1-2877b33b9288}">
      <IDSymbol name="MyMenuGroup" value="0x1020" />
      <IDSymbol name="ApplyCodeGenerationCommandId" value="0x0100" />
    </GuidSymbol>
  </Symbols>
</CommandTable>
```

Figure 5-12. *Updated* `.vsct` *file*

Notice that we have a new `CommandFlag` added with the value `DynamicVisibility`. Apart from this, the only new section that is added in the `vsct` file is that of `VisibilityConstraints`. Notice that the `VisibilityItem` element has the GUID matching the GUID of the button and id matching that of command, indicating that the visibility of the command is being defined here. The context property of `VisibilityItem` element is set to a GUID that is defined in the `GuidSymbol` element in the Symbols section.

5. Next, we will add a class to the project. This class will be responsible to generate the C# code from the JSON file content. Let us name that class `JsonToCSharpCodeGenerator.cs`. Now the question comes: How would we convert the JSON to C# code?

6. Well, there is a library named `NJsonSchema.CodeGeneration.`
    `CSharp`, which generates the C# file from the schema. We will
    leverage this library for code generation. To do so, we will install
    the `NJsonSchema.CodeGeneration.CSharp` NuGet package, by
    doing a right-click on the project references and then clicking
    Manage NuGet Packages... This will open the NuGet Package
    Manager window as shown in Figure 5-13.

Figure 5-13.   *Install* `NJsonSchema.CodeGeneration.CSharp` *package*

7. Under the Browse tab, search for `NJsonSchema.CodeGeneration.`
    `CSharp`, and then install this package. You can also make use
    of Package Manager Console to install this package if it is
    convenient.

Generating the Code

Before we write the code in `JsonToCSharpCodeGenerator` class, let us discuss the
different types involved in code generation. The important types are illustrated in
Figure 5-14.

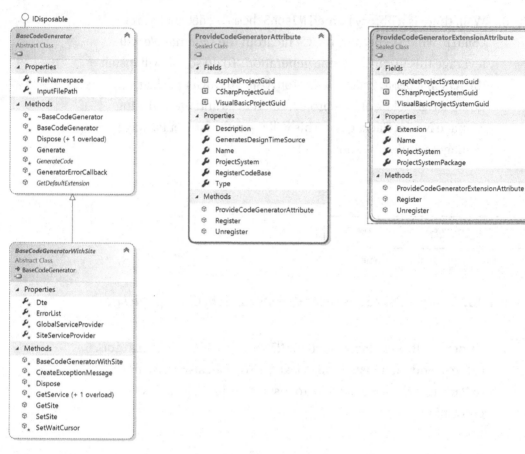

Figure 5-14. *Types for code generation*

All these types reside in `Microsoft.VisualStudio.TextTemplating.`
`VSHost.15.0.dll`, which is already included in the SDK. The types and their purpose are described in the "Class References" section at the end of this chapter.

We can create a code generator by deriving it from the `BaseCodeGenerator` or `BaseCodeGeneratorWithSite` abstract class and register this code generator with our package class using the `ProvideCodeGenerator` and `ProvideCodeGeneratorExtension` attributes. This is what we will do in the following steps. What we have discussed is a small portion of the code generation type system. Visual Studio has a rich set of APIs for text templating and transformation, and I would recommend readers to read the documentation of `Microsoft.VisualStudio.TextTemplating.VSHost` namespace from the official Microsoft documentation at `https://learn.microsoft.com/en-us/dotnet/api/microsoft.visualstudio.texttemplating.vshost?view=visualstudiosdk-2022.`

Writing the Code Generation Class

We will derive JsonToCSharpCodeGenerator from the BaseCodeGeneratorWithSite abstract class and implement the abstract methods as shown in the following code. The gist of the code is discussed immediately after the code snippet.

```
[Guid("f0ff9543-4996-4be8-9061-c57131998819")]
public class JsonToCSharpCodeGenerator : BaseCodeGeneratorWithSite
{
    public const string Name = nameof(JsonToCSharpCodeGenerator);

    public const string Description = "Generates the C# class from
    JSON file";

    public override string GetDefaultExtension()
    {
        ThreadHelper.ThrowIfNotOnUIThread();
        // Next two lines are only for demonstration.
        var item = (ProjectItem)GetService(typeof(ProjectItem));
        var ext = Path.GetExtension(item?.FileNames[1]);
        return $".cs";
    }

    protected override byte[] GenerateCode(string inputFileName, string
    inputFileContent)
    {
        ThreadHelper.ThrowIfNotOnUIThread();
        string document = string.Empty;

        try
        {
            document = ThreadHelper.JoinableTaskFactory.Run(async () =>
            {
                var text = File.ReadAllText(inputFileName);

                var schema = NJsonSchema.JsonSchema.
                FromSampleJson(text);
                var generator = new CSharpGenerator(schema);
```

```
                    return await System.Threading.Tasks.Task.
                    FromResult(generator.GenerateFile());
            });
        }
        catch (Exception exception)
        {
            LogException(ex);
        }

        return Encoding.UTF8.GetBytes(document);
    }
}
private void LogException(Exception ex)
{
    ThreadHelper.ThrowIfNotOnUIThread();
    // Write to output window.
    var outputWindowPane = GetService(typeof(SVsGeneralOutputWindow
    Pane)) as IVsOutputWindowPane;
    outputWindowPane?.OutputStringThreadSafe($"An exception occurred
    while generating code {ex}.");

    // Show in error list.
    GeneratorErrorCallback(false, 1, $"An exception occurred while
    generating code {ex}.", 1, 1);
    ErrorList.ForceShowErrors();
    ErrorList.BringToFront();
}
```

Code discussion:

- There is a GUID attribute decorated on the class to uniquely identify this code generator.

- We have defined two constants for Name and Description. These are needed when registering this code generator with our package class.

- The method GetDefaultExtension gets the default file extension that is given to the output file generated by the generator. Here we will return ".cs" as the extension as we wish to generate the C# file. However, I have also illustrated how we can name the extension from the selected file name. For that, we make use of GetService API and get the selected project item. From the selected item, we can get the file extension of the selected file.

- The method GenerateCode, as the name suggests, generates the code. It has two input parameters inputFileName and inputFileContent that contain the file name and content of the selected input file.

- In this method, we get the content from the file and pass this content to the NJsonSchema.JsonSchema.FromSampleJson API to get its schema. We then pass this schema to the CSharpGenerator constructor to construct the CSharpGenerator object. Finally, we invoke the GenerateFile API of the generator object to get the generated code.

- The code generation of C# class is dependent on the JSON file. If JSON is not valid, it may result in an exception, which if not handled can crash the extension. So, we have put this entire code generation block in the try block. In case of an exception, we need to let the users of our extension know that an exception has occurred. To do so, we fetch the reference to the General Output Windowpane and display the exception message in the output window. Recall that our base class has a property of ErrorList, which represents the Visual Studio ErrorList. We also display this error message in this ErrorList and bring it to focus. This is done in LogException method.

- Finally, the return type of GenerateCode method is byte[], so we convert the generated code to byte[]. The underlying framework takes care of processing this byte[] and generating the C# file.

- Next, we need to associate this code generator with our package. To do so, we will use the `ProvideCodeGenerator` attribute on the package class as shown in the next code snippet:

```
[ProvideCodeGenerator(typeof(JsonToCSharpCodeGenerator),
JsonToCSharpCodeGenerator.Name, JsonToCSharpCodeGenerator.
Description, true)]
```

This constructor of `ProvideCodeGenerator`, used earlier, has the following signature:

```
public ProvideCodeGeneratorAttribute(Type type, string name, string
description, bool generatesDesignTimeSource)
```

The first three parameters of the constructor are self-explanatory. The last parameter is `generatesDesignTimeSource` of type Boolean, which specifies if the code generator provides the design-time source code.

- We also want the command "Generate C# Code" to appear only for JSON files and not for any other file types. Recall that we have already added a `VisibilityItem` element in the vsct file. However, we still need to make changes in the package class and command class to honor it. In the package class, we add one more attribute named `ProvideUIContextRule`, which creates a rule-based UI context entry that is activated when the specified expression is evaluated as true. This is shown in the next code listing:

```
[ProvideUIContextRule(PackageGuids.guidVisibilityContextString,
name: "Context",
expression: JsonToCSharpCodeGenerationPackage.JsonExt,
termNames: new[] { JsonToCSharpCodeGenerationPackage.JsonExt },

termValues: new[] { "HierSingleSelectionName:." +
JsonToCSharpCodeGenerationPackage.JsonExt + "?$" })]
```

The constructor has the signature:

```
public ProvideUIContextRuleAttribute(string contextGuid, string name,
string expression, string[] termNames, string[] termValues, uint delay = 0)
```

It has six parameters:

- contextGuid of type string: This is a GUID string and its value should be the same as the GUID for the context defined in the vsct file. This is the GUID of the UI context to be created. It is worth noting that PackageGuids class used to specify the GUID for this parameter is autogenerated by the VSIX Synchronizer extension.

- Name of type string: It defines the name of the context rule.

- Expression of type string: This parameter defines the expression to be evaluated for determining the state of the UI context.

- termNames of type string array: This defines the term names used in the expression.

- termValues of type string array: This defines the term values used in the expression. In this case, it has a format of "HierSingleSelectionName:.json?$". This value will evaluate to true whenever the selection in the active hierarchy of project is a single item and the name of the selected item matches the .NET regular expression ".json?$". So, the value will be true if a single json file is selected.

- Delay of type unit (unsigned int): It is an optional parameter. It defines the delay, in milliseconds, before activating the UI context.

With this, the changes for package class are complete. The changes are summarized as follows:

```
[ProvideCodeGenerator(typeof(JsonToCSharpCodeGenerator),
JsonToCSharpCodeGenerator.Name, JsonToCSharpCodeGenerator.
Description, true)]
  [ProvideCodeGeneratorExtension(JsonToCSharpCodeGenerator.Name,
  JsonToCSharpCodeGenerationPackage.JsonExt)]
   [ProvideUIContextRule(PackageGuids.guidVisibilityContextString,
       name: "Context",
       expression:JsonExt,
       termNames: new[] {JsonExt },

       termValues: new[] { "HierSingleSelectionName:." +JsonExt + "$" })]
```

```
[ProvideMenuResource("Menus.ctmenu", 1)]
public sealed class JsonToCSharpCodeGenerationPackage : AsyncPackage
{
    public const string JsonExt = "json";
}
```

Updating the Command Class

Now we will update the command class to make the following changes:

- Modify the command to honor the VisibilityConstraints defined in the vsct file.

- Apply the custom tool property on the JSON file to use our JSON to C# code generator.

Let's get started:

1. So first we will define a private static field named dte of type DTE2. In the static InitializeAsync method, of the command class, we will get the reference to the DTE2 and assign it to the static dte field. Next, we get a reference to OleMenuCommandService and pass it to the constructor of this command class. The updated InitializeAsync method is shown in the next code listing:

```
public static async Task InitializeAsync(AsyncPackage package)
{
    // Switch to the main thread - the call to AddCommand in
        ApplyCodeGenerationCommand's constructor requires
    // the UI thread.

    await ThreadHelper.JoinableTaskFactory.
    SwitchToMainThreadAsync(package.DisposalToken);
    dte = (DTE2)await package.GetServiceAsync(typeof(DTE));
    Assumes.Present(dte);
```

```
OleMenuCommandService commandService = await package.
GetService
Async(typeof(OleMenuCommandService)) as OleMenuCommandService;

Instance = new ApplyCodeGenerationCommand(package,
commandService);
}
```

2. In the constructor of the command class, we will modify the
    code to set the Supported flag of the command to false. Since the
    CommandFlag is set to DynamicVisibility, the control then falls
    back to vsct file, wherein the command is shown only based on
    the context. This updated method is shown in the following code.
    The changes are highlighted for easy reference.

```
private ApplyCodeGenerationCommand(AsyncPackage package,
OleMenuCommandService commandService)
{
        this.package = package ?? throw new
        ArgumentNullException(nameof
        (package));

        commandService = commandService ?? throw new
        ArgumentNullException
        (nameof(commandService));
        var menuCommandID = new CommandID(CommandSet, CommandId);
        var menuItem = new MenuCommand(Execute, menuCommandID);

        commandService.AddCommand(new OleMenuCommand(Execute,
        menuCommandID)
        {
          Supported = false,
        });
}
```

3. Finally, we will modify the command button event handler
    to set the Custom tool property of the JSON file with our
    JsonToCSharpCodeGenerator. The following code does this:

```
private void Execute(object sender, EventArgs e)
{
    ThreadHelper.ThrowIfNotOnUIThread();
    ProjectItem item = dte.SelectedItems.Item(1).ProjectItem;
    if (item != null)
    {
        item.Properties.Item("CustomTool").Value =
        JsonToCSharpCodeGenerator.Name;
    }
}
```

With this, we are done with the code changes to generate a C# class from JSON in our
extension.

Running the Extension

Let's run the extension. A new experimental instance of Visual Studio will launch. Open/
create a new project and add a JSON file to it as shown in Figure 5-15.

```
{
  "Book": {
    "Name": "Visual Studio Extensibility Development",
    "Subject": "Technology",
    "Publisher": "Apress",
    "Inspiration": "Mads Kristensen",
    "Pages": 400,
    "ChapterCount": 10,
    "Year": 2023,
    "Author": "Rishabh Verma"
  }
}
```

Figure 5-15. *JSON file*

Right-click the JSON file, and a new context menu item named "Generate C# class" will show up as shown in Figure 5-16.

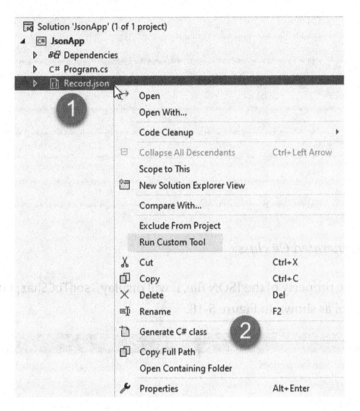

Figure 5-16. *Generate C# class*

Click "Generate C# class." It will generate a C# class for the selected JSON as shown in Figure 5-17.

Figure 5-17. *Generated C# class*

If we check the property of the JSON file, it will display `JsonToCSharpCodeGenerator` as the Custom Tool as shown in Figure 5-18.

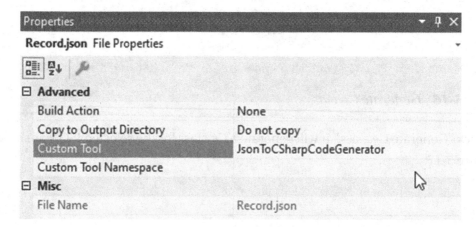

Figure 5-18. *Custom Tool*

You can also run the command "**Run Custom Tool**" to generate the code as this command runs the custom tool assigned to the file. This can be seen in the context menu shown in Figure 5-16. Once the custom tool is set, triggering the build of the project also runs the custom tool and generates the code.

Now, this is the happy path. What happens in case of an error? For example, the JSON file may not be well formed. In that case, we need to make the user of our extension aware that there is an error that needs their attention, by displaying the error in the error list and bringing it to focus in the Visual Studio IDE. To simulate this scenario, we remove a comma from the JSON file to make it invalid and save the file. On saving the file, our code generator executes and tries to generate the code. Since JSON is not valid, it encounters an error. That error is displayed in the Visual Studio Error List as well as Output window. This is illustrated in Figure 5-19.

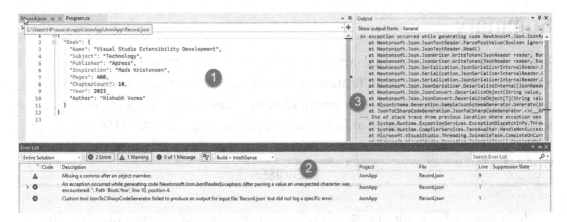

Figure 5-19. *Error in code generation*

And that's a wrap. Our extension has successfully achieved the intended objective. The displayed output might not be as polished as Visual Studio's native display we saw earlier in the chapter that is attributed to the underlying library we've employed for this demonstration. Our C# class and its properties are decorated with attributes and do require usNewtonsoft.Json NuGet package to be installed, but overall, it does a decent job. This concludes our sample extension, showcasing the execution of single-file code generation. Our code generator produces a nested C# file upon modification of the JSON file or when our designated command is executed. Yet, this extension merely scratches the surface. The realm of possibilities for code generation using extensibility and the .NET compiler platform is boundless. There are possibilities of code generation using extensibility and .NET compiler platform like generate tests for a method/class, generate client for an API, generate documentation from a class, etc. This extension, however, serves as a stepping stone and a guiding compass in that direction.

For those interested in exploring further, the Visual Studio Extensibility samples have a good sample on Single File Generator at `https://github.com/microsoft/VSSDK-Extensibility-Samples/tree/master/SingleFileGenerator`.

Also, one of the extensions that we are using in our extension development VSIX Synchronizer is also a great sample extension to explore and learn. The source code for VSIX Synchronizer can be seen at `https://github.com/madskristensen/VsixSynchronizer`.

Summary

In this chapter, we've expanded our horizons by developing a couple more extensions and learned how to display notifications within Visual Studio. We also saw how we can generate code, making use of code generator in our extension. In the next chapter, we will develop extensions related to code analysis, refactoring, and `IntelliSense`.

EXERCISES

The following activities are recommended to deepen the knowledge and understanding of the fundamentals we discussed in this chapter:

1. Familiarize yourself with the alert, notification system, and progress for Visual Studio by reading this great documentation at `https://learn.microsoft.com/en-us/visualstudio/extensibility/ux-guidelines/notifications-and-progress-for-visual-studio?view=vs-2022`.

2. When will you use the following to get the user's attention: (a) InfoBar, (b) Status bar, (c) Output Window, (d) Modal Dialog, and (e) Toast Notification?

3. Explore and debug the code of the following extensions: (a) Single File Generator, `https://github.com/microsoft/VSSDK-Extensibility-Samples/tree/master/SingleFileGenerator,` (b) VSIX Synchronizer, `https://github.com/madskristensen/VsixSynchronizer.`

4. List out the learnings from debugging and exploring the code of the preceding extensions.

5. Write a code generator that generates the documentation xml file of a C# class. Can you generate multiple files?

6. Explore and learn the Text Template Transformation Toolkit (T4) template and explore how T4 can be used to generate the code.

7. Explore and list five Custom Tools that you have encountered so far. What do these custom tools do?

Class References

Infobar Type System

- IVsInfoBarHost: It defines a host control that knows how to lay out an infobar. This is generally a tool windowpane or the main window of Visual Studio to host the infobar. It exposes the following methods.

Method Name	Description
AddInfoBar	This method adds an infobar to be displayed by the host. Infobars are displayed in the order in which they are added to the host. This method takes IVsUIElement as the parameter from which IVsInfoBarUIElement derives.
RemoveInfoBar	Removes an infobar from the infobar host control. This method also takes IVsUIElement as the parameter.

- IVsInfoBarUIElement: As the name suggests, this type defines the UI element of InfoBar. The methods exposed by IVsInfoBarUIElement are as follows.

Method Name	Description
Advise	This method subscribes to UI events for the InfoBar. It has two parameters. The first parameter is named eventSink. The type of eventSink is IVsInfoBarUIEvents and describes the events to subscribe to, while the second parameter is an out parameter named cookie of type uint. This method returns Microsoft.VisualStudio.VSConstants.S_OK (an integer) if the operation succeeds; otherwise, it returns an error code.
Close	This method requests the InfoBar to close itself by raising its OnClosed event. Returns Microsoft.VisualStudio.VSConstants.S_OK (an integer) if the operation succeeds; otherwise, it returns an error code.
get_DataSource	Gets the data source for this element. It takes data source as an input and returns Microsoft.VisualStudio.VSConstants.S_OK if the method succeeds, while it returns an error code if it fails.
GetUIObject	Gets the implementation-specific object (e.g., a Microsoft.VisualStudio.Shell.Interop.IVsUIWpfElement or a Microsoft.VisualStudio.Shell.Interop.IVsUIWin32Element). It has an out parameter named ppUnk of type object and returns Microsoft.VisualStudio.VSConstants.S_OK on success and an error code in case of failure.
put_DataSource	Binds the specified data source to this element. If the method succeeds, it returns Microsoft.VisualStudio.VSConstants.S_OK. If it fails, it returns an error code.
Translate Accelerator	Translates keyboard accelerators. If the method succeeds, it returns Microsoft.VisualStudio.VSConstants.S_OK. If it fails, it returns an error code.
Unadvise	Unsubscribes from UI events for the InfoBar. It takes an unsigned int parameter named cookie as the parameter and returns S_OK if the operation succeeded; otherwise, it returns an error code.

- IVsInfoBarUIFactory: This factory is responsible for the creation of Infobar. The methods exposed by this type are the following.

Method Name	Description
CreateInfoBar	Creates an infobar UI element by taking in a parameter of type IVsInfoBar.

- IVsInfoBar: It represents the data needed to construct an
  IVsUIElement representing an infobar. Infobars can have an icon, a
  set of spans of text, action elements, and an optional close button.
  The members of IVsInfoBar are listed in the next table.

Property Name	Description
ActionItems	Gets the collection of action items displayed in the infobar. It is of the type IVsInfoBarActionItemCollection.
Image	Gets the image displayed in the infobar. It is of the type ImageMoniker.
IsCloseButton Visible	Determines whether or not the InfoBar supports closing. Returns true if the InfoBar supports closing; otherwise, it returns false.
TextSpans	Gets the collection of text spans displayed in the infobar. Any IVsInfoBarActionItem spans in this collection will be rendered as a hyperlink. It is of type IVsInfoBarTextSpanCollection and returns the collection of text spans displayed in the infobar.

- InfoBarModel: This class creates a data model implementing
  IVsInfoBar, for use with IVsInfoBarUIFactory.CreateInfoBar. It
  implements the interface IVsInfoBar. The members of InfoBarModel
  are the following.

Method Name	Description
InfoBarModel	There are multiple overloads of constructors exposed by the usInfoBarModel to construct an infobar. There are overloads to construct an infobar with 1. A simple message. 2. A simple message and a separate panel of action buttons or links. 3. A message involving formatted text. 4. A message involving formatted text and a separate panel of action buttons or links.
ActionItems	Gets the collection of buttons or links to display.
Image	Gets the moniker for the image to display in the infobar.

(*continued*)

Method Name	Description
IsCloseButton Visible	Gets whether or not the infobar can be closed by the user.
TextSpans	Gets the message to display in the infobar.

- IVsInfoBarUIEvents: It handles user gestures in an infobar. The following methods are exposed by this type.

Method Name	Description
OnActionItemClicked	Handles the event raised when an action item on an infobar is clicked. It takes an infobar and action item as parameters.
OnClosed	Handles the event raised when the close button on an infobar is clicked. This method takes infobar as a parameter.

- IVsInfoBarTextSpan: This represents a span of text inside an IVsInfoBar. Multiple spans of text can be concatenated together, in the same way as a rich text document. The following properties are defined in this type.

Property Name	Description
Bold	Determines whether the text is bold.
Italic	Determines whether the text is italic.
Text	Gets the text for the span.
Underline	Determines whether the text is underlined.

- IVsInfoBarActionItem: This represents a clickable action span inside an IVsInfoBar, rendered by default as a hyperlink. Action items can have contextual data associated with them and have a click callback on the IVsInfoBarUIEvents interface. The properties of IVsInfoBarActionItem are as follows.

Property Name	Description
ActionContext	Gets the user-provided context associated with the hyperlink. This contextual data can be used to identify the hyperlink when it's clicked. The type of this property is dynamic.
Bold	Determines whether the text is bold.
IsButton	Determines whether this action item should be rendered as a button. By default, action items are rendered as a hyperlink.
Italic	Determines whether the text is italic.
Text	Gets the text associated with the action item.
Underline	Determines whether the text is underlined.

- IVsInfoBarActionItemCollection: This represents a collection of action items. Its members are as follows.

Method Name	Description
GetItem	Gets the action item stored at a specific index in the collection.
Property Name	**Description**
Count	Gets the number of action items in the collection.

- IVsInfoBarTextSpanCollection: It represents a document comprised of spans of text. Its members are as follows.

Method Name	Description
GetSpan	Gets the span stored at a specific index in the collection.
Property Name	**Description**
Count	Gets the number of spans in the collection.

Code Generation Types

- BaseCodeGenerator: It is an abstract class that implements the interfaces IVsSingleFileGenerator and IDisposable. This class is a managed wrapper for Visual Studio's concept of an IVsSingleFileGenerator which is a custom tool invoked during the build which can take any file as an input and provide a compilable code file as output. The important and nontrivial members of this class are as follows.

Property Name	Description
FileNamespace	Gets the namespace of the file.
InputFilePath	Gets the file path of the input file.
Method Name	**Description**
GenerateCode	This method does the work of generating code from the given input file.
GenerateError Callback	This method communicates an error via the shell callback mechanism, should an error occur in generating code.
GetDefault Extension	This method gets the default extension of the output file generated from this code generator.

- BaseCodeGeneratorWithSite: This abstract class derives from the BaseCodeGenerator class and exists to be co-created in a preprocessor build step. It also implements an interface IObjectWithSite. The important members of this class are listed in the next table.

Property Name	Description
Dte	Gets the DTE object.
ErrorList	Gets the Visual Studio ErrorList object.
GlobalServiceProvider	Provides a wrapper on the global service provider for Visual Studio.

(continued)

Property Name	Description
SiteServiceProvider	Gets a wrapper on the containing project system's service provider. This is a limited service provider that can only reliably provide `VxDTE::SID_SVSProjectItem SID_SVSWebReferenceDynamicProperties IID_IVsHierarchy SID_SVsApplicationSettings`.

Method Name	Description
CreateException Message	This is the method to create an exception message given an exception.
GetService	This method gets a service, by either providing its type or GUID.
SetWaitCursor	This method sets the wait cursor until the end of this generation.

- ProvideCodeGeneratorAttribute: This attribute class is meant to provide registration of a code generator. This class derives from the RegistrationAttribute class, which itself derives from the Attribute class. This attribute can be decorated only on classes and is meant to be placed on the package class. The important members of this attribute class are listed in the following table.

Field Name	Description
AspNetProjectGuid	GUID of the ASP.Net Project System package
CSharpProjectGuid	GUID of the C# Project System package..
VisualBasicProjectGuid	GUID of the Visual Basic Project System package.

Property Name	Description
Description	Gets a human-readable description of the generator.
GenerateDesign TimeSource	Gets a value indicating whether to flag this code generator as providing design-time source code.
Name	Gets the name of the code generator.

(*continued*)

Field Name	Description
RegisterCodeBase	Gets a value indicating whether or not to register the generator using a code base.
Type	Gets the type implementing the code generator.
TypeID	Overrides the TypeID property in order to let the Registration Attribute derived classes to work with System. ComponentModel.TypeDescriptor.GetAttributes. An attribute derived from this one will have to override this property only if it needs a better control on the instances that can be applied to a class.

Method Name	Description
Register	The method to register the generator.
Unregister	The method to unregister the generator and delete the keys.

- ProvideCodeGeneratorExtensionAttribute: This attribute class is meant to provide registration of a code generator against a specific file extension. This class derives from RegistrationAttribute class. This attribute can be decorated only on classes and is meant to be placed on the package class. This attribute works in addition to the ProvideCodeGenerator attribute to set up the default application of the specified generator to the files with provided extension. The important members of this attribute class are listed in the following table.

Field Name	Description
AspNetProjectGuid	GUID of the ASP.Net Project System package.
CSharpProjectGuid	GUID of the C# Project System package.
VisualBasicProjectGuid	GUID of the Visual Basic Project System package.

Property Name	Description
Extension	Gets the extension to bind the named generator to.

(continued)

Field Name	Description
Name	Gets the name of the generator to add an extension for.
ProjectSystem	Gets the project system that this code generator is registered with.
ProjectSystemPackage	Gets the package implementing the project system that this code generator is registered with.
Method Name	**Description**
Register	The method to register the generator.
Unregister	The method to unregister the generator and delete the keys.

CHAPTER 6

Developing Real-World Extensions for Visual Studio Editor

In our journey so far, we've not extended the core part of Visual Studio that is predominantly used by the developers – the code editor. The Visual Studio editor offers a rich set of extension points, and most of its parts are extensible via the Managed Extensibility Framework (MEF). In fact, there are so many extensibility points exposed by the editor that covering each of these in details would require a book in itself. Fortunately for us, Microsoft has already documented these extensibility points and features in great depth. In this chapter, we will discuss the extensibility points of the Visual Studio editor and develop extensions for code analysis, fixes, and refactoring.

In the pages that follow, we'll go into the details of `IntelliSense`, understanding how it works under the hood, and also write an extension to provide custom `IntelliSense`.

Imagine having an artificial intelligence (AI) collaborator right at your fingertips, ready to assist with your coding challenges. We'll introduce you to ChatGPT, a powerful AI language model that can understand and generate code snippets. We'll discuss how we can integrate ChatGPT into our Visual Studio extension, enabling it to provide real-time suggestions and explanations and even generate code on demand.

Before we can start extending the Visual Studio editor, it is important to understand the editor, its subsystems, features, and extensibility points. In the next section, we discuss the editor and then dive into extending it.

© Rishabh Verma 2024
R. Verma, *Visual Studio Extensibility Development*, https://doi.org/10.1007/978-1-4842-9875-6_6

Visual Studio Editor

The Visual Studio editor is undeniably the most frequently used component of Visual Studio. This is the space where developers write, view, edit, and debug the code in any of the supported programming languages. Figure 6-1 visually depicts the Visual Studio editor for the C# language and its different elements.

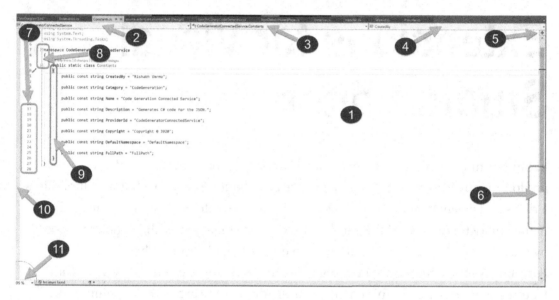

Figure 6-1. *Visual Studio C# code editor*

These elements are numbered for easy reference and identification. The numbered items are discussed next. They are the following:

1. Code editor: At the heart of this interface lies the core editor region where the document is edited and displayed. The key feature IntelliSense also comes into the picture in this region. Right-clicking in this area triggers a context menu, which we have already seen and discussed in prior chapters.

2. Project drop-down: This drop-down displays the currently active project that corresponds to the open file. If an orphan file is opened in Visual Studio, this drop-down displays "Miscellaneous Files."

3. Types drop-down: This drop-down lists all the types defined in the currently active document. It displays the selected value as the type that is being edited or is active, that is, where the cursor is placed.

4. Members drop-down: All members ranging from constructors and fields to properties and methods of the currently selected or active type are listed in this drop-down.

5. Window splitter: This is used to split the code windows.

6. Scrollbar: It is used to navigate easily to the specific section of the code window and bring the section of the window into view. Figure 6-1 displays the vertical scrollbar. Depending upon the code, you may also see a horizontal scrollbar in the bottom of the editor.

7. Line number: It displays the position of each line within the file.

8. Selection margin: This is the place between line numbers and the outline indicators. When we modify the code, those lines are highlighted with a color on the left side of the code editor. The selection margin is used to show code changes and allow you the ability to select an entire line of code with just one click.

9. Brace completion: The editor provides the feature to have brace completion and highlights the corresponding opening/closing brace when the other one is selected.

10. Indicator margin: This is the thin gray area on the left side of the editor. It is the area where breakpoints and bookmarks are marked for the line of code.

11. Zoom level: This can be used to zoom in or out of the code editor to view the larger or smaller font size in the editor.

Now we have seen a high-level overview of the Visual Studio editor. It is time to discuss the subsystems of the editor.

Editor Subsystems

The Visual Studio editor comprises different modules or subsystems that take care of the separation of concerns between the user interface and the data that is bound to the editor, that is, the text. Figure 6-2 depicts the four high-level subsystems of the Visual Studio editor. If you come from a web development background, you may find it easy to remember these subsystems if you draw an analogy with the Model View Controller (MVC) design pattern. Broadly speaking, there are four subsystems.

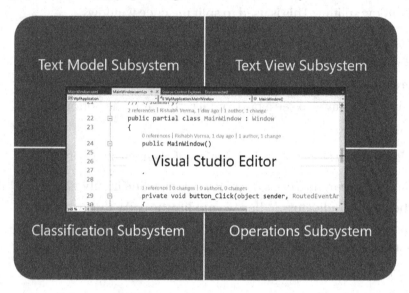

Figure 6-2. *Editor subsystems*

Text Model Subsystem

It represents the data model to be displayed in the editor. This subsystem is responsible for representing the text to be displayed in the editor as well as its manipulation and projection. This subsystem provides the types for the following features:

- Service to associate text with the file and manage reading and writing the file in the file system

- A differencing service that finds minimal differences between two sequences of objects

- Projection system that provides a way for combining text from multiple text buffers

Figure 6-3 illustrates the namespaces that contain the types describing the preceding features.

- ▪▪ Microsoft.VisualStudio.Text.Data
  - ▷ { } Microsoft.CodeAnalysis
  - ▷ { } Microsoft.VisualStudio.Text
  - ▷ { } Microsoft.VisualStudio.Text.Differencing
  - ▷ { } Microsoft.VisualStudio.Text.Document
  - ▷ { } Microsoft.VisualStudio.Text.Projection
  - ▷ { } Microsoft.VisualStudio.Text.Utilities
  - ▷ { } System.Runtime.CompilerServices

Figure 6-3. *Text, Differencing, and Projection*

We can see in Figure 6-3 all the classes that we are referring to reside in `Microsoft.VisualStudio.Text.Data.dll`. There are three different namespaces, which handle the previously discussed aspects. If we will expand these namespaces, we notice that they contain a number of types. Discussing each of them is outside the scope of this book. A few of the important types that can be seen in the `Microsoft.VisualStudio.Text` namespace are ITextChange, ITextChange2, ITextChange3, ITextEdit, ITextVersion, ITextVersion2, ITextSnapshot, IUndoEditTag, IDeletedTag, ITextBuffer, etc., which have methods to manipulate, order, and track the text data. Figure 6-4 illustrates a few of the classes comprising the text model subsystem.

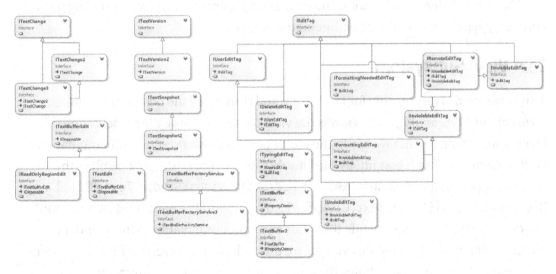

Figure 6-4. *Some of the types for text manipulation*

The "Class References" section at the end of this chapter provides a high-level overview of the important members of the text model subsystem.

All these types depend on .NET Framework base classes and MEF. Likewise, Differencing and Projection namespaces also have a number of types, which we will not dive into. But we will see the details of the types as we need them.

When we work with a file in Visual Studio, we know what kind of file it is. It can be a C# code file or an XML file, JSON file, or a csproj file, Visual Basic code file, and so on. One way for us to identify them is the file extension. Seeing the extension, we can identify the file type. However, from an extensibility point of view, what happens if we need to add a new custom file type, say, for example, a .verma file, and want to support it in Visual Studio and have C# `IntelliSense` support for these file types?

Visual Studio defines what is called a ContentType, which can handle these scenarios. A content type is a technique to define different types of contents like text, code, data, binary, and so on, or a technology type like C#, JSON, XML, etc. Many editor features and extensibility points are tied to the content type. For example, if we open a C# file in the editor, we see three drop-downs for Project, type, and members at the top, while they disappear when we open a JSON or XML or text file. Similarly, the syntax highlighting, coloring, and `IntelliSense` also differ for all these file types. This is because different content needs different handling, and defining these extensibility features based on content type takes care of this.

The "Class References" section summarizes the important types comprising the content types along with their documentation URLs.

Text View Subsystem

This subsystem is responsible for formatting and displaying the text in the editor. In terms of our MVC analogy, text view is the view part comprising the presentation layer of the editor. All that we see in the editor are **W**indows **P**resentation **F**oundation (WPF) elements. This is essentially the UI subsystem of the editor that displays the text. The types in this subsystem reside in `Microsoft.VisualStudio.Text.UI.dll` and `Microsoft.VisualStudio.Text.UI.Wpf.dll`. The assembly's name ending with WPF contains the WPF elements, while the other one contains a platform-independent element. Hence, the types of this system are divided into two layers: WPF and platform independent. Figure 6-5 illustrates the namespaces of a text view subsystem.

```
▪▪ Microsoft.VisualStudio.Text.UI
  ▷ { } Microsoft.CodeAnalysis
  ▷ { } Microsoft.VisualStudio.Commanding
  ▷ { } Microsoft.VisualStudio.Text
  ▷ { } Microsoft.VisualStudio.Text.Adornments
  ▷ { } Microsoft.VisualStudio.Text.BraceCompletion
  ▷ { } Microsoft.VisualStudio.Text.BraceCompletion.Implementation
  ▷ { } Microsoft.VisualStudio.Text.Classification
  ▷ { } Microsoft.VisualStudio.Text.Differencing
  ▷ { } Microsoft.VisualStudio.Text.Editor
  ▷ { } Microsoft.VisualStudio.Text.Editor.Commanding
  ▷ { } Microsoft.VisualStudio.Text.Editor.Commanding.Commands
  ▷ { } Microsoft.VisualStudio.Text.Editor.MultiCaret
  ▷ { } Microsoft.VisualStudio.Text.Editor.OptionsExtensionMethods
  ▷ { } Microsoft.VisualStudio.Text.Formatting
  ▷ { } Microsoft.VisualStudio.Text.IncrementalSearch
  ▷ { } Microsoft.VisualStudio.Text.Operations
  ▷ { } Microsoft.VisualStudio.Text.Outlining
  ▷ { } Microsoft.VisualStudio.Text.Tagging
  ▷ { } Microsoft.VisualStudio.Text.UI.Adornments
  ▷ { } Microsoft.VisualStudio.Utilities
  ▷ { } System.Runtime.CompilerServices
▪▪ Microsoft.VisualStudio.Text.UI.Wpf
  ▷ { } Microsoft.CodeAnalysis
  ▷ { } Microsoft.VisualStudio.Core.Imaging
  ▷ { } Microsoft.VisualStudio.Text.Adornments
  ▷ { } Microsoft.VisualStudio.Text.Classification
  ▷ { } Microsoft.VisualStudio.Text.Differencing
  ▷ { } Microsoft.VisualStudio.Text.Editor
  ▷ { } Microsoft.VisualStudio.Text.Editor.DragDrop
  ▷ { } Microsoft.VisualStudio.Text.Editor.OptionsExtensionMethods
  ▷ { } Microsoft.VisualStudio.Text.Formatting
  ▷ { } Microsoft.VisualStudio.Text.OverviewMargin
  ▷ { } Microsoft.VisualStudio.Text.UI.Wpf
  ▷ { } Microsoft.VisualStudio.Text.Utilities.Automation
  ▷ { } System.Runtime.CompilerServices
```

Figure 6-5. *Namespaces of a text view subsystem*

Notice that in both of these assemblies, a few of the namespaces are common; this is anticipated as one would contain platform-independent implementation, while the other will have WPF-specific implementation. A couple of the important types of this subsystem are ITextView and IWpfTextView, which reside in the `Microsoft.VisualStudio.Text.Editor` namespace. It also has types for formatting, inserting, searching, outlining, brace completion, tagging, scrolling, etc.

The "Class References" section summarizes a few of the important types of the text view subsystem.

Classification Subsystem

When we type C# code in the Visual Studio editor, it does a great job of segregating the keywords, comments, base classes, using directives, etc. by assigning different colors to them. This is made possible by the classification subsystem of the editor, which categorizes the text into different classes and maps the text to the font properties. Types for tagging, which is a way of adding markers to the span of texts, are also defined in this subsystem. The types of this subsystem are defined in `Microsoft.VisualStudio.Text. Logic.dll` as shown in Figure 6-6.

```
■-■ Microsoft.VisualStudio.Text.Logic
  ▷ { }  Microsoft.CodeAnalysis
  ▷ { }  Microsoft.VisualStudio.Editor
  ▷ { }  Microsoft.VisualStudio.Text
  ▷ { }  Microsoft.VisualStudio.Text.Classification
  ▷ { }  Microsoft.VisualStudio.Text.Configuration
  ▷ { }  Microsoft.VisualStudio.Text.Differencing
  ▷ { }  Microsoft.VisualStudio.Text.Document
  ▷ { }  Microsoft.VisualStudio.Text.Editor
  ▷ { }  Microsoft.VisualStudio.Text.Editor.OptionsExtensionMethods
  ▷ { }  Microsoft.VisualStudio.Text.Operations
  ▷ { }  Microsoft.VisualStudio.Text.PatternMatching
  ▷ { }  Microsoft.VisualStudio.Text.Tagging
  ▷ { }  Microsoft.VisualStudio.Text.Utilities
  ▷ { }  System.Runtime.CompilerServices
```

Figure 6-6. *Types of a classification subsystem*

The information from the classification subsystem is used by the view subsystem to format the text and display it in the font mapped from the classification format.

Operations Subsystem

As the name suggests, this subsystem is responsible for all the editor operations, commands, and behaviors. The types of this subsystem are defined in multiple assemblies, a few of which we have seen earlier.

Let's discuss the editor features and extensibility points in the next section.

Editor Features

The Visual Studio editor is very rich and full of features. The editor features are nicely designed to keep them extensible. To do so, each feature has abstractions and implementations. A few of their important features and a brief discussion are summarized next.

Tags

They are used to tag or mark a span of text. Tagging is displayed visually by highlighting, coloring, outlining, or underlining a text or by displaying graphics or pop-ups. For example, the syntax highlighting is done via classifier, so it is a kind of tag. Tagging can also be used to display errors like compilation errors. A few of the types used for tagging are as follows:

- `TextMarkerTag`: Used for highlighting text.

- `OutliningRegionText`: For displaying the outlines.

- `ErrorTag`: For displaying errors. A lot of features of the editor are based on tags. Figure 6-7 shows an error tag (squiggle) highlighted.

```
var name = "Some name";
```

Figure 6-7. *Error tag in action*

Classifier

A classifier, as the name suggests, categorizes or classifies the text. Classifiers are defined for a content type by implementing the IClassifier interface since there can be multiple classifications or categories. They are defined by the `IClassificationType` interface. A classifier may classify the code text as comment, or a keyword or identifier, just like we classify the English alphabet as vowels, consonants, and so on. The instance of classifier type is called a classification. Then there are classifier aggregators, which also act as classifiers as they break the text into a set of classifications. The text formatting of the editor is based on text classification. The text is classified as a keyword, literal, comment, identifier, etc., and the text view subsystem formats, highlights, and colors the text based on classification. Figure 6-8 illustrates different colors used to mark different parts of the C# code. This happens via classification.

```
/// <summary>
/// Gets the name of type.
/// </summary>
/// <param name="key">The key as string</param>
/// <param name="keyValuePairs">The dictionary</param>
/// <returns>The name as string</returns>
1 reference | 0 changes | 0 authors, 0 changes
private static string GetClassNameOfType(string key,
    IEnumerable<KeyValuePair<string, string>> keyValuePairs)
{
    foreach (var item in keyValuePairs)
    {
        var name = "Some name";
        var className = item.Key;
```

Figure 6-8. *Different classifications and different colors*

Adornments

The literal meaning of the word adornment is decoration or ornament. Similarly, in
the context of the Visual Studio editor, any text decoration or graphic, apart from the
font and color of the text, is referred to as adornment. The red and green squiggle on
the piece of code for error and warning are a great example of adornment. A tool tip
is another adornment. Since they show up in the editor UI, which is WPF based, any
adornment should derive from the UIElement and implement ITag. Figure 6-9 depicts a
tool-tip adornment for string when we hover over the string keyword in the editor.

Figure 6-9. *The tool-tip adornment*

Projection

Projection is a technique for combining text from multiple text buffers and constructing
a different text buffer. So, using projection, the text from different buffers can be
combined in such a way to show the entire text from the buffers or just show a part of text
and hiding the other part. When we use the outlining feature of the Visual Studio editor,
we can either collapse or expand the section of code. This is achieved by projection of
text buffers. Figure 6-10 shows the collapsed piece of code, which is done internally via
projection.

```
/// <summary> Gets the name of type.
1 reference | 0 changes | 0 authors, 0 changes
private static string GetClassNameOfType(string key,
    IEnumerable<KeyValuePair<string, string>> keyValuePairs)...
```

Figure 6-10. *Collapsed code block*

Outlining

This is a known feature of the editor. We can expand or collapse a section of code
block in the editor. Outlining is defined as a kind of tag, just like adornment.
OutliningRegionTag defines a region of text that can be expanded or collapsed. The
type IOutliningManagerService provides an IOutliningManager that can enumerate,
expand, or collapse the different blocks of text represented by the ICollapsible object,
to expand or collapse the section of code in the Visual Studio editor. This is shown in
Figure 6-11. The highlighted section is the outline, which can be collapsed.

```
2 references | 0 changes | 0 authors, 0 changes
private static string Join(string prefix, string name)
{
    return (string.IsNullOrEmpty(prefix) ? name : prefix + "." + name);
}
```

Figure 6-11. *Outlining in Visual Studio editor*

Operations

As the name suggests, this is used to automate the interaction of the editor. Earlier
Visual Studio had support for Macros, which used to be the preferred way of automating
the repetitive tasks in Visual Studio including editor. To automate interaction with the
editor, we first import the IEditorOperationsFactoryService to access operations on
a text view. Then this object can be used to modify the selection or change the scrollbar
position and so on as needed. Figure 6-12 displays the scrollbar, split window, caret, and
tool tip in action.

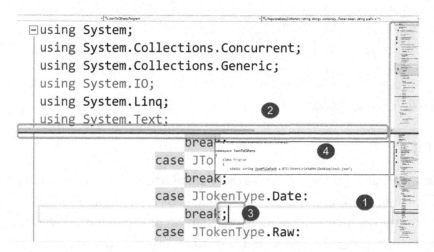

```
⊟using System;
 using System.Collections.Concurrent;
 using System.Collections.Generic;
 using System.IO;
 using System.Linq;
 using System.Text;
```

```
         break
    case JTo
         break;
    case JTokenType.Date:
         break;
    case JTokenType.Raw:
```

Figure 6-12. *Scrollbar, split window, caret, and tool tip in action (in the order of numbering)*

IntelliSense

If we will look at the most used features of the Visual Studio editor, IntelliSense would definitely feature among the toppers. It's basically the contextual intelligent sense of the editor that supports statement completion, signature help, quick info, and light bulb-style refactorings. The statement completion feature provides a pop-up list of possible completions for the method names, APIs, or other markup elements as applicable in the context. IntelliSense is invoked when a user types a period (.) or (Ctrl + .). Behind the scenes, this initiates a completion session that displays a list of potential completions. A user can select one of those or dismiss the list altogether. The type ICompletionBroker is responsible for creating and triggering the ICompletionSession, which displays the possible list of items contained in the type CompletionSet computed by the type ICompletionSource for a given session.

Figure 6-13 demonstrates completion suggestions.

```
67                    return string.Empty;
```
int string.Compare(string strA, string strB) (+ 9 overloads) | Compare
Compares two specified string objects and returns an integer that indicates their relative position in the sort order. | CompareOrdinal
```
69                                              Concat
70                    key = key.Trim();         Concat<>
                                                Copy
71                    var parentClassAnd        Empty
                                                Equals          ke
72                    if (parentClassAnd        Format          out
                                                Intern
```

Figure 6-13. *Completion suggestions*

Figure 6-14 shows light bulb-style refactoring in Visual Studio. We will learn to implement both these features later in this chapter.

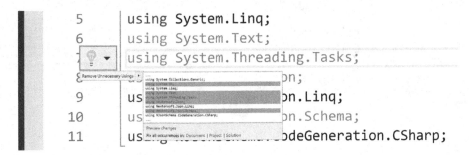

Figure 6-14. *Light bulb-style refactoring*

All these features and more are very well documented in the online Visual Studio editor documentation, and I highly encourage readers to spend some time and read this detailed documentation at `https://learn.microsoft.com/en-us/visualstudio/extensibility/inside-the-editor?view=vs-2022`.

Next, we will look at the various extensibility points exposed by the Visual Studio editor.

Editor Extensibility

The Visual Studio editor is highly extensible and provides extension points that can be used to extend the editor as **Managed Extensibility Framework** (MEF) component parts. The editor features that we discussed in the last section are all extensible. For a few of these features, Visual Studio extensibility templates provide direct item templates, while for a few others, we need to do custom coding by adding classes manually and deriving from the right interfaces and classes. Visual Studio offers extensibility item templates for classifier, margin, adornment, and viewport adornment. This can be seen by adding an item to an extensibility project and choosing Extensibility ➤ Editor in the left panel of the Add New Item dialog as shown in Figure 6-15.

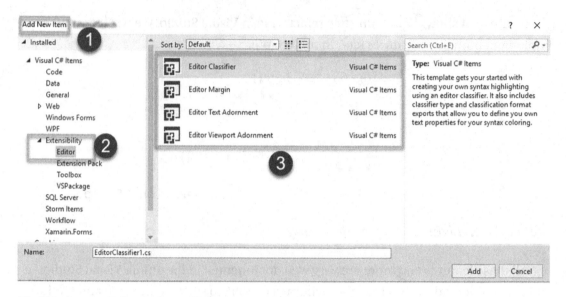

Figure 6-15. *Editor extensibility item templates*

If we choose any of these item templates, then build, and debug/deploy the extension, we have a working extension demonstrating the editor feature extension. When we add any of these item templates, it does a bunch of things in the background, like adding code files, references, and adds an asset node of type `MefComponent` in the `vsixmanifest`, etc. However, to customize the feature based on our requirements, we need to modify code, but just to see how the feature can be extended and wire up these templates are a great start. I would encourage all readers to try out each of these templates and see how the MEF exports and imports are decorated to the types and how everything wires up. Apart from these features, there are a number of other features for which there is no template provided. Covering each of these extensibility points would require a book in itself and hence they are outside the scope of this book. The great news, though, is that extending all of these features is very well documented, and even code walkthrough with a step-by-step process to extend the editor features are provided as needed. I would highly recommend readers to read the following Visual Studio documentation on extending language and editor services at `https://learn.microsoft.com/en-us/visualstudio/extensibility/language-service-and-editor-extension-points?view=vs-2022`.

In the next section, we develop an extension that runs a live code diagnostic analyzer on the C# editor and shows a red squiggle as we make any violation and also suggests a code fix.

Diagnostic Analyzer with Code Fix

One might naturally wonder about the necessity of a real-time diagnostic analyzer. Visual Studio comes with numerous code analysis and diagnostic analyzers built in, so you may already have known and used diagnostic analyzers. Recall that while developing extensions in earlier chapters, we encountered a squiggle below our code whenever the code was required to be executed on the main/UI thread, as shown in Figure 6-16.

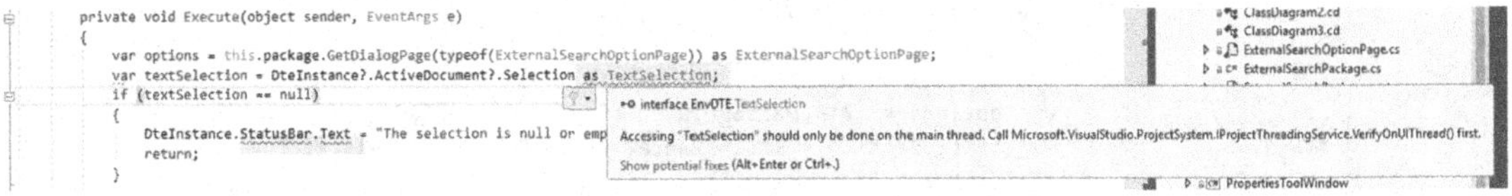

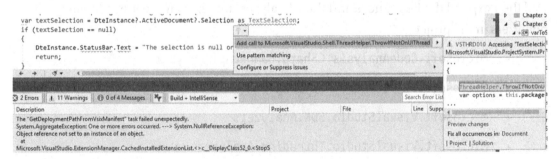

Figure 6-16. Diagnostic analyzer in action

This is achieved by means of an analyzer, which now comes by default in the VSIX project templates. We see a tool tip and light bulb when we hover over the squiggle. This is essentially the code fix. When we click on the down marker beside the light bulb, we see the suggestion to fix the issue. Clicking the suggestion fixes the issue. The suggestion also offers to show the preview of code fix in the method under discussion or for fixes of all such occurrences in the document, project, or solution as shown in Figure 6-17.

Figure 6-17. Code fix

Clicking preview changes displays a nice dialog that shows how the code would look after the code fix is added. If we are happy with code changes, we can click Apply or else cancel by clicking the Cancel button. This is shown in Figure 6-18.

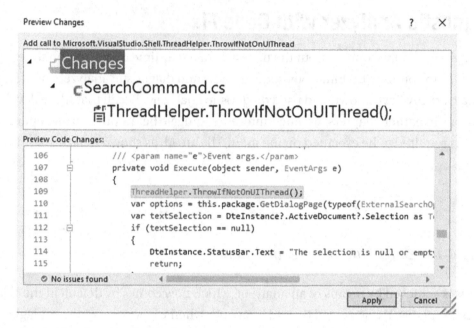

Figure 6-18. *Preview code fix changes*

Cool and awesome! Right!

If I open the extension project (created from VSIX template) in the solution explorer and then expand the References and then Analyzers node, I can see the following analyzers in the project:

- `Microsoft.CodeAnalysis.CSharp.BannedApiAnalyzers`

- `Microsoft.ServiceHub.Analyzers`

- `Microsoft.VisualStudio.SDK.Analyzers`

- `Microsoft.VisualStudio.Threading.Analyzers`

- `Microsoft.VisualStudio.Threading.Analyzers.CSharp`

Figure 6-19 displays the analyzers that come in the VSIX template along with their expanded set of rules.

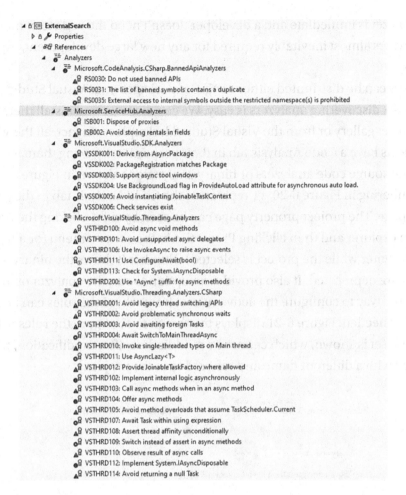

Figure 6-19. *Code analyzers in the VSIX project*

Leveraging the live feedback provided by the analyzer, while coding, we developers can avoid a lot of issues that may otherwise remain uncaught or may get caught in code reviews, or worse, in production. So, diagnostic analyzers can make the adoption of best practices, coding standards, and team guidelines rather easy, especially in a large team. The severity of each rule can be determined by the rule author.

Another great thing about analyzers, unlike other static code analysis tools like FxCop of earlier times, is that they don't require your code to be compiled and assembled to be generated for it to give the feedback. On one hand, due to the late or delayed feedback provided by old static analysis tools, many times teams had to take the tough call to let go of the FxCop code analysis findings without fixing as they used to be provided very late in the game. This used to increase the technical debt. On the other hand, feedback from an analyzer is immediate and a developer doesn't need the code to compile. This makes analyzers almost inevitably required for any new large development, especially in large teams.

Analyzers can be distributed either as NuGet packages or as Visual Studio extensions. So, discovering analyzers is easy. We can discover and install them either from the NuGet gallery or from the Visual Studio Marketplace. In fact, all the Visual Studio projects have a Code Analysis tab in their properties; by using them, we can configure the source code analyzers or binary analyzers as shown in Figure 6-19. If we see the numbering in Figure 6-20, #1 represents the Code Analysis tab in the project properties page. The project property page can be seen by right-clicking the project in the solution explorer and then clicking Properties in the context menu (or alternatively pressing Alt+Enter while the project is selected). Number 2 shows the binary analyzers section that are deprecated. It also provides an option to run the analyzer on build. And #3 displays the way to configure the active ruleset from where the rules can be selected/unselected as needed. Figure 6-21 displays the screen to configure the ruleset. (Here Microsoft ruleset is shown, which cannot be modified, so after modification, this ruleset can be saved with a different name and referred to in the project.)

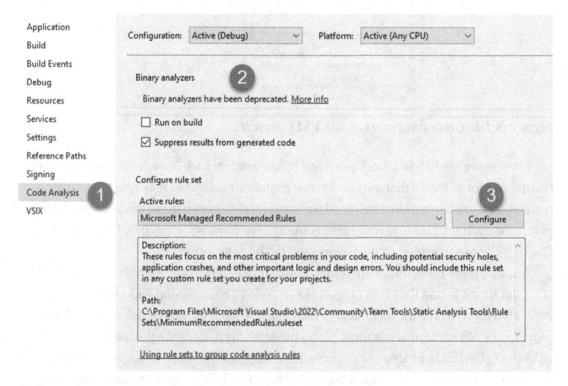

Figure 6-20. *Configure analyzers in project properties*

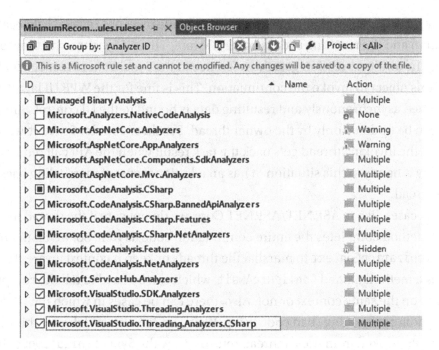

Figure 6-21. *Configure analyzer ruleset*

Writing a Diagnostic Code Analyzer with Code Fix

Visual Studio has a project template that makes it easier for us to write a diagnostic analyzer. So next, we will develop a diagnostic code analyzer with a code fix.

async await is very widely used in most modern web, desktop, or cross-platform apps developed on C#. Though .NET (and .NET Core) doesn't have SynchronizationContext, .NET full framework has it, and if .NET or .NET full framework class library is consumed by a .NET Framework application, SynchronizationContext plays an important role in determining the performance and also if the application can run into deadlock or not. How? Different types of applications have different threading models, like WPF/Windows forms app requires that only the owning thread can modify the UI control or update its value. If we try to update the UI control in any other thread, we will get an exception.

ASP.NET/ASP.NET Core doesn't have such restrictions. This is taken care of at the compiler level by a class named SynchronizationContext. When we mark any method as async, the compiler transforms this method code into a type that implements a state machine, which can be invoked multiple times and can start execution from different places. In this async method, when an await statement is encountered, the compiler

245

essentially hooks up the remainder of the method code in a `ContinueWith` delegate or a continuation and the resulting code is context aware. Thus, if `SynchronizationContext` is present, the await expression gets the reference to the `SynchronizationContext` object and uses this object to invoke the continuation. This is fine for the WPF UI layer, as an API is invoked asynchronously and resulting data is bound to the UI control. Since UI controls can be updated only by the owner thread, `SynchronizationContext` would ensure that the invoking thread gets back the task result when the API call returns. Though this is handy in this situation, it has an additional cost of marshaling back to the invoking thread.

In most cases, like in ASP.NET/ASP.NET Core, we do not care if the thread invoking the async method completes the entire continuation code as well. So, we do not require the `SynchronizationContext` to marshal the threads or keep it context aware. To do so, there is a method named `ConfigureAwait`, which can be used to tell the compiler to continue on the same context or not. Also, there can be cases in which the UI thread is blocked doing something (bad code using .Wait() or .Result), and during this time, the async API invoked from the UI thread returns. Now the `SynchronizationContext` would try to return the execution back on the captured context, that is, on the UI thread, which is blocked on some other blocking call, resulting in a deadlock. Therefore, it is recommended that all library methods must use `.ConfigureAwait(false)` with the await statement so that situations leading to deadlock or poor performance can be avoided.

We will write a simple diagnostic analyzer, which will check if our await statement has `ConfigureAwait(false)` or not. If it doesn't, then it would display a squiggle. We will also provide a simple code fix to address this issue by appending a call to `ConfigureAwait(false)`. Though this rule now comes built in with the analyzers, we still go ahead with this analyzer as we are developing it for learning and demonstration purposes.

We come across various terms and jargons while we develop our code analyzer, so let us quickly see these terms as shown in Table 6-1.

Table 6-1. *Commonly Used Code Analysis Terms*

Term	Description
Diagnostic	A compiler error or a warning or a violation of code pattern, along with the location where it occurred.
Analyzer	A class that reports a diagnostic. It is an instance of a type that derives from DiagnosticAnalyzer.
Code fixer	A class that provides code fixes for compiler or analyzer diagnostics. It is an instance of type that derives from CodeFixProvider.
Code refactoring	A type that provides source code refactorings. It is an instance of type derived from CodeRefactoringProvider.
Code action	Refers to code fix or code refactoring action.
Equivalence key	We will see this in action, whenever we register any code action. It represents a string value representing an equivalence class of all the code actions registered. Two or more code actions are treated as equivalent if they share the same equivalence key values and are generated by the same code fixer or refactoring.
FixAll provider	A class that provides FixAll occurrences code fix. It is an instance of type derived from FixAllProvider.
FixAll occurrences code fix	A code action returned by FixAllProvider.GetFixAsync, which fixes all or multiple occurrences of diagnostics fixed by the corresponding code fixer, for a given FixAllScope.

Setting Up the Project

Let's get started with our diagnostic analyzer coding. The followings steps should be completed to develop a diagnostic analyzer using Visual Studio 2022:

1. Open Visual Studio 2022 and create a new project. Search for the project template "Analyzer with Code Fix" as shown in Figure 6-22.

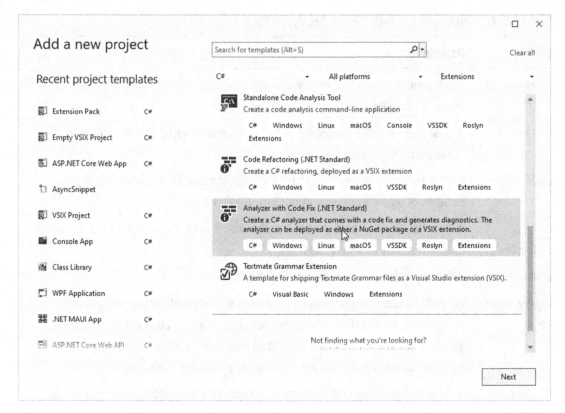

Figure 6-22. *Analyzer with Code Fix*

2. Give the project a meaningful name, and then click the Create
    button as shown in Figure 6-23.

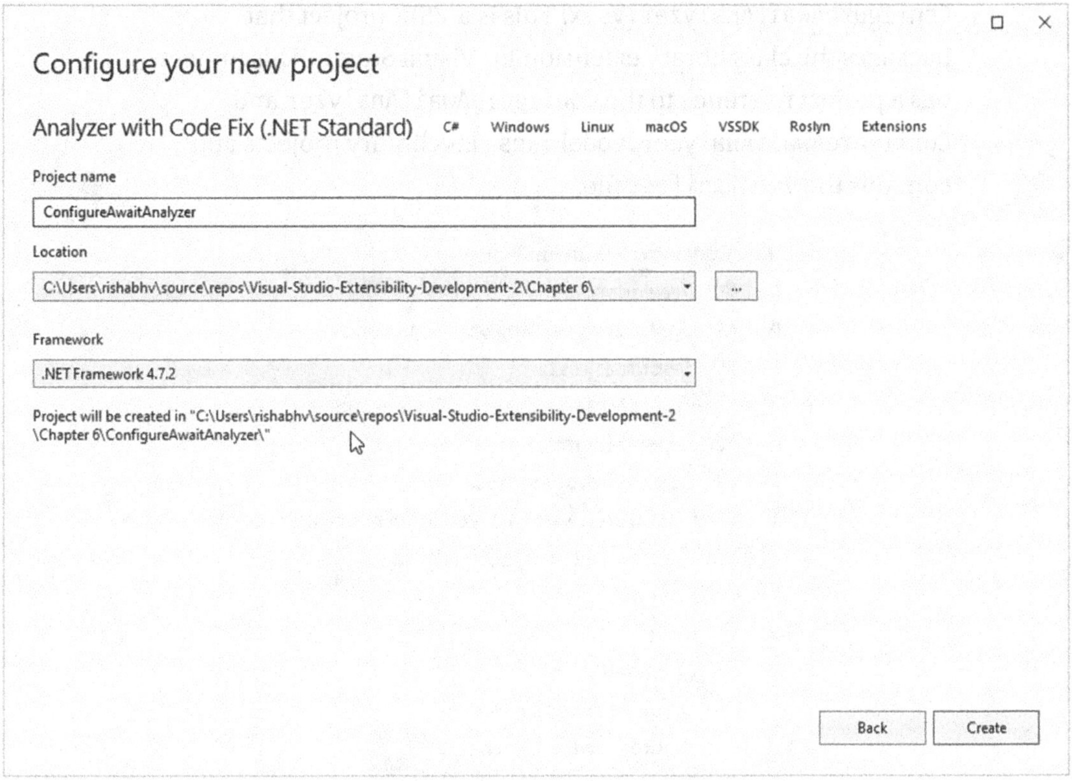

Figure 6-23. *ConfigureAwaitAnalyzer project*

This will add five projects as shown in Figure 6-24. The projects are as follows:

- `ConfigureAwaitAnalyzer.csproj`, which is a class library project: This is where we write our diagnostic analyzer class. This project also contains the resource file for localization.

- `ConfigureAwaitAnalyzer.CodeFixes.csproj`: This class library project hosts the code fix provider and resource file for localization.

- `ConfigureAwaitAnalyzer.Package.csproj`: This class library project contains the PowerShell scripts to install and uninstall the analyzer.

- `ConfigureAwaitAnalyzer.Test`, which is a test project: This project can be used to test the diagnostic analyzer as well as code fix.

- `ConfigureAwaitAnalyzer.Vsix`: This is a VSIX project that packages the class library extension for Visual Studio. This project has a project reference to the `ConfigureAwaitAnalyzer` and `ConfigureAwaitAnalyzer.CodeFixes` class library projects and contains the `vsixmanifest` file.

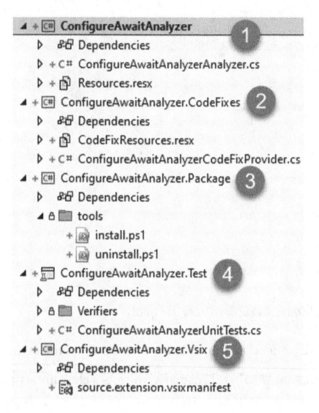

Figure 6-24. *Added projects*

This `VSIXManifest` file defines the four important Asset nodes in the Asset section, which wires up the code analyzer when the MEF component parts are resolved. The code for these nodes is shown next:

```
<Assets>
  <Asset Type="Microsoft.VisualStudio.MefComponent" d:Source="Project"
  d:ProjectName="ConfigureAwaitAnalyzer" Path="|ConfigureAwaitAnalyzer|"/>
  <Asset Type="Microsoft.VisualStudio.Analyzer" d:Source="Project"
  d:ProjectName="ConfigureAwaitAnalyzer" Path="|ConfigureAwaitAnalyzer|"/>
```

```
<Asset Type="Microsoft.VisualStudio.MefComponent"
d:Source="Project" d:ProjectName="ConfigureAwaitAnalyzer.CodeFixes"
Path="|ConfigureAwaitAnalyzer.CodeFixes|"/>
<Asset Type="Microsoft.VisualStudio.Analyzer" d:Source="Project"
d:ProjectName="ConfigureAwaitAnalyzer.CodeFixes"
Path="|ConfigureAwaitAnalyzer.CodeFixes|"/>
</Assets>
```

The UI for these changes in the vsixmanifest editor in Visual Studio is shown in Figure 6-25.

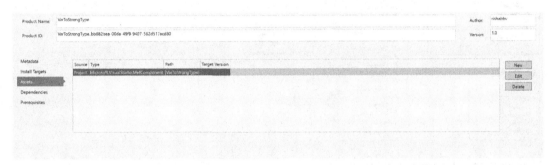

Figure 6-25. *Assets in VSIX manifest*

For the folks advocating test-driven development (TDD), writing unit tests may be the way to start. But I belong to a different school of thought, and hence, I will first write the analyzer and then the unit tests. The code generated from the template is already a working code analyzer. However, it just detects if the type name contains a lowercase letter or not. If it does, a squiggle is shown. Before we edit the ConfigureAwaitAnalyzerAnalyzer.cs file to write our diagnostic, we should first understand the existing code. Also, we should rename the file as it has repeated Analyzer in the name. Figure 6-26 displays the class diagram of the diagnostic analyzer. We see the following in the class diagram:

- The analyzer class is a class, and it derives from another abstract class named DiagnosticAnalyzer.

- The base class DiagnosticAnalyzer has two members of interest in addition to the members exposed by System.Object. They are

  - SupportedDiagnostics

  - Initialize

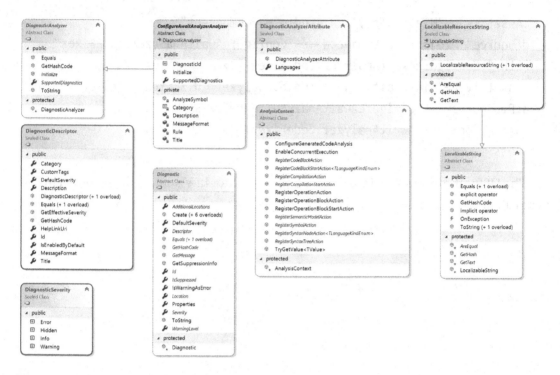

Figure 6-26. *Diagnostic Analyzer*

SupportedDiagnostics

This is an abstract read-only property of the type `ImmutableArray<Diagnostic Descriptor>`. The deriving class would provide the diagnostics that are supported by the analyzer. `DiagnosticDescriptor` is a sealed class defined in the `Microsoft.CodeAnalysis` namespace, which provides a description about a Diagnostic. Diagnostic is another abstract class defined in `Microsoft.CodeAnalysis` namespace, which represents a diagnostic, such as a compiler error or warning, along with the location where it occurred. It provides static methods to create a Diagnostic with multiple overloads. Both of these types are shown in the preceding class diagram. The members of these types are simple to understand and are very intuitive as we will see in the coding a little later. However, for the sake of completion, the important members of `DiagnosticDescriptor` and Diagnostic class are summarized in the "Class References" section.

Initialize

This is an abstract method that gets invoked once at the start of session to register the actions in the analysis context. It has a parameter named context of type AnalysisContext, which is shown as an abstract class in the preceding class diagram. This is where we register the diagnostic action for our analyzer. Analyzer initialization can use an AnalysisContext to register actions, which can be executed at any of the compilation's start or end, completion of parsing of code document, or completion of semantic analysis of code or a symbol.

The important members of the AnalysisContext abstract class are described in the "Class References" section. More detailed documentation can be read online at https://learn.microsoft.com/en-us/dotnet/api/microsoft.codeanalysis. diagnostics.analysiscontext?view=roslyn-dotnet.

The other types are LocalizableResourceString, which derives from the abstract class LocalizableString and is used for localization as this resource string may be formatted differently depending upon culture. If you do not want your analyzer to be localizable, you can choose the normal strings as well. There is an attribute named DiagnosticAnalyzerAttribute that can be decorated on the class. Placing this attribute on a type causes it to be considered a diagnostic analyzer.

Now that we know the different types and their members involved in the diagnostic analyzer code, let us tweak the code of the diagnostic analyzer to look at the await statements that doesn't have a ConfigureAwait method invoked.

Coding the Diagnostic Analyzer

To achieve this, we must tap into the capabilities of Roslyn, the .NET Compiler platform. Roslyn provides two types of models to work with code, namely, SyntaxTree and SemanticModel:

- SyntaxTree can be generated by parsing the code and is object model representation of the code. It is immutable, meaning it cannot be modified. Modifying the SyntaxTree gives a new SyntaxTree object. It doesn't have compilation information. It understands the code, for example, Console, as just a text identifier or literal.

- The compilation information is provided by another model called the SematicModel, which is also immutable and understands the code, for example, Console, as a type like System.Console.

To identify whether `ConfigureAwait` is invoked or not, `SyntaxTree` or syntactic analysis is enough. To do so, we first need to identify await statements and then check if it invokes the `ConfigureAwait` method or not. For simplification, Visual Studio introduces a valuable resource: the Syntax Visualizer tool window. To open this window, navigate to the top menu bar and then click View ➤ Other Windows ➤ Syntax Visualizer. This will open a tool window, which we can pin on one of the sides of Visual Studio. I have pinned it on the left side as it makes easier for me to see its content while I edit the code. While I type code on the editor or click a line in the editor, it displays the corresponding node in the `SyntaxTree` of the node, in the Syntax Visualizer window, as shown in Figure 6-27.

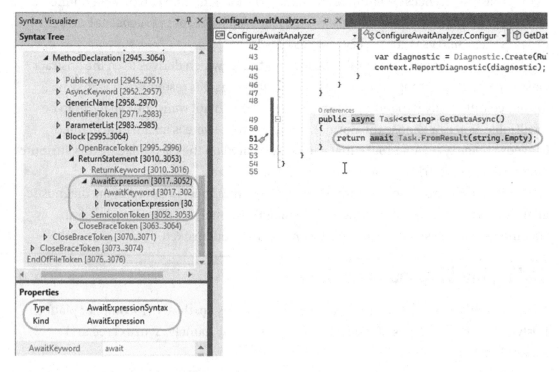

Figure 6-27. *Syntax Visualizer*

Notice that I have written a simple async method in the editor, which has an await statement without a call to `ConfigureAwait`. The directed graph of this method is shown in Figure 6-28. As we can see, it is so detailed that the entire code can be reconstructed back from this information, so we can surely find out how to look for await statements without `ConfigureAwait`. If we click the await statement in the editor and look for a highlighted node in the Syntax tree in the Syntax Visualizer window, we can find out the node to be looked in the Syntax tree for finding the await statement. In this case, I find that the await statement is represented by `AwaitExpression` in the Syntax tree. If we add a `ConfigureAwait` invocation, it is represented as an `IdentifierName` token inside a `SimpleMemberAccessExpression`.

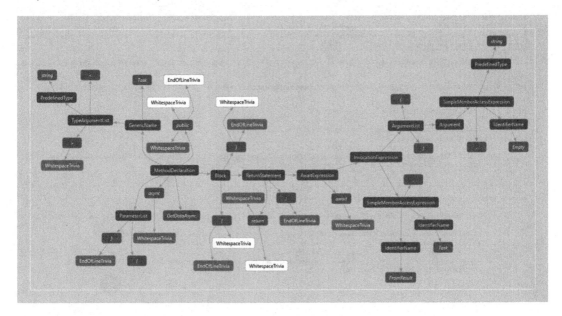

Figure 6-28. *Directed graph of async method*

With this information, we are ready to modify the code.

1. In our Diagnostic class, we will first provide the DiagnosticId. We shouldn't use ids starting with CA as they are used by Microsoft, so I will make use of RV001 (RV as in Rishabh Verma); you can choose some other string of your choice. Next, I will modify the resource file to add a proper title, message format, and description as shown in Figure 6-29.

Name	Value	Comment
AnalyzerDescription	await statement must make use of ConfigureAwait	An optional longer localizable description of the diagnostic.
AnalyzerMessageFormat	Method name '{0}' does not have ConfigureAwait	The format-able message the diagnostic displays.
AnalyzerTitle	await statement missing ConfigureAwait	The title of the diagnostic.

Figure 6-29. *Resource file updated with diagnostic title, description, and message format*

2. The other changes are highlighted in Figure 6-30.

```
[DiagnosticAnalyzer(LanguageNames.CSharp)]
2 references
public class ConfigureAwaitAnalyzer : DiagnosticAnalyzer
{
    public const string DiagnosticId = "RV001";                                    1

    // You can change these strings in the Resources.resx file. If you do not want your analyzer to be localize-able, you can use regula
    private static readonly LocalizableString Title = new LocalizableResourceString(nameof(Resources.AnalyzerTitle), Resources.ResourceM
    private static readonly LocalizableString MessageFormat = new LocalizableResourceString(nameof(Resources.AnalyzerMessageFormat), Res
    private static readonly LocalizableString Description = new LocalizableResourceString(nameof(Resources.AnalyzerDescription), Resourc
    private const string Category = "Reliability";                                 2

    private static readonly DiagnosticDescriptor Rule = new DiagnosticDescriptor(DiagnosticId, Title, MessageFormat, Category, Diagnosti

    0 references
    public override ImmutableArray<DiagnosticDescriptor> SupportedDiagnostics { get { return ImmutableArray.Create(Rule); } }

    0 references
    public override void Initialize(AnalysisContext context)
    {
        context.ConfigureGeneratedCodeAnalysis(GeneratedCodeAnalysisFlags.None);
        context.EnableConcurrentExecution();
        // TODO: Consider registering other actions that act on syntax instead of or in addition to symbols
        // See https://github.com/dotnet/roslyn/blob/main/docs/analyzers/Analyzer%20Actions%20Semantics.md for more information
        context.RegisterSyntaxNodeAction(AnalyzeAwaitStatements, SyntaxKind.AwaitExpression);    3
    }

    1 reference
    private void AnalyzeAwaitStatements(SyntaxNodeAnalysisContext context)
    {
        if (!context.Node.DescendantNodes().OfType<IdentifierNameSyntax>().Any(j => j.Identifier.ValueText.Equals("ConfigureAwait")))
        {
            var containingMethod = context.Node.Ancestors().OfType<MethodDeclarationSyntax>().FirstOrDefault();
            if (containingMethod != null)
            {
                var diagnostic = Diagnostic.Create(Rule, context.Node.GetLocation(), containingMethod.Identifier.ValueText);
                context.ReportDiagnostic(diagnostic);
            }
        }                                                                          4
    }
}
```

Figure 6-30. *Code changes for ConfigureAwait analyzer*

I have changed the category to Reliability and modified the Initialize method to register a SyntaxNode action with the context. The code will invoke AnalyzeAwaitStatements method whenever it encounters an AwaitExpression.

The code for AnalyzeAwaitStatements is as follows:

```
private void AnalyzeAwaitStatements(SyntaxNodeAnalysisContext context)
{
        if (!context.Node.DescendantNodes().
        OfType<IdentifierNameSyntax>().Any(j => j.Identifier.ValueText.
        Equals("ConfigureAwait")))
        {
            var containingMethod = context.Node.Ancestors().OfType<Method
            DeclarationSyntax>().FirstOrDefault();
            if (containingMethod != null)
            {
```

```
            var diagnostic = Diagnostic.Create(Rule, context.Node.
            GetLocation(), containingMethod.Identifier.ValueText);
            context.ReportDiagnostic(diagnostic);
        }
    }
}
```

The code is simple to understand. The parameter of our method is of type
SyntaxAnalysisContext, which is a struct and contains the properties to get
SyntaxNode, Compilation, ContainingSymbol, SemanticModel, and Options properties
from the context. It also has a method named ReportDiagnostic that can be used to
report a diagnostic. Since we have registered our action when an AwaitExpression
is encountered, we will always get an AwaitExpression as the parameter of our
method. We have already seen earlier that ConfigureAwait code would appear as an
IdentifierName inside the SimpleMemberAccessExpression, so we look for descendant
nodes of AwaitExpression and search for Identifier named ConfigureAwait. If
it is found, there is no issue; otherwise, we create a diagnostic object and call the
ReportDiagnostic method on the context object and pass the diagnostic object as the
parameter.

Running the Diagnostic Analyzer

This completes the code for our diagnostic analyzer. We can test it by selecting the VSIX
project in solution explorer and then start debugging. We see unit testing as a way to test
the extension a little later. In the newly opened experimental instance of Visual Studio,
we will create a new console app and write a few async methods, which do not have
ConfigureAwait(false) invocation in the await statements. If our diagnostic analyzer is
coded correctly, we should see a squiggle. The sample code for our test project is shown
in Figure 6-31.

```
    0 references
    static void Main(string[] args)
    {
        Console.WriteLine("Hello World!");
    }

    0 references
    private static async Task<int> GetDataAsync()
    {
        return await Task.FromResult(2);
    }

    0 references
    private static async Task MethodAsync()
    {
        await Task.Delay(500);
    }
}
}
```

Figure 6-31. *Await statements without* `ConfigureAwait(false)`

The diagnostic analyzer is shown in action in Figure 6-32. See the squiggle under the await statements and in the error list also; we can see the error code RV001 with the description and title of this diagnostic. The line number of the issues is also displayed. Cool! And all this is done with just a few lines of code.

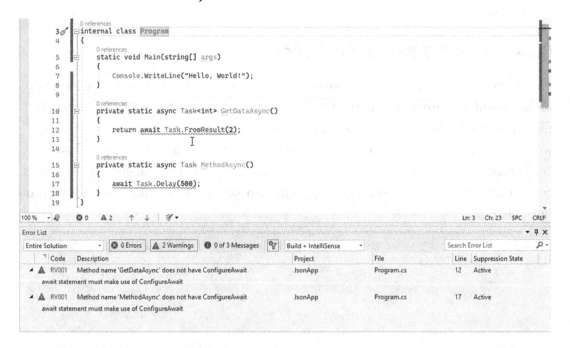

Figure 6-32. *Diagnostic analyzer in action*

Writing a Code Fix

Next let us write the code fix for this analyzer. The default code fix provider can be modified to suit our needs. Code fix provider code is rather straightforward as it has a fixed format. The `ConfigureAwaitAnalyzerCodeFixProvider` class derives from the abstract class `CodeFixProvider`. The class diagram of `CodeFixProvider` and other types relevant to the code fix provider is shown in Figure 6-33.

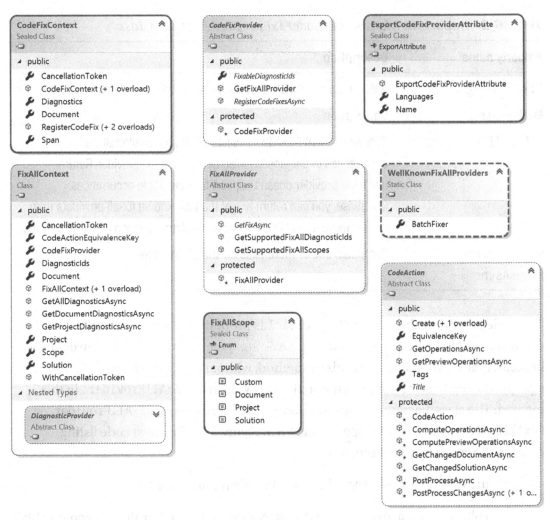

Figure 6-33. *Code fix provider*

Let us discuss this diagram as it exposes a wealth of information needed to implement a code fix provider that displays a light bulb-style code fix suggestion when we hover over the diagnostic. Deriving from the `CodeFixProvider` class marks the `ConfigureAwaitAnalyzerCodeFixProvider` class to be treated as a code fix provider. Here, we specify the title that should appear while fixing the code and implement the members of the abstract class `CodeFixProvider`. The important properties and methods of this class are discussed in brief in Table 6-2.

Table 6-2. *Important Members of CodeFixProvider Abstract Class*

Property name	Description
FixableDiagnosticIds	A list of diagnostic IDs that this provider can provide fixes for.
Method name	**Description**
GetFixAllProvider	Gets an optional `FixAllProvider` that can fix all/multiple occurrences of diagnostics fixed by this code fix provider. Returns null if the provider doesn't support fix all/multiple occurrences. Otherwise, you can return any of the well-known fix-all providers from `WellKnownFixAllProviders` or implement your own fix-all provider.
RegisterCode FixesAsync	Computes one or more fixes for the given context.

While overriding the `FixableDiagnosticIds` property, we return the same diagnostic ids that we created in our diagnostic analyzer, and we will keep the default implementation of `GetFixAllProvider` method, without any code change. We return a property called BatchFixer from the static class `WellKnownFixAllProviders` in this method. The class diagrams of type `WellKnownFixallProviders`, `FixAllProvider`, `FixAllContext`, and `FixAllScope` are shown in Figure 6-33. The next code listing displays the code we have discussed:

```
private const string title = "Use ConfigureAwait";

public sealed override ImmutableArray<string> FixableDiagnosticIds
{
```

```
    get { return ImmutableArray.Create(ConfigureAwaitAnalyzer
    Analyzer.DiagnosticId); }
}
public sealed override FixAllProvider GetFixAllProvider()
{
    // See https://github.com/dotnet/roslyn/blob/master/docs/
    analyzers/FixAllProvider.md for more information on Fix All
    Providers
    return WellKnownFixAllProviders.BatchFixer;
}
```

The main action happens in the RegisterCodeFixesAsync method, which registers a code fix on the CodeFixContext instance. The CodeFixContext class provides the context for the code fixes. The important members of CodeFixContext are documented in Table 6-3.

Table 6-3. *Important Members of CodeFixContext Class*

Property name	Description
CancellationToken	The cancellation token to support cancellation.
Diagnostics	Immutable array of diagnostics to be fixed.
Document	Document corresponding to the span to be fixed.
Span	Text span within the document to be fixed.
Method name	**Description**
RegisterCodeFix (multiple overloads)	Add supplied action to the list of fixes that will be offered to the user.

The CodeFixContext is available as a parameter to the RegisterCodeFixesAsync method that we will override. In this method, we would be calling the RegisterCodeFix method of the context, which takes a CodeAction as the parameter. A code action is an action produced by CodeFixProvider or a CodeRefactoringProvider. The important members of CodeAction abstract are documented in Table 6-4.

Table 6-4. *Important Members of CodeAction Abstract Class*

Property name	Description
EquivalenceKey	Two code actions are treated as equivalent if they have equal non-null EquivalenceKey values and were generated by the same CodeFixProvider or CodeRefactoringProvider.
Tags	Descriptive tags from WellKnownTags. These tags may influence how the item is displayed.
Title	A short title describing the action that may appear in a menu.
Method name	**Description**
ComputeOperations Async	Override this method if you want to implement a CodeAction subclass that includes custom CodeActionOperations.
ComputePreview OperationsAsync	Override this method if you want to implement a CodeAction that has a set of preview operations that are different than the operations produced by ComputeOperationsAsync(Cancel lationToken).
Create	Creates a CodeAction for a change to a single document or many documents in a solution. Use the document overload of factory when the change is inexpensive to compute, or else use the solution overload.
GetChangedDocument Async	Computes changes for a single document. Override this method if you want to implement a CodeAction subclass that changes a single document.
GetChangedSolutionAsync	Computes all changes for an entire solution. Override this method if you want to implement a CodeAction subclass that changes more than one document.
PostProcessAsync	Apply post-processing steps to a single document: reducing nodes annotated with Annotation Formatting nodes annotated with Annotation.
PostProcessChangesAsync	Apply post-processing steps to a document or solution changes, like formatting and simplification.

Now, let's proceed to complete the implementation of the `RegisterCodeFixesAsync` method. We need to do the following things:

1. Obtain the root node from the `SyntaxTree`. This is necessary to locate the AwaitExpressionSyntax that requires correction by utilizing `ConfigureAwait`.

2. Retrieve the diagnostic information and the location span where the fix needs to be applied.

3. Using the preceding collected pieces of information, identify the AwaitExpressionSyntax that requires correction.

4. Register the code action on the context object by providing the title, `EquivalenceKey`, and a `Func<CancellationToken, Task<Document>>` that will make the code fix and return the modified document.

The code for the method would now look like the following code listing:

```
public sealed override async Task RegisterCodeFixesAsync(CodeFixContext
context)
        {
            var root = await context.Document.GetSyntaxRootAsync(context.
            CancellationToken).ConfigureAwait(false);

            // TODO: Replace the following code with your own analysis,
            generating a CodeAction for each fix to suggest
            var diagnostic = context.Diagnostics.First();
            var diagnosticSpan = diagnostic.Location.SourceSpan;
            // Find the type declaration identified by the diagnostic.

            var declaration = root.FindToken(diagnosticSpan.Start).Parent.
            AncestorsAndSelf().OfType<AwaitExpressionSyntax>().First();
            // Register a code action that will invoke the fix.
            context.RegisterCodeFix(
                CodeAction.Create(
```

```
            title: title,
            createChangedDocument: c => ConfigureAwaitFalseAsync
            (context.Document, declaration, c),
            equivalenceKey: title),
        diagnostic);
}
```

Next, we need to define the method `ConfigureAwaitFalseAsync`, which needs to append `ConfigureAwait(false)` to the await expression. We have passed the document, declaration, and cancellation token parameters to this method. Appending `ConfigureAwait(false)` is straightforward if we again make use of the Syntax Visualizer tool window. We can write an await statement with `ConfigureAwait(false)` and without `ConfigureAwait(false)`, and we can come to know what all changes in `SyntaxTree` are desired to achieve this. If this sounds like work, you can also make use of this great online tool called RoslynQuoter (`http://roslynquoter.azurewebsites.net/`), which can be used to generate the code snippet of Roslyn. This is developed by Kirill Osenkov who is a Microsoft employee. This may require you to play around a little bit, but in time you should get comfortable with it.

I always make use of replace nodes method to replace an existing code statement/expression to how it should be and so I created an await expression with `ConfigureAwait(false)` and then replaced that node in the document and returned the new document back. (Remember Syntax trees and most Roslyn-based constructs are immutable.) The complete code listing for `ConfigureAwaitFalseAsync` is shown in the following snippet:

```
private async Task<Document> ConfigureAwaitFalseAsync(Document document,
ExpressionSyntax expression, CancellationToken cancellationToken)
    {

        return await this.ConfigureAwaitAsync(document, expression,
        SyntaxKind.FalseLiteralExpression, cancellationToken).
        ConfigureAwait(false);
    }

    private async Task<Document> ConfigureAwaitAsync(Document
    document, ExpressionSyntax invocationExpression, SyntaxKind
    configureAwaitLiteral, CancellationToken cancellationToken)
    {
```

```
MemberAccessExpressionSyntax memberAccessExpression
Syntax = SyntaxFactory.MemberAccessExpression(SyntaxKind.
SimpleMemberAccessExpression, invocationExpression,
SyntaxFactory.IdentifierName("ConfigureAwait"));

SyntaxToken syntaxToken = SyntaxFactory.Token(SyntaxKind.
OpenParenToken);
List<ArgumentSyntax> argumentSyntaxes = new
List<ArgumentSyntax>()
{

    SyntaxFactory.Argument(SyntaxFactory.LiteralExpression
    (configureAwaitLiteral))
};

InvocationExpressionSyntax invocationExpressionSyntax =
SyntaxFactory.InvocationExpression(memberAccessExpress
ionSyntax,
SyntaxFactory.ArgumentList(syntaxToken, SyntaxFactory.Separated
List<ArgumentSyntax>(argumentSyntaxes), SyntaxFactory.Token
(SyntaxKind.CloseParenToken)));

var root = await document.GetSyntaxRootAsync(cancellationToken).
ConfigureAwait(false);

SyntaxNode syntaxNode = SyntaxNodeExtensions.ReplaceNode
<SyntaxNode>(root, invocationExpression,
invocationExpressionSyntax);
return document.WithSyntaxRoot(syntaxNode);
}
```

The method ConfigureAwaitFalseAsync calls another private method named ConfigureAwaitAsync with the provided parameters and returns the modified Document after applying the ConfigureAwait(false) configuration. The main work happens in ConfigureAwaitAsync method.

ConfigureAwaitAsync is a private method. It starts by creating a MemberAccessExpressionSyntax named memberAccessExpression, which represents a member access operation. In this case, it creates an expression like invocationExpression.ConfigureAwait. Then, it creates a list of ArgumentSyntax objects, containing a single argument that represents the configureAwaitLiteral parameter. This argument corresponds to the value SyntaxKind.FalseLiteralExpression. Next, it constructs an InvocationExpressionSyntax named invocationExpressionSyntax representing the method invocation of ConfigureAwait with the argument false, like ConfigureAwait(false). It retrieves the syntax root of the provided Document asynchronously and assigns it to the root variable. After that, it replaces the invocationExpression in the syntax tree with the invocationExpressionSyntax, effectively adding ConfigureAwait(false) to the code. Finally, it returns a new Document with the modified syntax tree.

With this, coding for our code fix provider methods is done. There might be instances where you would want to use ConfigureAwait(true), for example, to continue an operation on the main/UI thread in a WPF or Windows Forms application. This is equivalent to not adding a ConfigureAwait call at all. Therefore, exercise caution and ensure that you understand the specific locations where the change is truly necessary when using the code fix provider. Before we test, let us quickly discuss an attribute that is decorated on the code fix provider class, so that it can be exported as a code fix provider and resolved as an MEF component part. The attribute name is ExportCodeFixProvider, which is shown in the class diagram in Figure 6-33. The updated code with the decorated attribute would look like the following snippet:

```
[ExportCodeFixProvider(LanguageNames.CSharp, Name = nameof(ConfigureAwait
AnalyzerCodeFixProvider)), Shared]
    public class ConfigureAwaitAnalyzerCodeFixProvider : CodeFixProvider
    {...}
```

There are just three parameters in the attribute: first language, name of code fix provider, and optional additional languages to which the code fix provider applies.

There is another attribute applied to the class named Shared. It indicates that instances of this class can be shared across multiple code fix requests. This helps improve performance and memory usage by reusing instances of the code fix provider rather than creating a new one for each code fix request.

Now, we are ready for testing. First, let us debug the extension (by selecting the VSIX project in solution explorer and start debugging) and then we will see how we can also leverage the test project to test the analyzer and code fix provider. In the new experimental instance, let us go back to our test console app, which we used for checking our code analyzer. Now, when we hover over the squiggle, we will see a light bulb-style icon. Clicking it shows the available code actions/fixes for that diagnostic as shown in Figure 6-34.

```
  2
               0 references
  3    ⊟internal class Program
  4     {
               0 references
  5    ⊟        static void Main(string[] args)
  6             {
  7                 Console.WriteLine("Hello, World!");
  8             }
  9

               0 references
 10    ⊟        private static async Task<int> GetDataAsync()
 11             {
 12                 return await Task.FromResult(2);
 13             }
 14

               0 references
 15    ⊟        private static async Task MethodAsync()
 16             {
 17 💡 ▾            await Task.Delay(500);
 18
 19
```

Use ConfigureAwait	▸	⊙ ⚠ Method name 'MethodAsync' does not have ConfigureAwait
Introduce constant	▸	Lines 16 to 18
Add argument name 'millisecondsDelay'		{
Convert to binary		await Task.Delay(500);
Convert to hex		await Task.Delay(500).ConfigureAwait(false);
Use expression body for method		}
Introduce parameter for '500'	▸	Preview changes
Suppress or configure issues	▸	Fix all occurrences in: Document | Project | Solution | Containing Member
		| Containing Type

Figure 6-34. *Code fix in action*

We see a context menu item as Use ConfigureAwait, and on hovering it, it displays a nice expanded view showing the DiagnosticId (RV001) and diagnostic title with the code before and after the fix. It also provides hyperlinks to Preview changes and to fix all the occurrences in Document, Project, and Solution. If we click the context menu item (Use ConfigureAwait), it updates the code in the editor and the await statement now uses ConfigureAwait(false).

There are a couple of things to consider while developing the extension. Firstly, the template for the "Analyzer with Code Fix" appends the suffix "Roslyn" instead of the regular "Exp". As a result, the extension is deployed as a distinct instance with a name ending in "Roslyn".

Secondly, if you are progressing through the steps and building the extension incrementally, it's advisable to also increment the version in the VSIXManifest. For instance, you can transition from 1.0.0 to 1.0.1 and so forth. This practice ensures that the latest modifications are accurately reflected within the extension. Updating the version is covered in Chapter 4.

Testing the Extension

We can initiate a new instance of Visual Studio to test the extension, similar to what we've done for previous extensions. However, you'll discover that debugging the extension for testing purposes can quickly become laborious and time-consuming. This is primarily because testing via debugging involves a series of time-consuming steps. Every minor code alteration prompts the extension to be built, followed by the launch of an experimental instance. Then, we must load our test project in the experimental instance of Visual Studio and wait for its complete loading before proceeding to validate that the changes are satisfactory.

To alleviate this tedious process, there exists a test project that we can capitalize on to test both the diagnostics and code fix provider. The most appealing aspect is that to test any of our analyzers or code fix providers, we need to make only a few changes to the default test project:

- The code against which we want to test our analyzer/code fix provider. For example, given that our analyzer targets await statements, we will write code featuring an await statement without `ConfigureAwait(false)`.

- The expected result, which is of type `DiagnosticResult`. Generally, we will need to specify the location of code in the expected diagnostic, which can be easily identified while specifying the code to test.

- If we want to create more tests, we can just copy and paste the existing test and change the test code and expected result.

The class diagram of the important types in the unit test project concerning Diagnostics and `CodeFixProvider` for C# is shown in Figure 6-35. I have excluded the refactoring and Visual Basic types for brevity. We have four main classes: `ConfigureAwaitAnalyzerUnitTest`,

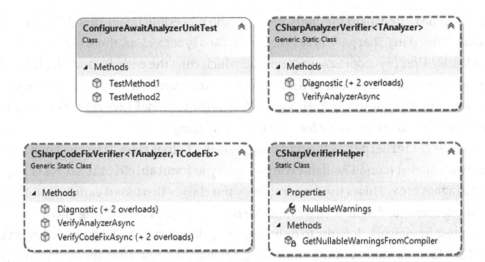

Figure 6-35. *Class diagram of unit testing project types*

`CSharpAnalyzerVerifier<TAnalyzer>`, `CSharpCodeFixVerifier<TAnalyzer, TCodeFix>`, and `CSharpVerifierHelper`. The test project makes use of the MSTest and hence references `Microsoft.VisualStudio.TestTools.UnitTesting` namespace.

The `CSharpAnalyzerVerifier<TAnalyzer>`, `CSharpCodeFixVerifier<TAnalyzer, TCodeFix>`, and `CSharpVerifierHelper` classes are utility classes used in testing C# diagnostic analyzers and code fix providers. They assist in setting up and executing tests for your analyzers and verifying the correctness of your code fixes. Let us discuss these classes:

`CSharpAnalyzerVerifier<TAnalyzer>` class is used to set up and run tests for C# diagnostic analyzers. This is a partial static class and is defined across multiple files. You provide a generic type parameter TAnalyzer, which is expected to be your custom diagnostic analyzer, and this class provides methods to verify that the analyzer produces the expected diagnostic results for specific code snippets. It has two main methods: (1) Diagnostic (+2 overloads), which returns a `DiagnosticResult` object representing an expected diagnostic, and (2) `VerifyAnalyzerAsync`, which runs the analyzer on the given source code and verifies that it produces the expected diagnostics. There is corresponding class for Visual Basic named `VisualBasicAnalyzerVerifier<TAnalyzer>` which does the same for Visual Basic language.

`CsharpCodeFixVerifier` class is used to set up and run tests for code fix providers in C#. This is a partial static class and is defined across multiple files. It provides methods for testing code fix providers that are designed to fix issues identified by diagnostic analyzers. It has three main methods shown in the preceding image. In addition to the methods defined in `CSharpAnalyzerVerifier<TAnalyzer>` class, there are a couple of overloads of `VerifyCodeFixAsync` method which runs the code fix provider on the provided source code and verifies that it produces the expected fixed code. There is corresponding class for Visual Basic named `VisualBasicCodeFixVerifier<TAnalyzer, TCodeFix>` which does the same for Visual Basic language.

`CSharpVerifierHelper` as the name suggests is a helper class. It has just one static property of interest named NullableWarnings of type `ImmutableDictionary<string, ReportDiagnostic>`. This is used internally by the classes discussed earlier. By default, the compiler reports diagnostics for nullable reference types as Warning and the analyzer test framework defaults to only validating diagnostics at `DiagnosticSeverity` of Error. This dictionary contains all compiler diagnostic IDs related to nullability mapped to `ReportDiagnostic.Error`, which is then used to enable all of these warnings for default validation during analyzer and code fix tests.

`ConfigureAwaitAnalyzerUnitTest` class will be our test entry point. It has two methods `TestMethod1` and `TestMethod2` created from a template that follows the two common patterns for an analyzer and code fix unit test. `TestMethod1` shows the pattern for a test that ensures the analyzer doesn't report a diagnostic when it shouldn't. `TestMethod2` shows the pattern for reporting a diagnostic and running the code fix. The template uses `Microsoft.CodeAnalysis.Testing` packages for unit testing.

The testing library supports a special markup syntax, including the following:

[|text|]: This indicates that a diagnostic is reported for text. By default, this form may only be used for testing analyzers with exactly one `DiagnosticDescriptor` provided by `DiagnosticAnalyzer.SupportedDiagnostics`.

> {|ExpectedDiagnosticId:text|}: This indicates that a diagnostic
> with Id ExpectedDiagnosticId is reported for text.

Unit testing of analyzer and code fix provider can be very involved and can have multiple scenarios to take care. We may need to check when a diagnostic should show and when it shouldn't show and related edge cases, so the detailed discussion of unit testing is outside the scope of current discussion. However, this discussion should be a good starting point for the readers to get started with the unit testing of the diagnostic analyzer and code fix provider. For further progress, this documentation should help https://learn.microsoft.com/en-us/dotnet/csharp/roslyn-sdk/tutorials/how-to-write-csharp-analyzer-code-fix#build-unit-tests.

Microsoft has a comprehensive walkthrough on creating a diagnostic analyzer with code fix in their official documentation. It can be seen at `https://learn.microsoft.com/en-us/dotnet/csharp/roslyn-sdk/tutorials/how-to-write-csharp-analyzer-code-fix`.

Distributing the Extension

Now, we have our diagnostic analyzer and code fix provider coded and tested. It still needs to be shared with others, so that it can be used. The analyzer can be distributed either as a NuGet package or as an extension. To create a NuGet package, we need to modify the project properties of our `CodeFixes` class library project, so right-click the class library project and then click navigate to Properties. Under the Package tab, tick on the check box for Generate NuGet package on build. This is shown in Figure 6-36. Update the other metadata information with appropriate values. Next, when we build the class library, the NuGet package for the analyzer (and code fix provider) would be generated. You can either upload this in the NuGet library or in your local NuGet feed or share with your teams as needed. Note that if you package the `CodeAnalyzer` project, only the `CodeAnalyzer` will be packaged, while on generating the package from `CodeFixes` project, both `CodeAnalyzer` and `CodeFixes` will be packaged.

On building the VSIX project, the Visual Studio extension (vsix) would be generated. As discussed, many times in previous chapters, do not forget to update the `VSIXManifest` with the appropriate metadata information like crisp description, name, tags, and icons as that is the first impression of your analyzer to the end user.

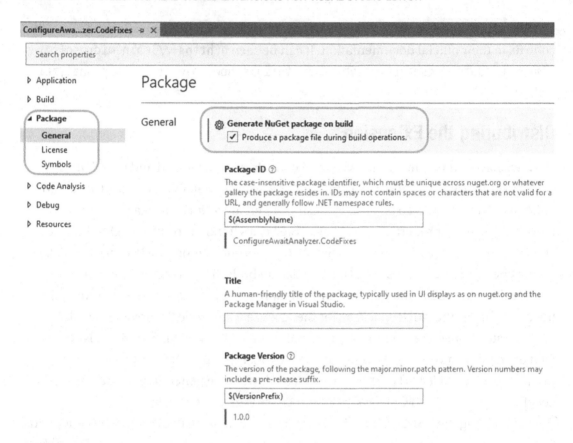

Figure 6-36. *NuGet package metadata*

This concludes our first diagnostic analyzer and code fix extension. In the next section, we will quickly code an extension for code refactoring.

Code Refactoring Extension

In our coding quest with C#, we've all encountered the use of "var" or have actively utilized it. A divergence of opinion exists concerning whether "var" should be employed or not. I've frequently engaged with coding purists who argue that "var" compromises the code's readability. It's important to remember that code is crafted for human comprehension, and readability is a pivotal consideration. Compilers and machines can understand unreadable code as well. There is no definitive right or wrong answer to this matter; it's more a question of convenience. While I personally lean toward using "var", the majority of my team held a different viewpoint. They advocated for the replacement of all occurrences of "var" with the respective strongly typed names.

Serving as the team's tooling expert, I undertook the responsibility of refactoring the entire solution – a colossal task comprising 240+ projects and over 1,000 files. The goal was to systematically replace every instance of "var" with its corresponding explicit data type. Thanks to Roslyn and its code refactoring capabilities, I managed to accomplish this feat through the implementation of a Visual Studio extension.

In this section, we will discuss a simple code refactoring that would replace the var declarations to their corresponding explicit strong type. Though Visual Studio now comes with this refactoring already built in, we will still go ahead with this extension as an educational opportunity. This approach will grant us insights into code refactoring via a straightforward example. Certain aspects in this code refactoring extension will be similar to our earlier extension on the code analyzer and code fix provider, so we will not delve into the intricacies of those sections. Let us develop this code refactoring extension by following these steps:

1. Launch Visual Studio and create a new project of type Code Refactoring as shown in Figure 6-37. Click the Next button.

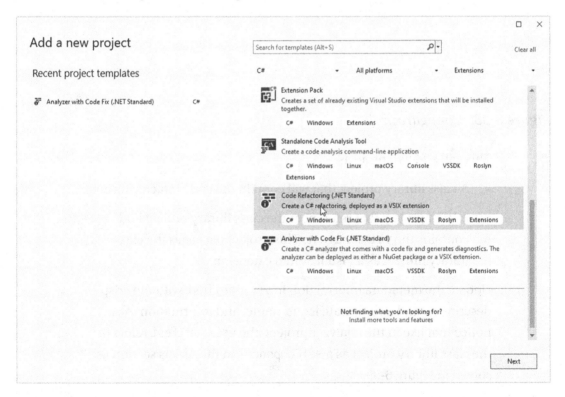

Figure 6-37. *Code Refactoring project*

2. Provide a valid name and location to the project and click the Create button as shown in Figure 6-38.

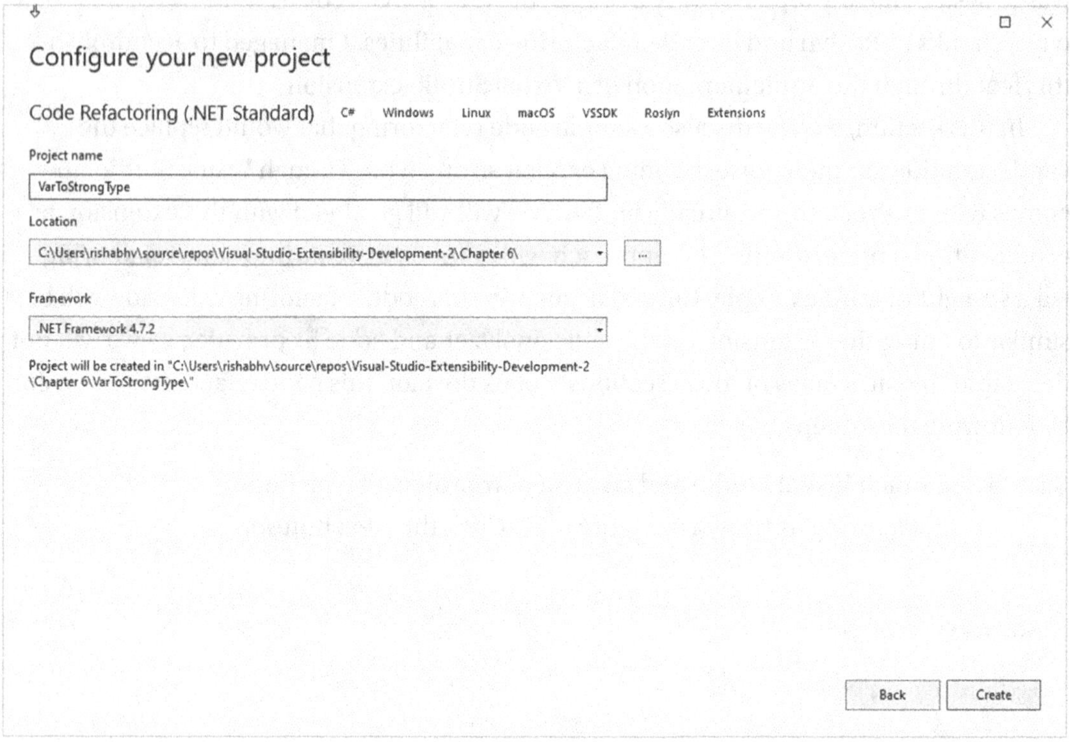

Figure 6-38. *Configure project*

This will add two projects:

- A class library project that will contain the code refactoring code.

- A VSIX project that references the class library project and contains the vsixmanifest. This project packages the class library project as a Visual Studio extension.

3. Update the metadata information in vsixmanifest with the crisp description and appropriate icons, name, and information. Also notice that like in the analyzer project, the vsixmanifest refers to the class library project as a MefComponent in the Assets section as shown in Figure 6-39.

```
<PackageManifest Version="2.0.0" xmlns="http://schemas.microsoft.com/developer/vsx-schema/2011">
  <Metadata>
    <Identity Id="VarToStrongType..119f0054-5268-4f39-b2ad-ac586921b0b9" Version="1.0" Language="en-US" Publisher="Rishabh Verma"/>
    <DisplayName>Var To Strong Type</DisplayName>
    <Description xml:space="preserve">This is a sample code refactoring extension for the .NET Compiler Platform ("Roslyn").</Description>
  </Metadata>
  <Installation>
    <InstallationTarget Id="Microsoft.VisualStudio.Community" Version="[15.0,)" />
  </Installation>
  <Dependencies>
    <Dependency Id="Microsoft.Framework.NDP" DisplayName="Microsoft .NET Framework" Source="Manual" Version="[4.5,)" />
  </Dependencies>
  <Assets>
    <Asset Type="Microsoft.VisualStudio.MefComponent" Source="Project" ProjectName="VarToStrongType" Path="|VarToStrongType|"/>
  </Assets>
  <Prerequisites>
    <Prerequisite Id="Microsoft.VisualStudio.Component.CoreEditor" Version="[15.0,)" DisplayName="Visual Studio core editor" />
    <Prerequisite Id="Microsoft.VisualStudio.Component.Roslyn.LanguageServices" Version="[15.0,)" DisplayName="Roslyn Language Services" />
  </Prerequisites>
</PackageManifest>
```

Figure 6-39. *Assets section has class library project as* MefComponent.

Coding the Extension

The default code refactoring provider class that comes up from the template is a working sample of code refactoring, though it doesn't do anything meaningful. So, we can update the same code if we understand what needs to be done. Figure 6-40 displays the class diagram of the important types used by the VarToStrongTypeCodeRefactoringProvider class.

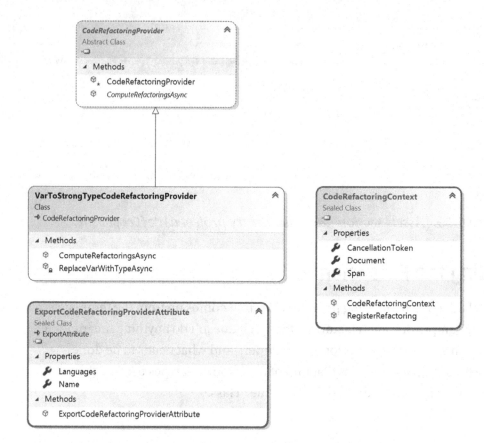

Figure 6-40. *Class diagram of types used for code refactoring*

Notice that there is a striking similarity between the code fix provider and code refactoring provider. The refactoring provider class VarToStrongTypeCodeRefactoringProvider derives from the abstract class CodeRefactoringProvider that has just one abstract method named ComputeRefactoringsAsync. This method takes a parameter of type CodeRefactoringContext, which provides a context for refactoring, and we register our code action on this context. Finally, we decorate the refactoring provider with an attribute named ExportCodeRefactoringProvider to export this code refactoring provider and resolve it as an MEF component by the hosting environment, to display UI for the refactorings. The types are very similar to the code fix provider, and their properties and methods are also similar, so we will not go into documentation of these types. However, they can be read online at https://learn.microsoft.com/en-us/dotnet/api/microsoft.codeanalysis.coderefactorings?view=roslyn-dotnet.

We have just one method to update in our `VarToStrongTyperefactoringProvider` class, namely, `ComputeRefactoringsAsync`. Here we need to provide a light bulb-style suggestion to change the declaration of type from var to its corresponding type. So, we first need to find a way to find out var declarations. To do so, we will again make use of the Syntax Visualizer tool window. We will write some variable declarations and initializations using the var keyword and notice how they show up in the `SyntaxTree`, so that we can find out the node to be searched in `SyntaxTree` for var declarations. Based on this exercise, I found out that variable declarations in methods can be identified by `LocalDeclarationStatementSyntax` as shown in Figure 6-41.

Figure 6-41. *Syntax Visualizer and local declaration*

We notice that for the var declaration, Name property of `IdentifierName` inside `VariableDeclaration` is var. Recall that var cannot be used at class level, so the `LocalDeclarationStatement` should be able to find all the local declarations, and then if we can find if it's a var, we know we need to take some action. To identify the LocalDeclarationStatement (or for any other nodes), we first need to find the root node or the compilation unit root. This is often (if not always) the first step while working with SyntaxTrees. Once we have a root, we can find the descendant nodes of type that we are looking for. This is shown in the next code listing:

```
var root = await context.Document.GetSyntaxRootAsync(context.
CancellationToken).ConfigureAwait(false);
IEnumerable<LocalDeclarationStatementSyntax> nodes = root.
DescendantNodes().OfType<LocalDeclarationStatementSyntax>();
```

Now, we have a collection of nodes that represents the local declarations. Next, we need to identify if they are var declaration or not. If we look at the properties of var IdentifierName, we see that it has a property named `IsVar`, which is set to true. This is shown in Figure 6-42. Using this, we can easily identify var declarations. And once we identify them, we can show the refactoring action to replace it with a strong type by registering the code action for refactoring.

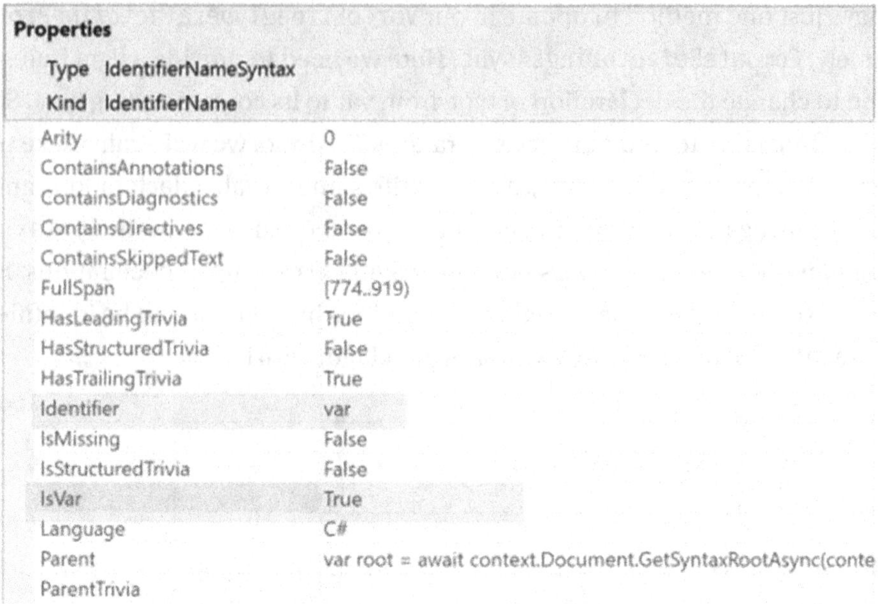

Properties	
Type IdentifierNameSyntax	
Kind IdentifierName	
Arity	0
ContainsAnnotations	False
ContainsDiagnostics	False
ContainsDirectives	False
ContainsSkippedText	False
FullSpan	[774..919]
HasLeadingTrivia	True
HasStructuredTrivia	False
HasTrailingTrivia	True
Identifier	var
IsMissing	False
IsStructuredTrivia	False
IsVar	True
Language	C#
Parent	var root = await context.Document.GetSyntaxRootAsync(conte
ParentTrivia	

Figure 6-42. *IsVar property*

The code listing for this change is shown in Figure 6-43.

```
var root = await context.Document.GetSyntaxRootAsync(context.CancellationToken).ConfigureAwait(false);
IEnumerable<LocalDeclarationStatementSyntax> nodes = root.DescendantNodes().OfType<LocalDeclarationStatementSyntax>();

foreach (var node in nodes)
{
    if (!node.Declaration.Type.IsVar)
    {
        continue;
    }

    // For any type declaration node, create a code action to replace with type
    CodeAction action = CodeAction.Create("Replace var with Type", c => this.ReplaceVarWithTypeAsync(context.Document, node, c));

    // Register this code action.
    context.RegisterRefactoring(action);
}
```

Figure 6-43. *Identifying var declarations and registering code refactoring action*

Now we need to define the ReplaceVarWithTypeAsync method, which takes the Document, LocalDeclarationStatementSyntax, and cancellation token as parameters and returns the modified and updated document with refactored code. In this method, we need to identify the actual type of var declaration and then replace the var node with that type node in the SyntaxTree and then return the document. Finding the type or getting a value is the answer that SyntaxTree cannot provide, so we need to use the Semantic model and SymbolInfo to get this information. We will do the following things in this method:

278

1. Obtain the root of the SyntaxTree, so that we can replace the var type node with the type node.

2. Obtain the semantic model of the document, so that we can identify the type of var declaration.

3. Obtain the symbol information of the declaration type from the semantic model.

4. Create a new node, which has the explicit type of declaration (to replace the var node).

5. Get the var declaration node from the local declaration statement (to replace it).

6. Replace the var node on the root object with the new node of explicit type. This will return the new modified root object.

7. Return the document with this new modified root object.

The complete code of this method is shown in Figure 6-44.

```csharp
1 reference
private async Task<Document> ReplaceVarWithTypeAsync
    (Document document,
    LocalDeclarationStatementSyntax varDeclaration,
    CancellationToken cancellationToken)
{
    SyntaxNode root = await document.GetSyntaxRootAsync(cancellationToken);

    // Get the symbol representing the type to be renamed.
    SemanticModel semanticModel = await document.GetSemanticModelAsync(cancellationToken);
    SymbolInfo typeSymbol = semanticModel.GetSymbolInfo(varDeclaration.Declaration.Type);
    var newIdentifier = SyntaxFactory.IdentifierName(typeSymbol.Symbol.ToDisplayString());

    IdentifierNameSyntax varTypeName = varDeclaration.DescendantNodes().OfType<IdentifierNameSyntax>().FirstOrDefault();
    LocalDeclarationStatementSyntax newDeclaration = varDeclaration.ReplaceNode(varTypeName, newIdentifier);
    SyntaxNode newRoot = root.ReplaceNode(varDeclaration, newDeclaration);
    return document.WithSyntaxRoot(newRoot);
}
```

Figure 6-44. ReplaceVarWithTypeAsync method

Testing the Refactoring

To test our refactoring, we will debug the extension. Select the VSIX project and start debugging. In the experimental instance of Visual Studio, create a new console project for our testing. Write some code that does the variable declaration and assignment, making use of the var keyword. If all works fine, we will see the squiggle under the variable declarations as shown in Figure 6-45.

```
0 references
static void Main(string[] args)
{
    var a = 2;
    var author = "Rishabh Verma";
    Console.WriteLine("Hello, World!");
}
```

Figure 6-45. *Variable declarations using the var keyword*

When we hover over the squiggle, we see a light bulb-style code suggestion as shown in Figure 6-46. It also displays the fixed code.

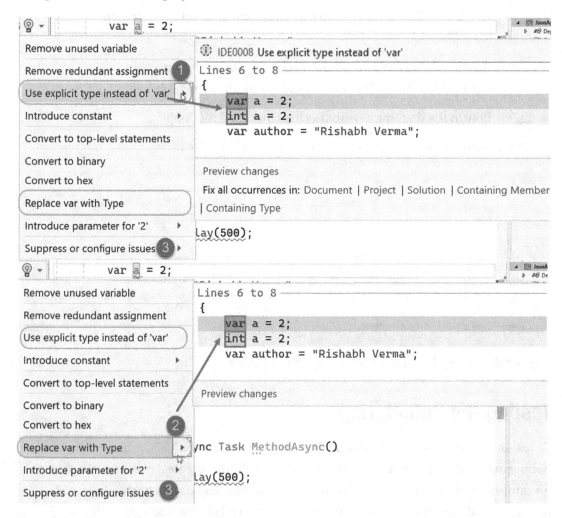

Figure 6-46. *Light bulb suggestion*

There are three important takeaways from this figure:

- There is already a refactoring that comes up with Visual Studio to use the explicit type instead of var. The #1 in the preceding figure shows the built-in Visual Studio refactoring.

- There is a Suppress or configure issues menu item (#3 in the preceding figure) that can be leveraged to get rid of squiggles or suggestions by configuring or suppressing the code action. This action makes an entry in the editorconfig file and provides a great way to have the same and consistent experience across the team.

- We can see the fixed code (**int a = 2;** immediately below **var a = 2;**). There is a link named "Preview changes," which can be used to preview the changes as shown in Figure 6-47.

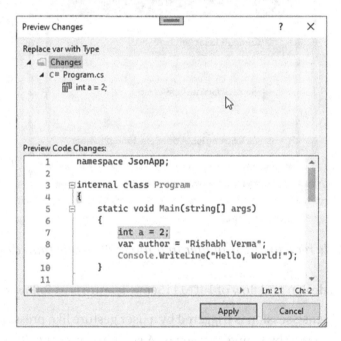

Figure 6-47. *Preview changes*

This completes our refactoring extension that can be used to refactor the var declarations to their corresponding types. This is easy to learn and implement. We just need to override and implement one method. This is summed up in a simple code map diagram in Figure 6-48.

Next, let us have a brief discussion on IntelliSense.

IntelliSense

No discussion on Visual Studio editor can go without touching upon IntelliSense. In the "Editor Extensibility" section of this chapter, there are links and code walkthroughs from the official Visual Studio documentation site, which walks through the code to extend IntelliSense. Let's quickly discuss the high-level approach to extend the IntelliSense and write an extension to extend the IntelliSense of the code comment.

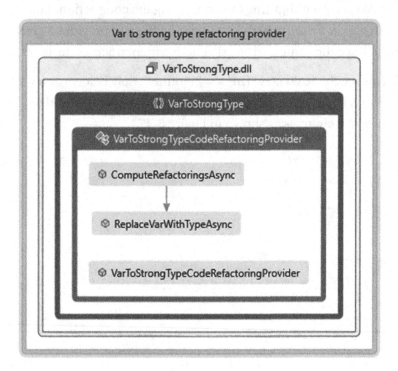

Figure 6-48. *Code refactoring provider in a nutshell – code map diagram*

The high-level design and flow of IntelliSense feature is as follows:

- IntelliSense session is triggered by a user gesture like pressing a key combination or by typing characters. A session represents the entire sequence of events right from the triggering point until the selection is committed or canceled.

- An IntelliSense controller is responsible for deciding when a session will start and end. It also decides when the item is committed or canceled.

- An IntelliSense source provides the content and decides the best match.

- An IntelliSense presenter is responsible for displaying the content.

To create an extension for IntelliSense, several key components need to be developed: a completion source and a completion source provider. These components work in conjunction and are enhanced by the utilization of attributes that define crucial metadata such as content type, order, and name. To better understand this process, let's delve into creating a simple yet illustrative extension that showcases how IntelliSense can be extended. To prevent our extension from interfering into the built-in Visual Studio IntelliSense, we will extend the IntelliSense while writing the comment. For the purpose of demonstration, we will trigger the completion when there is a specific trigger of my initials RV. Whenever the comment starts with // RV, our completion will be triggered. Let us see the steps to achieve this extension:

1. Launch Visual Studio 2022 and create a new project. Search for the project template "VSIX Project". Give the project a meaningful name like CommentIntelliSense or similar and then click Create button.

2. Next, we will add a class named CommentCompletionSource which implements the IAsyncCompletionSource interface. The instance of this class initializes the AsyncCompletionSession first by calling the InitializeCompletion method and then provides the CompletionItems through GetCompletionContextAsync. The code for class is shown in Figure 6-49. The important aspects of the code are labeled and described for easy comprehension:

   - #1: The class implements the IAsyncCompletionSource interface.

   - #2: The CommentCompletionSource class begins by initializing a static ImageElement field named _icon. This icon represents the visual aspect of the completion item and is associated with a specific identifier. The KnownMonikers.Cloud.ToImageId() method retrieves the image identifier for a cloud icon, and "elementIcon" provides a unique label for this image.

- #3: In the constructor of the `CommentCompletionSource` class, an `ImmutableArray<CompletionItem>` named `_commentItems` is populated. This collection will store the comment suggestions that will be presented to the developer. The three books authored by me are added as `CompletionItem` instances, each associated with the _icon we defined earlier for demonstrating that icons can be shown in suggestions. These books simulate the type of comment suggestions we want to offer.

- #4: To determine when the comment completion process should be activated, the `InitializeCompletion` method plays a vital role. By examining the text within the current line, this method decides whether to enable participation in the comment completion process. If the text contains the trigger // RV checked by the `HasRvTrigger` extension method on the text, the participation is enabled; otherwise, it's disabled.

- #5: To enhance the user experience, the `GetCompletionContextAsync` method is implemented. This method takes into account the user's context and triggers the presentation of comment suggestions that if the current line is not empty and contains a specific trigger ("// RV"), the `_commentItems` collection is returned, offering the list of available comment suggestions. Otherwise, an empty context is returned.

- To add a tool tip for each of the suggestion, we can implement the `GetDescriptionAsync` method.

3. Next, we will add a class named `CommentCompletionSourceProvider` which implements the `IAsyncCompletionSourceProvider` interface. This class is responsible for supplying the necessary completion source to the Visual Studio environment, ensuring that comment suggestions are available when needed. The code for class is shown in Figure 6-50. It is decorated with `[Export(typeof(IAsyncCompletionSourceProvider))]` attribute. This attribute indicates that the class exports the `IAsyncCompletionSourceProvider` type, which is an essential interface for providing asynchronous code completion sources. This declaration marks the class as a participant

in Visual Studio's extensibility framework. To refine the scope of
the completion source, the [ContentType("CSharp")] attribute is
applied to the class. This attribute identifies that the code completion
source is tailored for C# code files, ensuring that the suggestions are
relevant to C# development. A Lazy<CommentCompletionSource>
named _source is defined. This Lazy wrapper ensures that the
CommentCompletionSource instance is created only when required,
improving performance and resource utilization.

```
1 reference
internal class CommentCompletionSource : IAsyncCompletionSource   1
{
    private static readonly ImageElement _icon = new ImageElement(KnownMonikers.Cloud.ToImageId(), "elementIcon");
    private ImmutableArray<CompletionItem> _commentItems;
                                                          2
    0 references
    public CommentCompletionSource()
    {
        var list = new List<CompletionItem>
        {                                                         3
          new CompletionItem("Book 1 - .NET Core 2.0 By Example.", this, _icon),
          new CompletionItem("Book 2 - Parallel Programming With C# and .NET Core", this, _icon),
          new CompletionItem("Book 3 - Visual Studio Extensibility Development", this, _icon)
        };
        _commentItems = list.ToImmutableArray<CompletionItem>();
    }
}

    0 references
    public Task<CompletionContext> GetCompletionContextAsync(IAsyncCompletionSession session,
        CompletionTrigger trigger, SnapshotPoint triggerLocation, SnapshotSpan applicableToSpan,
        CancellationToken token)
    {                                                         5
        var containingLine = triggerLocation.GetContainingLine();
        var text = containingLine.Extent.GetText();

        if (!string.IsNullOrWhiteSpace(text) && text.IndexOf("// RV", StringComparison.OrdinalIgnoreCase) >= 0)
        {
            // Show list of available comments.
            return Task.FromResult(new CompletionContext(_commentItems));
        }

        return Task.FromResult(CompletionContext.Empty);
    }

    0 references
    public CompletionStartData InitializeCompletion(CompletionTrigger trigger, SnapshotPoint triggerLocation,
        CancellationToken token)
    {
        var containingLine = triggerLocation.GetContainingLine();
        var text = containingLine.Extent.GetText();           4
        if (text.HasRvTrigger())
        {
            return CompletionStartData.ParticipatesInCompletionIfAny;
        }

        return CompletionStartData.DoesNotParticipateInCompletion;
    }
```

Figure 6-49. CommentCompletionSource code

```
[Export(typeof(IAsyncCompletionSourceProvider))]
[ContentType("CSharp")]
[Name("Comment completion source")]
0 references                                    I
internal class CommentCompletionSourceProvider : IAsyncCompletionSourceProvider
{
    private readonly Lazy<CommentCompletionSource> _source = new Lazy<CommentCompletionSource>();

    0 references
    public IAsyncCompletionSource GetOrCreate(ITextView textView) => _source.Value;
}
```

Figure 6-50. *CommentCompletionSourceProvider code*

4.   Next, we need to wire up the Package with
     CommentCompletionSource. We add these two attributes to the
     Package class: ProvideAutoLoad and ProvideLanguageService.
     By using the [ProvideAutoLoad] attribute, the package is
     configured to automatically load in certain contexts. In this
     case, the package is set to load when the solution is not
     present (VSConstants.UICONTEXT.NoSolution_string) using
     the BackgroundLoad flag. This indicates that the package
     will load in the background when there's no active solution,
     enhancing resource efficiency. The [ProvideLanguageService]
     attribute is instrumental in bringing custom language service
     capabilities to Visual Studio. In this instance, the attribute links
     the CommentCompletionSource class, which is responsible for
     comment IntelliSense, with the C# language service. The third
     parameter of ProvideLanguageService is of type integer for
     languageResourceId which is used for localization. However, we
     are not worrying about the localization here, so we can use any
     valid integer value. One of the common values used is 106 for C#
     language service localization. The code for the two attributes in
     shown next:

     ```
     [ProvideAutoLoad(VSConstants.UICONTEXT.NoSolution_string,
     PackageAutoLoadFlags.BackgroundLoad)]
     [ProvideLanguageService(typeof(CommentCompletionSource),
     "C#", 106)]
     ```

5. As a final step, we need to update the VSIXManifest with the
    following code in the Assets section, in addition to regular
    metadata that we have updated in all the prior extensions:

```
<Asset Type="Microsoft.VisualStudio.MefComponent" Source="Project"
ProjectName="%CurrentProject%" Path="|%CurrentProject%|" />
```

This XML code defines an MEF component asset associated with
a Visual Studio project, where the asset's path and project name
are set to the current project.

The coding is now done and the extension is ready to be tested.
Hit the debug button that launches a new experimental instance
of Visual Studio. Open any C# project and type a comment
containing // RV and press Ctrl+Space and see our comment
suggestions launch. For other comments, the IntelliSense isn't
triggered. This is shown in Figure 6-51.

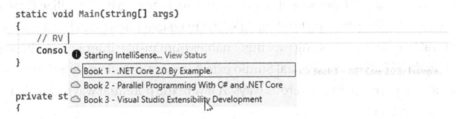

Figure 6-51. Comment suggestion in action.

This concludes our IntelliSense extension. Additionally, there are a few examples
from Mads Kristensen's extensions that will make implementation easier. One such
extension is VSCT IntelliSense, which can be debugged to gain understanding and
learn how to implement an extension on IntelliSense. The code for the extension can
be found at https://github.com/madskristensen/VsctIntellisense.

IntelliCode

Visual Studio 2022 comes up with an optional but recommended component called
IntelliCode. It should be installed by default in the Visual Studio installation if the
Visual Studio Extension development workload is selected. This was already discussed
in the starting chapters. When we trigger IntelliSense in Visual Studio 2022, it first

displays the members starting with ★ to help us with code completions. This is because of IntelliCode! It lists the most commonly used members first and then the other members. This is an awesome feature if you are writing code for a type that is not well known to you and you need to explore. With the help of IntelliCode, you already know that members starting with ★ are the most used ones and then you can use them and explore them to find the APIs and properties that you want to use. This is the power of telemetry that is collected on the API usage. On top of it, IntelliCode has a machine learning model that keeps getting trained with the usage patterns from the number of repositories, which follows best practices, so that the recommendations are good.

Enhance Visual Studio Using ChatGPT

Artificial intelligence has taken the world by storm in the last year or so, making rapid strides and impacting the technology landscape in a major way. ChatGPT is one of the prime examples. Others, such as Google Bard and Bing Chat, also exist. However, we will focus on ChatGPT because it offers an API, making it easier to utilize ChatGPT as a service. ChatGPT, powered by OpenAI's advanced language model, is a cutting-edge natural language processing tool that enables human-like interactions through text. Leveraging ChatGPT as a Visual Studio extension can significantly enhance the development experience in numerous ways. A few of the potential ways ChatGPT can add value are as follows:

- ChatGPT can provide valuable insights and explanations for code, helping developers understand complex logic, design patterns, and best practices.

- It can identify potential issues, suggest improvements, and offer guidance on code quality, making it a valuable companion for code reviews.

- ChatGPT can analyze code snippets and offer optimization suggestions to improve performance, readability, and maintainability.

- Developers can receive tailored recommendations for enhancing their code, leading to more efficient software development.

- ChatGPT can assist in identifying potential errors, vulnerabilities, and edge cases in the code.

- It can provide advice on writing effective unit tests and offer testing strategies, ultimately improving code reliability.

- Developers can write code more efficiently and with greater confidence, reducing debugging and refactoring efforts.

In summary, leveraging ChatGPT as a Visual Studio extension empowers developers with intelligent assistance, improving code quality, development speed, and knowledge transfer, making it a compelling choice for developers aiming to enhance their coding experience.

Let's explore how we can quickly create an extension that leverages ChatGPT to enhance the developer experience by performing various tasks such as code review, code explanation, and code optimization. The same can be expanded to add other functionalities like test generation as needed. But that is left to the readers as an exercise.

We will start by adding commands for these operations and grouping them in a submenu. Next, we will obtain the selected code and send it to the OpenAI API with the appropriate prompt based on the selected operation. After receiving the response, we will display it in the Output Window. The developer can stay within the IDE and harness the power of AI with just a single click. Let's proceed with the development of this extension.

1. Launch Visual Studio 2022 and create a new project. Search for the "VSIX Project" project template, and give the project a meaningful name like AICompanion or a similar name. Then, click the "Create" button.

2. Before we proceed with the code, let's sign up for access to the ChatGPT API and obtain an API key. To do this, visit `https://platform.openai.com/` and sign up. As of writing this chapter, I received a $5 free credit that can be used for making API calls (Figure 6-52).

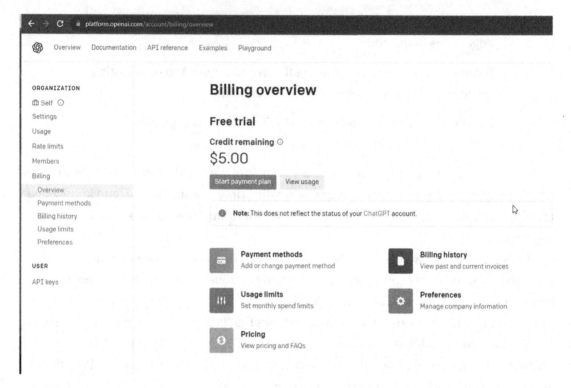

Figure 6-52. *$5 free credit*

3.   The next step is to generate an API key to make calls to the OpenAI API. Navigate to `https://platform.openai.com/account/api-keys` and create a new secret key. Ensure you copy it and securely store it because the key won't be displayed again after you close the dialog (Figure 6-53).

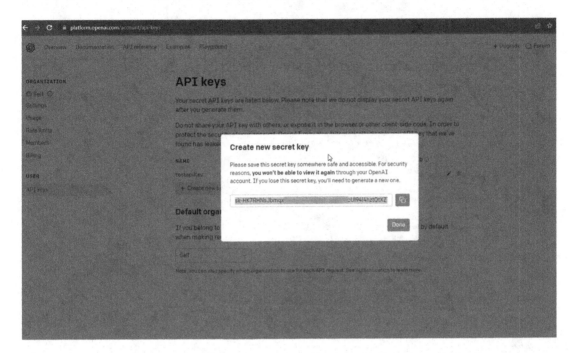

Figure 6-53. *Create new secret key*

4. After obtaining the API key, there are multiple ways to make
    the API calls. We can use the raw HttpClient or choose from
    various NuGet packages available for this purpose. It's a matter of
    preference. For this demonstration, we'll use the OpenAI package
    to abstract the complexities of making API calls. Please note that
    this is not an official NuGet package from OpenAI. It is maintained
    at https://github.com/OkGoDoIt/OpenAI-API-dotnet. So, let's
    install OpenAI NuGet package in our project.

5. Before we dive into making the API calls, let's first create the
    commands for "Review code," "Explain code," and "Optimize
    code." Since we'll be selecting within the editor and then invoking
    one of these commands, we need to add these commands to
    the code editor context menu. To add a command, right-click
    the project, add new item, and choose the "Command" item
    template under Extensibility. For a detailed step-by-step guide
    on adding a command, please refer to the extension developed in
    Chapter 4. We will create three commands, namely, "ReviewCode",

"ExplainCode", and "OptimizeCode". Once created, we will update the vsct file to group these three commands under a submenu named "ChatGPT" in the code window context menu. The code required for this are shown in Figure 6-54.

```xml
<CommandTable xmlns="http://schemas.microsoft.com/VisualStudio/2005-10-18/CommandTable" xmlns:xs="http://www.w3.org/2001/XMLSchema">
  <!--This is the file that defines the IDs for all the commands exposed by VisualStudio. -->
  <Extern href="stdidcmd.h" />
  <!--This header contains the command ids for the menus provided by the shell. -->
  <Extern href="vsshlids.h" />
  <Include href="KnownImageIds.vsct"/>      (2)
  <Commands package="guidAICompanionPackage">
    <Menus>
      <Menu guid="guidAICompanionPackageCmdSet" id="SubMenu" priority="0x0100" type="Menu">
        <Parent guid="guidAICompanionPackageCmdSet" id="MyMenuGroup"/>
        <Strings>
          <ButtonText>ChatGPT</ButtonText>              (3)
          <CommandName>ChatGPT</CommandName>
        </Strings>
      </Menu>
    </Menus>
    <Groups>
      <Group guid="guidAICompanionPackageCmdSet" id="MyMenuGroup" priority="0x0600">
        <Parent guid="guidSHLMainMenu" id="IDM_VS_CTXT_CODEWIN" />    (4)
      </Group>
      <Group guid="guidAICompanionPackageCmdSet" id="SubMenuGroup" priority="0x1100">
        <Parent guid="guidAICompanionPackageCmdSet" id="SubMenu" />    (5)
      </Group>
    </Groups>

    <Buttons>
      <Button guid="guidAICompanionPackageCmdSet" id="CodeReviewCommandId" priority="0x0100" type="Button">
        <Parent guid="guidAICompanionPackageCmdSet" id="SubMenuGroup" />   (6)
        <Icon guid="ImageCatalogGuid" id="CodeReview" />
        <Strings>
          <ButtonText>Review code</ButtonText>   (7)
        </Strings>
      </Button>
      <Button guid="guidAICompanionPackageCmdSet" id="cmdidExplainCommand" priority="0x0100" type="Button">
        <Parent guid="guidAICompanionPackageCmdSet" id="SubMenuGroup" />   (8)
        <Icon guid="ImageCatalogGuid" id="SourceControlExplorer" />
        <Strings>
          <ButtonText>Explain code</ButtonText>    (9)
        </Strings>
      </Button>
      <Button guid="guidAICompanionPackageCmdSet" id="cmdidOptimizeCommand" priority="0x0100" type="Button">
        <Parent guid="guidAICompanionPackageCmdSet" id="SubMenuGroup" />   (10)
        <Icon guid="ImageCatalogGuid" id="OptimizePivotTable" />
        <Strings>
          <ButtonText>Optimize code</ButtonText>    (11)
        </Strings>
      </Button>
    </Buttons>
  </Commands>

  <Symbols>
    <!-- This is the package guid. -->
    <GuidSymbol name="guidAICompanionPackage" value="{c4e9c827-5b52-4758-8ddf-62dc1b91769c}" />

    <!-- This is the guid used to group the menu commands together -->
    <GuidSymbol name="guidAICompanionPackageCmdSet" value="{ad3824a4-3a82-43a9-8462-79d84e77c8bb}">
      <IDSymbol name="MyMenuGroup" value="0x1020" />
      <IDSymbol name="SubMenu" value="0x1100"/>
      <IDSymbol name="SubMenuGroup" value="0x1120"/>      (1)
      <IDSymbol name="CodeReviewCommandId" value="0x0100" />
      <IDSymbol value="4129" name="cmdidExplainCommand" />
      <IDSymbol value="4130" name="cmdidOptimizeCommand" />
    </GuidSymbol>
  </Symbols>
</CommandTable>
```

Figure 6-54. *VSCT file changes*

The changes are labeled to make it easy to follow them. Let's discuss these changes:

- #1: We create two new IDSymbol elements, namely, SubMenu and SubMenuGroup, for the SubMenu, as we will be grouping these commands under a ChatGPT submenu.

- #2: We include KnownImageIds.vsct to leverage the 4K + images that come with Visual Studio.

- #3: We add a new Menu named ChatGPT. Please carefully note the id and guid attributes as well as the Parent element.

- #4: Since we want to add the commands to the code editor context menu, we update the Group parent id to IDM_VS_CTXT_CODEWIN.

- #5: To group the commands, we create a new Group with id SubMenuGroup. Note that its parent is set to SubMenu created in step #3.

- #6: We set the Parent element of the "Review Code" button to the SubMenuGroup. Similarly, #8 and #10 do the same for "Explain Code" and "Optimize Code" buttons.

- #7: We set the icon and update the botton text for the "Review Code" button. Similarly, #9 and #11 do the same for the "Explain Code" and "Optimize Code" buttons.

6. After selecting the code, the flow for each of the operations remains the same, with only the prompt sent to the OpenAI API being different. Therefore, it makes perfect sense to centralize this code in a class and then reuse that class in the three command handlers. We achieve this by adding a class named Helper. This class will perform the following:

- Retrieve the OpenAI API key from an Environment Variable or a configuration variable or the User Options Dialog. Avoid hard-coding the key at all costs. For simplicity, we will read an Environment Variable named OpenAIAPIKey, so ensure that this

Environment Variable is correctly set before using the extension. You can refer to Chapter 4, and consider making this a user input in the Options.

```
private static string s_apiKey = Environment.GetEnvironment
Variable("OpenAIAPIKey");
```

- Obtain access to the DTE2 instance and Output Window. We retrieve the service from the package only for the initial call.

```
DteInstance = DteInstance  ?? await package.
GetServiceAsync(typeof(DTE)) as DTE2;
OutputWindow = OutputWindow ?? await package.GetServiceAsync
(typeof(SVsGeneralOutputWindowPane)) as IVsOutputWindowPane;
```

- Obtain the selected text from the code editor. If no code is selected, it will display a message in the StatusBar indicating that no text is selected and avoid making the API call.

```
private static string GetSelectedText()
{
    if (!(DteInstance?.ActiveDocument?.Selection is
    TextSelection textSelection))
    {
        DteInstance.StatusBar.Text = "The selection is null or
        empty.";
        return string.Empty;
    }
    return textSelection.Text?.Trim();
}
```

- Invoke the OpenAI API passing the prompt and selected code.

```
private static async Task<string> AskChatGptAsync(string
prompt, string selectedText)
{
    var openai = new OpenAIAPI(s_apiKey);
    var query = $"{prompt} {selectedText}";
```

```
CompletionRequest completionRequest = new CompletionRequest
{
    Prompt = query,
    Model = OpenAI_API.Models.Model.DavinciText,
    MaxTokens = 1024
};

var completions = await openai.Completions.CreateCompletion
Async(completionRequest);
StringBuilder result = new StringBuilder();
foreach (var completion in completions.Completions)
{
    result.Append(completion.Text);
}
return result.ToString();
}
```

- Process the response and display it in an Output Window.

```
private static void ShowInOutputWindow(string message)
{
    ThreadHelper.ThrowIfNotOnUIThread();
    OutputWindow.OutputStringThreadSafe(message);
    OutputWindow.OutputStringThreadSafe(Environment.NewLine +
    "----------------------------------");
    OutputWindow.Activate();
}
```

- Define methods to pass the correct prompt to the OpenAI API.

```
internal static async Task ReviewSelectedCodeAsync()
{
    var prompt = "Review the code and suggest improvements";
    await AskChatGptAsync(prompt);
}
```

```
internal static async Task ExplainSelectedCodeAsync()
{
    var prompt = "Explain the code in detail";
    await AskChatGptAsync(prompt);
}

internal static async Task OptimizeSelectedCodeAsync()
{
    var prompt = "Optimize the code in detail";
    await AskChatGptAsync(prompt);
}
```

- Wire up the Helper method in the individual command handlers. This will be performed in all the three command handlers. The snippet from `CodeReviewCommand` is shown next. The same needs to be replicated for other command handlers.

  In the `InitializeAsync` method, call `InitializeAsync` method of the Helper class to initialize the DTE and Output Window. This is achieved with the following code:

  ```
  await Helper.InitializeAsync(package);
  ```

  Finally, set up the event handler by updating the `Execute` method as follows:

  ```
  private async void Execute(object sender, EventArgs e)
  {
      await Helper.ReviewSelectedCodeAsync();
  }
  ```

  With this, the coding changes are complete and we are ready to run the extension. You can find the complete source code in the book's GitHub repository.

7. Debug the project, and a new Visual Studio experimental instance will launch. Open a project in the experimental instance, open a code file, and select a piece of code. Right-click, and you will see the updated context menu with a new "ChatGPT" menu item, as shown in Figure 6-55.

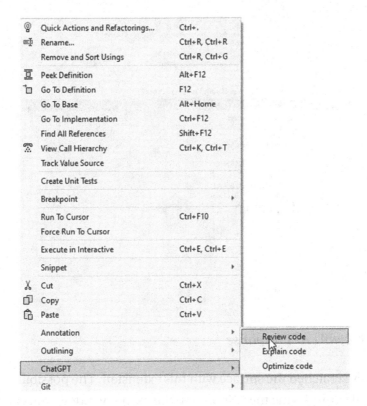

Figure 6-55. *ChatGPT commands*

8. Click "Review code" to see the Output Window (ChatGPT AI
    Assistant). It will display improvement suggestions from your
    AI companion. Figure 6-56 illustrates the selected code (#1),
    the ChatGPT AI Assistant Output Window (#2), and the OpenAI
    response (#3). Here's to a great and productive developer
    experience.

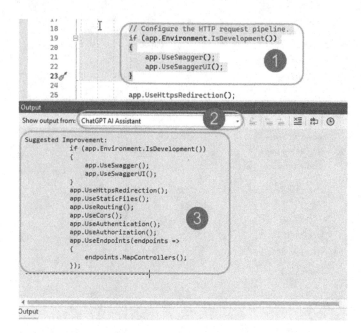

Figure 6-56. *OpenAI API response*

We have only scratched the surface with this extension. The possibilities are limitless. Instead of displaying the response in the output window, you can insert it into the editor or present it as a light bulb or refactoring suggestion. We leave this open for curious readers to explore and unleash their creativity. Please keep in mind that there is a cost associated with each API call. With this productivity-enhancing extension, we conclude this chapter.

Summary

In this chapter, we delved into the Visual Studio editor, exploring its subsystems, features, and extensibility points. We went through various documentation links and conducted code walkthroughs to extend editor features. Subsequently, we delved into diagnostic code analyzers and code fixers, gaining an understanding of their development. We then saw how to write unit tests to validate the functionality of both analyzers and code fix providers. We developed our second extension for code refactoring and learned to show light bulb-style code suggestions. Our journey further led to a concise discussion on IntelliSense, during which we conceived an extension to enhance comments, exemplifying the method of execution. Additionally, we received a brief introduction to IntelliCode. Finally, we concluded this chapter by writing an extension that harnesses the capabilities of ChatGPT to elevate developer efficiency in coding, comprehension, and optimization tasks. In the next chapter, we will develop a few more Visual Studio extensions that include code snippets, project, and item templates.

EXERCISES

The following activities are recommended to deepen your knowledge and understanding of the fundamentals we discussed in this chapter:

1. Familiarize yourself with the editor of Visual Studio by reading this great documentation at `https://learn.microsoft.com/en-us/visualstudio/extensibility/inside-the-editor?view=vs-2022#operations-subsystem`.

2. Write a diagnostic analyzer to identify unnecessary directives in a C# file.

3. Write a code fix provider for the preceding diagnostic.

4. Write the unit tests to verify the diagnostic analyzer and the code fix provider written earlier.

5. Write a code refactoring extension to sort the using directives.

6. Debug and learn the flow of implementing `IntelliSense` by debugging the following extension: `https://github.com/madskristensen/VsctIntellisense`.

Class References
Text Model Subsystem

Type name	Description
ITextBuffer	This represents a mutable sequence of UTF-16 (encoding used by System.String type in .NET) characters. The position in the buffer represents the sequence of the character starting from index 0. Any thread can edit the text buffer unless a thread takes its ownership by calling its method TakeThreadOwnership, after which only that thread can edit the buffer. As buffer represents a sequence of characters, which can be changed frequently, the buffer goes through a lot of changes during this journey and so many versions of the buffer are created. In fact, a new version is created every time the buffer is edited. Read about its properties, methods, and other members at https://learn.microsoft.com/en-us/dotnet/api/microsoft.visualstudio.text.itextbuffer?redirectedfrom=MSDN&view=visualstudiosdk-2022.
ITextBufferFactoryService	This is the factory service to create empty text buffers or a text buffer initialized from a string or TextReader. The documentation is available at https://learn.microsoft.com/en-us/dotnet/api/microsoft.visualstudio.text.itextbufferfactoryservice?redirectedfrom=MSDN&view=visualstudiosdk-2022.
ITextDocument	The text buffer can be persisted to the file system as an ITextDocument if needed. Its members and their documentation can be seen at https://learn.microsoft.com/en-us/dotnet/api/microsoft.visualstudio.text.itextdocument?redirectedfrom=MSDN&view=visualstudiosdk-2022.

(continued)

Type name	Description
ITextSnapshot	This type provides a read-only access to the snapshot of the ITextBuffer. This represents the content of the version of the text buffer. Since this is a read-only and immutable representation of the text buffer, it is thread-safe and can be accessed by any thread, even if the text buffer represented by it continues to be edited.
	The documentation can be read at https://learn.microsoft.com/en-us/dotnet/api/microsoft.visualstudio.text.itextsnapshot?redirectedfrom=MSDN&view=visualstudiosdk-2022.
SnapshotPoint	It is a struct that represents an immutable position of a character in the snapshot.
	The members of this struct are documented at https://learn.microsoft.com/en-us/dotnet/api/microsoft.visualstudio.text.snapshotpoint?redirectedfrom=MSDN&view=visualstudiosdk-2022 .
ITextSnapshotLine	This interface represents the line of text from the snapshot. Documentation can be read at https://learn.microsoft.com/en-us/dotnet/api/microsoft.visualstudio.text.itextsnapshotline?redirectedfrom=MSDN&view=visualstudiosdk-2022.
SnapshotSpan	This struct represents the immutable text span of a snapshot. The members of this struct are documented at https://learn.microsoft.com/en-us/dotnet/api/microsoft.visualstudio.text.snapshotspan?view=visualstudiosdk-2022.
NormalizedSnapshot SpanCollection	A collection of spans that are sorted by a start position, with adjacent and overlapping spans combined.
	The type is documented at https://learn.microsoft.com/en-us/dotnet/api/microsoft.visualstudio.text.normalizedspancollection?view=visualstudiosdk-2022.

(continued)

Type name	Description
ITextEdit	This type represents the set of editing operations on a text buffer. Only one ITextEdit object can be instantiated for a text buffer at any given time, and all its edits must be performed on the owning thread. Text edits can be canceled by calling the Cancel or Dispose method of ITextEdit.
	Documentation URL for this type is at https://learn. microsoft.com/en-us/dotnet/api/microsoft. visualstudio.text.itextedit?view=visualstudios dk-2022.
ITextChange	Describes a single contiguous text change operation on the text buffer.
	https://learn.microsoft.com/en-us/dotnet/api/ microsoft.visualstudio.text.itextchange?view=v isualstudiosdk-2022
ITrackingPoint	This type represents the position of a character in the text buffer. It can be accessed from any thread.
	The documentation of this type is available at https:// learn.microsoft.com/en-us/dotnet/api/ microsoft.visualstudio.text.itrackingpoint?vie w=visualstudiosdk-2022.
ITrackingSpan	A span of text in an ITextBuffer that grows or shrinks with changes to the text buffer. The span may be empty. It can be accessed from any thread.
	https://learn.microsoft.com/en-us/dotnet/api/ microsoft.visualstudio.text.itrackingspan?view =visualstudiosdk-2022

Content Types

Type Name	Description
ContentTypeDefinition	This sealed class defines the content type.
	Documentation URL is at https://learn.microsoft.com/en-us/dotnet/api/microsoft.visualstudio.utilities.contenttypedefiniti on?view=visualstudiosdk-2022.
IContentType RegistryService	This type represents the service that contains the definitions of different content types.
	This type of documentation is available at https://learn.microsoft.com/en-us/dotnet/api/microsoft.visualstudio.utilities.icontenttyperegistryservice?view=visualstudiosdk-2022.
ContentTypeAttribute	This attribute associates a file extension with the specific content type.
	This type is documented at https://learn.microsoft.com/en-us/dotnet/api/microsoft.visualstudio.utilities.contenttypeattribute?view=visualstudiosdk-2022.

Text View Types

Type Name	Description
ITextView	Represents a view of text in an ITextBuffer. It is the base class for a platform-specific interface that has methods to allow the formatted text to be rendered.
TextViewModel	Gets the ITextViewModel of the text view.
ITextViewModel	Gets a read-only list of the ITextViewLine objects rendered in the view.
ITextViewMargin	Represents the margin that is attached to an edge of an ITextView.
IWpfTextView MarginProvider	Creates an IWpfTextViewMargin for a given IWpfTextViewHost.

(continued)

Type Name	Description
IWpfTextViewHost	Contains an IWpfTextView and the margins that surround it, such as a scrollbar or line number gutter.
ITextViewLine	Represents text that has been formatted for display in a text view.
IFormattedLineSource	Generates formatted line from text snapshots.

Diagnostic Analyzer

- DiagnosticDescriptor: https://learn.microsoft.com/en-us/ dotnet/api/microsoft.codeanalysis.diagnosticdescriptor?vie w=roslyn-dotnet

Property Name	Description
Category	The category of the diagnostic (like Design, Naming, etc.).
CustomTags	Custom tags for the diagnostic.
DefaultSeverity	The default severity of the diagnostic.
Description	An optional longer localizable description for the diagnostic.
HelpLinkUri	An optional hyperlink that provides more detailed information regarding the diagnostic.
Id	A unique identifier for the diagnostic.
IsEnabledByDefault	Returns true if the diagnostic is enabled by default.
Message Format	A localizable format message string, which can be passed as the first argument to Format(String, Object[]) when creating the diagnostic message with this descriptor.
Title	A short localizable title describing the diagnostic.
Method name	**Description**
GetEffective Severity	Gets the effective severity of diagnostics created based on this descriptor and the given CompilationOptions.

Diagnostic: https://learn.microsoft.com/en-us/dotnet/api/microsoft. codeanalysis.diagnostic?view=roslyn-dotnet

Property Name	Description
Additional Locations	Gets an array of additional locations related to the diagnostic. Typically, these are the locations of other items referenced in the message.
Default Severity	Gets the default DiagnosticSeverity of the diagnostic's DiagnosticDescriptor.
Descriptor	Gets the diagnostic descriptor, which provides a description about a Diagnostic.
Id	Gets the diagnostic identifier. For diagnostics generated by the compiler, this will be a numeric code with a prefix such as "CS1001."
IsSuppressed	Returns true if the diagnostic has a source suppression, that is, an attribute or a pragma suppression.
IsWarning AsError	Returns true if this is a warning treated as an error; otherwise, it returns false.
Location	Gets the primary location of the diagnostic, or None if no primary location.
Properties	Gets property bag for the diagnostic. It will return Empty if there is no entry. This can be used to put diagnostic specific information you want to pass around, for example, to the corresponding fixer.
Severity	Gets the effective DiagnosticSeverity of the diagnostic.
WarningLevel	Gets the warning level. This is 0 for diagnostics with severity Error; otherwise, it is an integer between 1 and 4.

AnalysisContext

Member Name	Description
ConfigureGenerated CodeAnalysis	Configure analysis mode of generated code for this analyzer. Non-configured analyzers will default to an appropriate default mode for generated code. It is recommended for the analyzer to invoke this API with the required GeneratedCodeAnalysisFlags setting.

(continued)

Member Name	Description
EnableConcurrent Execution	Enable concurrent execution of analyzer actions registered by this analyzer. An analyzer that registers for concurrent execution can have better performance than a nonconcurrent analyzer. However, such an analyzer must ensure that its actions can execute correctly in parallel.
RegisterCodeBlockAction	Register an action to be executed after semantic analysis of a method body or an expression appearing outside a method body. A code block action reports Diagnostics about code blocks.
RegisterCodeBlock StartAction	Register an action to be executed at the start of semantic analysis of a method body or an expression appearing outside a method body. A code block start action can register other actions and/or collect state information to be used in diagnostic analysis, but cannot itself report any Diagnostics.
RegisterCompilationAction	Register an action to be executed for a complete compilation. A compilation action reports Diagnostics about the Compilation.
RegisterCompilation StartAction	Register an action to be executed at compilation start. A compilation start action can register other actions and/or collect state information to be used in diagnostic analysis, but cannot itself report any Diagnostics.
RegisterOperation Action	Register an action to be executed at completion of semantic analysis of an IOperation with an appropriate Kind. An operation action can report Diagnostics about IOperations and can also collect state information to be used by other operation actions or code block end actions.
RegisterOperation BlockAction	Register an action to be executed after semantic analysis of a method body or an expression appearing outside a method body. An operation block action reports Diagnostics about operation blocks.

(continued)

Member Name	Description
RegisterOperation BlockStartAction	Register an action to be executed at the start of semantic analysis of a method body or an expression appearing outside a method body. An operation block start action can register other actions and/or collect state information to be used in diagnostic analysis, but cannot itself report any Diagnostics.
RegisterSemantic ModelAction	Register an action to be executed at completion of semantic analysis of a document, which will operate on the SemanticModel of the document. A semantic model action reports Diagnostics about the model.
RegisterSymbolAction	Register an action to be executed at completion of semantic analysis of an ISymbol with an appropriate Kind. A symbol action reports Diagnostics about ISymbols.
RegisterSymbol StartAction	Register an action to be executed at the start of semantic analysis of an ISymbol and its members with an appropriate Kind.
RegisterSyntax NodeAction	Register an action to be executed at completion of semantic analysis of a SyntaxNode with an appropriate Kind. A syntax node action can report Diagnostics about SyntaxNodes and can also collect state information to be used by other syntax node actions or code block end actions.
RegisterSyntax TreeAction	Register an action to be executed at completion of parsing of a code document. A Syntax tree action reports Diagnostics about the SyntaxTree of a document.
TryGetValue	Attempts to compute or get the cached value provided by the given valueProvider for the given text. Note that the pair {valueProvider, text} acts as the key. Reusing the same valueProvider instance across analyzer actions and/or analyzer instances can improve the overall analyzer performance by avoiding recomputation of the values.

CHAPTER 7

Snippets, Templates, and More...

So far, we have developed and discussed a diverse range of extensions, spanning custom commands, tool windows, notifications, code generation, code editor, IntelliSense, code analysis, and refactoring. As a developer, we spend most of our time in coding, developing, and debugging, so in this chapter, we will look at ways by which we can enhance our productivity while coding and debugging. We will begin with a discussion on code snippets, then move on to project and item templates. Next, we will have a look at adding a connected service provider. Finally, will discuss a generic approach to debug an extension. Let's get things underway!

Code Snippets

The cardinal rule of boosting productivity dictates that tasks done repeatedly should be automated, as long as the cost of automation doesn't outweigh its benefits. As software developers, the lion's share of our time is spent in coding, so anything that can make us more productive is particularly enticing. While coding in C#, we do a lot of repetitive tasks, for example, defining properties in plain old CLR object (POCO) classes, writing "try-catch" blocks or iteration loops like "for", "foreach", "while", and many more. These constructs are very frequently used in our day-to-day C# coding. So, it would be highly productive, efficient, and time-saving if we don't have to write the entire structure of these constructs every time we use them. Fortunately, the Microsoft Visual Studio team already has taken cognizance on this aspect and introduced "Code Snippets."

The dictionary defines a "snippet" as a brief extract or a small piece. In the realm of coding, code snippet means a small piece or block of code that can be inserted and used in the code-enhancing coding efficiency. The piece of code can be a method, method block, property, or an entire class. Code snippets can be seamlessly inserted via a context menu in the code editor or from a specific key combination. Code snippets may have placeholders that can be replaced with appropriate names or types that make them very flexible. Therefore, code snippets are very handy and can save a lot of time in coding and development. Visual Studio code snippets are tied to a specific language so we have snippets organized for C#, C++, VB, etc.

In this section, we see code snippets in action, learn the anatomy of code snippets, and then develop a couple of code snippets.

Visual Studio 2022 ships with numerous code snippets. To see the list of code snippets, we can open the "Code Snippets Manager" by the navigation shown in Figure 7-1. Click the top Tools menu and then click Code Snippets Manager. Alternatively, you can also use the key combination Ctrl+K, Ctrl+B.

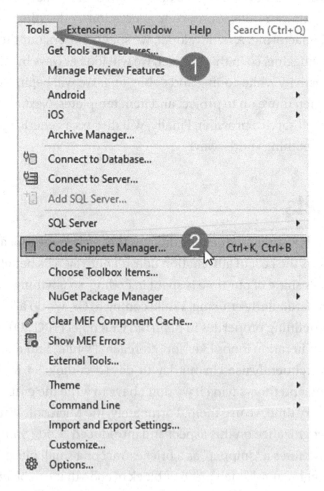

Figure 7-1. *Open Code Snippets Manager*

This will launch the Code Snippets Manager as shown in Figure 7-2. The important sections of the manager UI are labeled with numbers in the figure. The numbers are described as follows.

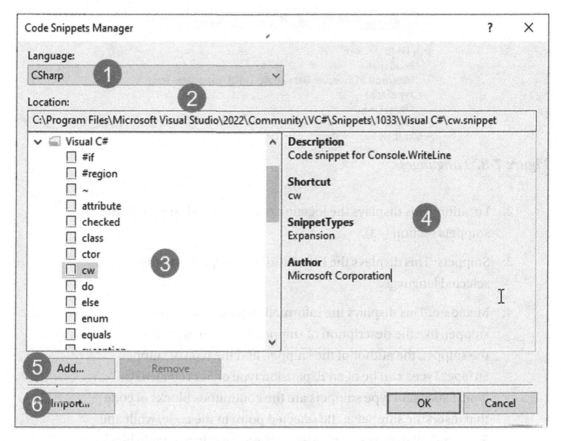

Figure 7-2. *Code Snippets Manager*

1. Language: This drop-down specifies the language for which the snippets will be displayed. In Figure 7-2, the selected language is C#. Figure 7-3 shows the supported languages in my code snippets manager.

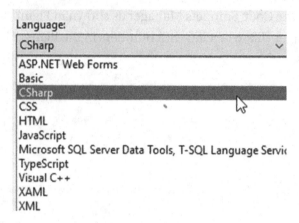

Figure 7-3. Languages

2. Location: This displays the location of the selected snippet in the snippets section (#3).

3. Snippets: This displays the list of available snippets for the selected language.

4. Metadata: This displays the information about the selected snippet, like the description of snippet, the shortcut to use the snippet, the author of the snippet, and the type of snippet. SnippetTypes can be of an Expansion type or SurroundsWith type. Expansion type snippets are the continuous blocks of code that insert the snippet at the selected point in the code, while the SurroundsWith type snippet can enclose the selected code block with the snippet like tryf (try finally). We will discuss them in a short while.

5. Add and Remove: You can add a directory containing snippets from the file system by clicking the "Add" button. You can select a folder and click the "Remove" button to remove that folder.

6. **Import**: This is to import the snippet files.

   A few of the commonly used C# snippets with their description are shown in Table 7-1.

Table 7-1. *Commonly Used C# Code Snippets*

Snippet	Description
~	The snippet for destructor
class	The snippet for class
ctor	The snippet for constructor
cw	The snippet for `Console.Writeline( )`
do	The snippet for do-while loop
enum	The snippet for enum
equals	The snippet for implementing Equals( ) according to guidelines
exception	The snippet for exception
for	The snippet for "for" loop
forr	The snippet for reverse for loop
foreach	The snippet for foreach loop
if	The snippet for if condition
indexer	The snippet for property indexer
interface	The snippet for interface
lock	The snippet for lock synchronization construct
prop	The snippet for property with automatic getter and setter
propfull	The snippet for property with backing field
propg	The snippet for Code snippet for an automatically implemented property with a "get" accessor and a private "set" accessor
switch	The snippet for switch statement
try	The snippet for try catch
tryf	The snippet for try finally
using	The snippet for using block
while	The snippet for while loop

Now that we have seen the commonly available and frequently used C# code snippets, let us watch them in action.

For this demonstration, I will be working on a console application. Inside my static void Main, I wish to iterate over a loop, perform some manipulations, and subsequently display the results in the console. To keep the application safe from an ungraceful exit due to exceptions, I also want to wrap the code inside a try-catch block and log the exception. This sounds like a very simple program and should not take more than a few minutes to get coded and operational. We will see how using code snippets makes it even faster and easy.

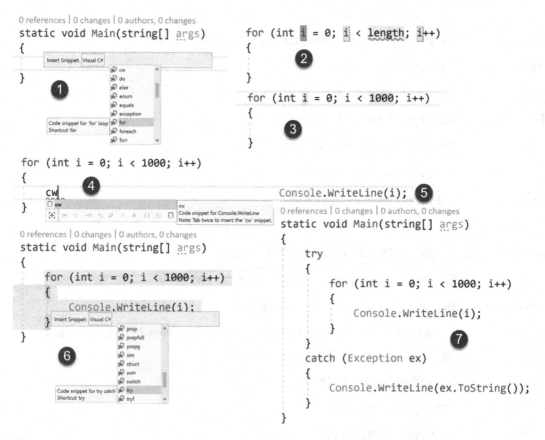

Figure 7-4. *Using code snippets*

Figure 7-4 illustrates how the code for our discussed scenario can be written using code snippets. The steps are numbered in the image for easy comprehension:

1. In the static void Main (snippet shortcut svm) of my console application, I invoke the insert snippet command, by the right-click context menu or by using the key combination Ctrl+K, Ctrl+X. Then under Visual C# language category, I click "for" in the IntelliSense displaying available snippets. This step illustrates one way of triggering the snippet, that is, by invoking the Insert Snippet command.

2. The code for the for loop gets inserted. Notice that the formatting of the variable length and i is different. This is because they are the placeholders and their values can be edited/modified. So, I just edit the value of length variable and press enter.

3. This displays the updated code of the for loop.

4. Now we need to print the loop variable in the console. To do so, we will use another way to consume the snippet and that is to use the snippet shortcut. So, we will directly type cw as the shortcut of the snippet and then tab twice.

5. This will generate the code for Console.WriteLine(), to which we pass the loop variable.

6. Our loop code is done. We need to wrap it up inside a try-catch block for defensive coding. To do so for illustration, I will select the entire loop code and invoke the Snippet ➤ Surrounds With either from the right-click context menu (Snippet ➤ Surround With) or by using the key combination Ctrl+K, Ctrl+S, and then choosing try from the drop-down and pressing enter. This will surround the selected code with the try block.

7. This is our final code that meets our simple requirement and is ready.

We just saw how to make use of snippets and get super productive in writing our code faster. In the next section, we will see the anatomy of a code snippet. We'll also explore how we can create code snippets for our project-specific scenarios. Moreover, we'll discuss how we can share the snippets, to enhance collaboration.

Anatomy of a Code Snippet

Code snippets are really just XML files. If you open the location (depicted by #2 in Figure 7-2) in Windows file explorer, you will see a bunch of .snippet files in the directory. Let us open the `for.snippet` file in Visual Studio. This is illustrated in Figure 7-5.

Figure 7-5. *Opening* for.snippet *XML file*

We will utilize the "`for.snippet`" file to understand the structure of a snippet file. Let's explore the structure of the code snippet XML file. The first line declares that the snippet file is indeed an XML file. Its root element is named `CodeSnippets` and it adheres to a schema specified in its xmlns attribute. Visual Studio has a great support for `IntelliSense` to author snippet files. This is illustrated in Figure 7-6. When we open the tag inside the `CodeSnippets` root element (#2), `IntelliSense` presents the available applicable element, which in this case is just `CodeSnippet`. This is in line with the convention that Microsoft consistently follows: a collection and then individual elements inside it. CodeSnippet has a required attribute named Format, which takes the string in "x.x.x" format, representing the version (where x is a numeric value, e.g., 1.0.0). Likewise, the CodeSnippet element can have a Header element (#3), and a Header element can have many metadata tags for the snippet like Author, Description, HelpUrl, Keywords, Shortcut, SnippetTypes, and Title (#4). Once the Header element is closed and we open a tag, we will see the Snippet element (#5), which contains the actual code snippet. Snippet can have following child elements: Code, Declaration, Imports, and References (#6). Putting it all together, the entire snippet is shown in #7.

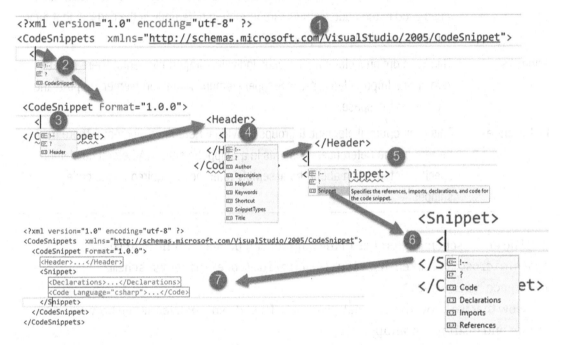

Figure 7-6. *Snippet XML Structure*

Though the elements are self-explanatory, let us quickly discuss the important child elements of the Snippet element as knowing them is essential to understand and author a snippet. See Table 7-2.

Table 7-2. *Child Elements of Snippet Element*

Element Name	Description
Code	This is a required element. It specifies the code that you want to insert into a documentation file. There must be exactly one Code element in a Snippet element.
Declarations	This is an optional element. It specifies the literals and objects that make up the parts of a code snippet that you can edit. There may be zero or one Declarations element in a Snippet element. The literals and objects defined in the declarations, when used in the Code element, are formatted differently in the code so that they can be easily identified as placeholders.
Imports	This is an optional element. It groups individual Import elements. There may be zero or one Import element in a Snippet element. An Import element imports the specified namespace.
References	This is an optional element. It groups individual Reference elements. There may be zero or one References elements in a Snippet element. A Reference element specifies information about the assembly references required by the code snippet.

The entire schema reference of the snippet can be read online at `https://learn.microsoft.com/en-us/visualstudio/ide/code-snippets-schema-reference?view=vs-2022`.

Now that we know the internal structure of a code snippet, let us see how we can author and distribute a snippet.

Developing and Distributing Code Snippets

In this section, we will develop a snippet from scratch and discuss other possible approaches to create snippets.

Snippet file is just an XML, so we can easily author a snippet file and package it as an extension to distribute it to others. Surprisingly, Visual Studio 2022 doesn't ship with a code snippet for async methods, which are very widely used now. Let us look at the high-level steps to author a snippet to write async methods quickly. We will write a snippet for async method, which has a return type. Here are the steps to do so:

1. Create an **Empty** VSIX project. Provide a valid name and location for the project. Note the emphasis on Empty as that is a different template from the ones we have used in the previous chapters. In my case, I have named it AsyncSnippet.

2. Generally, we will not create and ship a single snippet but several snippets at a time. Also, if we look at how built-in Visual Studio snippets are grouped in the file system (see Figure 7-2), they are grouped in a folder or directory. So, we will create a new subfolder (named async or anything you want) in our project.

3. Next, we will add the following two files to the async folder:

    a. `async.snippet`: The code snippet file

    b. `async.pkgdef`: To register the snippet

4. Ensure that you hit the F4 button on each of the preceding files in the Solution Explorer and update the properties as shown in Figure 7-7.

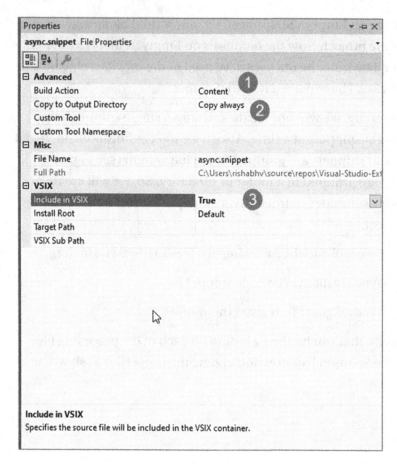

Figure 7-7. *Properties*

5. Next, update the .vsixmanifest file. Just like for every extension, provide valid and crisp metadata information. It's important to update the Assets section of the manifest to include the pkgdef file as an asset, so that the snippet can be registered. The updated Assets section is shown in Figure 7-8.

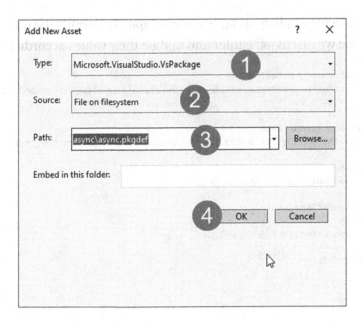

Figure 7-8. *Add pkgdef as Asset*

6. Now, we need to update the `.snippet` and `.pkgdef` files (as they are empty), and we will be done with our snippet extension. Let's update the `.pkgdef` file first as shown in Figure 7-9.

```
[$RootKey$\Languages\CodeExpansions\CSharp\Paths]
"Async"="$PackageFolder$"
```

Figure 7-9. *.pkgdef file code*

Taking the clue from this file, we can see that to add snippet for other languages, we need to replace the CSharp with appropriate supported language. This will create an entry in the registry as discussed earlier. The folder in which the snippet is kept is the second line, which is set to the "$PackageFolder$".

Now, we will create the async snippet. To leverage the IntelliSense support of Visual Studio, let us first add the root element CodeSnippets and specify its schema in the xmlns attribute of this element to http://schemas.microsoft.com/VisualStudio/2005/CodeSnippet. The root element now looks as follows:

```
<CodeSnippets xmlns="http://schemas.microsoft.com/VisualStudio/2005/
CodeSnippet">
```

Now IntelliSense will help us author the snippet. Let's open the tags and we will get all the tags that we discussed earlier and update their values accordingly.

```xml
<?xml version="1.0" encoding="utf-8" ?>
<CodeSnippets xmlns="http://schemas.microsoft.com/VisualStudio/2005/CodeSnippet">
  <CodeSnippet Format="1.0.0">
    <Header>
      <Author>Rishabh Verma</Author>
      <Description>The snippet to author async method with a return type.</Description>
      <Keywords>
        <Keyword>async</Keyword>
        <Keyword>non-void return types</Keyword>
      </Keywords>
      <Shortcut>async</Shortcut>
      <SnippetTypes>
        <SnippetType>Expansion</SnippetType>
      </SnippetTypes>
      <Title>async</Title>
    </Header>
    <Snippet>
      <Declarations>
        <Literal>
          <ID>returnType</ID>
          <Default>int</Default>
          <ToolTip>The return type of the method.</ToolTip>
        </Literal>
        <Literal>
          <ID>methodName</ID>
          <Default>MyMethod</Default>
          <ToolTip>The name of the method</ToolTip>
        </Literal>
      </Declarations>
      <Imports>
        <Import>
          <Namespace><![CDATA[System.Threading.Tasks]]></Namespace>
        </Import>
      </Imports>
      <Code Language="csharp">
        <![CDATA[public async Task<$returnType$> $methodName$Async()
        {
            return await Task.FromResult(default($returnType$));
        }]]></Code>
    </Snippet>
  </CodeSnippet>
</CodeSnippets>
```

Figure 7-10. *async.snippet file*

Because we want the return type and method name to appear as a placeholder so that we can change their values, we will declare these as literals. Also, to use Task constructs, we need a reference to the System.Threading.Tasks namespace, which is defined under the Namespace element inside Import element. The complete snippet is shown in Figure 7-10. It is very easy to understand.

We are done with our first snippet extension. If we debug the extension and see the Code Snippets Manager in the new experimental instance that launches, we see a new folder named async for the CSharp language. This is shown in Figure 7-11.

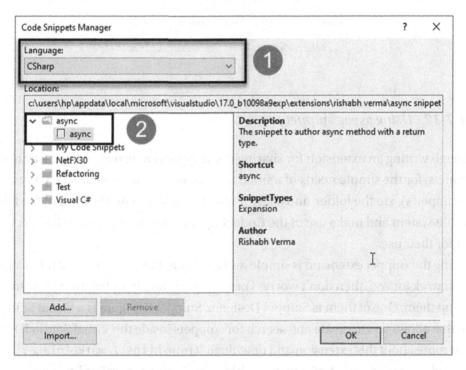

Figure 7-11. *New async folder and snippet*

To use the snippet, either use the right-click context menu command in the code editor to insert the async snippet, or even simpler, just type async and press the tab key twice, and the code would be inserted at the insertion point marker as shown in Figure 7-12. The highlighted code shows the code inserted by the snippet. Notice the difference in color shades for int and MyMethod, re-emphasizing the point that these literals are placeholders. Also notice that the using directive for System.Threading. Tasks is added at the top automatically.

```
using System.Threading.Tasks;
namespace JsonApp
{
    0 references
    internal class Program
    {
        0 references
        static void Main(string[] args)
        {
            Console.WriteLine("Hello, World!");
        }

        0 references
        public async Task<int> MyMethodAsync()
        {
            return await Task.FromResult(default(int));
        }
    }
}
```

Figure 7-12. *Using async snippet*

Though writing an extension for sharing the snippet is a recommended way to share the snippets, for the simple needs of a small team or individual developers, you can just create snippet(s), zip the folder, and share it with them. They can then unzip the folder in their file system and make use of the Code Snippets Manager to add or import the snippet for their use.

Writing the snippet extension is simple and easy, but if writing it from scratch appears too much work for you, then don't worry. There are tools and templates available to help us develop them. One of them is Snippet Designer. Snippet Designer is a Visual Studio plug-in that allows you to create and search for snippets inside the Visual Studio IDE. You can read more about this extension and download it from `https://marketplace.visualstudio.com/items?itemName=vs-publisher-2795.SnippetDesigner2022`.

Templates can be helpful in enhancing productivity and save us from doing repetitive tasks. We will discuss templates in the next section. Visual Studio exposes two types of templates: project templates and item templates.

Project and Item Templates

Visual Studio project and item templates offer reusable stubs that provide users with fundamental boilerplate code and structures that can be customized for their specific purposes. While working on various samples in this book, we have made use of various project and item templates while creating extensions. These templates have really eased a lot of our work, which otherwise would have taken a lot of time and repetitive code and tasks. Just to reiterate, all the projects that I develop and work on are based on some template or the other. When we create a new project in Visual Studio, it is based on a template. When we add a new item in a project, there we make use of an item template. Since we have used the templates so many times and know their importance, let us directly see ways to create a project and item template. In the preceding section, we created an extension for a snippet. Let us see how we can create a template out of that extension project. The steps are as follows:

1. On the top menu, click Project ➤ Export Template as shown in Figure 7-13.

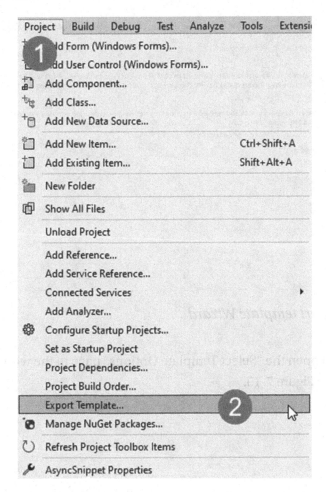

Figure 7-13. *Export Template*

2. This will open the "Export Template Wizard" dialog as shown in Figure 7-14. From here, we can create a Project template as well as an Item template. Right now, we will create a project template (item template will be created later), so we will select the project template in the dialog. Toward the bottom of the dialog, select the project from which the template would be created. This is shown in Figure 7-15. After choosing the right project, click the Next button.

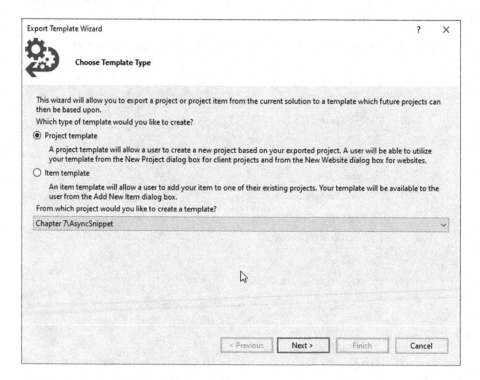

Figure 7-14. *Export template Wizard*

3. This will open the "Select Template Options" page in the wizard as shown in Figure 7-15.

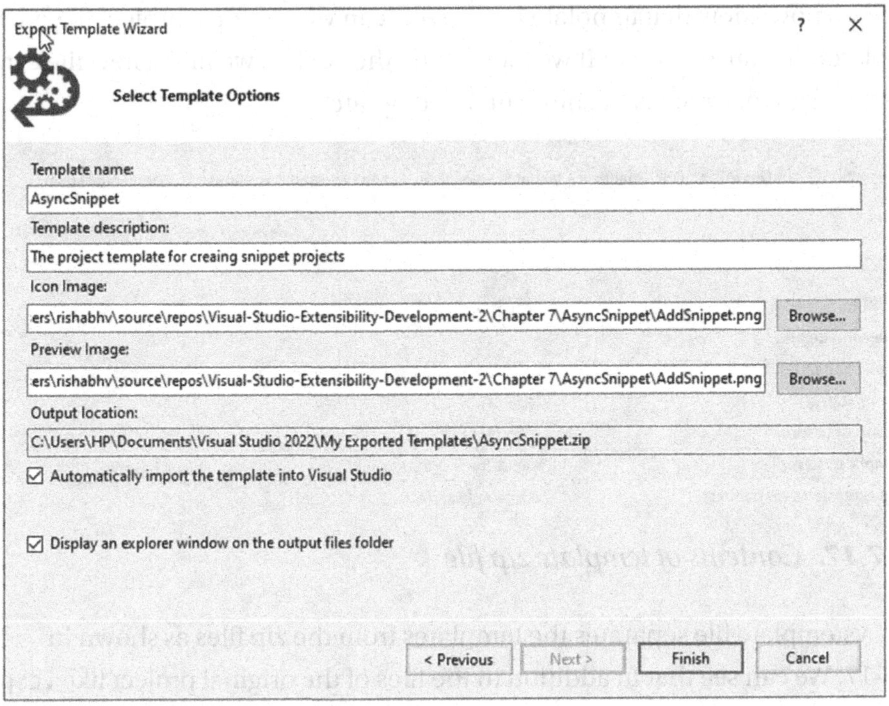

Figure 7-15. *Select Template Options page*

Here we can specify the name of the template, its description, icon image, preview image, and if the template should be imported into Visual Studio. This metadata information would be used to display the template name, description, icon, and preview image when we create a new project from the template. I have also checked the check box to display the explorer window after the template is generated. Click the Finish button.

The template is now successfully exported from the selected project and imported in Visual Studio. Since the check box to display explorer window was ticked, a windows file explorer window would open the directory where the exported template zip is generated. This is shown in Figure 7-16.

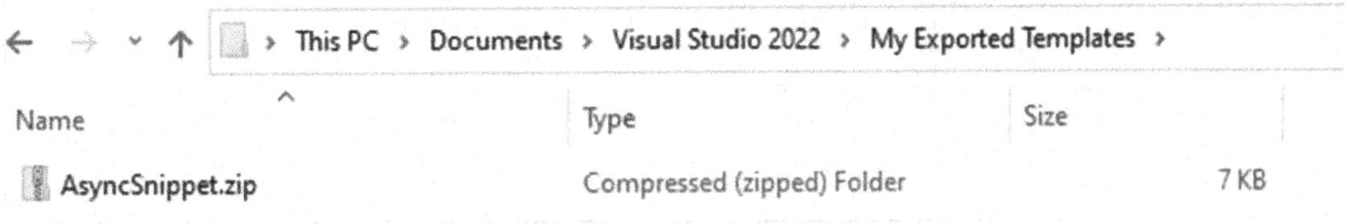

Figure 7-16. *Exported template location and exported project zip*

Since we now know that template is a zip file, can we just zip a project to generate the template? The answer is no. If we look inside the zip file, we find a new file extension called .vstemplate, which is the heart of the template.

Name	Type	Compressed size	Size
ASYNC	File folder		
PROPERTIES	File folder		
__PreviewImage.png	PNG File	1 KB	1 KB
__TemplateIcon.png	PNG File	1 KB	1 KB
AddSnippet.png	PNG File	1 KB	1 KB
AsyncSnippet.csproj	C# Project File	2 KB	4 KB
MyTemplate.vstemplate	Project/Item Template File	1 KB	2 KB
source.extension.vsixmanifest	Extension Manifest	1 KB	2 KB

This PC > Documents > Visual Studio 2022 > My Exported Templates > AsyncSnippet.zip

Figure 7-17. *Contents of template zip file*

This .vstemplate file separates the templates from the zip files as shown in Figure 7-17. We can see that in addition to the files of the original project like .csproj, .png, .vstemplate, etc., there are a couple of images added for a preview image, an icon, and a .vstemplate file that is a project/item template file.

Let us see the contents of a .vstemplate file. The structure of the .vstemplate file is shown in Figure 7-18.

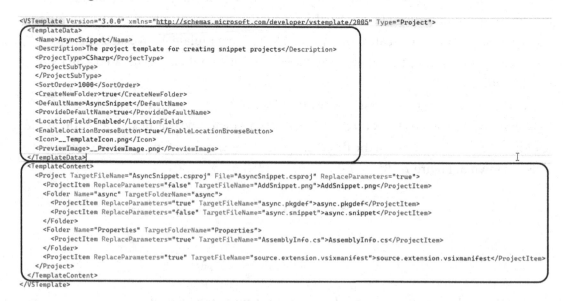

```
<VSTemplate Version="3.0.0" xmlns="http://schemas.microsoft.com/developer/vstemplate/2005" Type="Project">
  <TemplateData>
    <Name>AsyncSnippet</Name>
    <Description>The project template for creating snippet projects</Description>
    <ProjectType>CSharp</ProjectType>
    <ProjectSubType>
    </ProjectSubType>
    <SortOrder>1000</SortOrder>
    <CreateNewFolder>true</CreateNewFolder>
    <DefaultName>AsyncSnippet</DefaultName>
    <ProvideDefaultName>true</ProvideDefaultName>
    <LocationField>Enabled</LocationField>
    <EnableLocationBrowseButton>true</EnableLocationBrowseButton>
    <Icon>__TemplateIcon.png</Icon>
    <PreviewImage>__PreviewImage.png</PreviewImage>
  </TemplateData>
  <TemplateContent>
    <Project TargetFileName="AsyncSnippet.csproj" File="AsyncSnippet.csproj" ReplaceParameters="true">
      <ProjectItem ReplaceParameters="false" TargetFileName="AddSnippet.png">AddSnippet.png</ProjectItem>
      <Folder Name="async" TargetFolderName="async">
        <ProjectItem ReplaceParameters="true" TargetFileName="async.pkgdef">async.pkgdef</ProjectItem>
        <ProjectItem ReplaceParameters="false" TargetFileName="async.snippet">async.snippet</ProjectItem>
      </Folder>
      <Folder Name="Properties" TargetFolderName="Properties">
        <ProjectItem ReplaceParameters="true" TargetFileName="AssemblyInfo.cs">AssemblyInfo.cs</ProjectItem>
      </Folder>
      <ProjectItem ReplaceParameters="true" TargetFileName="source.extension.vsixmanifest">source.extension.vsixmanifest</ProjectItem>
    </Project>
  </TemplateContent>
</VSTemplate>
```

Figure 7-18. *The structure of vstemplate*

The content confirms that a vstemplate is an XML file. The root element of this XML file is named `VSTemplate`. It has an `xmlns` attribute, which ensures adherence to the `VSTemplate` schema. This attribute also enhances `IntelliSense` support for editing vstemplate files in Visual Studio.

The `Type` attribute of `VSTemplate` serves to specify the type of snippet, differentiating between Project and Item template. The `VSTemplate` element can have two child nodes, `TemplateData` and `TemplateContent`.

`TemplateData` node is responsible for housing the metadata information related to the template. This includes details like template name, description, project type, order, icon, preview image, etc.

The `TemplateContent` node holds the actual content of the template. For a Project template, this node will have a `Project` element, while an Item template will have a `ProjectItem` element. A `Project` element can have `ProjectItem`, `Folder`, etc. as the child nodes. Notice the attributes of each element. The `ReplaceParameter` attribute when set to true enables the parameter replacement of the corresponding `Project` or `ProjectItem` element. The detailed structure of vstemplate can be read online at `https://learn.microsoft.com/en-us/visualstudio/extensibility/visual-studio-template-schema-reference?view=vs-2022`.

Next time, when we open a new instance of Visual Studio and search for a "Snippet" project type, we will see the newly exported template as shown in Figure 7-19.

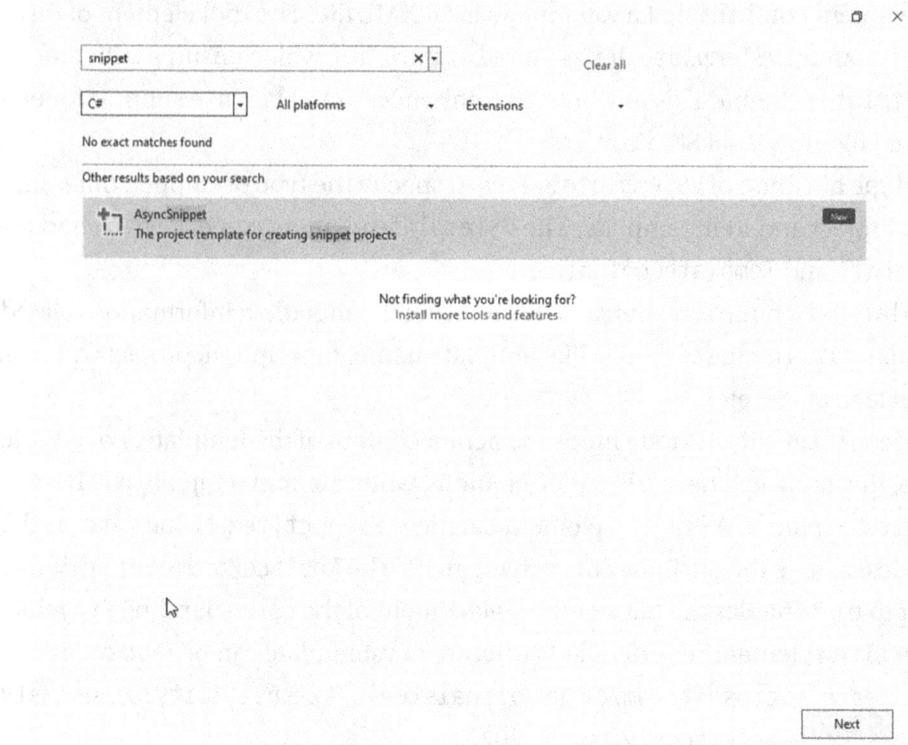

Figure 7-19. *Snippet Project type*

Notice that we can see the icon, name, and description of the template as we had specified. We can edit the name in the next dialog, and the created project will be an exact replica of the snippet project from which the template was exported. This is a great boilerplate project for us to start any snippet extension project, and we can just edit the snippet and get it ready for testing and shipping.

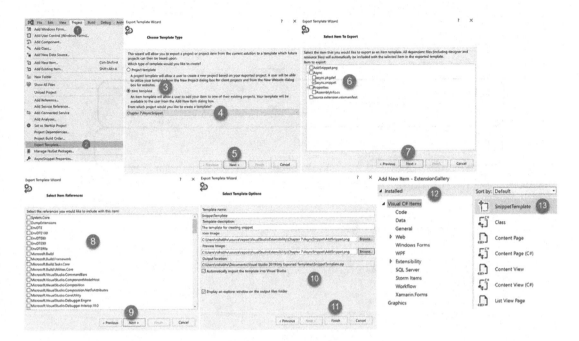

Figure 7-20. *Exporting Item template (.snippet) and using it*

Similarly, we can also export an item template, like the .snippet file item template or .pkgdef file template. The process is the same as that of exporting the project template, so we will not discuss it here. The entire process is summarized in Figure 7-20.

The figure is numbered to help you follow the process along with this image. Apart from exporting the project template and item template, Visual Studio 2022 also has first-class support to create the project and item templates. There are dedicated templates in the "Create new project" dialog to create a project template and item template from scratch. The generated template is in the form of a Visual Studio extension, so it can be easily shared and distributed to others as well. These templates can be seen in Figure 7-21. The documentation as well as walkthrough to create the templates are good enough for anyone to get started in almost no time. This documentation can be read at https://learn.microsoft.com/en-us/visualstudio/extensibility/creating-customproject-and-item-templates?view=vs-2022.

This is a very extensive topic and we have just discussed the tip of the iceberg, so I would highly recommend readers to thoroughly go through the URLs shared here and at last in the exercise.

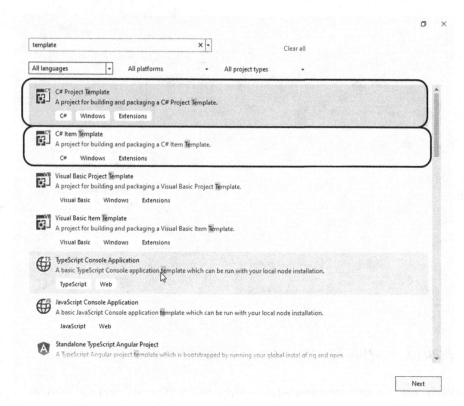

Figure 7-21. *Project and Item templates*

With this, we conclude our discussion on project and item templates. In the remainder of this chapter, we will have high-level discussion on "Connected Services" and debugging an extension.

Connected Services

If you have worked on any ASP.NET or ASP.NET Core projects, you would have come across the name of "Connected Services." In modern application development, services are everywhere. Whatever offerings that are in the IT world are being exposed as a service. Terms like infrastructure as a service, platform as a service, software as a service, and data as a service are frequently used. So, it is imperative more than ever to be easily able to integrate the services with your application. Connected Services were introduced to make it easier to integrate or connect applications to service providers that run in the cloud, or on premises. Azure and Google Cloud Platform are good examples or other third-party services hosted on premises may also fit the bill. Few examples of existing connected services extensions include Azure Application Insights, Azure Key Vault, Authentication with Azure Active Directory, Connect to Azure storage, etc.

The Connected Services feature can streamline the multiple steps required to establish a connection between a Visual Studio project and a service. What's particularly remarkable about the new Connected Services experience is its complete extensibility. Anyone has the capability to develop a Visual Studio extension that introduces a fresh Connected Service into the Add Connected Services dialog. Such a Connected Service holds the potential to facilitate connections from any Visual Studio application to any desired service. This model offers a wizard structure that makes it easier to get user inputs and required parameters to configure the code easily to connect with services. Visual Studio comes with a lot of available Connected Services that we can leverage out of the box as shown in Figure 7-22.

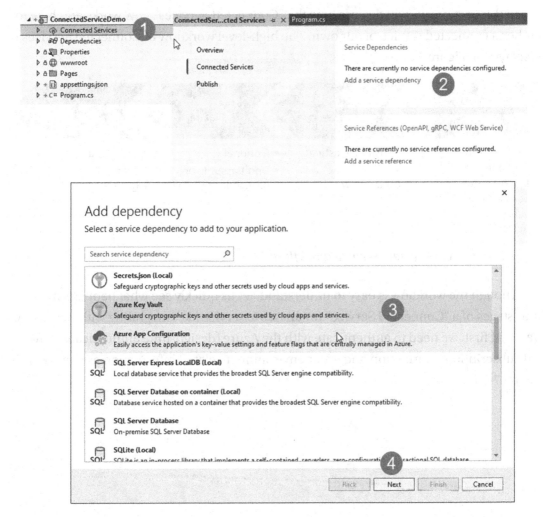

Figure 7-22. *Connected Services*

Connected Services has the following features:

- Enables easy integration of your project with the external or third-party services

- Configures your project as well as the service

- Guides you about next steps as it presents a Wizard

- Keeps the ownership of code with you, so even after integration you can change the code as required

- Can be shared as a Visual Studio extension and so it can be downloaded from the marketplace on demand as needed

In this section, we will discuss how the "Connected Services" flow works and how to author a connected service of our own. The high-level workflow of Connected Services is displayed in Figure 7-23.

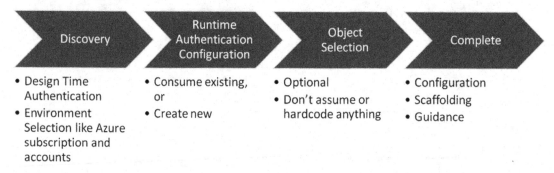

Figure 7-23. *Connected Service workflow*

Though the workflow is easy to understand, let us quickly see what happens in the four stages of a "Connected Service" for an Azure service like integrating with Azure Key Vault. At first, we need to authenticate with the Azure (design-time authentication) to get subscription information and other environment-related information as shown in Figure 7-24.

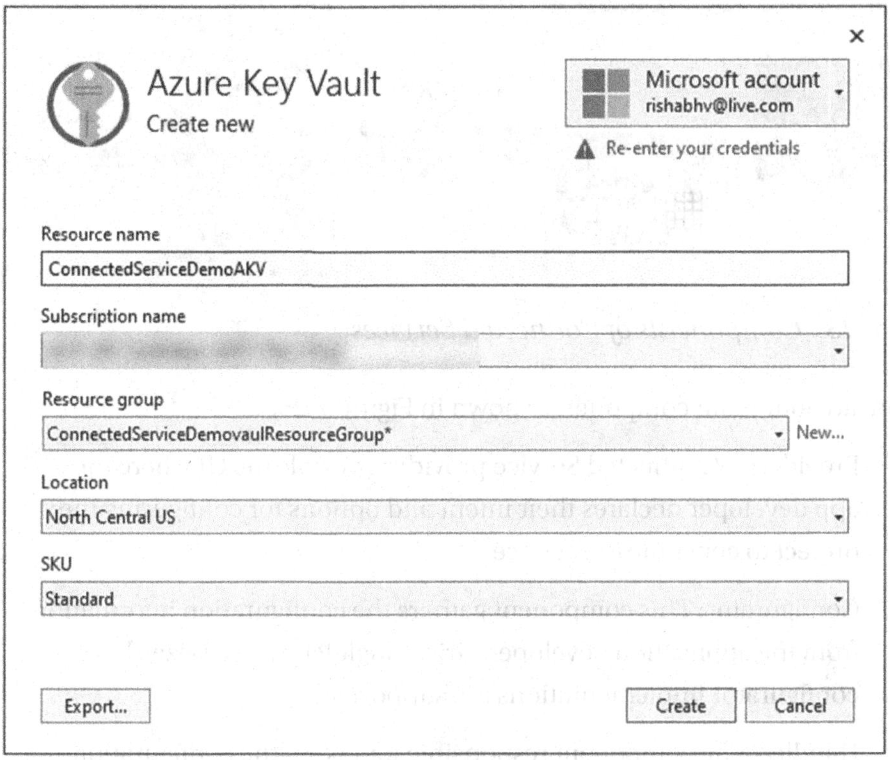

Figure 7-24. *Azure Key Vault Connected Service*

Next, we would add a new key vault (or use existing one), and to avoid hard-coding, we can extract these details into a configuration, which will be read at runtime, when the code runs. In a few of the services, we can have an optional step to select an object or class to keep things configurable without assuming or hard-coding anything. Finally, the code scaffolding is done, configurations are generated, and guidance for the next steps can be displayed in the wizard page. This way, in just a matter of few clicks, we can quickly integrate the services with our application, reducing the complexity to understand and do the difficult work. Given the benefits of Connected Services, it pays dividends to know how it works and how we can create one. Let us see the different components of Connected Services and a high-level overview of how they wire up and work. Figure 7-25 displays the high-level diagram of Connected Services.

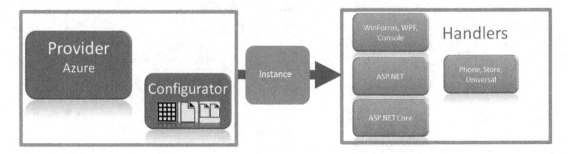

Figure 7-25. *Components of Connected Services*

There are four main components shown in Figure 7-25:

- Provider: A Connected Service provider controls the UI where the app developer declares their intent and options for configuring the project to consume the service.

- Configurator: This component gathers the configuration information from the application developer. Grid, SinglePage, and Wizard configurator implementations are supported.

- Handler: The component responsible for taking the configuration information that the app developer specifies in the configurator and modifying the service to be consumed and updating the project to consume the selected service. These modifications include adding values to app or app/web.config files, adding References, NuGet packages, scaffolding code, etc. Multiple handlers can be associated with a single provider to support different project types.

- Instance: The handoff between a provider and its handler is done in this component.

So, to make a Connected Service, we need to create a class each for the preceding components and then package it as an extension. The high-level steps to create a Connected Service extension are as follows:

1. Create an empty VSIX project.

2. Add a reference to ConnectedService SDK, by adding a NuGet package reference of "Microsoft.VisualStudio. ConnectedServices" to the project. This is required to get the types for implementing Connected Services.

3. Implement `Configurator` class. It can be one of the following:

    a. Single page

    b. Single page with grid

    c. Wizard

    d. No UI

    It is generally easy to implement a Wizard, by deriving it from the `ConnectedServiceWizard` class. Implement a constructor that takes the `ConnectedServiceProviderContext` as a parameter. This is passed by the framework. Override the `GetFinishedServiceInstanceAsync` method. For every page that you wish to display in the wizard, create a wizard page view model by deriving the class from the `ConnectedServiceWizardPage`. Implement the constructor of this view model page, which takes the `ConnectedServiceProviderContext` as a parameter. Create a WPF user control as the UI page to which the view model would bind. So, if you must display two pages in the wizard, there would be two WPF user controls and two view model classes. Since the wizard as well as view model page have access to `ConnectedServiceProviderContext`, the data can easily flow from one page to another and is also accessible to the wizard. A sample Wizard class is shown in Figure 7-26. The code for the WPF User control and the entire project can be seen in the code bundle of the book for this chapter.

```
2 references
internal class Wizard : ConnectedServiceWizard
{
    private readonly ConnectedServiceProviderContext _context;

    1 reference
    public Wizard(ConnectedServiceProviderContext context)
    {
        _context = context;
        Pages.Add(new WizardPage(_context));

        foreach (var page in Pages)
        {
            page.PropertyChanged += OnPagePropertyChanged;
        }
    }

    1 reference
    private void OnPagePropertyChanged(object sender, PropertyChangedEventArgs e)
    {
        IsFinishEnabled = Pages.All(page => !page.HasErrors);
        IsNextEnabled = false;
    }

    0 references
    public override Task<ConnectedServiceInstance> GetFinishedServiceInstanceAsync()
    {
        var instance = new Instance
        {
            Country = Pages.OfType<WizardPage>().FirstOrDefault()?.Country
        };

        return Task.FromResult<ConnectedServiceInstance>(instance);
    }
}
```

Figure 7-26. *Sample Wizard code*

4. Create a Provider class by deriving it from
    ConnectedServiceProvider and overriding the
    CreateConfiguratorAsync method. A sample Provider class is
    shown in Figure 7-27.

```
using Microsoft.VisualStudio.ConnectedServices;
using System;
using System.Reflection;
using System.Threading.Tasks;

namespace ConnectedService                    I
{
    [ConnectedServiceProviderExport(Constants.ProviderId)]
    1 reference
    internal class Provider : ConnectedServiceProvider
    {
        0 references
        public Provider()
        {
            Category = Constants.Category;
            Name = Constants.Name;
            Description = Constants.Description;
            Id = Constants.ProviderId;
            Name = Constants.Name;
            SupportsUpdate = true;
            Version = Assembly.GetExecutingAssembly().GetName().Version;
            MoreInfoUri = new Uri("https://rishabhverma.net");
        }

        0 references
        public override Task<ConnectedServiceConfigurator> CreateConfiguratorAsync(ConnectedServiceProviderContext context)
        {
            return Task.FromResult<ConnectedServiceConfigurator>(new Wizard(context));
        }
    }
}
```

Figure 7-27. *Sample Provider class*

5. Create a handler class by deriving it from the
    ConnectedServiceHandler class. A sample handler class which
    generates the code to fetch the universities of a country from an
    external service is shown in Figure 7-28. The detailed code can be
    seen in the GitHub repository of this edition of the book.

```
using Microsoft.VisualStudio.ConnectedServices;
using System.IO;
using System.Threading;
using System.Threading.Tasks;

namespace ConnectedService
{
    [ConnectedServiceHandlerExport(Constants.ProviderId, AppliesTo = "CSharp")]
    0 references
    public class Handler : ConnectedServiceHandler
    {
        0 references
        public override async Task<AddServiceInstanceResult> AddServiceInstanceAsync(ConnectedServiceHandlerContext context, CancellationToken ct)
        {
            var instance = (Instance)context.ServiceInstance;
            await context.Logger.WriteMessageAsync(LoggerMessageCategory.Information,
                $"Generating code to get universities of default country set as {instance.Country}");
            var csharpFilePath = await GenerateCSharpFileAsync(context, instance);
            await context.Logger.WriteMessageAsync(LoggerMessageCategory.Information, $"Generated {Path.GetFileName(csharpFilePath)}");
            var folderName = context.ServiceInstance.Name;
            var result = new AddServiceInstanceResult(folderName, null);
            return result;
        }

        0 references
        public override async Task<UpdateServiceInstanceResult> UpdateServiceInstanceAsync(ConnectedServiceHandlerContext context,
            CancellationToken cancellationToken)
        {
            var instance = (Instance)context.ServiceInstance;
            await context.Logger.WriteMessageAsync(LoggerMessageCategory.Information,
                $"Re-generating code to get universities of default country set as {instance.Country}");
            var csharpFilePath = await GenerateCSharpFileAsync(context, instance);
            await context.Logger.WriteMessageAsync(LoggerMessageCategory.Information, $"Re-generated code based on {csharpFilePath}");
            return await base.UpdateServiceInstanceAsync(context, cancellationToken);
        }

        2 references
        private async Task<string> GenerateCSharpFileAsync(ConnectedServiceHandlerContext context, Instance instance)[...]
    }
}
```

Figure 7-28. *Sample handler class*

6. Create an Instance class by deriving from
    ConnectedServiceInstance. This class will contain the instance
    of data that would be entered and displayed in the wizard pages.
    With all these classes implemented correctly, our connected
    service is ready. However, running it will not install the binaries,
    so let's make the changes to deploy the binary. This will be done
    by the .vsixmanifest file.

7. Update the vsixmanifest file with correct metadata information
    and update the Assets section of the manifest as shown in
    Figure 7-29.

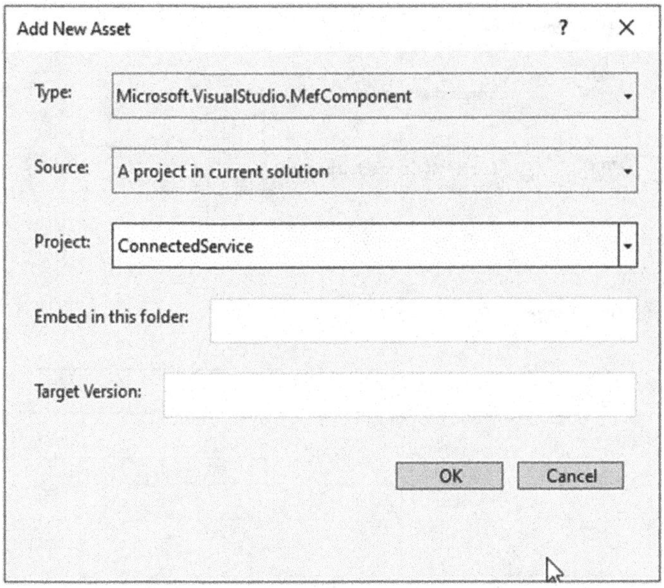

Figure 7-29. *Add new asset*

8. Since Connected Services is itself built as a Visual Studio extension, we'll also add a dependency on the Connected Services extension. Adding the dependency will warn developers attempting to uninstall the Connected Services extension that the Connected Service will no longer work. In the `source.extension.vsixmanifest` file, switch to the Dependencies tab and add a new dependency as shown in Figure 7-30.

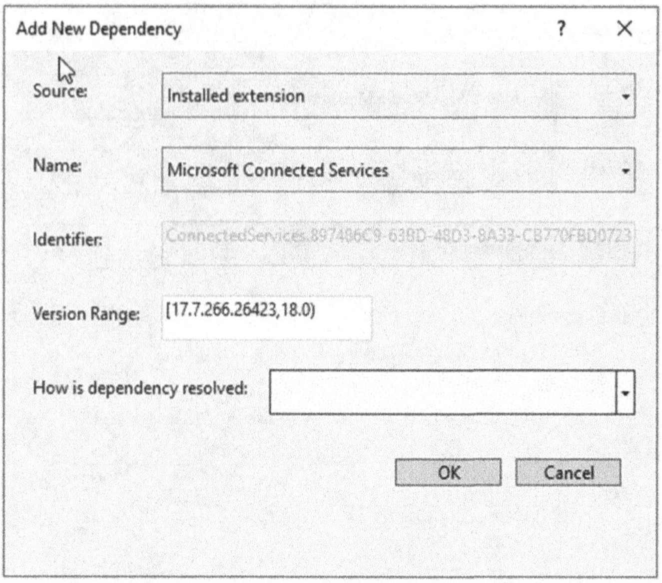

Figure 7-30. *Microsoft Connected Services dependency*

9.   With the changes done, we are now ready to run our connected
     service. So, if we debug the project, a new experimental instance
     will launch. Create/open a project in this experimental instance
     and then launch the Connected Service as shown in Figure 7-22.
     Our newly added University Connected Service will display in the
     "Other Services" section of the Connected Services (#2). Clicking
     the University Connected Service will display a Wizard page (#3)
     to input the Country. Clicking the Finish button (#4) in the page
     adds the generated code in the project and service is shown as
     "Configured" (#5). This is illustrated in Figure 7-31.

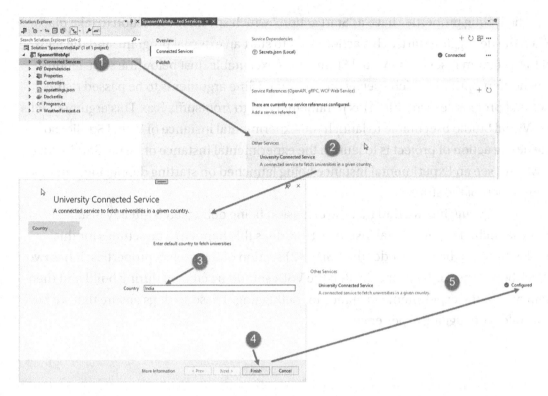

Figure 7-31. *New connected service*

This concludes our high-level overview of Connected Services. This also showcases that Connected Services extension can make it really easy for the end user to consume your services.

Debugging

Debugging constitutes an essential part of a developer's life and extensibility development is no different. When we use a template to create an extension, be it an empty VSIX project template, or a custom command template, or any other, the project properties are already set to enable debugging out of the box, but it is important to understand these settings. These can be seen by opening the properties of any extensibility projects and looking at the settings. Figure 7-32 displays the Debug and VSIX sections of the extensibility project properties.

The Debug properties have a "Start action," which specifies the action to take place when the debugging starts. This action is set to start an external program, and the path of this program is set to the Visual Studio 2022 executable. Just below the start action are the start options, which specify the command-line arguments to be passed to the external program executable. This parameter is set to /rootsuffix Exp. This argument tells the Visual Studio executable to launch the Experimental instance of Visual Studio. So, the debug action of project is to launch the experimental instance of Visual Studio; that is why we see an Experimental instance being launched on starting debugging. But this is just a part of the story.

While debugging, we find that the extension being debugged is already installed in the launched experimental instance. How does this happen? The settings for this deployment can be seen under the VSIX (#2) section of the project properties. It has two check boxes checked that specify that the VSIX should be created during build and then deployed to the experimental instance for debugging. These settings ensure that we have a seamless debugging experience.

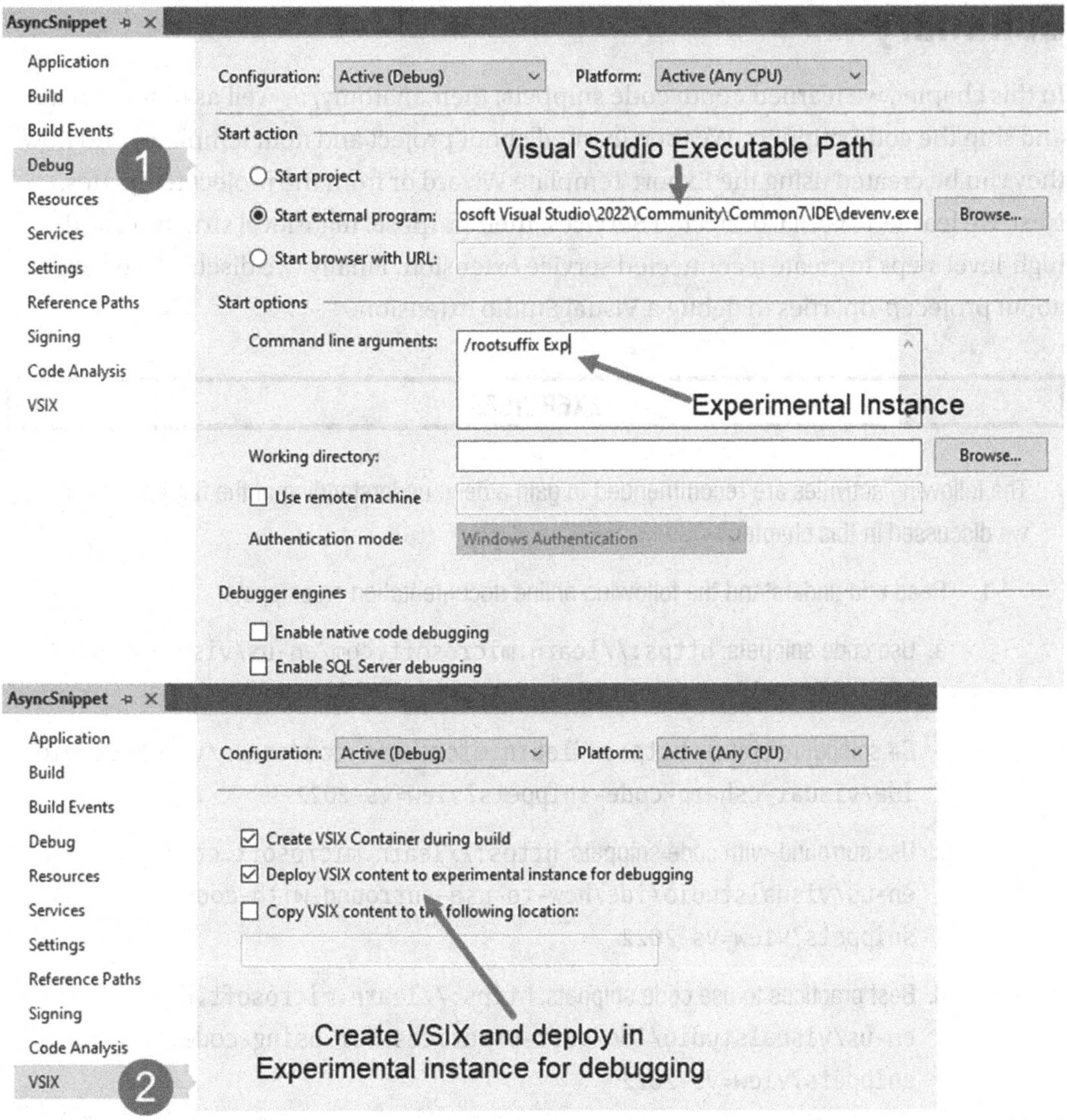

Figure 7-32. *Project properties*

Like most aspects of Visual Studio, the debuggers are also very extensible. Though discussing them is outside the scope of this book, here is a link that would be a good read to get started with debugger extensibility in Visual Studio:

https://learn.microsoft.com/en-us/visualstudio/extensibility/debugger/
visual-studio-debugger-extensibility?view=vs-2022

Summary

In this chapter, we learned about code snippets, their anatomy, as well as how to create and ship the code snippets. We then learned about project and item templates and how they can be created using the Export Template Wizard or from the project templates. Next, we learned about Connected Services, their purpose, high-level structure, and high-level steps to create a connected service extension. Finally, we discussed briefly about project properties to debug a Visual Studio extension.

EXERCISES

The following activities are recommended to gain a deep understanding of the fundamentals we discussed in this chapter:

1. Read and understand the following online documentation on snippets:

   a. Use code snippets: `https://learn.microsoft.com/en-us/visualstudio/ide/code-snippets?view=vs-2022`

   b. C# snippet reference: `https://learn.microsoft.com/en-us/visualstudio/ide/visual-csharp-code-snippets?view=vs-2022`

   c. Use surround-with code snippets: `https://learn.microsoft.com/en-us/visualstudio/ide/how-to-use-surround-with-code-snippets?view=vs-2022`

   d. Best practices to use code snippets: `https://learn.microsoft.com/en-us/visualstudio/ide/best-practices-for-using-code-snippets?view=vs-2022`

   e. Create code snippet: `https://learn.microsoft.com/en-us/visualstudio/ide/walkthrough-creating-a-code-snippet?view=vs-2022`

   f. Distribute code snippets: `https://learn.microsoft.com/en-us/visualstudio/ide/how-to-distribute-code-snippets?view=vs-2022`

   g. Code snippet functions: `https://learn.microsoft.com/en-us/visualstudio/ide/code-snippet-functions?view=vs-2022`

    h. Code snippets schema reference: `https://learn.microsoft.com/en-us/visualstudio/ide/code-snippets-schema-reference?view=vs-2022`

    i. Troubleshoot issues with snippets: `https://learn.microsoft.com/en-us/visualstudio/ide/troubleshooting-snippets?view=vs-2022`

2. Read the following links about Project and Item templates:

    a. Create project and item templates: `https://learn.microsoft.com/en-us/visualstudio/extensibility/creating-custom-project-and-item-templates?view=vs-2022`

    b. Troubleshooting discovery of templates: `https://learn.microsoft.com/en-us/visualstudio/extensibility/troubleshooting-template-discovery?view=vs-2022`

    c. Wizards: `https://learn.microsoft.com/en-us/visualstudio/extensibility/how-to-use-wizards-with-project-templates?view=vs-2022`

    d. Visual Studio template reference schema: `https://learn.microsoft.com/en-us/visualstudio/extensibility/visual-studio-template-schema-reference?view=vs-2022`

Continuous Integration and Hosting

So far, we have only discussed how to develop Visual Studio extensions. Equally important is understanding how to ship the extension to the Visual Studio Marketplace so that other Visual Studio users can also utilize the developed extension. In this chapter, we will learn how to publish our extension to the Visual Studio Marketplace, making it available to a wider audience.

With the DevOps getting more traction than ever before, we will explore how to establish an automated build setup for extension projects using the Azure DevOps build pipeline. We will then delve into leveraging Azure DevOps (ADO) to automate the process of publishing an extension to the marketplace. In addition to the Visual Studio Marketplace, there may be scenarios where hosting extensions in a private extension gallery becomes necessary to share extensions exclusively with a subset of users. Therefore, we will learn how to develop a private extension gallery and host extensions.

By the end of this chapter, readers should feel confident in

- Publishing extensions to the Visual Studio Marketplace

- Enabling continuous integration and deployment of extensions using Azure DevOps (ADO)

- Developing a private extension gallery and hosting extensions

Let's dive in!

© Rishabh Verma 2024
R. Verma, *Visual Studio Extensibility Development*, https://doi.org/10.1007/978-1-4842-9875-6_8

Visual Studio Marketplace

"Marketplace" refers to an open space where buyers and sellers trade products. The Visual Studio Marketplace serves as a comprehensive destination for all the extensions related to the Visual Studio family of products, including Visual Studio, Visual Studio Code, and Azure DevOps. This online platform serves as a hub where extension authors can publish and manage their extensions, while extension consumers can browse, search, and download extensions. The Visual Studio Marketplace can be accessed at the following URL: `https://marketplace.visualstudio.com/vs`. Figure 8-1 shows the user interface of Visual Studio Marketplace at the time of writing this chapter. Notice that at the top, there are tabs for the different products of the Visual Studio family (shown marked as #1).

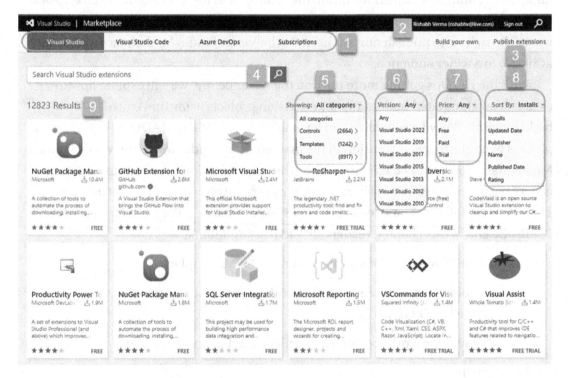

Figure 8-1. Visual Studio Marketplace

There are four tabs: Visual Studio, Visual Studio Code, Azure DevOps, and Subscriptions.

Clicking the first three tabs would navigate to the product-specific section displaying the extensions for the chosen product. In Figure 8-1, Visual Studio is selected as the product.

Number 2 displays the signed-in user. If the user is not signed in, the link to sign in will be displayed here. Users can sign in to the marketplace using their Microsoft email account (such as live/Hotmail/Outlook/msn, etc.). If you don't already have a Microsoft account, then it is a good opportunity to create one. It is important to notice that login to the marketplace is necessary only if you intend to publish or manage an extension. For browsing, searching, or downloading an extension, login isn't required.

Number 3 refers to the Publish extensions hyperlink. This provides the screen to enter the extension metadata, its icons, description, and VSIX file to be published. When we click the "Publish Extension" link for the very first time, the portal will navigate us to the "Create Publisher" page, where we can create our publisher profile as an individual or as an organization. The create publisher page is simple to use with intuitive field names as shown in Figure 8-2. It gathers basic information like name, unique identifier, description, domain name, logo, company website, LinkedIn, repository URL, and Twitter profile link, to name a few. Of all these fields, only name and ID are required fields, and the rest are optional. The values entered here display in the publisher profile page.

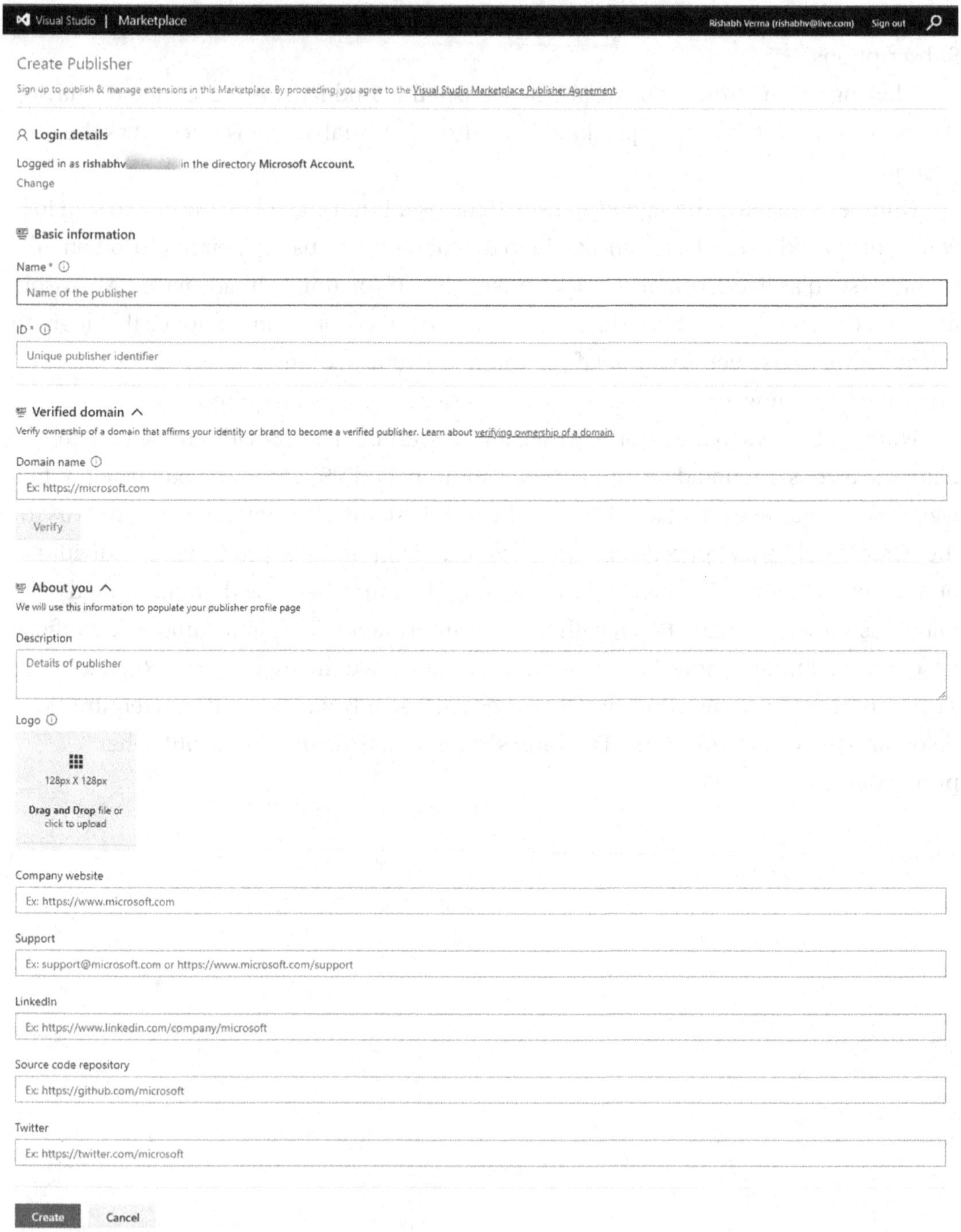

Figure 8-2. *Create a publisher page*

When we upload an extension in the marketplace, we can specify the category of extension as a control, template, or tool. The marketplace reads the VSIX file and finds out the supported Visual Studio versions for the uploaded extension. The tags are read from the VSIX as well, but publishers can edit the tags or add more. We can also select the pricing model of our extension, choosing among free, paid, or trial options. We will discuss publishing an extension in the marketplace shortly. However, these details provide enough understanding of the search and filtering criteria within the marketplace.

Coming back to Figure 8-1 to complete the discussion, #4 is the text box where you can type a text, name, publisher, etc. to search the marketplace. Numbers 5 through 8 show the various search criteria or filters that can be used to filter the search results. Number 5 is the categories filter. The possible values in the categories drop-down are "All categories," "Controls," "Templates," and "Tools." Needless to explain that choosing "All categories" will list the extensions of all the categories, choosing "Tools" will display the extensions that are categorized as tools, and so on. Likewise, we can filter the extensions on the supported Visual Studio version (marked as #6 in Figure 8-1) and price (#7). There is also an option for extension consumers to sort the extensions by various parameters. This "Sort by" drop-down filter is marked as #8 in Figure 8-1. Number 9 displays the search result count and all the extensions that match the search criteria. The possible values of all the filter drop-downs can also be seen in Figure 8-1.

To summarize, Visual Studio Marketplace is an online place for extension publishers and consumers to publish and consume extensions for the Visual Studio family of products. Visual Studio Marketplace provides an online platform that enables the following:

- Acquiring extensions: Extension users and consumers can browse, discover, download, and install extensions for Visual Studio, Visual Studio Code, and Azure DevOps. Extensions may be free, trial, or paid, and users may purchase the extensions.

- Publishing and managing extensions: Build, publish, and share extensions for the Visual Studio family of products with a wider community.

This completes our introduction to the Visual Studio Marketplace. In the next section, we will publish our extension to the Visual Studio Marketplace.

Publishing Extension to Visual Studio Marketplace

Let's assume that we have finished coding and testing our extension and it meets the criteria for a minimum viable product (MVP) and is prepared to deliver value to other users. Furthermore, we've successfully committed our code to the source control repository. With the VSIX package at our disposal, we're ready to publish this extension to the marketplace. Let us quickly discuss and see the steps to publish the extension:

1. Open the web browser of your choice and navigate to the Visual Studio Marketplace at `https://marketplace.visualstudio.com`.

2. Click the "Publish extensions" link shown in Figure 8-3.

Figure 8-3. *Visual Studio Marketplace*

3. If you are not signed into the marketplace, you would be redirected to sign in to Microsoft account screen as shown in Figure 8-4. You can either sign in with your Microsoft account (live/Hotmail/Outlook, etc.) or with your GitHub ID. If you don't have an account, then this is the time for you to create a Microsoft account. The links to create an account is displayed in the same dialog, as can be seen in Figure 8-4.

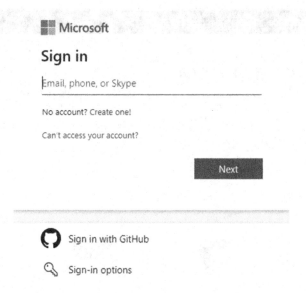

Figure 8-4. *Sign in*

4. After signing in with your Microsoft account for the very first time, you would be navigated to the "Create Publisher" page as shown in Figure 8-2. In this page, you would create the profile for yourself or for your company by providing the required information (Name, ID). The rest of the fields are not mandatory, but I would recommend that you accurately provide other information as well, to create a good publisher profile. Figure 8-5 shows my publisher profile in the marketplace. Click the "Create" button.

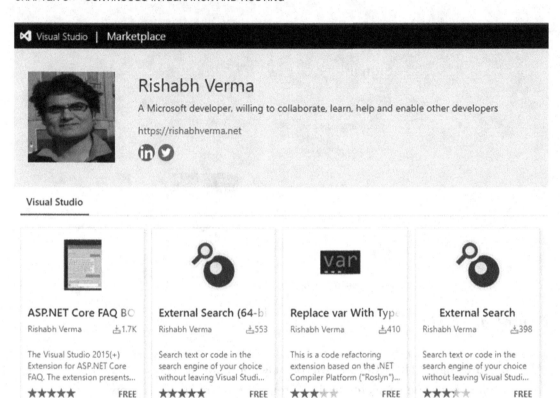

Figure 8-5. *Publisher profile page*

5. You will be redirected to the "Manage Extensions and Publishers" page. This is shown in Figure 8-6.

| Visual Studio | Marketplace | | | | | | Rishabh Verma (rishabhv@live.com) | Sign out |

Manage Publishers & Extensions

Need help? Contact Microsoft

+ Create publisher

Rishabh Verma (RishabhVerma)

Extensions   Details   Members   + New extension ∨

search

Name ↑	Version	Works with	Updated	Availability	Rating	Installs
ASP.NET Core ... ···	⊘ 1.0	2	6 years ago	Public	★★★★★ (1)	1703
External Search	⊘ 1.2	1	3 years ago	Public	★★★★☆ (3)	398
External Searc...	⊘ 2.0	1	2 years ago	Public	★★★★★ (2)	553
Microsoft.Hac...	⊘ 1.0	1	3 years ago	Not public	☆☆☆☆☆ (0)	0
Replace var Wi...	⊘ 1.0	1	6 years ago	Public	★★★☆☆ (4)	410
VS Search	⊘ 1.1	1	3 years ago	Not public	☆☆☆☆☆ (0)	0

Figure 8-6. *Manage Publishers and Extensions page*

6. In this page, you can create a publisher, update the publisher
    details, and see the list of extensions published by you, their
    ratings, and installations. We can create multiple publishers in the
    "Create Publisher" page. There may be multiple reasons to create
    multiple publisher profiles like creating one publisher profile for
    your personal use and one for your organization or team. You
    can also upload a new extension from this page. To upload a new
    extension, we will click the New extension drop-down and click
    Visual Studio as shown in Figure 8-7.

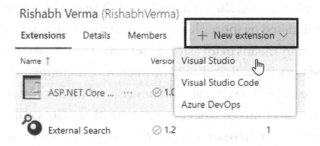

Figure 8-7. *New extension*

7. This will open the "New Visual Studio Extension" page, where we can upload the VSIX package or provide a link to the extension. This is shown in Figure 8-8. The page supports drag and drop, so you can drag and drop the extension file directly to upload it or you can click on the link to open the file browser and upload it.

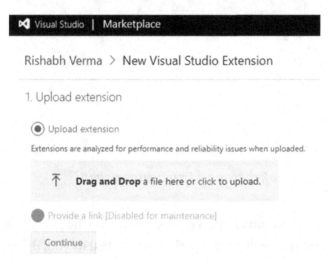

Figure 8-8. *New Visual Studio Extension page*

8. After the file is uploaded, click the "Continue" button. This will display additional details in the page. The uploaded VSIX would be parsed, and a few of the metadata fields would be populated with the `vsixmanifest` values like Display name, version, VSIX ID, logo, short description, and supported Visual Studio versions, to name a few. This is shown in Figure 8-9. The rest of the fields can be populated by the author. The mandatory fields are easily identifiable by means of an asterisk. Internal name and Overview are mandatory fields that should be filled with meaningful and crisp values. The Overview should be crisp yet descriptive so that users can easily find out what the extension does. Generally, a good practice is to have a crisp description of extension features along with images to back the description. I have seen few extensions making use of animated gif images that illustrate what the extension does. This is helpful for the user to make up their

mind to download an extension and use it. We can also specify the category of the extension to one of tools, controls, or templates. We can input the tags, pricing category, source control repository URL, and if questions and answers are enabled for this extension. Figure 8-9 shows the part of New Visual Studio Extension page.

Visual Studio | Marketplace

Rishabh Verma > New Visual Studio Extension

1. Upload extension

Extensions are analyzed for performance and reliability issues when uploaded.
ConnectedService.vsix ✎

2. Provide extension details

▣ **Basic information**

Internal name * ⓘ

universityConnectedService

Display name * ⓘ

ConnectedService

Version * ⓘ

1.0

VSIX ID ⓘ

ConnectedService.3b8994c2-1e1b-4036-8b9b-c25cf7ad254a

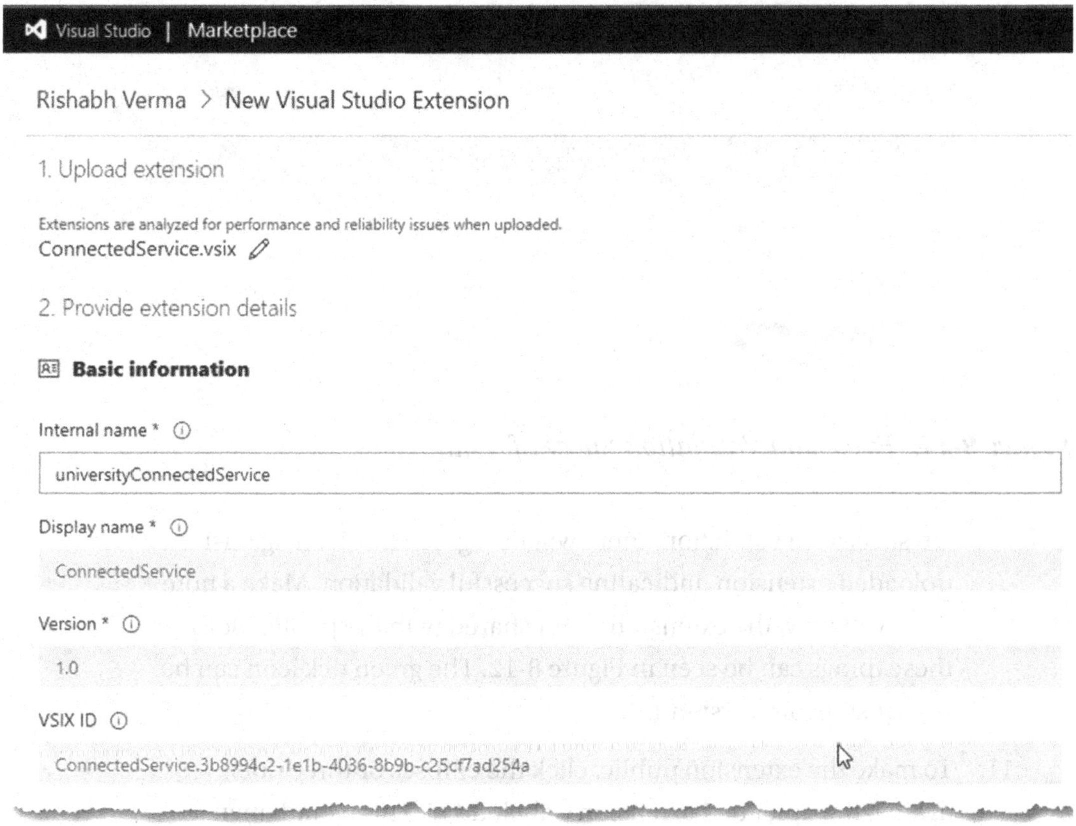

Figure 8-9. *New Visual Studio Extension page*

9. Once we are done updating the fields and happy with the updates, we can click the "Save & Upload" button. This will upload the extension. However, it would yet not be shared with the public for consumption.

ConnectedSer... ⋯   ▶ Verifying 1.0   1   just now   Not public   ★★★★★ (0)   0

Figure 8-10. *Verifying the extension*

As soon as we upload it, the marketplace runs the validation on the uploaded extension to check if the extension is fit for other users to download and use as shown in Figure 8-10.

10. The validation process runs for a while, and once the validation completes, you will receive an email notification that the extension validation was successful. This is shown in Figure 8-11.

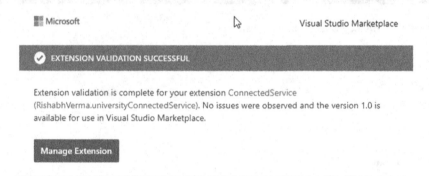

Figure 8-11. *Extension Validation Successful mail*

On successful validation, there will be a green tick icon against the uploaded extension, indicating successful validation. Make a note that even now, the extension is not shared with the public. Both these things can be seen in Figure 8-12. The green tick icon can be seen just before version 1.0.

11. To make the extension public, click the ellipses or three dots against the uploaded extension (labeled #1). This would open a context menu as shown in Figure 8-12. The context menu has the following items:

• View Extension: To view the uploaded extension page as it would show up to any user on the marketplace.

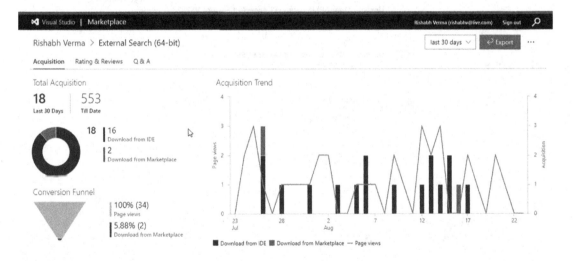

Figure 8-12. *Make extension public*

- Reports (#3 in Figure 8-12): To check the extension page views,
  downloads, conversion rates, and other statistics related to
  your extension for the last 30, 60, and 90 days. You can also
  export the report in the Excel format. This gives insights of how
  your extension is doing. A sample report screen is shown in
  Figure 8-13.

Figure 8-13. *Reports screen*

- Edit: To edit the extension page.

- Make Public (#2 in Figure 8-12): To make the extension visible to
  the public.

- Remove: To remove the extension.

12. Click the "Make Public" menu item, and it makes the extension listed publicly and available to all the users of the marketplace. This is shown in Figure 8-14.

Figure 8-14. *Publicly listed extension*

That's it! Our extension is now published and publicly listed in the Visual Studio Marketplace. The extension users can browse, search, and download it from the marketplace as well as from their Visual Studio IDE. This is shown in Figure 8-15.

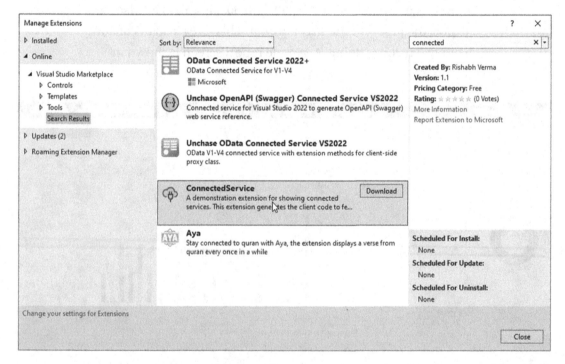

Figure 8-15. *Extension in Visual Studio Marketplace*

We have just discussed and learned to publish an extension in Visual Studio Marketplace. The publishing process is also documented well and can be read online at https://learn.microsoft.com/en-us/visualstudio/extensibility/walkthrough-publishing-a-visual-studio-extension?view=vs-2022.

With time, we may code some bug fixes in the extension or add new features and enhancements and may want to share this updated version with the community. To do so, we will follow the same steps, but instead of creating/uploading a new extension, we will edit the existing extension and upload the updated VSIX. Though the process is simple, it is still relatively lengthy and cumbersome to follow each time. Wouldn't it be cool to have it automated, that is, we just update and check in the code in the code repository and the rest is taken care automatically by the continuous integration pipeline? Let us see how we can achieve this using Azure DevOps (ADO).

Continuous Integration and Continuous Deployment

In this section, we will automate the manual steps we previously undertook to publish or update an extension in the Visual Studio Marketplace.

Our vision entails making changes in the extension code and subsequently checking in these code changes in the source control. This action should then trigger an automated build to generate an extension VSIX file. We can then conduct another round of testing on this VSIX (in addition to unit testing extensions in our local development environment). If you have unit tests written for the extension, even these unit tests can be automated in the build pipeline. Once our testing is complete and we're ready to publish the extension in the marketplace, our release pipeline will deploy the extension in the Visual Studio Marketplace.

With DevOps getting more traction than ever before, it is now essential for any software development to have continuous integration (CI) and continuous deployment (CD) integrated in the development life cycle, so that we can have faster releases of our software. Extensibility projects are no different.

Azure DevOps (ADO) is a leading DevOps tool from Microsoft, which makes it relatively easy to set up automated pipelines to build, test, and deploy code to any platform. We are going to use ADO for our discussion and for setting up CI/CD pipelines for our extensions. So, let's dive in. We assume at this point that we have already developed an extension (External Search) and its code is already checked in the GitHub public repository.

1. Launch the web browser of your choice and navigate to the Azure DevOps URL at `https://dev.azure.com/`. Log in with your Microsoft or GitHub account. It will take you to the landing page, which will have no projects at the time of first login and use. This is depicted in Figure 8-16.

Figure 8-16. *Azure DevOps landing page*

2. In the current UI (which may change with time), there is a button named "+ New project." Click this button to create a new project. The new project details are shown in Figure 8-17. After filling in the required details, click the "Create" button to create the project.

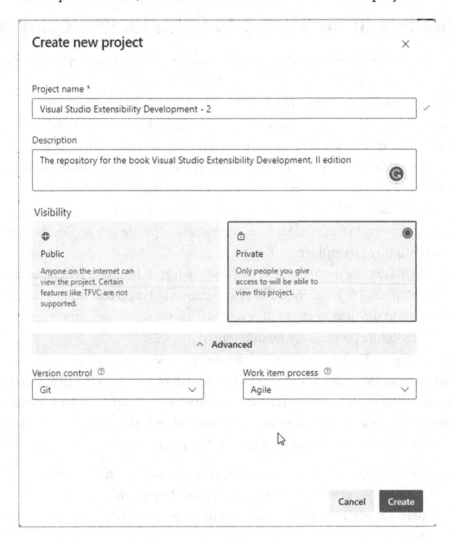

Figure 8-17. *Create new project*

3.   The project will get created and a new blank project dashboard
      page shows up. Click the pipelines on the left pane and then click
      the "Create Pipeline" button as shown in Figure 8-18.

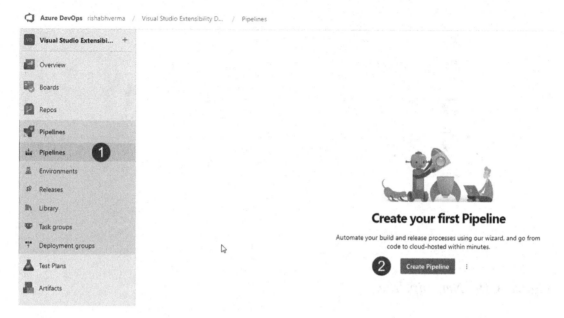

Figure 8-18. *Create pipeline*

4.   This action will bring up the "New Pipeline" page, prompting for
      the code location while offering predefined YAML (Yet Another
      Markup Language) templates for configuring the build pipeline
      based on various source control options. Though we can use
      YAML for GitHub to set up the pipeline, for simplicity and ease of
      use, we will opt for the classic editor that is more user interface
      oriented. Thus, we will proceed by clicking the "Use classic editor"
      link on the page as shown in Figure 8-19.

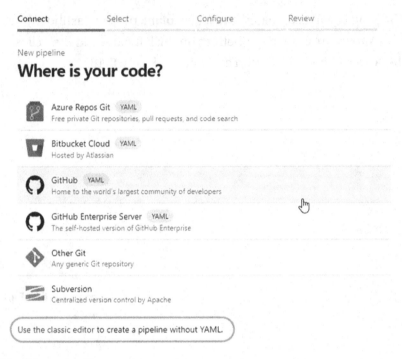

Figure 8-19. *New pipeline*

5. We would now need to select the source control repository. I selected GitHub. To list the repositories from GitHub, it will ask us for authorization. To do so, we can either provide a personal access token (PAT) or sign in using OAuth. Upon successful login or after providing PAT, we can select the repository and branch for which we need to set up the pipeline. After selecting the repository and branch, click the "Continue" button. This is shown in Figure 8-20.

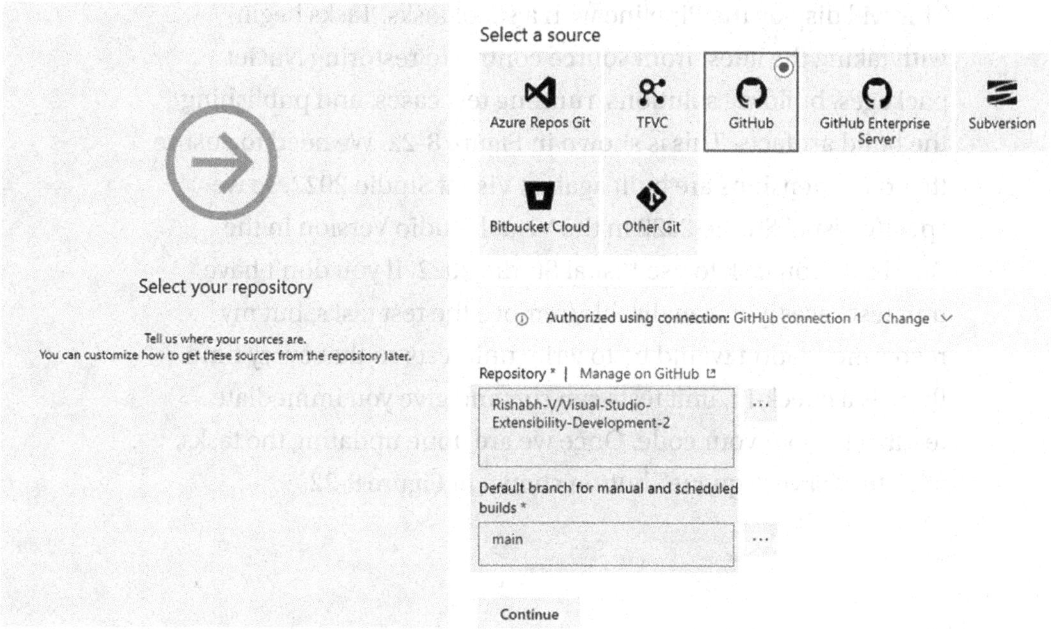

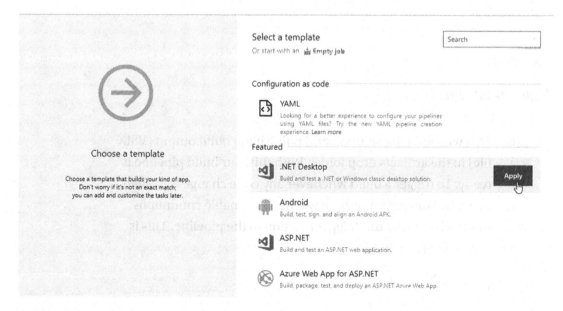

Figure 8-20. Select repository

6. This will display the screen to choose the template. Since we have
    a Visual Studio extension project, we will select the .NET Desktop
    template and click the "Apply" button as shown in Figure 8-21.

Figure 8-21. Choose a template screen

7. This will display the Pipeline with a set of tasks. Tasks begin
    with taking the latest from source control to restoring NuGet
    packages, building solutions, running test cases, and publishing
    the build artifacts. This is shown in Figure 8-22. We need to ensure
    that our extensions are built against Visual Studio 2022, so we
    specify Visual Studio 2022 in the Visual Studio Version in the
    Build solution task to use Visual Studio 2022. If you don't have
    unit test cases, you can disable/remove the test tasks, but my
    recommendation would be to write unit tests so that every time
    there is a check-in, unit tests can run and give you immediate
    feedback about your code. Once we are done updating the tasks,
    click the "Save & queue" button shown in Figure 8-22.

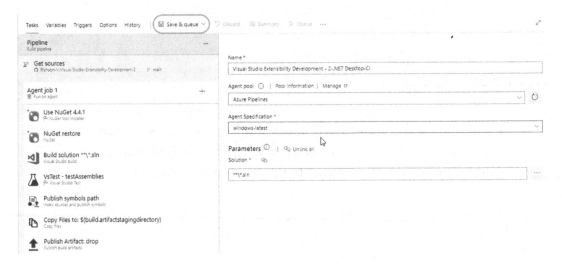

Figure 8-22. Pipeline page

8. This will build the solution and publish the build output (VSIX
    file) in the artifacts drop folder. With this, our build pipeline is
    ready. To trigger a build whenever any code change is pushed
    to the GitHub repository, we will need to enable continuous
    integration under the Triggers section of the pipeline. This is
    shown in Figure 8-23.

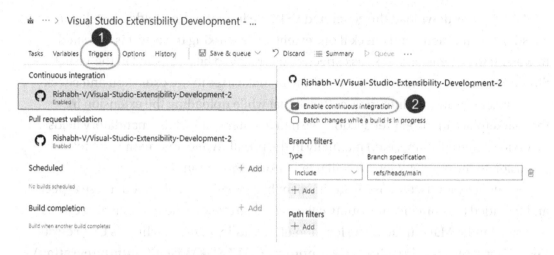

Figure 8-23. *Enable continuous integration*

9. Next time, when we check in the code, this build pipeline would
    get triggered, build the extension, and publish the VSIX file in
    the artifacts drop folder. Please see Figure 8-24, which shows the
    summary view of CI build. It shows that my code commit which
    had a message "chore: clean up and test CI" triggered a build. The
    figure shows the repository name and version at the time build
    was triggered and that the build was successful.

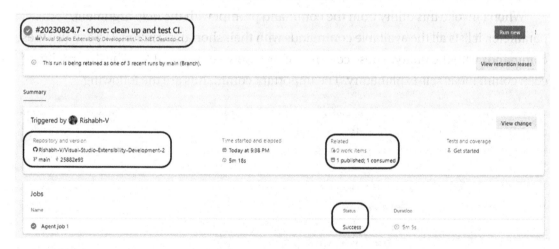

Figure 8-24. *Continuous integration run summary*

We can now download the generated VSIX file from the drop folder, install it in a testing environment, and check if our extension is working the way it is expected to work. If the extension works as expected, it is ready to be published in the Visual Studio Marketplace; if not, we will continue to make fixes in the extension and check-in to trigger continuous integration. Recall that while uploading the extension in the marketplace in the earlier section, we had to enter some of the mandatory fields (overview, internal name, etc.) manually in the portal. While automating the release of extension to the marketplace, we will need to keep this in mind.

Fortunately for us, the Visual Studio team has already thought about these aspects and included a command-line utility called VsixPublisher.exe to publish an extension to Visual Studio Marketplace. The location of this utility in my machine is **C:\Program Files\Microsoft Visual Studio\2022\Community\VSSDK\VisualStudioIntegration\Tools\Bin\VsixPublisher.exe**, so the path where you can find this utility in your machine is {VSInstallDir}\VSSDK\VisualStudioIntegration\Tools\Bin\VsixPublisher. exe, where {VSInstallDir} is the installation directory of your Visual Studio. We will make use of this utility to release extensions to the marketplace. Before we integrate this utility in our release pipeline, let us quickly discuss what this utility has to offer. This utility is well documented on the Microsoft docs site, and I will recommend readers to look at the documentation at https://learn.microsoft.com/en-us/visualstudio/ extensibility/walkthrough-publishing-a-visual-studio-extension-via-command-line?view=vs-2022 before starting the work on release pipeline.

When I invoke this utility from the command prompt with the help argument/ parameter, it lists all the available commands with their short description. We can use these commands with the utility. These commands are shown in Figure 8-25. The description of each command is self-explanatory. The important commands are the following.

```
C:\Program Files\Microsoft Visual Studio\2022\Community\VSSDK\VisualStudioIntegration\Tools\Bin>VsixPublisher.exe help
Vsix Publishing Tools 17.7.2189+bd7ee5fd3b
Copyright (C) Microsoft Corporation. All rights reserved.

  deleteExtension             Delete an extension from the marketplace.

  deletePublisher             Delete a publisher from the marketplace.

  help                        Show the usage text

  login                       Add a publisher to the known publishers list.

  logout                      Remove a publisher from the known publishers list.

  publish                     Publishes an extension.

  version                     Display the version of this program.
```

Figure 8-25. *VsixPublisher commands*

- deleteExtension: To delete an extension from the marketplace

- deletePublisher: To delete a publisher from the marketplace

- login: To add a publisher to the known publishers list

- logout: To remove a publisher from the known publishers list

- publish: To publish an extension

- In addition to these commands, there is

  - A help command, which displays the help text to use a command, and

  - A version command, which displays the version of the vsixpublisher.exe

  The documentation for using these commands can be seen in the tool by using the help command, or you can read the detailed usage documentation online (in the documentation link shared earlier). In Visual Studio 2019, there used to be an additional command createPublisher to create a publisher which is no longer available and one has to create a publisher directly in the Visual Studio Marketplace.

We want to upload the generated extension to the marketplace. So, for our use case, which is one of the most common scenarios, we will only need to use login and publish commands to log in to the marketplace and publish the extension, respectively.

The syntax for using login command is

```
VsixPublisher.exe login -personalAccessToken "{Personal Access Token}"
-publisherName "{Publisher Name}"
```

The login command requires two essential parameters: a personal access token (PAT) and the publisher name. The PAT serves as an authentication mechanism for the publisher. We have already seen the publisher name while creating a publisher in the marketplace earlier in this chapter. In the following section, we will delve into the process of obtaining the PAT. Upon executing the login command, the specified publisher name will be appended to the list of known publishers, and you will be successfully logged in under the publisher's identity.

Let us next see the syntax of `publish` command:

```
VsixPublisher.exe publish -payload "{path to vsix}" -publishManifest "{path
to vs-publish.json}"
```

The `publish` command mandates two essential parameters: specifically, payload and publishManifest. We can pass the path to the VSIX file or a hyperlink serving as a "more info URL." The publishManifest is a JSON file that contains all the metadata information that the marketplace needs to know to publish an extension.

Now that we know about the commands and publish manifest JSON, let us make necessary changes in our code to include a publish manifest JSON file as it would be needed to publish the extension. We need to add a readme.md file and a manifest.json file to the project structure. Ensure that these files are available in build output by setting the property "Copy to Output Directory" as "Copy always" for both these files. This will ensure that these files are always copied to the build output folder. Readme.md is a normal markdown file where you can specify the description about your extension in a regular markdown format.

The manifest format can be copied from the documentation URL, `https://learn.microsoft.com/en-us/visualstudio/extensibility/walkthrough-publishing-a-visual-studio-extension-via-command-line?view=vs-2022#publishmanifest-file`, and modified to describe your extension for the marketplace.

The manifest file code for our `AsyncSnippet` extension looks as shown in Figure 8-26.

```
{
  "$schema": "http://json.schemastore.org/vsix-publish",
  "categories": [ "coding" ],
  "identity": {
    "internalName": "asyncSnippet"
  },
  "assetFiles": [
    {
      "pathOnDisk": "AddSnippet.png",
      "targetPath": "AddSnippet.png"
    }
  ],
  "overview": "readme.md",
  "priceCategory": "free",
  "publisher": "rishabhverma",
  "private": false,
  "qna": true,
  "repo": "https://github.com/Rishabh-V/Visual-Studio-Extensibility-Development-2"
}
```

Figure 8-26. *Publish manifest JSON*

The publish manifest JSON mapping with Visual Studio Marketplace fields is shown in Figure 8-27.

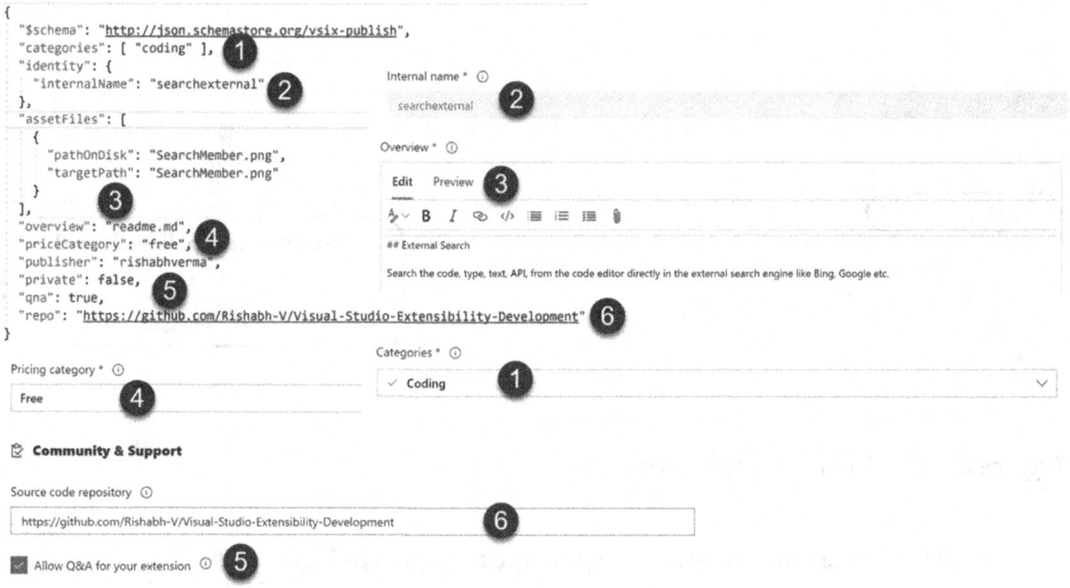

Figure 8-27. *Publish manifest JSON to marketplace mapping*

Though this is easy to understand (just match the number in JSON with the number in the UI), it is important to note the Overview section has a `readme.md` file created by us. All the images used by readme.md file are mentioned in the `assetFiles` collection of the JSON. The `private` value of `true` would keep the extension private. Please make a note that categories should contain the right and valid values, or else the publish will fail. Once these files are checked in GitHub, our continuous integration build would trigger. Validate that VSIX, images, `readme.md`, and publish manifest JSON files are existing in the build output.

Let us now build the release pipeline to publish the generated extension from the build pipeline to the Visual Studio Marketplace:

1. To create a release pipeline, click Releases in the left pane under Pipelines as shown in Figure 8-28. Click the "New pipeline" button to create a new release pipeline.

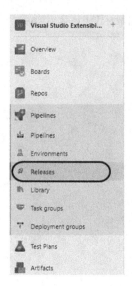

Figure 8-28. *New release pipeline*

2. This will create a new release pipeline as shown in Figure 8-29. Give this new release pipeline a meaningful name, like "Publish to Marketplace" or something else of your choice. Select an empty job template as there is no built-in template to publish VSIX to the marketplace. Then click "+ Add an artifact" and specify the source build pipeline from which this release will take the artifacts. If you have followed the previous steps, the source will show up in the drop-down. Since this is a simple demonstration, we will keep a single-stage release pipeline. So, rename the stage name to say, "Publish VSIX." Now, we will add tasks to the stage that would be responsible to take the extension VSIX, publishManifest as inputs from build, and publish the extension to the marketplace. As discussed, a little earlier, we can make use of the `VsixPublisher.exe` utility to publish the extension, so first, we need to have an agent in which Visual Studio is installed. We will then run the login and publish commands on the `VsixPublisher.exe` utility with proper parameters to publish the extension. So, let us next choose an agent that has Visual Studio installed.

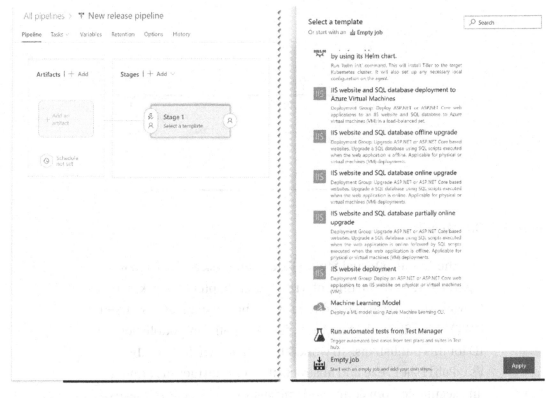

Figure 8-29. *Release pipeline*

3. Let's configure our Agent job. Select Azure Pipelines as the Agent Pool and windows-2022 or windows-latest as the Agent Specification. If we plan to use the `VsixPublisher.exe` utility, we can set the demand that Visual Studio must exist. This is illustrated in Figure 8-30.

4. Now, we have couple of options. We can either add a PowerShell task to get the path of `VsixPublisher.exe` and set the task environment variable with that path so that this variable can be used in the subsequent tasks for login and publishing the extension to the marketplace. But this is tedious as we first need to find the path of the executable and then execute the commands to login and publish. Fortunately, there is a predefined task called "Publish Visual Studio Extension" which can do the same job without us having to go through these hassles. We will leverage the same.

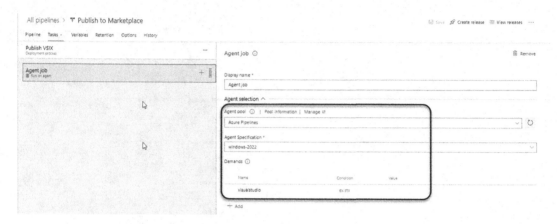

Figure 8-30. *Agent*

5. Add the "Publish Visual Studio Extension" task as depicted in
    Figure 8-31. As of the time of writing this chapter, the task is in the
    Preview state. We will need to provide the personal access token
    (PAT), VSIX file path, `manifest.json` file path, and publisher
    ID for this publish task to work. This task internally uses the
    `VsixPublisher.exe` and abstracts the complexities of running
    an executable from command line away from us. For the sake of
    completeness, let us quickly understand the steps. Click the "+"
    button on the Agent job (#1). This will display a list of available
    predefined tasks. Type "Publish Visual Studio" on the search
    text box (#2). This will filter and show the "Publish Visual Studio
    Extension" task. Click the "Add" button to add this task to our
    pipeline (#3). Click the "Publish Visual Studio Extension" (#4).
    This will display the task properties to be configured (#5).

6. To configure the publish task, provide your Publisher ID. The
    VSIX file path and Manifest file path can be picked from the build
    output by clicking the button next to the respective text box. Next,
    we will provide the Visual Studio Marketplace connection. This
    will ask for the PAT token. Therefore, let us first find the PAT.

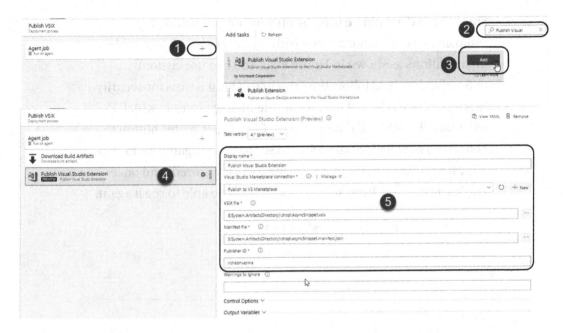

Figure 8-31. *Add tasks*

7. To get the PAT, click the top-right icon beside the user profile in the Azure DevOps site where we are currently working. Then click "Personal access tokens" as shown in Figure 8-32.

Figure 8-32. *Personal access tokens*

8. Since this PAT would be used by only me for publishing my
    extensions, I can create a token with full access for all accessible
    organizations as shown in Figure 8-33. You can use custom-
    defined scopes and follow the principle of least access for security
    reasons. I have selected the custom-defined expiration, which
    will make this PAT valid for one year. Click the "Create" button to
    generate a new PAT for the selected scopes and organizations. Do
    copy it as soon as it shows up, because it is not stored, and once
    you navigate away from screen, you will not be able to see it again.

Create a new personal access token   ✕

Name

> PATForPublish

Organization

> All accessible organizations   ⌄

Expiration (UTC)

> Custom defined   ⌄ | 8/22/2024   📅

Scopes
Authorize the scope of access associated with this token
Scopes ◉ Full access
       ○ Custom defined

Figure 8-33. *Create PAT*

9. To make use of this PAT in the publish task, let us go back to our
    release pipeline in the Publish Visual Studio Extension task. Click
    the "+ New" button shown in #5 section in Figure 8-31. Fill in the
    Personal Access Token copied in the last step. Provide a name in
    Service Connection name field and click the Save button as shown
    in Figure 8-34.

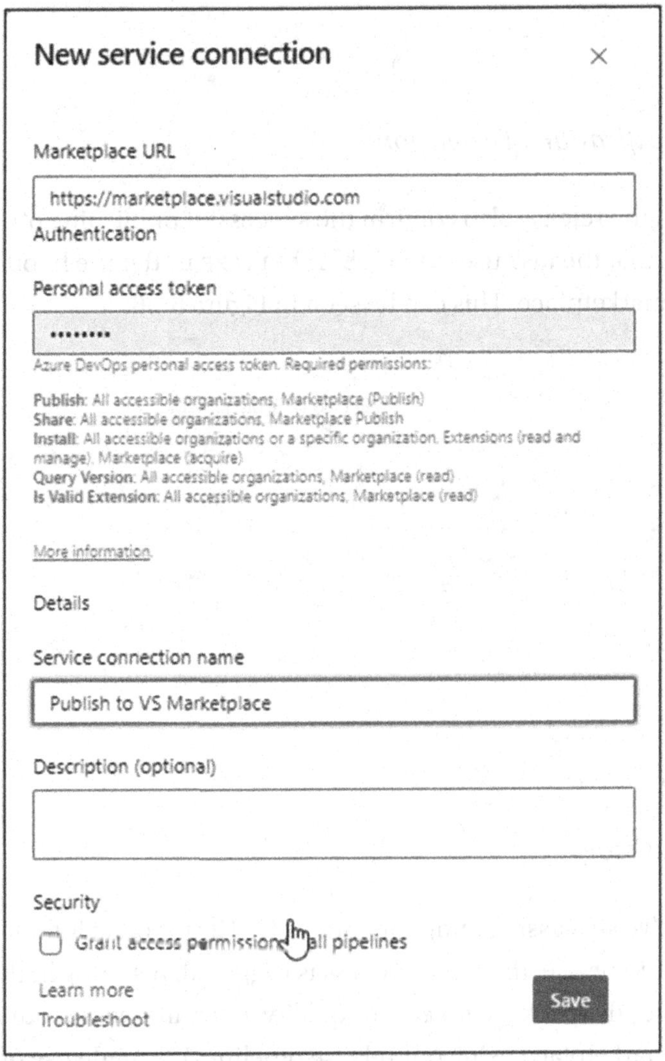

Figure 8-34. Visual Studio Marketplace connection

10. Save the tasks and create a new release and deploy. This will trigger a new release pipeline from the latest build. If all the parameters are correctly set, the release would succeed, and the extension gets published to the marketplace. Just like we saw while manually uploading the extension, there will be a verification triggered by the marketplace. This is shown in Figure 8-35.

Figure 8-35. *Verification of extension*

The logs from the release also confirm the successful publishing of extension. The logs also confirm that the task uses `VsixPublisher.exe` under the hood to publish the extension to the marketplace. This can be seen in Figure 8-36.

```
2023-08-24T16:15:48.9472894Z ##[section]Starting: Publish Visual Studio Extension
2023-08-24T16:15:48.9651713Z ========================================================================
2023-08-24T16:15:48.9651945Z Task         : Publish Visual Studio Extension
2023-08-24T16:15:48.9652026Z Description  : Publish Visual Studio extension to the Visual Studio Marketplace
2023-08-24T16:15:48.9652130Z Version      : 4.0.311
2023-08-24T16:15:48.9652191Z Author       : Microsoft Corporation
2023-08-24T16:15:48.9653423Z Help         : [More Information](https://marketplace.visualstudio.com/items?itemName=ms-devlabs.vsts-developer-tools-build-tasks)
2023-08-24T16:15:48.9653596Z ========================================================================
2023-08-24T16:15:49.9676089Z Logging in as 'rishabhverma'
2023-08-24T16:15:51.0144744Z [command]"C:\Program Files\Microsoft Visual Studio\2022\Enterprise\VSSDK\VisualStudioIntegration\Tools\Bin\VsixPublisher.exe" login -
personalAccessToken *** -publisherName rishabhverma
2023-08-24T16:15:55.9519565Z VSSDK: information VsixPub0041 : Publisher 'rishabhverma' is now logged-in.
2023-08-24T16:15:55.9520120Z Login successful.
2023-08-24T16:15:55.9520772Z Publishing 'D:\a\r1\a\drop\AsyncSnippet.vsix' to Visual Studio marketplace
2023-08-24T16:15:55.9554551Z [command]"C:\Program Files\Microsoft Visual Studio\2022\Enterprise\VSSDK\VisualStudioIntegration\Tools\Bin\VsixPublisher.exe" publish -
payload D:\a\r1\a\drop\AsyncSnippet.vsix -publishManifest D:\a\r1\a\drop\asyncSnippet.manifest.json -ignoreWarnings ""
2023-08-24T16:15:59.9797245Z VSSDK: information VsixPub0038 : Uploaded 'async Snippet' to the marketplace.
2023-08-24T16:15:59.9797765Z Published successfully.
2023-08-24T16:15:59.9798597Z Logging out publisher 'rishabhverma'
2023-08-24T16:15:59.9826794Z [command]"C:\Program Files\Microsoft Visual Studio\2022\Enterprise\VSSDK\VisualStudioIntegration\Tools\Bin\VsixPublisher.exe" logout -
publisherName rishabhverma -ignoreMissingPublisher
2023-08-24T16:16:01.7083404Z VSSDK: information VsixPub0042 : Publisher 'rishabhverma' has been logged-out.
2023-08-24T16:16:01.7084078Z Logout successful.
2023-08-24T16:16:01.7084409Z All done
2023-08-24T16:16:01.7216372Z ##[section]Finishing: Publish Visual Studio Extension
2023-08-24T16:16:01.7393163Z ##[section]Starting: Finalize Job
2023-08-24T16:16:01.7438519Z Cleaning up task key
2023-08-24T16:16:01.7439928Z Start cleaning up orphan processes.
2023-08-24T16:16:01.7460219Z ##[section]Finishing: Finalize Job
2023-08-24T16:16:01.7550757Z ##[section]Finishing: Agent job
```

Figure 8-36. *Task logs*

Excellent! We've successfully implemented a CI/CD pipeline for our extension. Now, whenever we commit code, the build process is triggered, resulting in the generation of VSIX package. After the package meets our quality gates and passes our testing, we can publish it to the marketplace using our release pipeline. We made use of `VsixPublisher.exe` under the hood for publishing the extension.

Interestingly, there's another Azure DevOps extension that caught my attention: VsixTools. This extension offers an alternative approach for publishing our extension via the release pipeline. VsixTools boasts compatibility with various platforms, including Visual Studio Marketplace, Open VSIX Gallery (a gallery developed by Mads Kristensen for nightly extension builds), and even the MyGet VSIX feed. For more details and to download this extension, visit `https://marketplace.visualstudio.com/items?itemName=SamirBoulema.Vsix-Tools&targetId=64baaa2e-8a07-490c-b409-75352cb02a9e`.

CHAPTER 8   CONTINUOUS INTEGRATION AND HOSTING

A crucial point to highlight is that, for each update, we should increment the extension's version within the VSIXmanifest. Here, we have to do it manually, but we can easily write a script to increment the version based on the build pipeline parameter.

With this note, we will conclude our discussion on setting up a CI/CD pipeline for our extension. We had a reference to open VSIX gallery in this discussion, which we said is an open source gallery for nightly builds of extensions. In the next section, let's discuss private extension galleries.

Private Galleries

While Visual Studio Marketplace is the one-stop shop for sharing and consuming the extensions, there arise instances where extensions are tailored to specific business scenarios and are relevant only to selected developers or teams within an organization. There may be additional constraints such as enterprises safeguarding their proprietary business easing extensions from wider exposure. To cater to the preceding unique needs, Visual Studio has great support for private extension galleries, with the same capabilities of auto-updating the per-user extensions, just like Visual Studio Marketplace. So, if you develop extensions that are useful to your team members but may not be relevant or useful to others, then you can think of hosting your extensions in a private extension gallery. This approach not only ensures the relevance of your extensions to your team but also streamlines the distribution of updates, should you address bugs or introduce enhancements. In the next section, we will discuss the anatomy of a private gallery, so that we can then learn to create the gallery.

Anatomy of a Private Gallery

To understand the anatomy of a private gallery, let us take an example. Open your preferred web browser and navigate to the URL http://vsixgallery.com/. This will navigate us to the Open VSIX Gallery as shown in Figure 8-37. The gallery lists numerous extensions.

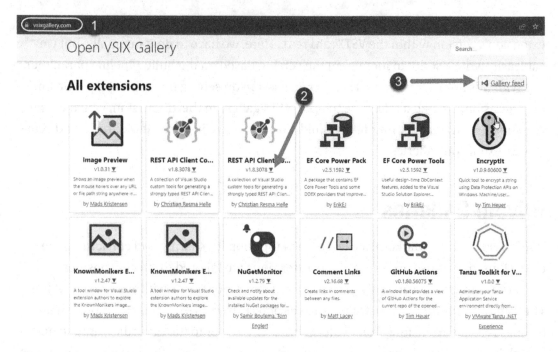

Figure 8-37. *Open VSIX Gallery*

There is a download button for each of the listed extensions. There exists a button for the Gallery feed. Click the "Gallery feed." This action will open the atom feed XML, which can be subscribed to via browsers, email, or various other clients. This feed XML (opened in Microsoft Edge and Google Chrome browsers side by side) is shown in Figure 8-38.

Atom feed is just a data feed that contains structured data and content of this feed can change or update frequently. This XML feed contains all the necessary metadata information that is essential for the Visual Studio infrastructure to display the extension and its information. If you read the XML, it's easy to understand that it has all the metadata information that we specify in our `vsixmanifest` file. Take note of the "subtitle" node within the XML, as it offers guidance on consuming this feed XML within Visual Studio.

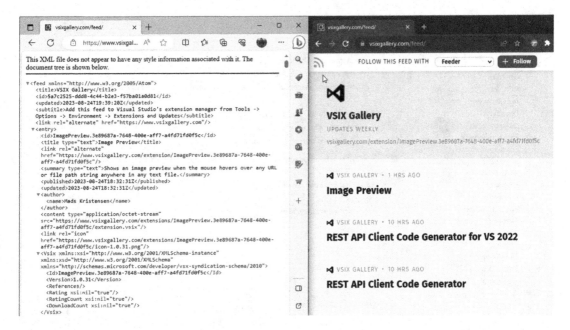

Figure 8-38. *Gallery feed*

To consume this feed XML in Visual Studio is easy. In your Visual Studio, open the Options dialog from the top Tools menu. You can alternatively use Search (Ctrl+Q) to search for Options. In the Options dialog, click Extensions under the Environment node in the left pane. Then click the Add button beside Additional Extension Galleries. Next, enter the Name and URL of the gallery as Open VSIX Gallery and `http://vsixgallery.com/feed/`, respectively, and click the Apply button. This flow is explained via numbered steps in Figure 8-39. For a detailed discussion and guide, refer to `www.vsixgallery.com/feedguide`.

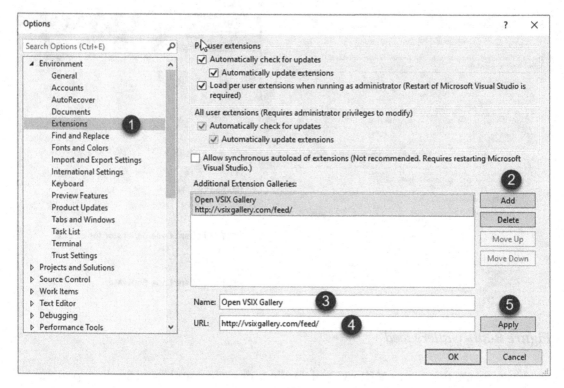

Figure 8-39. *Adding the Open VSIX Gallery*

Now, if we open the Manage Extensions dialog, we will see a new extension gallery under the online section with the name Open VSIX Gallery as shown in Figure 8-40. We can use this extension gallery in the same way as Visual Studio Marketplace. So, the crux of the matter is that all we need to create an additional extension gallery for Visual Studio is an Atom feed that describes all the metadata information about the extensions. If we can create a valid atom feed in the format discussed earlier with valid links to icons and vsix file, we can easily set up a private extension gallery. In the next section, we will quickly discuss various ways to create a private extension gallery.

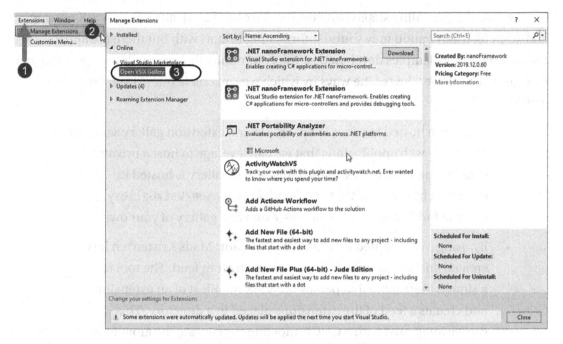

Figure 8-40. *Open VSIX Gallery in Manage Extensions dialog*

Creating Private Galleries

Based on our last discussion, it is safe to say that to create a private extension gallery, we need to do the following:

1. Place all the extensions (vsix files) that we want to be hosted in our gallery in a location that is accessible to the target audience of your gallery.

2. Parse the VSIX files and gather the metadata information of all the extensions.

3. Generate the Atom feed xml from the collected metadata information in the XML format discussed earlier.

If we do the preceding steps correctly, we can create a private gallery. VSIX parsing and atom feed generation may sound intimidating to start with but there are already utilities, tools, and samples developed by the community that we can leverage to achieve this easily. Let us see a few of the ways by which we can create our private extension gallery:

- By using a hosted service: There are several extension gallery samples created as web applications that we can leverage to host a private gallery. The source code of the Open VSIX Gallery is hosted in GitHub at `https://github.com/madskristensen/VsixGallery/`, and you can fork it and create a private extension gallery of your own.

- By using a tool named PrivateGalleryCreator: Mads Kristensen has created an open source utility to create an atom feed. The tool is a simple executable that parses the VSIX manifest of an extension and creates a feed of the extensions placed in a directory. This can be integrated with a CI/CD pipeline to generate the atom feed whenever a new code check-in is done. The tool is open source and you can see it in GitHub at `https://github.com/madskristensen/PrivateGalleryCreator`.

Other features of the tool and detailed steps to use it correctly can also be read from the same link.

- By using third-party hosted feeds: There are few public offerings for hosting private galleries as well. One quick and easy way to set up your private gallery quickly is `www.myget.org/vsix`. Just sign in and get started by creating your own feed and adding your extensions to the feed. The only downside I observed in this approach is that it is paid!

- Manually crafted atom feed xml: Though it is not something we will want to do; it can be one of the approaches that can be used to spawn a private gallery. Essentially, the atom feed format is fixed and we need to populate the right metadata values from the extension `vsixmanifest` into the atom feed, so copying a templated feed xml and updating the metadata values can also be a dirty but possible way to create an extension gallery.

We have discussed a few of the ways to quickly create a private extension gallery. It can be set up easily and quickly without needing much time. However, this is just one part of the story. We also need users to use these private galleries in Visual Studio, so integration with Visual Studio still needs to be done. In the next section, we will quickly discuss how to register a private gallery with Visual Studio.

Consuming Private Galleries

Figure 8-39 summarizes the steps needed to add a new extension gallery to the Visual Studio. This is easy to do, but is a manual process requiring way too many clicks and navigations that all our gallery users would need to follow. So why not have a Visual Studio extension that can accomplish this and take away all the manual steps? Let's see how we can create an extension to add a private gallery to Visual Studio. It's actually pretty simple to do so. The steps are as follows:

1. Open Visual Studio and create a new project using an empty VSIX project template.

2. Give a name and location to the project and click create. I have named my extension as "Extension gallery." This will create an empty VSIX project with just a vsixmanifest file as shown in Figure 8-41.

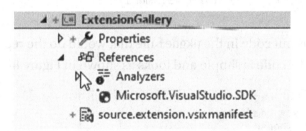

Figure 8-41. *Empty VSIX project*

3. Add a new file named "ExtensionGallery.pkgdef" to the project. This file is responsible for registering the private extension gallery with Visual Studio. Right now, it is just an empty file.

4. Like in every extension, update the source.extension. vsixmanifest file with the appropriate name, description, tags, icons, and other metadata information.

5. Navigate to the Assets section of the vsixmanifest file and add a new asset of type VsPackage as shown in Figure 8-42. Notice that source is set to "file on filesystem" and path is set to the pkgdef file we added earlier. Without this change, the extension would not be able to run registrations and hence will not work.

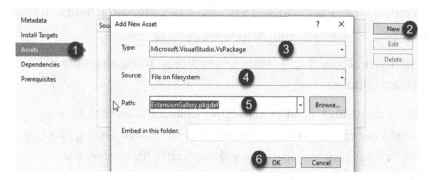

Figure 8-42. *Update asset section of* vsixmanifest

6. Now let us put code in the pkgdef file that would do the registry entries. The code is simple and looks as shown in Figure 8-43.

```
[$RootKey$\ExtensionManager\Repositories\{415e1d4b-02b9-4b24-a546-fbac239898cf}]
@="http://vsixgallery.com/feed/"
"Priority"=dword:00000056
"Protocol"="Atom Feed"
"DisplayName"="Rishabh Gallery"
```

Figure 8-43. *Pkgdef file content*

The code is simple; we are setting the extension gallery URL "http://vsixgallery.com/feed" at the path $RootKey$\ ExtensionManager\Repositories\{<A guid>} and then setting the other properties like priority, protocol, and DisplayName.

7. That's it! Coding for our extension gallery extension is done. Now, if we debug the extension, a new experimental instance of Visual Studio would open. In this instance, we will navigate to the "Manage Extensions" dialog and check the installed and online sections as shown in Figure 8-44.

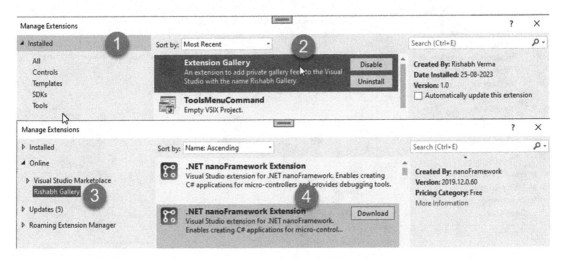

Figure 8-44. Installed and Online sections in Manage Extensions

In the Installed section, we confirm that the Extension Gallery extension is installed. And in the Online section, we find that we have a new gallery with the name "Rishabh Gallery," and we can see all the extensions from the Open VSIX Gallery listed and available to download.

8. If we navigate to the Options dialog and check the Extensions section, we will find that there is no entry in the "Additional Extension Gallery" section. This is because the new gallery is added directly at the registry! Figure 8-45 illustrates the empty section of Addition Extension Galleries.

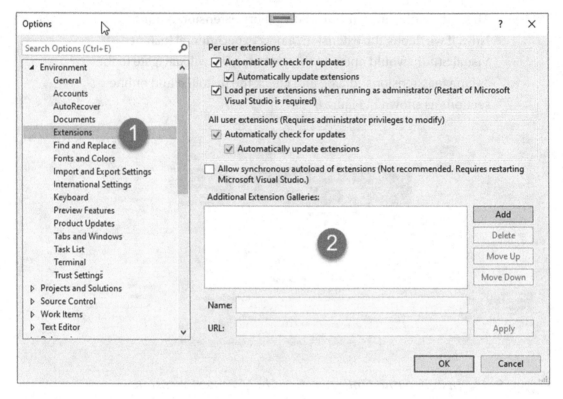

Figure 8-45. Empty "Additional Extension Galleries"

This concludes our discussion on the private galleries.

Summary

In this chapter, we learned the process of publishing a Visual Studio extension on the marketplace, extending its reach to a wider audience and the development community. We then wore a DevOps hat and created a CI and CD pipeline to build and deploy extensions. Finally, we discussed private extension galleries, their anatomies, and how we can create and consume the private galleries. With these insights, we'll wrap up our journey on a high note, equipped with enhanced skills and knowledge.

EXERCISES

The following activities are recommended to strengthen the knowledge gained from this chapter:

1. Read the documentation on publishing extensions at `https://learn.`
   `microsoft.com/en-us/visualstudio/extensibility/walkthrough-`
   `publishing-a-visual-studio-extension-via-command-`
   `line?view=vs-2022`.

2. Create an extension and publish it to Visual Studio Marketplace. (If you do not wish to share with the world, you can keep the extension private.)

3. Create a CI/CD pipeline for your developed extension. You may use the DevOps tool of your choice, so the pipeline may be Azure DevOps or AppVeyor or Jenkins or GitHub actions or any other tool of your choice.

4. Read the following resources on private galleries:

   a. `https://devblogs.microsoft.com/visualstudio/create-a-private-`
      `gallery-for-self-hosted-visual-studio-extensions/`

   b. `https://learn.microsoft.com/en-us/visualstudio/extensibility/`
      `private-galleries?view=vs-2022`

   c. `https://learn.microsoft.com/en-in/visualstudio/extensibility/`
      `how-to-create-an-atom-feed-for-a-private-gallery?view=vs-2022`

   d. `https://github.com/madskristensen/PrivateGalleryCreator`

   e. `https://github.com/madskristensen/VsixGallery/`

5. Set up a private gallery for your extensions. Create an extension to register this gallery with Visual Studio and share it with your friends or teammates.

CHAPTER 9

Tips and Tricks

In this chapter, we will discuss several practical tips that can enhance your experience with Visual Studio and aid in both developing and using its extensions. Some of these suggestions will also contribute to enhancing the professionalism of your extensions. We shall also discuss briefly the extensibility of Visual Studio Code. Finally, we will conclude this chapter and the book by showcasing a selection of the cool and valuable extensions that I personally find useful.

Tips and Tricks

A highly regarded Chinese philosopher, Confucius, once expressed the sentiment "I hear and I forget. I see and I remember. I do and I understand." So, nothing is as valuable as the hard-earned hands-on experience gained by developing the extensions. But we can always learn from the experience and learning of others who have tread on this journey of using and developing Visual Studio extensions. In this section, we will discuss a few of the handy things to know about using Visual Studio in general and also for developing Visual Studio extensions. Let's have a look at few I have learned and discovered.

VSIXManifest Metadata Values

Update a VSIXManifest file with concise and meaningful metadata values. As the adage goes, "First impression is the last impression." While I don't necessarily agree with this adage entirely, it's undeniable that a first impression carries lasting weight, and the same applies to Visual Studio extensions. When searching for or browsing through extensions on the Visual Studio Marketplace, the initial elements that capture our attention include the extension's name, description, icon, tags, and license, among others.

© Rishabh Verma 2024
R. Verma, *Visual Studio Extensibility Development*, https://doi.org/10.1007/978-1-4842-9875-6_9

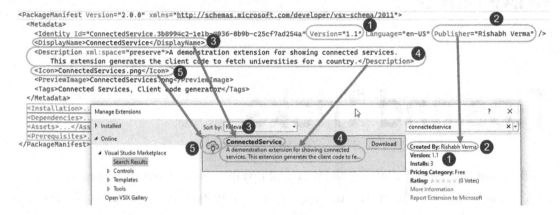

Figure 9-1. `.vsixmanifest` *file metadata values*

These values define the branding your extension to the end user and significantly impact the overall professionalism of your extension's appearance. Hence, these metadata values should always be updated with crisp, clear, meaningful, and precise information. Figure 9-1 illustrates the VSIXManifest XML and how the values specified within the XML nodes correspond to the extension that appears during an extension search. In the preceding image, the VSIXManifest-to-UI mapping is outlined next according to the provided numbering:

> #1: Version attribute – Version
>
> #2: Publisher attribute – Created by
>
> #3: DisplayName element – Extension name
>
> #4: Description element – Description
>
> #5: Icon element – Icon in UI

Name and Description

Extensions with appropriate names and precise descriptions are more likely to attract users, thereby increasing the likelihood of downloads and installations.

License

Just like any product, licensing holds a pivotal role in defining usage terms, liabilities, and warranties, if applicable. To begin comprehending and selecting an appropriate license for your extension, valuable resources can be explored at `https://github.com/github/choosealicense.com/tree/gh-pages/_licenses` or `https://choosealicense.com/` or `https://opensource.org/licenses/`.

Tags

While tags are optional and can be entered as semicolon-separated values, they prove beneficial for enhancing extension discoverability. Therefore, it's advisable to include a well-defined list of relevant tags.

Correct Target Version

Determine the target version of your extension and set it accurately in the `VSIXManifest` file. Before releasing your extension, understanding the desired target Visual Studio versions is crucial. Depending on the features (APIs) utilized in your extension, certain APIs might not be available in the prior versions of Visual Studio. Hence, it's advisable to thoroughly test your extension against the intended version range you wish to support (see Figure 9-2). We covered version ranges in Chapter 4; however, Mads provides a comprehensive blog post on version ranges that is highly recommended to read at `https://devblogs.microsoft.com/visualstudio/visual-studio-extensions-and-version-ranges-demystified/`.

After reading this blog, you can easily target your extension to a previous version (e.g., Visual Studio 2019).

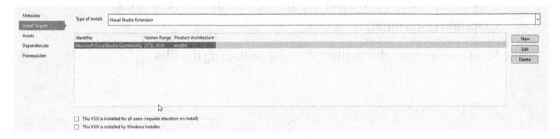

Figure 9-2.   Version Range

Packaging and Updating the Extension

Determine how you wish to package and update the extension. In most cases, shipping VSIX serves the purpose, but I have come across scenarios where the team wanted the installation via Microsoft Windows Installer (MSI) to package the extension as part of their suite of tools. The steps to achieve this are displayed in Figure 9-3. They are the following:

1. Navigate to the vsixmanifest file and click the "Install Targets" tab.

2. Tick the check box titled "The VSIX is installed by Windows Installer." This will add an attribute InstalledByMsi="true" on the Installation element in the VSIXManifest file. This tells the VSIX installer to not install this VSIX. If you attempt to install this extension, you will see the following error:

    Install Error : Microsoft.VisualStudio.ExtensionManager. InstallByMsiException: The InstalledByMSI element in extension <<Extension Name>> cannot be 'true' when installing an extension through the Extensions and Updates Installer. The element can only be 'true' when an MSI lays down the extension manifest file.

3. In the project properties page of your extension project, navigate to the VSIX section.

4. Tick the check box "Copy VSIX content to the following location" and enter the path where you want the VSIX content to be copied.

5. Build the extension project and navigate to the folder location specified in step #4. We will see the VSIX content copied in this location upon build.

The MSI installer can refer to this folder for packaging the files.

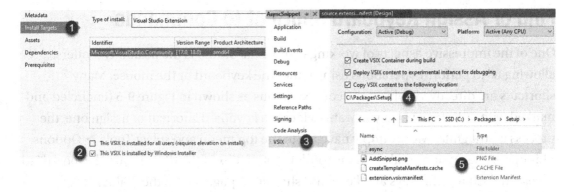

Figure 9-3. *Supporting MSI-based installations*

Use Extensibility Essentials 2022 Extension

As discussed in Chapter 4, the extension "Extensibility Essentials 2022" (see Figure 9-4) is highly recommended for all Visual Studio 2022 extension authors. It is an extension pack and has several useful extensions. You can read more about this extension in Chapter 4 or online at `https://marketplace.visualstudio.com/items?itemName=MadsKristensen.ExtensibilityEssentials2022`.

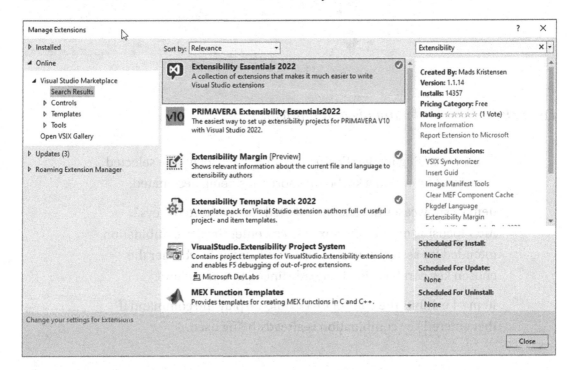

Figure 9-4. *Extensibility Essentials 2022*

Find or Assign Keyboard Shortcut to Commands

One of the impressive aspects of working with Visual Studio is the flexibility it offers, allowing us to perform operations using either the keyboard or the mouse. Many shortcuts are directly visible on the context menus as shown in Figure 9-5 (encircled and marked with #6). However, if you want to locate a keyboard shortcut or assign one, the process is straightforward. Simply navigate to the top menu and select Tools ➤ Options. This opens the Options dialog. In the top-left search box of the dialog, type "keyboard" to access the "Change hotkeys and keyboard shortcuts" page within the dialog.

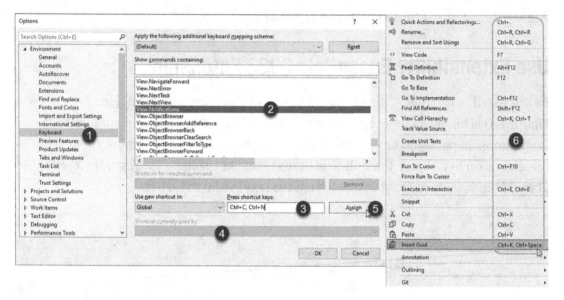

Figure 9-5. *Keyboard mapping and shortcuts*

In the preceding image (Figure 9-5), item #2 displays the selected command for which a keyboard shortcut is being designated.

Item #3 showcases the text box labeled "Press shortcut keys." After focusing on this text box, you can enter the key combination intended for assignment to a command, or verify whether the chosen key combination is already linked to a command.

Item #4 exhibits the control that would display the command if that entered key combination is already being used.

The #5 allows you to click the Assign button, enabling the assignment of the key combination to a command. If you wish to assign a shortcut to a command, you can also search for a command in the upper half of the section.

Run a Command

Once we're familiar with a command, situations may arise where we desire to execute the command, either directly within Visual Studio or from the extension under development. Here are several methods to execute a command:

- From the command window: Press Ctrl+Alt+A or navigate to the top-level menu bar and select View ➤ Other Windows ➤ Command Window. This action will open the Command window, wherein you can input a command. The Command window features IntelliSense support, making command input easier. After typing the command, press Enter to execute it. If the command is available in the current context, it will be executed; otherwise, a message indicating that the command is unavailable will be displayed. The IntelliSense support in Command window is shown in Figure 9-6.

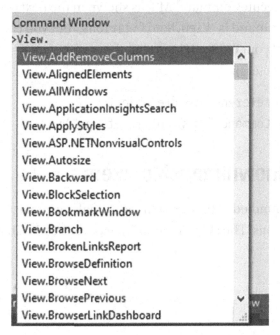

Figure 9-6. *Command Window*

- From an extension: Command Explorer extension can be used to execute a command as shown in Figure 9-7. Just click the Execute link beside the command. Again, it would execute only if it is available in the context.

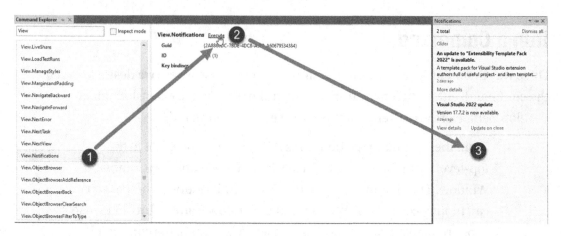

Figure 9-7. Execute command from Command Explorer

- From your extension code: Running a command from your extension code is simple; just get a reference to the DTE2 object and then invoke its ExecuteCommand API, as shown in the next code listing. Here the command is "`View.Notifications`," but you can use the command of your choice (along with the parameters if the command needs parameters):

```
// Get the reference to dte object
dte.ExecuteCommand("View.Notifications");
```

Make Use of KnownImageMonikers

Visual Studio comes bundled with over 4K images, making it logical to utilize these images in your extensions. The steps to do so were described in Chapter 5.

```
<CommandTable xmlns="http://schemas.microsoft.com/VisualStudio/2005-10-18/CommandTable" xmlns:xs="http://www.w3.org/2001/XMLSchema">
  <!--This is the file that defines the IDs for all the commands exposed by VisualStudio. -->
  <Extern href="stdidcmd.h"/>
  <!--This header contains the command ids for the menus provided by the shell. -->
  <Extern href="vsshlids.h"/>
  <Include href="KnownImageIds.vsct"/>   1
  ...
  <Commands package="guidExternalSearchPackage">
    ...
    ...
    <Groups>...</Groups>
    <!--Buttons section. -->
    ...
    <Buttons>
      ...
      <Button guid="guidExternalSearchPackageCmdSet" id="SearchCommandId" priority="0x0100" type="Button">
        <Parent guid="guidExternalSearchPackageCmdSet" id="MyMenuGroup" />
        <Icon guid="ImageCatalogGuid" id="Search" />   2
        <CommandFlag>IconIsMoniker</CommandFlag>
        <Strings>                              3
          <ButtonText>Search</ButtonText>
        </Strings>
      </Button>
    </Buttons>
  </Commands>

  <KeyBindings>
    <KeyBinding guid="guidExternalSearchPackageCmdSet" id="SearchCommandId" editor="guidVSStd97" key1="S" mod1="Alt">
    </KeyBinding>
  </KeyBindings>

  <Symbols>
    <!-- This is the package guid. -->        4
    <GuidSymbol name="guidExternalSearchPackage" value="{2f33e5a2-ff60-4424-b309-e57787c5d3fa}" />
    <!-- This is the guid used to group the menu commands together -->
    <GuidSymbol name="guidExternalSearchPackageCmdSet" value="{20580f36-35da-4d5f-95d6-d2d2d4df35fd}">
      <IDSymbol name="MyMenuGroup" value="0x1020" />
      <IDSymbol name="SearchCommandId" value="0x0100" />
    </GuidSymbol>
  </Symbols>
</CommandTable>
```

Figure 9-8. *Using known image monikers*

The following is a summary of how to make use of KnownImageMonikers:

1. In your vsct file, include the reference to KnownImageIds.vsct as shown in step 1 of Figure 9-8.

2. Add an Icon node with GUID set to ImageCatalogGuid and id corresponding to the id of the image you wish to use. If you use Extensibility Essentials 2022 extension, you will get to see a preview image.

3. Add a CommandFlag node and set it to IconIsMoniker.

4. Remove the Bitmaps nodes and references to Bitmaps in IDSymbol nodes.

Coding Is Easier with IntelliCode

Visual Studio ships with a cool feature IntelliCode that can save your time by putting the APIs that you are most likely to use on the top of the completion list. This applies to statement completion as well as to signature help. Figure 9-9 shows IntelliCode in action.

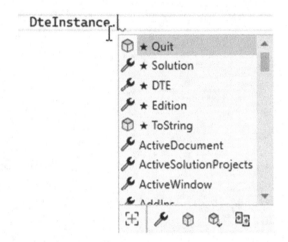

Figure 9-9. IntelliCode in action

Async Package and Background Loading

Derive your package class from AsyncPackage class (default in Visual Studio 2022 for creating any VSPackage) to enable loading of your package on a background thread and hence keeping the UI thread free and responsive. PackageRegistrationAttribute on the package class should explicitly set the AllowsBackgroundLoading property to true to opt into background loading behavior. This is a must to keep Visual Studio responsive while the extension loads. The following code listing demonstrates the code of VSPackage making use of AsyncPackage and background loading:

```
[PackageRegistration(UseManagedResourcesOnly = true,
AllowsBackgroundLoading = true)]
public sealed class DemoPackage : AsyncPackage
{}
```

For a detailed discussion on background loading, please read this official documentation at https://learn.microsoft.com/en-us/visualstudio/extensibility/how-to-use-asyncpackage-to-load-vspackages-in-the-background?view=vs-2022.

Use async All the Way

Proper usage of `async await` is crucial for maintaining non-blocking operations and a responsive UI. Incorrect implementation can lead to threads not being freed as expected. Thus, it's essential to ensure all methods in a call chain follow `async await` principles. Specifically:

- Avoid sync over async: This can lead to blocking and potential deadlocks. So, avoid using `Task.Result` and `Task.Wait`.

- Avoid async over sync: This can create false asynchrony and often leads to scalability problems (although this might be manageable in extensions). So, when we wrap a synchronous method in `Task.Run` like `Task.Run(SynchronousMethod)`, it will queue the work item to the `ThreadPool`. Since the method is actually synchronous, the thread will be blocked till the method returns. A large number of requests to such methods can potentially lead to scalability issues as the threads will be blocked.

Make Use of Analyzers

Your extension code must ensure that Visual Studio SDK is used correctly, and threading rules are strictly followed. To help facilitate this, Visual Studio 2022 default extension templates come up with the analyzers `Microsoft.VisualStudio.SDK.Analyzers` and `Microsoft.VisualStudio.Threading.Analyzers`. Please ensure that you take care of any warnings or errors detected by these analyzers.

Get a Service

In every extension that I ever wrote, I have always needed to make use of an existing service, so it's important to know how to get a service. To get a service, we always need to have an instance of `IServiceProvider`. The package class itself implements `IServiceProvider`, so inside the `AsyncPackage` code, we already have it. In command classes, we have a property of type `ServiceProvider` or a Package. In such cases, we can make use of the `GetService` API of the `ServiceProvider` to get the service we want as shown in the next code listing:

```
myUIShell = myPackage.GetService(typeof(IVsUIShell)) as IVsUIShell;
```

From a tool window class or other non-VSPackage classes, we can make use of the static GetGlobalService method of the Package class. This method tries to get the requested service from the cached service provider that is initialized the first time any VSPackage is sited. The documentation for this can be read at https:// learn.microsoft.com/en-us/visualstudio/extensibility/how-to-get-a-service?view=vs-2022.

Provide a Service

To expose your service to be used by other extensions or VSPackages, read the following documentation at https://learn.microsoft.com/en-us/visualstudio/extensibility/how-to-provide-a-service?view=vs-2022.

Make Use of Options Page

Consider using an options page for your extension if something in your extension needs a setting or can be configured. Avoid hard-coding at all costs. This is shown in Chapter 4.

Localize the Extension

Extensions can be localized in the target language. All we need to do is to create a .vsixlangpack file for the target language and then put it in the correct folder. The complete documentation is available at https://docs.microsoft.com/en-us/visualstudio/extensibility/localizing-vsix-packages?view=vs-2022.

InstalledProductRegistration Attribute

Perhaps you want to see your extension in the About Microsoft Visual Studio dialog, shown in Figure 9-10. In the top-level menu, click Help and then click About Microsoft Visual Studio to see the About dialog. To see your extension in this dialog, you must decorate your package class with the InstalledProductRegistration attribute like this:

```
[InstalledProductRegistration("<The name of my extension>","<Description of
my extension>","<Version of my extension>")]
```

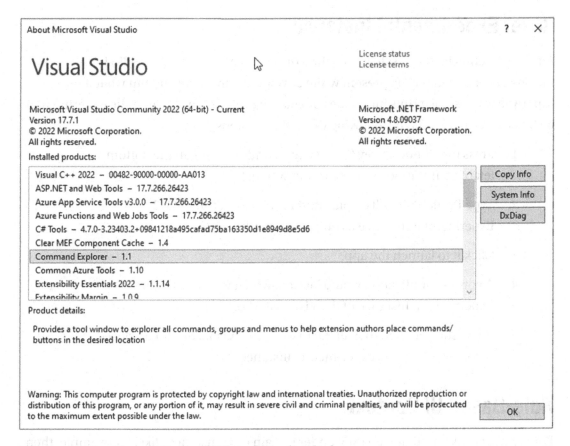

Figure 9-10. *About Microsoft Visual Studio dialog*

Consider to Use Ngen for Better Performance

Ngen is a utility that creates the native images, which are files containing the machine processor architecture–specific binary code and installs them in the native image cache of the local computer. The runtime can use this native image from the cache instead of using a just-in-time (JIT) compiler to perform a compilation of the original assembly. The steps to enable Ngen in your extension are listed in the following documentation at https://docs.microsoft.com/en-us/visualstudio/extensibility/ngen-support?view=vs-2022.

Reset Experimental Instance

An experimental instance safeguards the normal instance of Visual Studio from the buggy code that may be present while developing an extension. But what if my experimental instance runs into issues or gets corrupted? We can reset the experimental instance of Visual Studio by following these simple steps:

1. Press the Windows key (or click the Windows icon on the bottom left of your Windows 10 operating system).

2. Type Reset. This will display Reset the Visual Studio 2022 Experimental Instance as one of the results.

3. Click it to launch the app.

4. A console application would launch, which would reset the Experimental Instance of the Visual Studio.

5. It is recommended that all the instances of Visual Studio be closed before resetting the experimental instance.

Rule-Based UI Context

For creating packages that load only under certain circumstances like, for example, then a command should show up only when a specific file extension is opened, Microsoft came up with a concept of UI contexts. We used UI Context while discussing code generators. For a thorough documentation on rule-based UI context, please read the online documentation at `https://learn.microsoft.com/en-us/visualstudio/ extensibility/how-to-use-rule-based-ui-context-for-visual-studio- extensions?view=vs-2022`.

Use Syntax Visualizer

If you work with the .NET compiler platform (Roslyn), do make use of Syntax Visualizer to understand the SyntaxTree.

Look at Sample Extensions

Microsoft has built numerous Visual Studio extension samples that can be used as a reference to build your own extensions. These samples can be seen at `https://github.com/Microsoft/VSSDK-Extensibility-Samples`.

Add Sound Effects

You can add an element of excitement to your coding experience by incorporating sound effects into your build and debugging processes. Beyond the novelty, this can prove beneficial when working on extensive applications that require substantial build or debugging times. While your application is building or you're awaiting a breakpoint to trigger, you can engage in other tasks. Once the build completes or the breakpoint activates, a sound will play, signaling you to return to your work. Implementing this feature is straightforward, as demonstrated in Figure 9-11.

Figure 9-11. *Assign sound to Visual Studio build events and breakpoint hit event*

Press the Windows key on your keyboard, then type "Change System sounds," and click the corresponding item (#1 in the figure). This will open the dialog for configuring the sound theme. Within the Program Events section, locate "Microsoft Visual Studio" (#2 in the figure). You'll find four Visual Studio events listed: "Breakpoint Hit," "Build Canceled," "Build Failed," and "Build Succeeded." Depending on your preference, choose one of these events and assign a sound to it. Test the configuration to ensure your liking, and then apply the sound. The next time you launch a new instance of Visual

Studio and experience one of your configured events, the selected sound will play. Neat! There's also a programmatic method to achieve this using an extension. The DTE object offers an Events property that enables subscribing to events and triggering sounds. Mads Kristensen's extension "Farticus" serves as a great reference for this. You can download it from `https://marketplace.visualstudio.com/items?itemName=MadsKristensen.Farticus`, and the GitHub source link is available for you to explore the code.

OFF TOPIC

Allow me to share an amusing anecdote about an incident involving the Farticus extension. Perhaps this story might inspire you to inject some enjoyment into your team dynamics. One of our regional architects had come to visit our office and so our team was sitting in a conference room for a week. One of my colleagues was conducting a proof-of-concept work on a relatively smaller solution and was in a stage where he used to build often to check his changes incrementally. At a point when he momentarily stepped away from his desk for a discussion, we took the opportunity to install the Farticus extension in his Visual Studio environment. Strategically, we removed a semicolon from one of the code statements just before the workday concluded. The following morning, my friend entered the conference room early, joined only by our visiting regional architect. As he began his work and initiated a solution build, the absence of the semicolon triggered a build failure. This, in turn, prompted the installed Farticus extension to emit a resounding, comical sound. My friend got nervous and had no idea as to what was happening. He built again and the same loud farting sound played. Disturbed by the sound, the architect yelled "Wonderful!" and my friend was left rather embarrassed. He eventually realized it was the build failure that was making the noise and muted his laptop speakers. However, this story soon spread like a wildfire, and we had lots of fun!

Digitally Sign Your Extension

Though not required, but to secure your extension from any third-party or unsolicited modification, you can digitally sign your VSIX package by the steps mentioned in the online documentation at `https://learn.microsoft.com/en-us/visualstudio/extensibility/signing-vsix-packages?view=vs-2022`.

Create a VS Extension Pack

If you wish to package your multiple extensions in one extension, you can create an extension pack, just like the Extensibility Essentials 2022 extension pack. Creating an extension pack is easy and supported by means of a template in Visual Studio 2022. Please note that only extensions that are published in the marketplace or extension gallery can be packaged in the extension pack. The steps are shown in Figure 9-12.

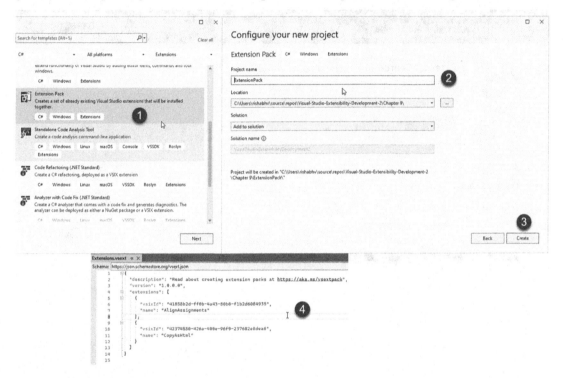

Figure 9-12. *Create an extension pack*

The steps are the following:

1. Add a new project of type Extension Pack.

2. Name the project and location.

3. Click the "Create" button to create the project.

4. Open the Extensions.vsext file. Provide the vsixId and name of the extensions that you wish to package in the extensions collection. The vsixId can be copied from the marketplace by clicking the CopyID link as shown in Figure 9-13.

5. Build and publish or install the extension. It is this simple to create an extension pack.

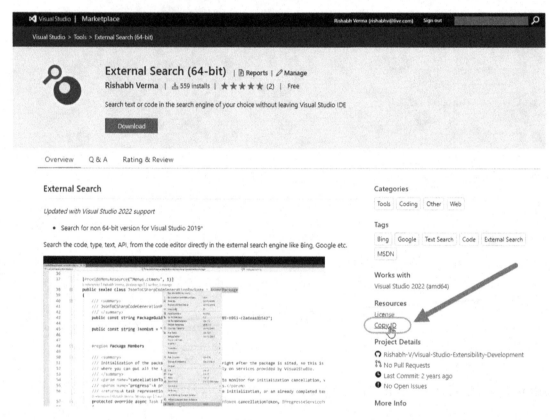

Figure 9-13. *Copy ID in marketplace*

Use the Checklist

A checklist is important to ensure that your extension follows the guidelines and best practices to make your extension professional and great. Do read and make use of it religiously. Read the documentation at https://gist.github.com/madskristensen/731 0c0d61694e323f4deeb5a70f35fec.

Visual Studio Performance Manager

On the search/quick launch of Visual Studio, type "Visual Studio Performance Manager" to find out extensions and tool windows that are impacting the startup up times and other glitches like Solution load, typing, unresponsive, crashes, etc. Alternatively, on the top menu, you can select Help ➤ Visual Studio Performance Manager. This navigation is shown in Figure 9-14. Visual Studio Performance manager UI is depicted in Figure 9-15.

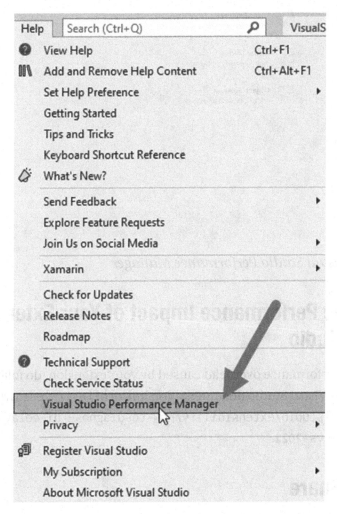

Figure 9-14. *Navigate to Visual Studio Performance Manager*

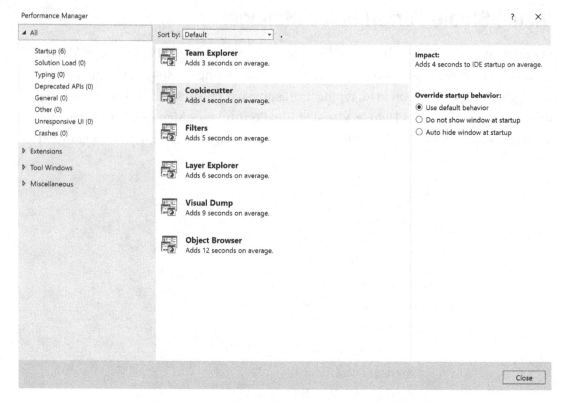

Figure 9-15. *Visual Studio Performance Manager*

Measure the Performance Impact of Your Extension on Visual Studio

To measure the performance overhead caused by your extension, do follow the steps mentioned in this Visual Studio documentation link at `https://learn.microsoft.com/en-us/visualstudio/extensibility/how-to-diagnose-ui-delays-caused-by-extensions?view=vs-2022`.

Live Code Share

Visual Studio has a cool feature named live code share that you can leverage to collaborate with your peer developers for peer programming, debugging, and review and also share your code without the receiver needing to clone the repository. Do give it a try.

Quick Launch/Search

As the name implies, quick launch is designed for swiftly accessing tool windows, commands, options, and more in order to save time. Positioned at the top of Visual Studio, it can be activated by either clicking the Search box at the top or by pressing Ctrl+Q. I have had numerous occasions where I was struggling to find a setting or command and quick launch came to my rescue, so much so that now that I always make use of quick launch for all my searches. It is shown in Figure 9-16.

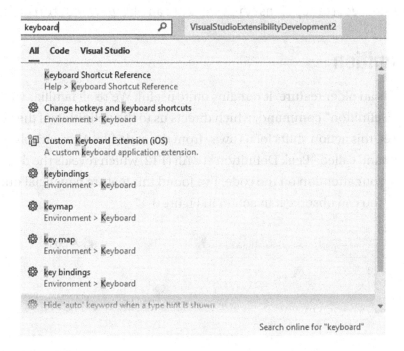

Figure 9-16. *Quick launch*

Close Tool Window

Often, when managing multiple tool windows, my Visual Studio interface becomes cluttered with numerous open windows. Manually closing them individually by clicking the close button can be quite laborious. To streamline this process, I employ the keyboard shortcut Shift+Esc; and voilà, my workspace is once again organized and free from unnecessary clutter. This keyboard shortcut is linked to the window's close command, providing an efficient way to tidy up the workspace.

Use EditorConfig File

We can make portable and custom editor settings by adding an editorconfig file to our project. This can also be used to enforce consistent coding styles for everyone that works in the code base. EditorConfig settings take precedence over global Visual Studio text editor settings. There is already an item template to add an editorconfig file and an extension to provide IntelliSense support to the edit editorconfig file. Read more about editorconfig at https://learn.microsoft.com/en-us/visualstudio/ide/create-portable-custom-editor-options?view=vs-2022 and https://editorconfig.org/.

Peek Definition

Although this is an older feature, it remains quite useful. We're all familiar with F12 or the "Go to Definition" command, which directs us to the definition of the chosen type or API. Yet, this action shifts focus away from the code file. Alternatively, there's another command called "Peek Definition" or Alt+F12, which reveals the definition while keeping your attention on the code. I've found this feature beneficial during development. You can observe it in action in Figure 9-17.

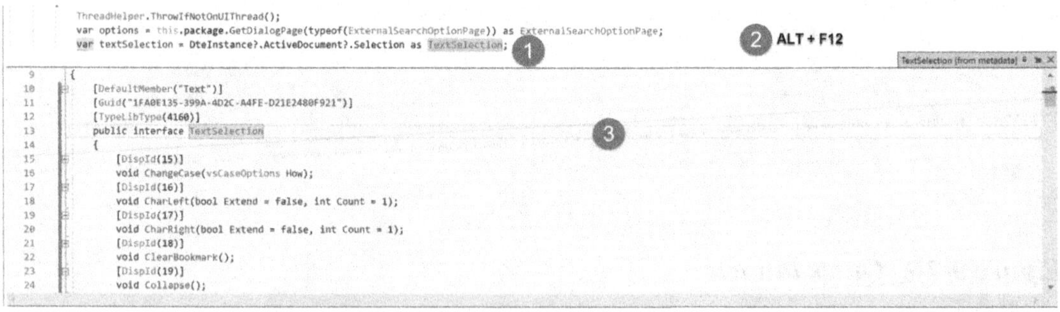

Figure 9-17. *Peek Definition*

Customize Scrollbar

The Visual Studio editor scrollbar is extensible and customizable as discussed in Chapter 6. Do try out these customizations by searching for scrollbar in the search (quick launch) and then trying different options. Figure 9-18 displays the steps to display the map mode of the scrollbar with a wide source preview tool tip. The image contains numbering, which lists the steps to achieve this.

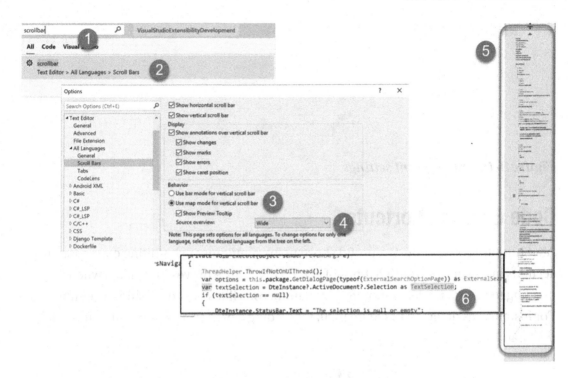

Figure 9-18. *Scrollbar customization*

Conditional Breakpoints, Tracepoints, and Data Breakpoints

Employ conditional breakpoints, dependent breakpoints, temporary breakpoints, tracepoints, and data breakpoints to enhance your debugging process. Press F9 to insert a breakpoint on a line, creating a basic breakpoint. To transform it into a conditional breakpoint, right-click the breakpoint and add a condition. This will cause the breakpoint to trigger only when the specified condition evaluates to true. Additionally, you can configure an action to output a message to the output window upon hitting the breakpoint, converting it into a tracepoint. Removing the breakpoint after its first hit results in a temporary breakpoint. Enabling a breakpoint to activate only when another breakpoint is hit creates a dependent breakpoint. During debugging, performing a quick watch on fields, variables, or properties allows you to halt the debugger solely when the value changes; these are referred to as data breakpoints. Breakpoint settings are depicted in Figure 9-19. For an in-depth exploration and official documentation on using breakpoints, data breakpoints, and tracepoints, refer to `https://docs.microsoft.com/en-us/visualstudio/debugger/using-breakpoints?view=vs-2022`.

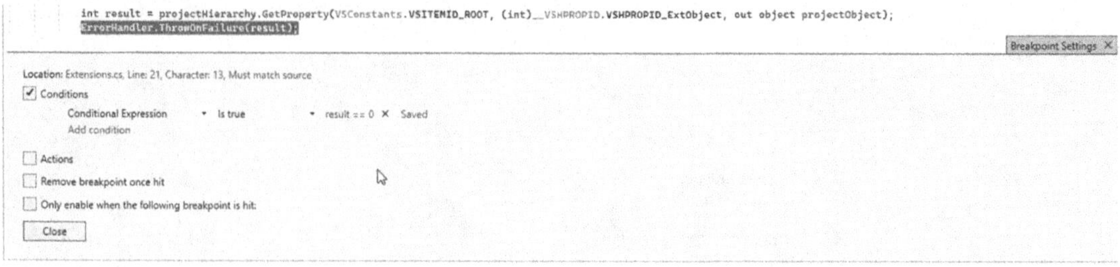

```
int result = projectHierarchy.GetProperty(VSConstants.VSITEMID_ROOT, (int)__VSHPROPID.VSHPROPID_ExtObject, out object projectObject);
ErrorHandler.ThrowOnFailure(result);
```

Breakpoint Settings ✕

Location: Extensions.cs, Line: 21, Character: 13, Must match source

☑ Conditions

    Conditional Expression   ▼   Is true   ▼   result == 0   ✕   Saved
    Add condition

☐ Actions
☐ Remove breakpoint once hit
☐ Only enable when the following breakpoint is hit

  Close

Figure 9-19. Breakpoint settings

Code Editing Shortcuts

Alt+Shift+up/down arrow is a useful shortcut for simultaneously editing corresponding
sections of text across multiple lines of code. This feature proves invaluable when
needing to insert, delete, or modify text in numerous lines of code within the editor.
For instance, as depicted in Figure 9-20, I'm adding a private access modifier to all field
declarations.

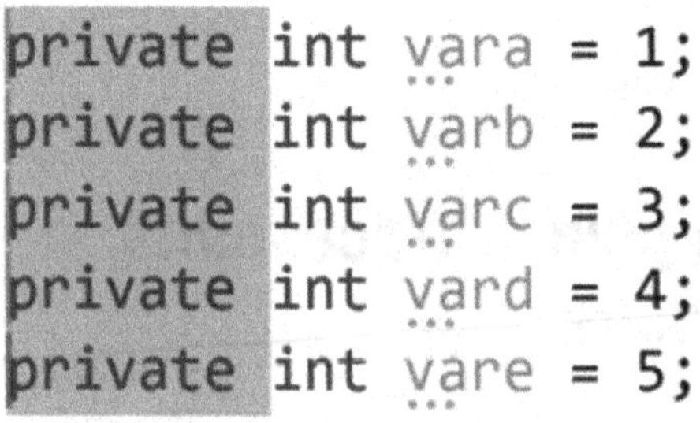

```
private int vara = 1;
private int varb = 2;
private int varc = 3;
private int vard = 4;
private int vare = 5;
```

Figure 9-20. Editing multiple lines of code text

Make Use of Snippets

Visual Studio ships with several snippets that can make your coding faster and easier.
You can use the Insert snippet command (Ctrl+K, Ctrl+X) to insert a snippet or Surround
with command (Ctrl+K, Ctrl+S) to surround a portion of code with a snippet.

Make Use of Code Map

Code map is a cool feature to visualize how your code is layered along with its dependencies without needing to browse through the entire code. Figure 9-21 shows the code map diagram for the code of this book. To create a code map diagram, we need the Enterprise edition of Visual Studio. Though you can open the code map diagrams in Professional and Community editions, you cannot edit the diagrams in these editions.

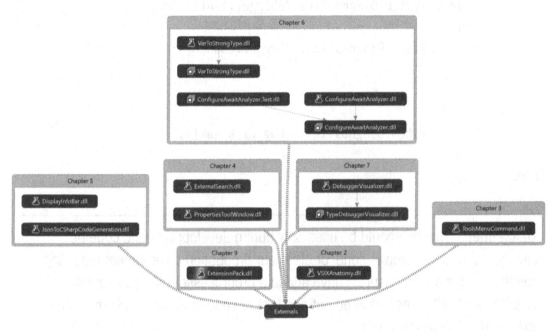

Figure 9-21. *Code map diagram*

Use IntelliTest to Write and Maintain Better Tests

Testing is an important part of developing and shipping any software. IntelliTest makes it easier to test your code with proper test scenarios. It is available only in the Enterprise version of Visual Studio, but I would highly recommend this feature. To read more about IntelliTest, read the documentation at https://learn.microsoft.com/en-us/visualstudio/test/intellitest-manual/introduction?view=vs-2022.

Programmatically Attach or Break the Debugger in Your Code

You can programmatically attach or break the debugger in your application to be debugged, by the following snippet:

```
#if DEBUG
            if (!System.Diagnostics.Debugger.IsAttached)
            {
                System.Diagnostics.Debugger.Launch();
            }
            else
            {
                System.Diagnostics.Debugger.Break();
            }
#endif
```

Disclaimer   This tip should be used only during development and code be reverted after debugging is done, or else your production environment may stop running. As a safety measure, I have added a preprocessor directive, which requires a DEBUG constant to be defined for the code to execute, which will not exist in Release mode builds.

C# Interactive Window

A C# Interactive window is a great place to experiment and play around with code and APIs and can be helpful in cases where we need to perform quick prototyping or checking the output of a function without wanting to create a new project. It is based on the .NET Compiler platform (Roslyn) and provides a read–eval–print-loop (REPL) to get the live evaluation and feedback on our code as we type. It has support for syntax coloring, highlighting as well as IntelliSense support, to make it easier to use. There are a couple of ways to execute code in the Interactive window. On the top-level menu in Visual Studio, click View ➤ Other Windows ➤ C# Interactive. This will launch the Interactive window. Another way is to right-click the code editor and then click "Execute in Interactive." This will also launch the C# Interactive window. This window is just like an editor with IntelliSense support so you can write the code with ease and execute it. A simple program to declare two variables and then sum them and check the sum is shown highlighted in Figure 9-22. The other numbers on the image indicate the two different ways to launch the Interactive window as discussed.

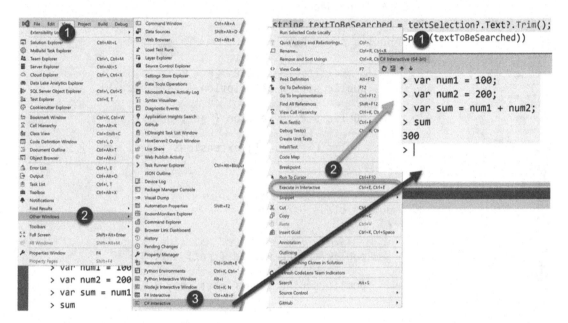

Figure 9-22. *C# Interactive window*

Paste Special for XML and JSON

If you work with web APIs, XML, or JSON, then Paste Special may be of great use to you for converting XML or JSON into corresponding C# classes. To do so, open the file in Visual Studio where you wish the C# classes to be pasted. Then copy the JSON/XML and in the top-level menu of Visual Studio, click Edit ➤ Paste Special ➤ Paste JSON as classes as shown in Figure 9-23.

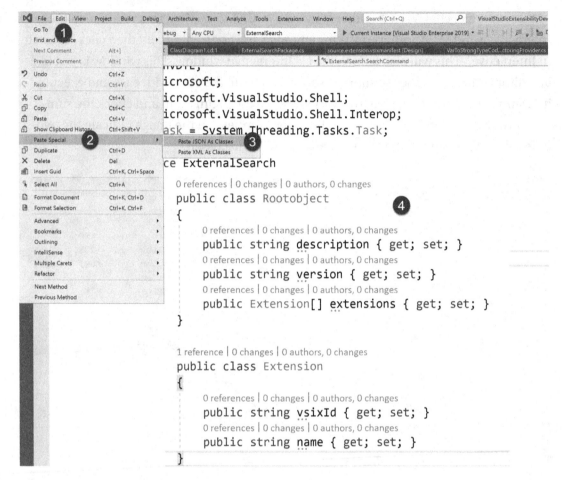

Figure 9-23. *Paste Special command*

Go to All

Use Ctrl+, or Ctrl+T, to quickly find files, classes, methods, and symbols across your solution (Figure 9-24).

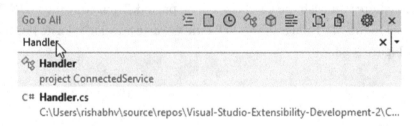

Figure 9-24. *Go to All*

Improve Solution Load Performance

For enhancing the performance of a project or solution load, go to Tools ➤ Options ➤ Project and Solutions, and uncheck the "Restore Solution Explorer project hierarchy state on solution load" option. This action will not restore the previous state of the solution upon opening the VS 2022 IDE, leading to improved loading performance of the solution. This is labeled #1 in Figure 9-25.

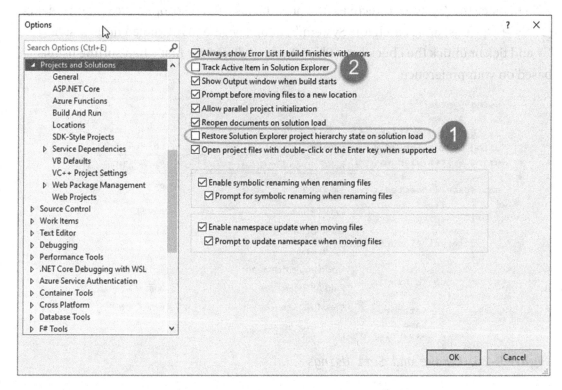

Figure 9-25. *Improve solution load performance*

Improve Navigation

Item #2 in Figure 9-25 shows the setting to enable the "Track Active Item in Solution Explorer" feature. Once enabled, as you navigate through your code or switch between different files, the Solution Explorer will automatically adjust to show the active item. This feature is particularly helpful for improving navigation and efficiency when dealing with complex solutions or projects with many files and folders.

Remove and Sort usings

Frequently, we encounter instances where numerous unused using directives are needlessly referenced in code. To optimize your code base, consider removing these unused directives and arranging the remaining ones. This practice not only improves code readability but also minimizes clutter. Utilize the shortcut Ctrl+R, Ctrl+G, or access the feature through the context menu for seamless execution. You may customize if you wish to place the "System" directives first or at the last. To do so, open the Options dialog (Tools ➤ Options) and search for "System." Then, navigate to Advanced node inside C# and tick or untick the check box "Place 'System' directives first when sorting usings" based on your preference.

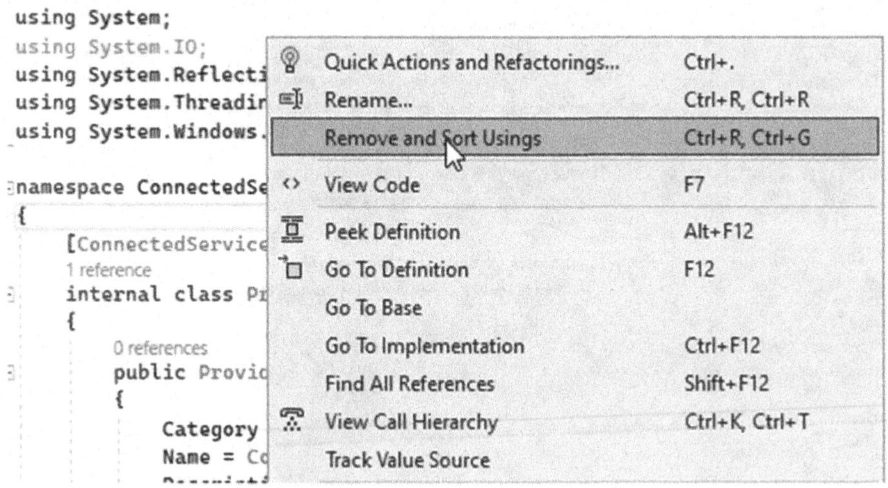

Figure 9-26. Remove and Sort Usings

Use Toolbox

During live coding sessions, presentations, or training, the need often arises for using specific code snippets. Typically, these snippets are copied to a notepad file and then pasted into the Visual Studio IDE. However, a more efficient approach that eliminates the need for context switching can be accomplished through the Toolbox. The Toolbox, traditionally employed for housing Windows Forms and WPF controls, can also serve as a repository for code snippets. To do this, select the desired code in the code editor, then drag and drop the selection onto the Toolbox. The snippet will be stored within the Toolbox. When you require the snippet, position the cursor where insertion is needed, and click the stored snippet. This approach eliminates unnecessary steps and is demonstrated in Figure 9-27.

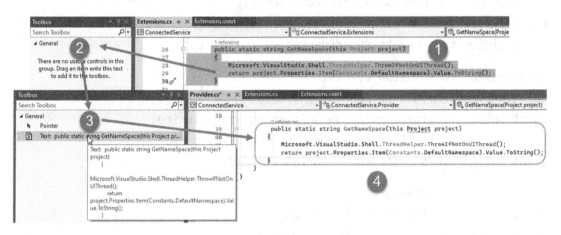

Figure 9-27. *Use toolbox to store snippets*

Use Extensibility Templates

https://marketplace.visualstudio.com/items?itemName=MadsKristensen.
ExtensibilityItemTemplates2022 – This template pack is another fantastic extension for extensibility authors, offering a wide range of valuable project and item templates. These templates simplify the process of adding commands, tool windows, and more. Additionally, a community-maintained guide is available to assist you in utilizing these templates at www.vsixcookbook.com.

Tap On to Events

We can tap into solution, project, build, debugger, command, and document events to execute our code when these events occur. For instance, if we desire to trigger code execution upon build completion, we can link our code to the Build Completed event. The following code snippet demonstrates how to connect with build and solution events. Similar approaches can be employed for handling other events as well.

```
// Get the DTE Instance.
var dte = await package.GetServiceAsync(typeof(DTE)) as DTE2;

// Get the events object.
var events = dte.Events as EnvDTE80.Events2;
var solutionEvents = events.SolutionEvents;
var buildEvents = events.BuildEvents;

// Subscribe to solution events.
solutionEvents.Opened += OnSolutionOpened;
solutionEvents.BeforeClosing += OnSolutionBeforeClosing;
solutionEvents.AfterClosing += OnSolutionAfterClosing;
solutionEvents.ProjectAdded += OnProjectAdded;

// Subscribe to build events.
buildEvents.OnBuildDone += OnBuildDone;
buildEvents.OnBuildBegin += OnBuildBegin;

// Define event handlers.
private void OnBuildBegin(vsBuildScope Scope, vsBuildAction Action)
{
    // Handle build begin event.
}

private void OnBuildDone(vsBuildScope Scope, vsBuildAction Action)
{
    // Handle build done event.
}

private void OnProjectAdded(Project Project)
{
    // Handle project added event.
}

private void OnSolutionAfterClosing()
{
    // Handle solution after closing event.
}
```

```
private void OnSolutionBeforeClosing()
{
    // Handle solution before closing event.
}
private void OnSolutionOpened()
{
    // Handle solution opened event.
}
```

Activity Log

To log activity for debugging purposes when your extension is facing issues or when investigating pkgdef, use the /log argument when launching Visual Studio. When launching Visual Studio, simply type "devenv.exe / log" in the command prompt, and it will create an Activity Log, which is a valuable resource for investigating issues. You can find the ActivityLog.xml at "%APPDATA%\Microsoft\VisualStudio<Visual_Studio_Version>\ActivityLog.xml."

The following links are valuable reads: https://devblogs.microsoft.com/visualstudio/troubleshooting-extensions-with-the-activity-log/

https://devblogs.microsoft.com/visualstudio/troubleshooting-pkgdef-files/

GitHub Examples and Documentation

This is a feature starting with Visual Studio 2022 17.6. You can find examples and documentation for the API directly within the Visual Studio IDE. Simply hover over the API, and the tool tip will display "GitHub Examples and Documentation." Click the link, and a new tool window will open, showing GitHub usage examples from public repositories and reference documentation. This feature makes it incredibly easy for developers to learn and utilize new APIs. You can also use the keyboard shortcut Ctrl+Alt+' after placing the cursor on the intended API to achieve the same.

GitHub and Visual Studio

The Git experience in Visual Studio 2022 is significantly enhanced with features such as branch comparison, line staging, commit checkout, multi-repo branching, item linking to commits, and referencing issues or pull requests (PRs). Be sure to take advantage of these fantastic features. To learn more about Git features in Visual Studio, read `https://devblogs.microsoft.com/visualstudio/introducing-new-git-features-to-visual-studio-2022/`.

Migrate Visual Studio 2019 Extensions to Visual Studio 2022

Visual Studio 2022 differs from Visual Studio 2019 as it is a 64-bit application, while Visual Studio 2019 is 32-bit (x86). Additionally, there are several breaking changes between the two versions. Consequently, extensions that were functional in Visual Studio 2019 might or might not work seamlessly in Visual Studio 2022. Addressing this could entail minor or substantial adjustments, depending on the extent of API usage. For guidance on migrating extensions from Visual Studio 2019 to 2022, refer to this informative article:

`https://learn.microsoft.com/en-us/visualstudio/extensibility/migration/update-visual-studio-extension?view=vs-2022`

Share Feedback with Microsoft

Should you run into any issue in Visual Studio, first check for updates and ensure that you are running the latest, greatest version of Visual Studio. However, you can also report a problem or share a feature suggestion with Microsoft directly from Visual Studio. On the top-right part of Visual Studio, click the Send Feedback icon. This will display a context menu where you can either report a problem or suggest a feature. Clicking any of these items will launch Visual Studio feedback dialog, where you can report a problem (post login). This is shown in Figure 9-28.

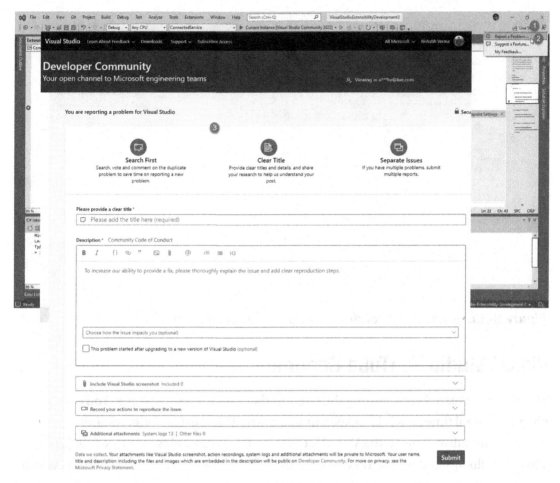

Figure 9-28. *Share feedback with Microsoft*

Ask the Experts

Gitter is a platform for software developers. It is an open source chat and networking medium for communities to interact and thrive by messaging and sharing content. The Visual Studio Extensibility team and extension authors from community are on the Gitter platform at `https://gitter.im/Microsoft/extendvs`. In case you run into an issue or want some expert help, do post out to this group. The group is very active, so it's highly likely that you will receive a solution to your problem in this forum. Other forums to ask questions, like Stack Overflow, are useful as well. Figure 9-29 shows the Microsoft extendvs community on gitter.im.

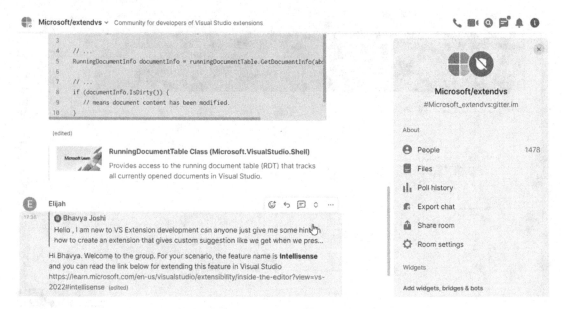

Figure 9-29. *Microsoft extendvs community on* `gitter.im`

Visual Studio YouTube Channel

The Microsoft team keeps posting the latest updates on the Visual Studio YouTube channel several times a week, so keep updated with the latest and greatest from Microsoft by subscribing to the Visual Studio YouTube channel (see Figure 9-30). To get Visual Studio tips and tricks, there is a playlist named Visual Studio Tips & Tricks. Watch this channel `www.youtube.com/@visualstudio`.

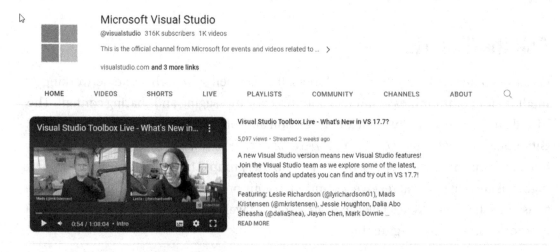

Figure 9-30. *Microsoft Visual Studio YouTube channel*

Tips on Twitter

Microsoft is using Twitter to share tips on being more productive with the Visual Studio IDE at the #vstip hashtag and encourages the community to share their tips as well with the same hashtag. Figure 9-31 shows this.

Figure 9-31. #vstip to find tips on Twitter

So, if you wish to find cool Visual Studio tips on Twitter, just search Twitter for #vstip. Also, if you come across a cool tip that you want to share with the community, do tweet the tip with the #vstip hashtag.

Subscribe to Blogs

The Visual Studio team (including the extensibility team) keeps sharing the latest, greatest, and cool features about the Visual Studio (and extensibility). Do subscribe to the blogs to keep yourself abreast with them. The URL for the extensibility team blog is `https://devblogs.microsoft.com/visualstudio/category/extensibility/` and shown in Figure 9-32.

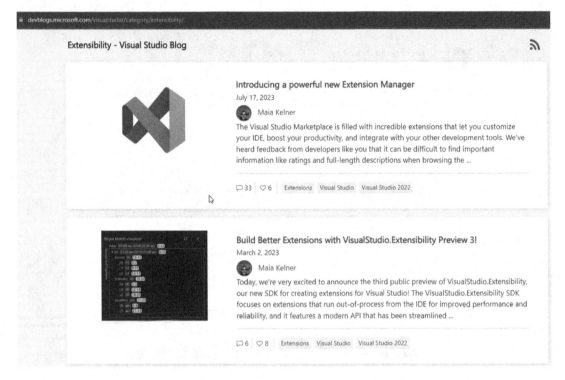

Figure 9-32. *Visual Studio Blog*

Visual Studio is highly extensible and has a lot of features, so no number of tips and tricks can do full justice to our great and beloved IDE. However, the last few tips provide the way to keep getting the latest tips and tricks on Visual Studio. So, we close the discussion on tips and tricks on this note. In the next section, let us discuss briefly about the Visual Studio Code editor and its extensibility.

Visual Studio Code

Visual Studio Code is a free, open source, and cross-platform code editor that can be extended with plug-ins to meet your needs. It includes support for debugging, embedded Git control, syntax highlighting, extension support, intelligent code completion, snippets, and code refactoring, which makes it a very potent code editor. It is a lightweight editor and can be used for development in Windows, Linux, and macOS as well. It has very quickly become the favorite and preferred code editor of many programmers and software engineers, not only for C# but for other languages as well. So, a question may come to the reader's mind that why shouldn't we move completely to Visual Studio Code instead of Visual Studio altogether? Make a note that Visual Studio is an integrated development environment (IDE), while Visual Studio Code is an editor, just like Notepad is an editor. So Visual Studio Code is much more lightweight, fast, and fluid with great support for debugging and has embedded Git control. It is a cross-platform editor and supports Windows, Linux, and Macintosh. Debugging support is good and has rich IntelliSense and refactoring. Like most editors, it is keyboard centric. It is a file and folders-based editor and doesn't need to know the project context, unlike an IDE. There is no File | New Project support in Visual Studio Code as you would be used to in Visual Studio IDE. Instead, Visual Studio Code offers a terminal, through which we can run dotnet command lines to create new projects. It can be downloaded and installed from https://code.visualstudio.com/. See Figure 9-33.

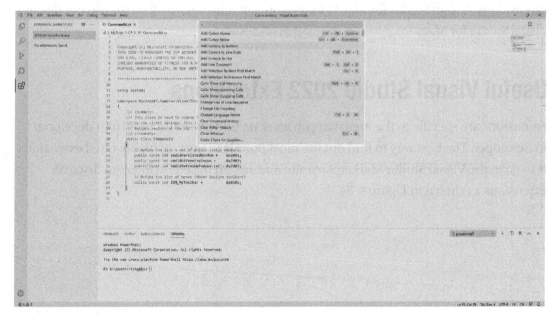

Figure 9-33. *Visual Studio Code*

Like Visual Studio, Visual Studio Code is highly extensible. Almost every component of Visual Studio Code is extensible and can be enhanced through the Extension API. Many core features of the Visual Studio Code are added as extension and use the same Extension API.

Just like Visual Studio extensions can be downloaded and installed from the marketplace, Visual Studio Code extensions can also be downloaded and installed from the marketplace. The URL is `https://marketplace.visualstudio.com/vscode`. Notice vscode at the end of this URL; this specifies the product for which extensions would display. At the time of writing this section, there are more than 51K Visual Studio Code extensions at the marketplace.

Visual Studio code is built on open source framework named Electron, developed and maintained by GitHub. Electron is used for developing Node.js-based applications, and hence to develop extensions for Visual Studio Code, you need to have Node.js installed. We will not be diving into coding VS Code extensions in this brief discussion, but curious and enthusiastic readers can read the following official documentation to start developing Visual Studio Code extensions at `https://code.visualstudio.com/api`.

The code samples for Visual Studio Code extensions are available at `https://github.com/Microsoft/vscode-extension-samples`.

With this, we will conclude our brief discussion on Visual Studio Code and its extensibility. Visual Studio for Mac is now deprecated by Microsoft so we will not discuss Visual Studio for Mac.

Useful Visual Studio 2022 Extensions

Extensions are specific to the area that you work on and so would vary from developer to developer. The best way to find out the most popular, latest, or highly rated extensions is to go to the Visual Studio Marketplace site and search based on filters to discover extensions as shown in Figure 9-34.

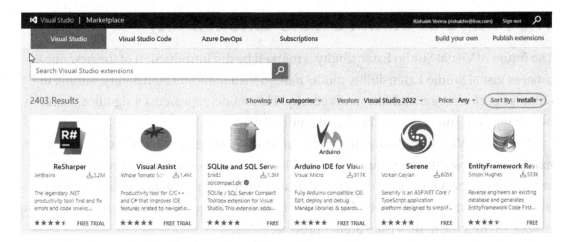

Figure 9-34. *Visual Studio 2022 extensions*

I generally work on extensions, .NET Core, installers, and general web and desktop development, so the extensions I use are specific to these areas. Here is the list of my most useful Visual Studio 2022 extensions:

- Extensibility Essentials 2022: For all my extensibility needs.

- CodeMaid: CodeMaid is an open source Visual Studio extension to clean up and simplify our C#, C++, F#, VB, PHP, PowerShell, R, JSON, XAML, XML, ASP, HTML, CSS, LESS, SCSS, JavaScript, and TypeScript coding.

- WiX Toolset extension: To develop and work on Windows Installer projects.

- Snippet Designer: This extension allows you to create and search for snippets inside the IDE.

- .NET Portability Analyzer: This evaluates portability of assemblies across .NET platforms.

- ILSpy: It integrates the ILSpy decompiler into Visual Studio.

- Visual Studio Show Inline Errors: This extension displays compiler errors, warnings, and other messages in the line they occur.

- GitHub Extension for Visual Studio: A Visual Studio extension that brings the GitHub Flow into Visual Studio.

Next, let us discuss the future of Visual Studio extensibility in brief.

The Future of Visual Studio Extensibility

The future of Visual Studio Extensibility is marked by the introduction of the new out-of-process Visual Studio Extensibility model named VisualStudio.Extensibility, aiming to enhance performance, stability, and security. This model represents a significant shift in how extensions interact with the Visual Studio IDE.

Until now, Visual Studio has the traditional in-process extensibility model, where extensions run within the same process as Visual Studio. This has sometimes led to issues like performance degradation and instability due to potential conflicts. The new out-of-process model addresses these concerns by allowing extensions to run in separate processes from the main Visual Studio process.

The key benefits include enhanced stability, improved performance, isolation, security and compatibility, to name a few.

With extensions running independently in their own processes, crashes or issues in one extension are less likely to affect the overall stability of the IDE. The separation of extension processes from the main IDE process reduces the impact of resource-intensive extensions on Visual Studio's performance. The out-of-process model provides better isolation, preventing extension conflicts that can arise when multiple extensions share the same process. This model enhances security by limiting the scope of interaction between extensions and the core Visual Studio environment. This enables better compatibility with different versions of Visual Studio, as extensions are less tightly coupled with the IDE's internal components.

Developers creating extensions based on this new extensibility model will need to adapt to the new out-of-process model. The approach to communication between the extension process and the Visual Studio IDE will change, requiring the use of interprocess communication (IPC) mechanisms. Currently, when we install an extension, we need to restart the Visual Studio. However, with the new extensibility model, this will no longer be needed as the extensions are isolated from the Visual Studio process.

Migrating existing extensions to the out-of-process model may involve making code adjustments to accommodate the new communication model. Developers should also ensure their extensions adhere to best practices for IPC and resource management.

The new extensibility model is currently in preview state and can be tried out using this GitHub documentation: `https://github.com/microsoft/VSExtensibility/`. Also, this YouTube playlist is a great introduction to the new extensibility model: `www.youtube.com/watch?v=L5zYUZvWnJE&list=PLReLO99Y5nRc6m-CLanAhWGO3_7DD_1Nu&ab_channel=MicrosoftVisualStudio`.

This concludes our discussion for this section, chapter, and the book. If you come across a cool tip or useful extension, do share it with the community with a #vstip hashtag.

Summary

In this chapter, we explored several valuable tips and tricks for working with Visual Studio and developing Visual Studio extensions. We also delved into Visual Studio Code and its extensibility capabilities. Additionally, we highlighted a selection of useful extensions that I personally use and appreciate. Finally, we concluded the chapter by taking a glimpse into the future of Visual Studio extensibility.

Index

Printed in the United States
by Baker & Taylor Publisher Services